FATHER ABRAHAM

ALSO BY RICHARD STRINER

Washington Past and Present: A Guide to Our Nation's Capital
(with Donald R. Kennon)

Art Deco

The Civic Deal: Re-Empowering Our Great Republic

FATHER ABRAHAM

LINCOLN'S RELENTLESS STRUGGLE TO END SLAVERY

RICHARD STRINER

OXFORD

UNIVERSITY PRESS

2006

OXFORD

UNIVERSITY PRESS

Oxford University Press, Inc., publishes works that
further Oxford University's objective of excellence
in research, scholarship, and education.

Oxford New York
Auckland Cape Town Dar es Salaam Hong Kong Karachi
Kuala Lumpur Madrid Melbourne Mexico City Nairobi
New Delhi Shanghai Taipei Toronto

With offices in
Argentina Austria Brazil Chile Czech Republic France Greece
Guatemala Hungary Italy Japan Poland Portugal Singapore

Published by Oxford University Press, Inc.
198 Madison Avenue, New York, NY 10016
www.oup.com

Oxford is a registered trademark of Oxford University Press

Library of Congress Cataloging-in-Publication Data
Striner, Richard, 1950–
Father Abraham : Lincoln's relentless struggle to end slavery / Richard Striner.
p. cm.
Includes bibliographical references and index.
ISBN-13: 978-0-19-518306-1
ISBN-10: 0-19-518306-1
1. Lincoln, Abraham, 1809–1865—Views on slavery.
2. Lincoln, Abraham, 1809–1865—Relations with African Americans.
3. Slaves—Emancipation—United States. I. Title.
E457.2.S89 2006
973.7'092—dc22
2005023083

1 3 5 7 9 8 6 4 2
Printed in the United States of America
on acid-free paper

To my wife, Sara Jane, and all my family

Contents

Acknowledgments

I WISH TO THANK the following people for their contributions to the book. I am deeply grateful to James M. McPherson, Eric Foner, David Grimsted, Harold Holzer, Michael Burlingame, Herman Belz, Robert Cleary, and my wife, Sara Striner, for their willingness to review the manuscript in whole or in part. I am especially indebted to my literary agent, John W. Wright, for his many helpful suggestions. At Oxford University Press, I will always be grateful to my editor, Peter Ginna, his assistant, Laura Stickney, and senior production editor Joellyn Ausanka for their many outstanding contributions to this book. I will always remember the encouragement provided by my family (especially my parents) and my friends Richard Berryman, Avis Black, Joan Nicolaysen, Jann Hoag, Laura Lieberman, Henry McKinney, and Carl Reddel. I will always be grateful to my graduate student Kevin Fields for his research assistance. Any errors in the book are my own.

FATHER ABRAHAM

Introduction

To WHAT EXTENT should Abraham Lincoln be regarded as our nation's "Great Emancipator"?

This book will show that Lincoln was a masterful anti-slavery leader. A moral visionary, Lincoln was also blessed with extraordinary talent in the orchestration of power. *Father Abraham* will argue that this rare combination of gifts in the leadership of Lincoln played a vital role in the extinction of American slavery. This book will challenge portrayals of Lincoln that misunderstand his character and therefore misunderstand what his leadership achieved.

For a long time, a significant number of historians have argued that Lincoln was a cautious or emotionally tepid man, who was driven by outside pressures and events into anti-slavery leadership. A host of recent commentators have suggested that Lincoln's contributions to the anti-slavery movement were almost unintentional.

Several years ago, historian Allen C. Guelzo contended in *The Washington Post* that Lincoln was a "reluctant recruit to the abolitionist cause," a "restrained" and "emotionally chilly" politician whose "unblinking eye for compromise" created an "ambiguous shadow" of a legacy.[1]

In his best-selling 1995 biography of Lincoln, historian David Herbert Donald talked of an "essential passivity" in Lincoln's nature, an alleged personality quirk that resulted in "reluctance to take the initiative and make bold plans." He contended that this "basic trait of character" was "evident throughout Lincoln's life."[2]

In Ken Burns's 1989 documentary television series *The Civil War*, historian Barbara Fields expressed impatient disdain for the reputation

1

of Lincoln as the Great Emancipator. Fields dismissed the Emancipation Proclamation as a gesture of moral catch-up: "The people most affected by the Emancipation Proclamation," she said, "obviously did not receive it as news because they knew before Lincoln knew that the war was about emancipation."[3]

To be sure, there are millions of Americans who continue to venerate Lincoln for patriotic reasons. Moreover, some prominent historians continue to defend Lincoln's record as an anti-slavery leader. James M. McPherson, for example, credits Lincoln's "superb leadership, strategy, and sense of timing as president, commander in chief, and head of the Republican Party" with the liberation of millions.[4]

But for many Americans, Lincoln these days is a strikingly ambiguous figure: a moody, strange, and mysterious sort of politician.

Even worse, he seemed to be *tricky* now and then—a mere vote-grubbing "pol"—and Americans are not very keen nowadays about "tricky" politicians in the White House. In the 1984 novel *Lincoln*, Gore Vidal portrayed Lincoln as a consummate power broker whose real motivations were elusive. And a steady outpouring of scholarly books depicts Lincoln as a "practical" man who was driven into acts of moral leadership by others.[5]

In contrast, according to public affairs scholar William Lee Miller, Lincoln was a *virtuous* leader on all the major issues of the day, and a leader of the highest ideals.[6]

In my own view, Abraham Lincoln was a great moral leader. But I believe we must acknowledge that the ethical politics of Lincoln depended on some very crafty methods. Moreover, the ethics and the tricky maneuverings of Lincoln were essentially harmonious—paradoxical as this may seem—and they should not be detached from one another as we analyze his politics.

This book will show that Lincoln was a rare man indeed: a fervent idealist endowed with a remarkable gift for strategy. An ethicist, Lincoln was also an artist in the Machiavellian uses of power. It was this combination of qualities that made Lincoln's contribution to the anti-slavery movement so fundamental, and, it may be argued, so demonstrably *necessary*.

Building upon the work of scholars such as Harry V. Jaffa, Don E. Fehrenbacher, LaWanda Cox, James M. McPherson, and William Lee Miller, *Father Abraham* argues that the qualities that some regard as problematical in Lincoln in no way detract from his greatness. To the contrary—they *establish* his greatness. A few other observations are in order in regard to the book. First, I approach Lincoln's rise to greatness as a story of expanding audacity; though he learned from other people, his genius developed as an ongoing process of mental self-discovery. His goals kept expanding as he tested how far he might go in his attempt to change history.

Second, Lincoln scholars are continuously confronted with a problem of source analysis. The sheer *craft* of Lincoln's ways demands critical analysis, even to the point of asking questions about his veracity. Historian LaWanda Cox has observed that "in striving for consent," Lincoln "would tailor an argument to fit his hearer. To develop public support or outflank opposition, he would at times conceal his hand or dissemble. . . ."[7] Indeed, Cox has argued that "Lincoln's style of presidential leadership was as often devious as forthright."[8] The challenge for historians is to find and analyze the overall pattern in which Lincoln's ploys were merely parts within a whole.

Third, chapters 4 through 7, devoted to the war years, address Lincoln's overlapping of political and military strategy. This extensive examination of military issues is important for two reasons: If, as the German military theorist Carl von Clausewitz argued so famously, the waging of war is a direct extension of politics, the Civil War is fraught with validation of his point. Much of Lincoln's moral strategy in politics, especially concerning the issue of slavery, was connected to his prosecution of the war. Furthermore, Lincoln's genius in power orchestration can never be fully understood if his military and civilian strategems are separated. His sheer capacity to *visualize* power, and his artistry in simultaneous best-case and worst-case contingency planning, will appear across the board in his presidential leadership.

Perhaps some words about my title—*Father Abraham*—are also in order. "We Are Coming, Father Abraham, Three Hundred Thousand More" was the title of a Union recruiting poem. It was later set to music by Stephen Foster and others. As the title of the poem made the rounds, "Father Abraham" took its place among the various nicknames for Lincoln. The derivation of the nickname was biblical: many hymns had long referred to the patriarch, the "father" of the Hebrew nation, as "Father Abraham." And when Lincoln's supporters began to compare him to Washington—as the second "Father of his Country"—the paternal theme deepened in its cultural resonance.

There is, of course, an extremely ironic difference in the fate of Abraham Lincoln and the fate of his biblical namesake. God tested the patriarch Abraham by telling him to sacrifice Isaac, his son. As Abraham prepared for the deed, God relented and spared him the sacrifice. "Venerable Father Abraham," wrote Søren Kierkegaard in 1843, "thou didst gain all and didst retain Isaac."[9] Though Lincoln "gained all," in a sense, he had to make a horrible sacrifice. Six hundred thousand were killed in the Civil War—including Lincoln himself—in a scourging of the nation that Lincoln, in his second Inaugural Address, proclaimed a wrathful judgment of the Lord.

Lincoln took responsibility for those in his charge: like a father, he sought to protect them, even (on occasion) from themselves. But alas, he could not forestall the sacrifice.

ONE

Lincoln and Slavery: The Problem

THEY HAD COME FROM ALL OVER the city of Chicago and vicinity to gather at the Tremont House hotel on the evening of July 10, 1858. They had come to hear the candidate, Lincoln.

Transcripts of the speech that he delivered that evening—and the newspaper texts included audience response—make it clear that his listeners were almost in a frenzy as he roused their turbulent emotions. While the speech was officially a kick-off address in his campaign for the United States Senate, its subjects were slavery and race.

Using patriotic and religious themes, Lincoln channeled his thoughts into searing incantations as he argued that white supremacy was poisoning the soul of America by slow degrees. White Americans were feasting on evil fruit, he declared, if they convinced themselves that their black fellow countrymen deserved nothing better than enslavement. What do such arguments amount to, Lincoln demanded, but "the arguments that kings have made for enslaving the people in all ages of the world?" Tyrants, he added sarcastically, "always bestrode the necks of the people, not that they wanted to do it, but because the people were better off for being ridden."

This was the argument, Lincoln said, of all the white supremacists who advocated slavery or said they didn't care about the issue. It was a vile, seductive, hypocritical, and sinful argument, Lincoln insisted. It was nothing less than "the same old serpent that says you work and I eat, you toil and I will enjoy the fruits of it. Turn [it] in whatever way you will—whether it come from the mouth of a King, as an excuse for enslaving the people of his country, or from the mouth of men of one race as a reason for enslaving the men of another race, it is all the same old serpent. . . ."

And where will it end, Lincoln asked—will it stop with the blacks? If Americans should choose to back away from "this old Declaration of Independence, which declares that all men are equal upon principle," if Americans indulged and abetted tyrannical behavior in violation of the principle, "it does not stop with the negro." Not at all: "If one man says it does not mean a negro, why [may] not another say it does not mean some other man?" And so the degradation would spread—the American Republic would degenerate.

Enough of such apostasy, Lincoln proclaimed as he worked his spell upon the crowd; if it comes to such a pass, it might be better to abandon the American experiment, to trash the Declaration and its eloquent phrases altogether if they stood for nothing.

"If that declaration is not the truth," Lincoln cried out at the speech's climax, "let us get the Statute book, in which we find it and tear it out! Who is so bold to do it! (Voices—'me' and 'no one,' etc.) If it is not true let us tear it out! (cries of 'no, no')."[1]

This is hardly the Lincoln that millions of Americans know from their schoolbook history. This is not the sort of Lincolnesque oratory chosen by a later generation for carving and enshrining on the walls of the Lincoln Memorial. Even Lincoln's extraordinary second Inaugural Address, with its stark Old Testament passages, renders but a muted distillation of the anger, the insistent vehemence, the sheer imperious brilliance of the Lincoln who could work those crowds with such impatient and charismatic fervor in the 1850s.[2]

People sanctify a very different Abraham Lincoln: the sorrowful and saintly "moderate" who put preservation of the Union first and who embraced anti-slavery goals as a means to that end. This Lincoln stereotype is quite pervasive in its influence. Even among academic scholars it remains influential. It is embraced by Lincoln admirers and Lincoln detractors alike.

Admirers praise Lincoln's wise "moderation," which could triumph over "extremism." Detractors (at least left-of-center detractors) revile Lincoln's "moderate" ways as pusillanimous compared to the anti-slavery militance of abolitionists like William Lloyd Garrison and Frederick Douglass.

Many believe that Lincoln "only wanted to save the Union" when the guns blazed away at Fort Sumter. They believe that he gradually came to "realize" how deeply the slavery issue was embroiled in the sectional tragedy—the tragedy that he had presumably tried to avert in his "House Divided" speech, the supposedly sorrowful, patient, and healing plea to de-escalate the tensions that were leading toward civil war.

But it was not so. Those who regard Lincoln's 1858 "House Divided" speech in this manner have probably never read much of it. If they did, they would swiftly encounter a sharp, insistent, and urgent warning that America's divided House was re-uniting in the worst possible way. The "House Divided" speech was a warning that the slavery system was on its way North unless Americans prevented the uniting of their "House" along pro-slavery lines.

By itself, preservation of the Union was an empty concept to Lincoln, unless the Union remained dedicated—or could forcibly be re-dedicated—to its founding principle that all men are created equal. If America *could* be re-dedicated to this fundamental principle, as Lincoln so fervently hoped, then there was justification for defending the Union's permanence. But if the nation should ever lose or repudiate that founding principle, the Union would become a monstrosity, better abandoned than patched up with "moderate" evasions or compromises of appeasement.

In fact, it might be better for decent men to leave the United States, Lincoln ruminated in the 1850s, if pro-slavery forces succeeded in uniting the nation their way. "Our progress in degeneracy appears to me to be pretty rapid," he wrote to a close friend in 1855. "As a nation, we began by declaring that '*all men are created equal.*' We now practically read it, 'all men are created equal, *except negroes.*'" Soon enough "it will read 'all men are created equal, except negroes, *and foreigners and Catholics.*' When it comes to this I should prefer emigrating to some country where they make no pretense of loving liberty—to Russia, for instance, where despotism can be taken pure, and without the base alloy of hypocracy [*sic*]."[3]

Right up to the outbreak of the Civil War, Lincoln talked this way and followed up with appropriate actions. Indeed, it was Lincoln's election itself that sparked the secession proclamations in the winter of 1860–61. The reason was clear to almost everyone: Lincoln had promised to support legislation that would stop the expansion of slavery. If Lincoln and his fellow Republicans succeeded in carrying out this promise—if Congress prevented the creation of new slave states in the West—the existing slave states would eventually be locked into permanent minority status in the Union, unable to block abolitionist legislation in Congress or stop an anti-slavery amendment of the Constitution.

Though Lincoln did not (until December 1861) reveal any plans that would push beyond the goal of slavery containment, there might be nothing to stop a Republican *successor* from adopting such a course of action, once the groundwork had been laid and the basic conditions were locked in place. After all, this was clearly a long-term struggle. Strategists on both sides of the issue engaged in long-term contingency planning, and they framed their short-term positions accordingly.

This was the reason, as the leaders in the slave states knew very well, why the strategy of slavery containment was a near-fatal threat to the "peculiar institution" of slavery. For as soon as the slave states were finally reduced to a minority faction in Congress and the nation at large, there might be nothing—nothing but the force of arms—that could hold abolitionism back from eventual victory.

Ever since the 1820s, American advocates of slavery had been keeping careful track of this political arithmetic, maintaining a vigilant and fearful watch upon the balance of the free and slave states. For years, Southern militants had threatened secession if the free states placed them in a "one-down" power position.

Lincoln resolutely stood up to these threats of secession and proposed to let the chips fall where they might. He would not back down one inch from his program of slavery containment. And this was merely the beginning of what Lincoln had in mind for America.

Lincoln fully intended to contain the institution of slavery as a prelude to phasing it out over time, perhaps through a gradual "buy-out" program. He hoped that the leverage provided by containing the slavery system would gradually soften resistance in the South to an offer of money in return for the liberation of slaves. He meant to place the institution of slavery "where the public mind shall rest in the belief that it is in [the] course of extinction," as he said in his "House Divided" speech.[4] Preservation of the Union was entirely subsumed in this overriding objective. Nothing was to stand in the way of it.

In December 1860, Lincoln killed a sectional compromise designed to preserve the Union and to stall the momentum of secession. This compromise (the Crittenden Compromise) would have permitted the continued expansion of slavery. Lincoln shot down this compromise to save the Union by instructing his fellow Republicans to "entertain no proposition for a compromise in regard to the *extension* of slavery.

The instant you do, they have us under again; all our labor is lost, and sooner or later must be done over. . . . Have none of it. The tug has to come & better now than later."[5] So the war began.

Concurrently, he took a fresh look at his options for phasing out slavery. Within a year, he took advantage of political moods and got Congress to authorize federal funds to encourage the gradual liberation of slaves. As a test case, Lincoln offered this voluntary phaseout package to the handful of border slave states that had not attempted secession.

What he hoped to achieve was the creation of a voluntary pilot program that would demonstrate, in embryonic form, the overall feasibility of phasing out slavery. But the border states turned him down.

Whereupon, Lincoln promptly and drastically revised his whole approach to the problem and accelerated his anti-slavery strategy.

Specifically, he turned from the border states to the slave states comprising the rebellious Confederate States, and there, in the name of preserving the Union, he instituted sweeping and immediate emancipation with no compensation for the rebels. This plan, as announced in the Preliminary Emancipation Proclamation of September 22, 1862, would take effect just as soon as his armies took control of rebellious territory (provided the Confederate States were still in a state of rebellion as of January 1, 1863). There was no turning back from this sacred commitment, Lincoln told both Houses of Congress in his annual message of December 1862.

Lincoln critics deride these achievements as "gradualism," suggesting his commitment to equality was tepid or equivocal. But consider the achievement of Lincoln-style gradualism in context.

It amounted to nothing less than this: Lincoln forced the United States, North and South, to turn the fundamental corner on slavery. His anti-slavery gradualism was flexible enough for very fast acceleration when the turbulent give-and-take of political and military strategy made it possible. It was also backed up with a heroic commitment on the order of six hundred thousand killed, including Lincoln himself, by the time the Civil War had ended.

In light of this, it behooves us to take a very serious look at the stereotype of Lincoln as a "moderate" who "only wanted to preserve the Union." In the first place, how could such a one-sided stereotype have developed at all?

If the written Lincoln record were consistently clear, then the stereotype would not have developed. It must now be admitted, however, that Lincoln made some statements in the course of the Civil War, especially in a famous open letter that he wrote to political journalist Horace Greeley in 1862, in which he explicitly declared that preservation of the Union was indeed his paramount goal in the struggle. Moreover, in the course of the Lincoln-Douglas debates of 1858, Lincoln even made statements (under pressure from Douglas) denying that he advocated social equality for blacks.

The "moderate" stereotype of Lincoln has elements of truth: his politics were surely different, for example, from those of the Radical Republicans, even though the Radicals and Lincoln had a great deal more in common than people might suppose.

The politics of Lincoln were complex and multifaceted. There was clearly a moderate *side* to Lincoln, just as there was clearly a *sense* in which his commitment to saving the Union was genuine, indeed quite passionate.

So the Lincoln record could be regarded plausibly as murky or even contradictory, at least on the surface. No wonder that distinguished historian Richard N. Current once consigned the seeming contradictions in Lincoln's career to the enigmatic nature of "the Lincoln nobody knows."

But such apparent contradictions in the record of Lincoln are not enigmatic. They are part of an extraordinary pattern of statecraft, one that Americans should now understand on its merits.

Pioneering research and interpretation by scholars in the past half-century—especially the work of Harry V. Jaffa, Don E. Fehrenbacher, James M. McPherson, LaWanda Cox, and William Lee Miller—has cleared away a vast amount of confusion spawned by the "moderate" Lincoln stereotype.

Lincoln was that rarest of all great men, a political ethicist who was also an extraordinary natural genius in the Machiavellian orchestration of power.[6] Lincoln forged a brilliant plan to propel abolitionism forward into gradual and incremental victory, to roll back the evil of slavery, to make it recoil upon itself until it died. But the strategy entailed a certain tactical cost that might pain many Lincoln admirers.

The fact should not be evaded: Lincoln chose sometimes to obscure the full truth about his mission in the Civil War years. Like any political virtuoso, he weighed both the content and tone of what he said at different places and times. When it served his purpose, he was capable of generating lawyerly hair-splitting rhetoric, at times to the brink of pettifoggery. He deliberately played up the constitutional case for preserving the Union while playing down his anti-slavery mission whenever he believed that the realities of politics and power made it necessary.

Lincoln gave a very misleading impression now and then to the effect that his wartime anti-slavery acts should be understood *only* as ploys with which to save the Union. To be sure, he was careful to phrase the proposition as a matter of constitutional law—as a matter of the constitutional *justification* for his anti-slavery actions, a justification that was certainly true enough on its level but surely not the *whole* truth—and to write key statements in a cunningly legalistic way.

He did this to pacify opponents of his anti-slavery program, opponents whose support he needed to win the Civil War and to achieve his full objectives for America. So he talked to them in terms they would respect.

In this manner, an enduring cult built up around the notion that "Lincoln only wanted to preserve the Union" in the Civil War. This is how the "moderate" stereotype of Lincoln developed and grew, notwithstanding the fact that it was after all Lincoln's own insistence on containing the institution of slavery that *triggered* the secession crisis (thereby jeopardizing the Union) in the first place.

If Lincoln only wanted to preserve the Union, then why did he oppose the Crittenden Compromise in 1860? Preservation of the Union (at least until the outbreak of secession) was relatively easy: just appease the slave-holding states and let slavery continue to expand. But Lincoln refused. Yet posterity regards him as primarily a Unionist, who freed the slaves in his endeavor to save the Union.

Such were the arts of this master politician who would use the necessity of saving the Union as a justification for saving the Union *his way*. It is obvious enough that if Lincoln had been willing to compromise on the issue of slavery expansion, the Union might very well have "held." But with the Union placed in serious peril, an occasion was provided for a very tough policy against the rebellious slave states.

This policy, of course, would develop into outright emancipation, thus extending the Republican anti-slavery agenda that had *caused* the Confederates to put the Union in peril. The logic of the Lincoln policies came full circle.

It is no special pleading, however, to observe that such behavior can be morally defensible in certain situations. Few politicians choose to blurt out their deepest intentions to everyone all the time. They may even choose on occasion to mask their full intentions to avert catastrophic possibilities.

Consider the case of Franklin Delano Roosevelt, who told an isolationist-leaning American public in 1939 and 1940 that America could stay out of World War II when in fact he believed the reverse and needed time to shape public opinion.

Were the tactical methods of Lincoln and FDR mere studies in guile? Or were they nothing less than grand demonstrations of the ethical calculus that strategists must always confront as they weigh lesser evils with greater?

However dismaying it may seem to admirers of Lincoln to acknowledge that he didn't always tell the "whole truth," his case must be judged not only in the context of moral ends that may justify otherwise questionable means but also in a clear-headed, wide-awake realization of the risks and the dangers Lincoln faced as he struggled to keep white supremacy at bay while phasing out slavery.

A powerful segment of Northern public opinion regarded Lincoln as a "nigger lover." The hate campaigns that were waged against Lincoln's policies were fearsome and ugly. The heart of Lincoln's strategy was simple and stunning: having captured the White House on terms that plunged the slave states into secession, Lincoln used the battle cry of saving the Union as a method for building a political and military power coalition that would break the power of the slave-holding states forever. This coalition extended necessarily beyond the Republican Party. It included white supremacist Democrats who would *only* support the Republican administration in a war over principles of Union.

But to keep that Union devoted to the principles essential to its highest meaning, Lincoln used a remarkable tactic that is far too little understood: he embraced the cause of saving the Union on two different levels at once.

At the highest level, Lincoln's mission to save the Union was a heartfelt imperative. For so long as the Union continued to embody the principles enshrined in the Declaration of Independence, it was for Lincoln a sacred vessel, a channel through which, as he said in his 1858

Chicago address, Americans could feel themselves to be "blood of the blood, and flesh of the flesh of the men who wrote that Declaration."[7]

Nonetheless, the mission of saving the Union would always be contingent for Lincoln on America's success in putting slavery "on the downhill," as he phrased it. The Union cried out for preservation as long as it stood for its founding ideals.

Lincoln's wartime rhetoric of saving the Union was intended on this highest level for those who agreed already with his anti-slavery ideals or for those who could at least be touched by his moral principles.

At a lower level—at the level of tactical dealings with those who supported slavery—Lincoln's Unionism was employed for a very different purpose, an essentially Machiavellian purpose, an ingeniously calculated strategy of transformation, a strategy that forced its own opponents into limited cooperation by dint of a patriotic cause that transcended their bigotry.

And this was the level at which Lincoln insisted, as he did in his 1862 letter, that his wartime anti-slavery measures were *only* designed to preserve the Union, a point which, though true as a justification, begged the larger question of what that Union would stand for in years to come.

This strategy was neither "insincere" nor "sincere" in conventional terms. It was political artistry developed for transcendent and practical purposes, artistry that was morally consistent, ethically justified, and paradoxically grounded in the craft of juxtaposing half-truth and truth for simultaneous transmission to very different groups of "players."

The genius behind all this—the orchestration of ideas and passion and power—has no real equal in American history. Call it moderate, conservative, radical, or liberal, as prompted by your own sensibilities. Call it any combination of personal or ideological principles that strike your fancy. It was nothing less than a *tour de force* of power in the service of freedom.

Moreover, as Lincoln strove in this high-risk manner to assure the success of his cause through the strategy of slavery containment, he worked experimentally to craft the best possible deal for American blacks in a post-Emancipation epoch. But he remained ever mindful that a white supremacist backlash could wipe away all the moral progress he had gained.

The backlash occurred in 1862 (in reaction to Lincoln's Emancipation Proclamation), and it recurred periodically until the Civil War was over. While it almost cost him the presidency in 1864, it cost him his life the next year. By then, the transformation he had wrought was irreversible in its essentials. But what "might have been" if he had lived is a very different matter, as we shall see.

To UNDERSTAND LINCOLN, some historical background is in order. For in many respects Lincoln's anti-slavery strategy built upon some older ideas that emerged in the age of the Founding Fathers, a number of whom viewed slavery as one of the fundamental issues that confronted the new nation.

At the Constitutional Convention, for example, James Madison acknowledged that "the States were divided into different interests not by their difference of size, but by other circumstances; the most material of which resulted partly from climate, but principally from [the effects of] their having or not having slaves."[8]

Well before the American Revolution, abolitionism had been taken up by Quakers. But in the Revolutionary and early National periods, it was "in the air" across the nation. The idealism unleashed by the American Revolution prompted most of the Northern states to embark upon abolishing or phasing out slavery between 1777 and 1804.

In the upper South as well, the anti-slavery cause made an impact. Indeed, one of the most famous expositors of anti-slavery principles in Revolutionary America was the Virginian Thomas Jefferson.

Many recent historians have indicted Jefferson-the-slaveholder on the charge of hypocrisy, a charge containing strong elements of truth. For present purposes, though, it behooves us to acknowledge that Jefferson, as the preeminent oracle of American freedom, made a powerful impact on Lincoln and many others.

The Jefferson who wrote the extraordinary lines of the Declaration of Independence was the Jefferson whom Lincoln revered. This was the Jefferson who proclaimed in a famous letter written just before he died that "the mass of mankind has not been born with saddles on their backs, nor a favored few booted and spurred, ready to ride them legitimately by the grace of God."[9]

This was the Jefferson who proposed a new constitution for Virginia in 1783, a constitution that would have forbidden the importation of "any more slaves to reside in this State, or the continuance of slavery beyond the generation which shall be living on the thirty-first day of December, one thousand eight hundred; all persons born after that day being hereby declared free."[10]

Other Virginians such as George Mason and George Washington hoped that the state of Virginia would phase out slavery. Washington worked behind the scenes in the 1790s to get the work started; meanwhile, he developed a plan to convert Mount Vernon to a well-rounded farm to be worked by free tenants. When his plans for Mount Vernon came to nought, he determined to free his slaves in his will. He predicted in private that the nation would have to face up to the issue and decide in favor of freedom, universal freedom. According to one reminiscence, he told a British visitor in conversations at Mount Vernon in 1797, "I can clearly foresee that nothing but the rooting out of slavery can perpetuate the existence of our union, by consolidating it in a common bond of principle."[11]

Washington also told Edmund Randolph—if notes of this second-hand account as set forth in the papers of Jefferson can be believed—that if North and South should ever divide on the issue of slavery during his lifetime, "he had made up his mind to move and be of the northern."[12]

The anti-slavery Founding Fathers were men of diverse sensibilities. Some of them were white supremacists, who nonetheless condemned slavery. A few regarded blacks as their equals. But most of them agreed that a phaseout program was the only realistic way to end slavery in light of the widespread prevalence of racial prejudice, combined with the enormous amount of money invested in slaves. So they did what they could on the national level to begin such a phaseout. The preliminary step was containment.[13]

Anti-Slavery Measures in the New American Nation

In 1784, Jefferson tried to lay the groundwork for such a policy in Congress (still meeting under the Articles of Confederation) when he introduced legislation setting forth the process whereby states would be created out of territory west of the Appalachians. Several states possessed colonial charters without a western boundary. Such states were expected by many to cede their western lands to the Union, and Virginia, while retaining Kentucky, had already ceded its western territories north of the

Ohio River to the Union in 1781. Other states, such as Georgia and the Carolinas, had not yet taken action on the issue.

In Jefferson's text for the Ordinance of 1784 slavery would have been forbidden in *all* common territories west of the Appalachians after 1800. This was deleted from the ordinance (it lost in Congress by the margin of one vote), but an anti-slavery provision was adopted in the stronger Northwest Ordinance of 1787. It bears noting, however, that the Northwest Ordinance was limited to the former Virginia lands above the Ohio River.

Another significant step was taken in 1787 to prevent the expansion of slavery. The Federal Constitution, which was being drafted at this time, gave the Federal Congress the power to shut off the importation of slaves after twenty years. Together, the Northwest Ordinance and the Constitution's importation cut-off provision were twin features of a policy hammered out piecemeal to contain the institution of slavery— a prelude to long-term phaseout. But a counter-movement against this policy had started already.

In 1790, the Federal Congress passed the Southwest Ordinance, covering western lands to be ceded by the states below Virginia. This ordinance did *not* forbid slavery below the Ohio River. In the same year, 1790, North Carolina ceded its western territories. Kentucky broke away from Virginia in 1792, and was admitted to the Union with a slave state constitution. Tennessee (created out of former North Carolina lands) was admitted as a slave state in 1796. Georgia ceded its western lands in 1802. The western lands of Georgia went the same way: Mississippi was admitted as a slave state in 1817, and Alabama was admitted as a slave state in 1819.

The expansion of slavery below the Ohio River was driven in part by "economics," that is, by visions of prodigious fortunes to be made through the cultivation and harvesting of cotton using Eli Whitney's new "gin." The movement to contain the evil of slavery was obviously hampered by the powerful appeal of the riches to be gained by expanding it.

There was, however, a different side to the pro-slavery movement of the 1790s: a fear that anti-slavery talk could incite a slave insurrection that would lead to a catastrophic race war. Events in the Caribbean convinced a great many owners of slaves in the United States that even casual talk of a long-term slavery phaseout was tantamount to playing with matches, as we would say, in the presence of gasoline.

The Caribbean events in question took place at "St. Dominique" (Santo Domingo), the island of Hispaniola comprising the present-day Dominican Republic and Haiti. From 1791 to 1804, a bloody slave insurrection ravaged the island, alarming scores of American slave owners. Nervous alarms pervaded Southern American ports, and the discovery in 1800 of an incipient slave revolt in Virginia (the Gabriel Prosser revolt) added to the scare.

For these reasons, pro-slavery leaders at the time viewed talk of a long-term anti-slavery program in the United States as dangerous folly. They argued that the presence of freed blacks was a permanent incitement to rebellion among the enslaved, for which reason a number of them proposed sending former slaves out of the country if their masters chose to free them.

Even before these tensions of the 1790s, Jefferson had expressed his belief that a long-term separation of the races was the only real scenario for abolition. He avowed that "deep-rooted prejudices entertained by the whites; ten thousand recollections, by the blacks, of the injuries they have sustained; new provocations; the real distinctions that nature has made; and many other circumstances, will divide us into parties, and produce convulsions, which will probably never end but in the extermination of the one or the other race," unless blacks and whites agreed to seek separate destinies in separate countries.[14]

This package of presuppositions was sufficiently widespread to influence the founding (in 1816) of the American Colonization Society, an anti-slavery group that proposed to repatriate thousands of slaves to Africa, the continent of their ancestors. Within a few years the nation of Liberia was founded as a promised land for former slaves.

This was the America into which Abraham Lincoln was born on February 12, 1809, in the slave state of Kentucky, a nation poised between advocates of slavery containment and advocates of slavery expansion. The two philosophies were reflected in rival formulae for state constitutions: free states above the Mason-Dixon and Ohio River border and slave states below the border. On each side of the line, Americans argued about the morality of enslavement. But the anti-slavery movement was generally centered on the strategy of colonization. Such was the overall situation before the great Missouri crisis broke out in 1819, when Lincoln was ten years old.

The Missouri Crisis and Its Aftermath

The state of Louisiana had been admitted to the Union as a slave state in 1812. But the rest of the Louisiana Purchase, which the United States had acquired from France in 1803, was in a state of limbo regarding slavery. Congress had not yet addressed the issue as to whether or not slavery should exist in the future states that would be created in the vast Louisiana Territory.

Still, the westward spread of American slavery continued. In 1819, a majority of voters and leaders of the territory of Missouri (whose population was 16 percent enslaved) petitioned Congress for admission as a slave state. In response, Congressman James Tallmadge, Jr., of New York proposed to amend the Missouri statehood bill by prohibiting the introduction of any more slaves into the state and by requiring the emancipation of slaves who were born in Missouri, after its statehood had been granted, when they reached the age of twenty-five. The Tallmadge amendments were passed in the House of Representatives but defeated in the Senate.

Almost immediately, the sectional difference over slavery erupted into fury, with Southern denunciations of the amendments as unconstitutional, and with threats of secession if the free states attempted to stop the institution of slavery from expanding.

In March 1820, Speaker of the House Henry Clay engineered the passage of a series of measures that would constitute the famous Missouri Compromise. Missouri would be admitted as a slave state, but some northern counties of Massachusetts would be organized into the new free state of Maine.

In 1820, the geopolitical balance of the free and slave states was even: eleven apiece. With the admission of Missouri and Maine into the Union, the delicate balance of power between the free states and the slave states would be preserved.

Or would it? In a critical development, Senator Jesse Thomas of Illinois proposed that Congress establish a dividing line that would run from east to west across the remainder of the Louisiana Territory, a line that would stipulate the outermost limit beyond which slavery would be prohibited.

This boundary line would extend due west from the *southern*, rather than the northern, border of the new state of Missouri. What this meant was that the free-state system got the lion's share of all the land that remained in the Louisiana Purchase. The free-state system would gradually overwhelm the slave-state system in its geographical magnitude, and hence in its representation in Congress. The Thomas Proviso passed, and the boundary line was established.

Thus the political war over slavery expansion began with the Missouri crisis, with the slave states emerging from the war's first engagement with their long-term power at risk. Though some politicians thought the compromise had settled the issue "forever," by the end of the decade pro-slavery leaders began to think about the worst-case picture if the free-state bloc should outnumber the slave states.

To be sure, pro-slavery Americans kept working to encourage the expansion of slavery where the Thomas Proviso permitted it: into Arkansas territory, for instance, just below the new state of Missouri, and into the newly independent nation of Mexico, whose province of Texas received a heavy new influx of American settlers, many of whom brought their slave property with them. But when Mexico abolished and prohibited slavery in 1829, the American settlers resisted all Mexican attempts to bring them into compliance. The importance of Texas to American struggles over slavery would soon be apparent.

Pro-slavery theorists were troubled by the prospect of being outnumbered by the free states. They worried about the growing abolitionist movement, fearing that a militant and abolitionist North might begin to wield the power of the federal government in ways that would insinuate an anti-slavery agenda into slave states by measured degrees.

These fears propelled one of the most spectacular ideological turnabouts in American history, the transformation of South Carolina's preeminent political leader John C. Calhoun from an ardent supporter of broad construction of the Constitution for the purpose of creating magnificent public works (a program he supported when he served as secretary of war under James Monroe) into a militant strict constructionist and states-rights advocate, shrilly committed to the platform that federal tariffs to finance internal improvements were an abrogation of the rights of the sovereign states. Such was the justification of the famous "nullification" campaign against the Tariff of 1828. This controversy, which erupted when Lincoln was about to turn twenty years old, was settled by another compromise brokered by Henry Clay in 1833.

The nullification controversy—a controversy over taxes, the rights of states, and the subtleties of constitutional logic—is generally offered as "Exhibit A" by the people who argue that the controversy over slavery could not possibly in and of itself have caused the Civil War, and that other issues, mostly economic and constitutional issues, were more fundamental.

But slavery *was* the central issue all the while, as the nullification leaders admitted. The nullification episode was largely a pretext—a symbolic rallying point—a flashpoint for agitation by which to generate leverage against the much larger formations of power that the agitators envisioned just over the horizon.

Calhoun admitted as much in his private correspondence. Notwithstanding his denunciation of the so-called Tariff of Abominations, in 1830 Calhoun confided: "I consider the Tariff, but as the occasion, rather than the real cause of the present unhappy state of things. . . . The truth can no longer be disguised, that the peculiar domestick institutions of the Southern States . . . [have] placed them in regard to taxation and appropriation in opposite relation to the majority of the Union; against the danger of which, if there be no protective power in the reserved rights of the states, they must in the end be forced to rebel, or submit to have . . . their domestick institutions exhausted by Colonization and other schemes, and themselves & children reduced to wretchedness."[15]

A fellow South Carolina "nullifier" named James Hamilton, Jr., made the same point: "I have always looked upon the present contest with the government, on the part of the Southern States, as a battle at the outposts, by which, if we succeeded in repulsing the enemy, *the citadel would be safe*. The same doctrines 'of the general welfare' which enable the general government to . . . appropriate the common treasure to make roads and canals . . . would authorize the federal government to erect the *peaceful* standard of servile revolt, to give the bounties for Emancipation here, and transportation to Liberia afterwards."[16]

The point was this: in light of the majority status that the free-state bloc had been gaining, the most militant slave-state leaders decided to prevent any sizable concentration of power—including the power to raise significant amounts of revenue—at the federal level, lest a newly powerful federal government fall into the hands of abolitionists, who would use their power to strike at the slavery system in all of the slave states. Historian William W. Freehling put it succinctly; the nullifiers feared that "the 'general welfare' clause would serve abolitionists as well as road builders."[17]

The most extreme Southern militants were dubious even of nullification. In 1830, a South Carolinian named John Richardson proclaimed the "absurdity of assuming the right to nullify Federal laws, *as a sovereign right reserved to the State*," when the rights of any state could be easily trumped through the power of a constitutional amendment, as soon as three-quarters of the states had chosen to ratify one. The sovereign powers of a state, he argued, could in turn be "controlled by three-fourths of the States."[18]

The 1830s

Slaveowners' fears became greater in the 1830s with the emergence of a radical new generation of abolitionists such as William Lloyd Garrison. And the outbreak at last of a full-fledged slave revolt—the 1831 Nat Turner Revolt in Virginia—quickened fears that had haunted the proslavery mind since the 1790s. Consequently, opinions on both sides of the issue became more militant during the 1830s, when Lincoln was beginning his political career.

The new abolitionists were militant in different degrees and in different ways. Some of them followed the philosophic lead of Garrison, who gradually expanded his anti-slavery principles to encompass a complete renunciation of force in human relationships, a radical and in many ways utopian worldview. Garrisonian abolitionists were increasingly non-political and even anti-political. But others, following the leadership of Theodore Dwight Weld, believed that the slavery system should be challenged not only through moral agitation but also political action.[19]

Weld, it bears noting, was happily married to an abolitionist woman from Charleston, South Carolina: Angelina Grimké, whose sister Sarah Grimké was also an abolitionist.

Many of the new abolitionists were sincere advocates of racial equality. They were therefore highly unpopular figures at a time in American history when mainstream culture was pervaded by the notions of white supremacy.

The idealism of the abolitionist movement grew steadily. The movement was augmented significantly by the participation of people such as Frederick Douglass, an escaped slave who became an important abolitionist leader in the 1840s and afterward. Free blacks (such as David Walker) had played a fundamental role in the abolitionist movement for a while.[20] But the leadership provided by former slaves was even more dramatic.

Foreign events, moreover, played a role in the issue once again: in 1833, British abolitionists succeeded in convincing Parliament to end the institution of slavery throughout the Empire. The goal was achieved through a program of gradual and compensated emancipation. This decisive event inspired the creation of the American Anti-Slavery Society.

Yet throughout the 1830s, the militance of the new abolitionist radicals was matched by a growing pro-slavery militance, such that John C. Calhoun declared in his notorious "Positive Good" speech of 1837 that the greatness of every superior civilization was grounded in the existence of a mud-sill class of degraded workers.[21] It was a militance that prompted several slave-holding states to pass laws against abolitionist speeches and rallies, against the publishing of abolitionist books, and against the possession of abolitionist literature. (It should be noted that nineteenth-century jurisprudence viewed the Bill of Rights as a bulwark against actions by the federal government, and not against actions by the states.)[22] It was a militance that prompted Southern postmasters to search and censor the mails in order to destroy abolitionist tracts. It was a militance that foisted a "Gag Rule" upon the Congress, a rule that from 1836 to 1844 prevented congressional discussion of abolitionist petitions by automatically tabling them.

In the South, the establishment of this new authoritarian "Cordon Sanitaire" forced the anti-slavery movement into hiding or out of existence.[23] In the North, the anti-slavery movement was approaching a crossroads. This was the political world in which Lincoln was rising in the state of Illinois as he approached the age of thirty.

In 1836, Texas achieved its independence from Mexico. Texas petitioned Congress for admission to the Union as a state—as potentially the largest state in the Union—and as a huge new bastion of slavery. Texas annexation hung in limbo for the next nine years, and the reason was obvious.

The 1840s

The sectional dispute over slavery continued in the 1840s, when Lincoln was elected to Congress. By the end of the decade the slavery issue was dominating the political life of the United States, and pro-slavery militants were threatening to break up the Union unless the abolitionist threat could be removed on a permanent basis.

The abolitionists themselves had become increasingly politicized. Some of them joined the new Liberty Party, whose nominee for the presidency in 1840 and again in 1844 was James G. Birney, a former slave owner. The Liberty Party succeeded in electing only one of its members to Congress (Gerrit Smith of New York). And yet a growing number of congressmen owed their elections to anti-slavery voters. For that reason, an anti-slavery bloc was emerging in Congress.

The most urgent dispute about slavery during the early 1840s was the issue of Texas. The issue had festered since 1836, when the Texans had broken away from Mexico and proclaimed their country an independent republic, at least until annexation to the United States could be achieved. In 1843, President John Tyler, a pro-slavery Virginian, appointed John C. Calhoun as his secretary of state, and the two of them forced the Texas issue by submitting an annexation treaty to the Senate. The Senate rejected this treaty, and the Texas question became a major source of controversy in the 1844 presidential election.

In 1844, the voters of the United States elected James K. Polk of Tennessee. Polk supported the annexation of Texas. But he believed that he could pacify the anti-Texas opposition by the time-honored methods of regional compromise. In a bid to appease anti-slavery sentiment, Polk suggested that the annexation of Texas be linked to the acquisition of the Oregon country, which the United States and Great Britain had occupied jointly pursuant to an 1818 treaty. Once again, the accession of additional land for the institution of slavery would be counter-balanced by an augmentation of land in which slavery would probably never take root—or so it seemed to conventional wisdom.

Upon Polk's election, lame-duck President Tyler proclaimed that a mandate for Texas annexation had been given. Through adroit maneuvering in Congress, Tyler was able to invite the Republic of Texas to join the United States in 1845.

Simultaneously, Florida, another slave state, joined the Union, and in quick succession, two more free states: Iowa, admitted to statehood in 1846, and Wisconsin, in 1847.

The years in which the old techniques of territorial balance could contain the slavery dispute were drawing to a close. A fundamental change had overtaken the anti-slavery movement, a change of over-powering magnitude. More and more, the movement's political power was centered in a broad coalition of anti-slavery whites who were not necessarily abolitionists at all, a coalition whose members often denied any interest in promoting racial equality. On the contrary, many of them were white supremacists, who saw slavery as an infringement of the liberties of *whites*.

It abridged white liberties by keeping poor whites from the best agricultural lands in the Southern states. It preempted the choicest plantations for the use of a selfish and arrogant elite. It abridged white liberties by spreading this system to the West, by sending out scores of would-be plantation nabobs, with thousands of enslaved black drudges in tow, to monopolize the great new Western empire and keep it from "the common man."

It abridged white liberties by censoring the words of Southern citizens who challenged the system, by stifling the voices of white representatives in Congress, by threatening murder and torture to any poor lout who presumed to think himself man enough to challenge the self-proclaimed lords and masters of Dixie. This, said the leaders of the "Free-Soil movement," was a threat to the liberties of all.[24]

It was something un-American, they said, and it threatened to pull the United States backward into Old World social conditions, back to medieval misery with lords of the manor in control, and their wretched vassals down below. Having started down the path to autocracy by tyrannizing blacks, the leaders of America's "Slave Power" were beginning to tyrannize whites. More and more, the militant protection of the slavery system was suppressing white freedom of speech, curtailing white freedom of the press, and threatening vocal white opponents of the system with beatings, whippings, and death.

In 1845, a dramatic development in Richmond, Virginia increased these fears even more. White workers at the Tredegar Iron Works called a strike for better hours and wages. The owner of the factory proceeded to fire them all and then rented—actually *rented*—enough slaves to run his factory effectively. American slavery was suddenly proven effective in industrial settings. And it had taken the jobs of white workers.[25]

Because of these fears and concerns, the anti-slavery bloc in Congress grew apace. And the Polk administration collided with its leaders when the president chose to pick a new territorial fight with Mexico.

Polk was indeed a believer in America's "Empire of Liberty." He meant to expand it to continental size by acquiring not only the Oregon country, but the Mexican province of California as well. His attempt to buy California from Mexico was quickly rebuffed. Unfazed, he proceeded to agitate relations with Mexico, ordering American troops onto land that was disputed by the Texans and Mexicans.

As the Mexican War erupted in 1846, the anti-slavery leaders in Congress took action. A Free-Soil Democrat from Pennsylvania named David Wilmot proposed a proviso to a war appropriations bill on August 8, 1846. The Wilmot Proviso declared "that, as an express and fundamental condition of the acquisition of any territory from the Republic of Mexico . . . neither slavery nor involuntary servitude shall ever exist in any part of said territory." The proviso was passed by the House of Representatives but killed in the Senate.

Once again, the territorial issue put slavery at the center of American politics. Southern newspapers praised California as a natural extension of Dixie and claimed that California was perfect for slavery.

But no sooner had Mexico consented to sell California and New Mexico in 1848 than gold was discovered in the streams of California, bringing in swarms of feisty "forty-niners." They got to California fast, most frequently in clipper ships racing south "around the Horn" and then up the west coast of South America. Before slave owners could make their way to California, the settlers applied for admission to the Union as a free state, and pro-slavery Southerners cried foul.

There had not been sufficient time, they protested, to give the South a real chance in California. Events had moved too quickly. Slave owners needed time to extend and to stabilize their Cordon Sanitaire. They needed time to convince a territorial legislature to pass a tough and effective slave code in order to prevent or suppress any slave insurrections and to catch any fugitive slaves.[26] The South was being pushed around, they declared—preempted in a fight for supremacy.

All the while, the slavery issue was tearing away at America's political parties. The Free-Soil movement was furious, its leaders reviling the Polk administration and its infamous "war to expand slavery." The

Wilmot Proviso was revived; over fifty different versions were passed by the House of Representatives between 1846 and 1850. But all of them were killed in the Senate, because the votes between the free- and slave-state blocs were equal.

To break the impasse, Polk suggested extending the Missouri Compromise line to the Pacific, which would turn California into *two* states. But most of the Free-Soil leaders and slave-state leaders wanted none of it.

In 1848, the Democratic Party nominated Senator Lewis Cass of Michigan for president. Cass tried to play it safe on the territorial problem by espousing "Popular Sovereignty," a policy that would allow white settlers to decide about the slavery issue themselves on a case-by-case basis. But the doctrine of Popular Sovereignty begged the crucial question as to *when* these settlers would have their say: *before* the institution of slavery had entered a territory (thus angering the owners of slaves), or *afterward*, when the institution might be very hard to dislodge, thus offending Free-Soilers?

Because of widespread contempt for this policy among the members of the Free-Soil movement, renegade Democrats bolted and joined with anti-slavery citizens across party lines to form a "Free-Soil Party" under the leadership of former President Martin Van Buren.

The other major party, the Whigs, selected a military hero as their candidate in 1848: General Zachary Taylor, "Old Rough and Ready." While Taylor belonged to neither party and had never even voted, he did own slaves, along with some large plantations in Mississippi and Louisiana, and his daughter (by that time deceased) had been married to Senator Jefferson Davis of Mississippi.

Free-Soil Whigs ("Conscience Whigs," as they called themselves) were sufficiently troubled by the nomination of Taylor to bolt from their party to the Free-Soil Party of Van Buren. But Taylor won the election, and he promptly astonished both Northerners and Southerners by siding with the Free-Soil movement.

Though Taylor owned slaves, he selected a prominent congressional anti-slavery leader, Senator William H. Seward of New York, as his adviser. Taylor proposed that California and New Mexico skip the territorial stage and be admitted as states—free states—immediately. The South was in an uproar.

In 1849 and 1850, Senator John C. Calhoun made it clear that the Union was in grave jeopardy. It was the slavery issue that threatened destruction of the Union, he warned. "I have, Senators," he thundered, "believed from the first that the agitation of the subject of slavery would, if not prevented by some timely and effective measure, end in disunion." In the current crisis, he predicted, "California will become the test question. If you admit her, under all the difficulties that oppose her admission, you compel us to infer that you intend to exclude us from the whole of the acquired territories, with the intention of destroying, irretrievably, the equilibrium between the two sections."[27]

Calhoun, like his fellow Southern "Fire Eaters," felt pushed to the brink by two related circumstances: first, the presidential power of Taylor, a military hero, a determined leader, and a newly revealed (or newly unmasked) adherent of the Free-Soil movement; and second, the loss to the slave-state bloc of the entire West Coast of North America. This situation prompted Calhoun to call for new and permanent measures to protect the interests of slavery. He warned that only an amendment of the Constitution for the permanent protection of slavery would appease Southern fears about the abolitionist threat.

Calhoun had barely a month to live when, on March 4, 1850, he called upon the North to agree to drafting the amendment. But the Constitution was not to be amended that year. Instead, Senator Henry Clay took his final bow as America's "Great Pacificator." He crafted yet another big regional compromise for passage by Congress.

1850

The Compromise of 1850, however, was a mess, and it satisfied no one. California would enter the Union as a new free state, but the slave-state system remained a possibility in all the newly acquired lands between Texas and California, which would henceforth be settled on the basis of "Popular Sovereignty."

To satisfy anti-slavery proponents, the slave trade would be ended in Washington, D.C. But to appease pro-slavery sentiment, a tough new Fugitive Slave Law would be passed to empower the federal government to catch runaway slaves.[28] This latter provision, importantly, showed that the defenders of slavery could jettison the doctrine of "states' rights" whenever they perceived the possibility of using the federal government's power to police their system.

President Taylor opposed this compromise, and urged its rejection emphatically. But then Taylor suddenly died of a digestive illness, and Vice President Millard Fillmore, his successor, supported the compromise. Congress passed it as a package of measures in August and September of 1850, after months of fiery debate.

But the sectional tensions emerged more powerfully than ever when a staunch pro-slavery Democrat, Franklin Pierce, won the presidency in 1852. Concurrently, the advocates of slavery began an audacious new counterattack on the Free-Soil movement. They attempted to expand the territorial reach of slavery to unheard-of dimensions. It was this campaign that propelled Lincoln into the maelstrom.

For over thirty years, the geopolitical struggle of the slave-state bloc and the free-state bloc had swerved back and forth, with each side probing and grasping for a method that would somehow guarantee protection to its own social system and preempt the menace of the other. Through most of this period, the intermittent struggles kept returning to a tense "equilibrium." But, by the 1850s, the days of equilibrium were over.

AS THE STRUGGLE OVER SLAVERY DEVELOPED, young Lincoln was a novice politician. He was quiet on the issue of slavery. But within him were tremendous reserves of audacity—and a powerful capacity for outrage. These qualities emerged full-blown after many years of reflection.

In the multitudinous studies of Lincoln produced since his death—all of the biographies and monographs, specialized studies, and assessments of his words and deeds—the complexities of Lincoln's personality continue to challenge us. He was the awkward-looking yokel from the backwoods who had a brilliant and penetrating mind. He was the blithe and gregarious spinner of yarns, the best raconteur in his surroundings, possessing a rich and boundless repertoire of earthy stories. But he was also a man who could suddenly withdraw into reveries, sinking at times into profoundly morbid spells, which he called "the hypos."

He was precocious, rebelling at a very early age against farm life and all of its tedium. He read constantly, absorbing Shakespearean drama, the works of Euclid, the poems of Byron and Robert Burns, and the Bible—though mostly to refute it at first, since his early religious views were decidedly skeptical.[29]

He taught himself surveying and law. He ran for public office in his twenties. An ardent follower of Henry Clay, he believed in heroic government. He advocated for public works and "internal improvements" that would build up the nation and provide its people with employment. In 1834 he was elected to the Illinois legislature at age twenty-five.

His political techniques could vary from conciliation and reason to the use of merciless ridicule (which led in one case to a challenge to a duel) to the droll and self-deprecating humor for which he would later become quite famous to the stirring and electrifying oratory that he put to such important use in later years.

His first public stance on the slavery issue took the form of a negative vote. Some slavery supporters had sent to the Illinois legislature a package of provocative resolutions affirming the constitutionality of slavery in states that permitted it while condemning anti-slavery agitation by abolitionists. Lincoln joined a small minority in voting "no" to these resolutions when the issue was considered in January 1837.

The minority was small because the attitudes of white supremacy were rampant in frontier America. Abolitionists were often reviled in the 1830s as the vanguard of "mongrelization." In November 1837, a pro-slavery mob in the town of Alton, Illinois, had murdered an abolitionist editor named Elijah Lovejoy.

This incident served as the backdrop to one Lincoln's most important early speeches, his address to the Young Men's Lyceum of Springfield, Illinois, on January 27, 1838, almost two months after Lovejoy's murder. Without mentioning the incident directly, Lincoln condemned mob rule, which he singled out as the greatest existing threat to the United States. But his speech went on to identify other potential threats to republics that might very well threaten America in days to come. Many of these threats were inherent in human nature, Lincoln observed.

The worst of them all was an emerging spirit of autocracy, whatever its symptoms. Throughout history, Lincoln observed, most republics had succumbed to the machinations of power mongers, to Napoleonic and Caesarian figures whose audacious ambition "thirsts and burns for distinction, and, if possible . . . will have it, whether at the expense of emancipating slaves, or enslaving freemen."

Consequently, asked Lincoln, is it really far-fetched for Americans "to expect, that some man possessed of the loftiest genius, coupled with ambition sufficient to push it to the utmost stretch, will at some time, spring up among us? And when it does, it will require the people to be united with each other, attached to the government and laws . . . to successfully frustrate his designs."[30]

It was the wide-ranging critic and novelist Edmund Wilson who perceived, in the early 1950s, that Lincoln's Lyceum Speech might have
been something truly extraordinary: that Lincoln might well have been
using this occasion to imagine for himself his own future role in American history, while doing it in terms that were *negative*, at least in part.

The towering "genius" envisioned by Lincoln, the ambitious leader
who imagined both the possibility of emancipating slaves and of enslaving free men, was an image as it seemed to Wilson that in some
ways attracted but also troubled the young politician.[31] In Wilson's
opinion, as Lincoln gave the speech he was in all probability conjuring
with his own inner urge to greatness.

On an obvious level, the Lyceum Speech was an oratorical set piece,
a reiteration of familiar political proverbs, which, since Napoleon's
rise and fall, had revived all the ancient warnings against the "Caesarian" threat to republics. On this level, certainly, the Lyceum Speech
was not unusual.

But if Wilson's observations have real psychological validity, the
Lyceum Speech was quite remarkable. It was nothing less, perhaps,
than a channel through which Lincoln poured out a secret knowledge
of his own latent talents in gathering and orchestrating power, while
expressing a guilt-ridden fear that these abilities amounted to hubris.

Writing several years after Edmund Wilson, political philosopher
Harry V. Jaffa examined the same speech and concurred on its importance. Indeed, said Jaffa, Lincoln "seems to have concentrated his whole
inner life upon preparing for the crisis foretold in the Lyceum speech."[32]

But for Jaffa, this speech was a philosophic "teaching," a warning by
an upcoming statesman that all truly free societies should ask of their
citizens a basic control of their passions. Republics, in order to protect
their inner nature, must require of their people an ethical restraint
against the surging projections of ego that could otherwise verge into
tyranny—whether it amounted to the tyranny that slave owners showed
to their slaves, or the tyranny of mobs lashing out against their helpless
victims, or the tyranny of would-be emancipating geniuses, believers
in heroic government, who, above all, must always remember to summon and wield their power in a manner that preserves their republic
instead of undermining its substance.

Whatever the meaning of this thought-provoking speech, Lincoln
resolutely continued to support the philosophy of Henry Clay, that
consummate believer in energetic government. Lincoln also supported

the Whig Party's national agenda for "internal improvements" and economic expansion.

In the economic depression that followed the Panic of 1837, for instance, Lincoln pushed for the creation of extensive public works to turn the economy around and ease unemployment, even if that meant financing them through deficit spending on occasion. By the end of the 1830s, Lincoln had risen to membership in the leadership "Junto" controlling his state's Whig organization.

Lincoln's service in the Illinois legislature ended in 1842. Shortly thereafter he began to prepare for a congressional career, and his efforts paid off with his election in 1846 to the House of Representatives. His service in Congress, which lasted from 1847 to 1849, coincided with his party's opposition to the Polk administration's foreign policy. Not only did Lincoln oppose the Mexican War as an act of shameful aggression, he also supported the Wilmot Proviso in its various incarnations.

Lincoln, like many Americans, had been turning his thoughts to the slavery issue more intensely in the 1840s. Moreover, an experience in 1841 affected his feelings on the issue profoundly. Traveling aboard an Ohio River steamer, he saw twelve slaves being shipped to the Deep South; they were chained together, he observed, "like so many fish upon a trot-line."[33] Years later, he said that the experience was "a continual torment to me," and that the slavery issue "had the power of making me miserable."[34]

By 1846, he had joined the Free-Soil movement within the Whig Party, and his opposition to slavery became more pronounced. In January 1849, he informed the House of Representatives that he would introduce legislation to abolish the institution of slavery in Washington, D.C. But when Lincoln sized up the prospects for passing such a bill, he gave up the venture as futile.

In his political orientation, Lincoln still remained devoted to the levelheaded principles of Henry Clay, his mentor. And Clay, in addition to supporting active government, took special pride in his role as the nation's impresario of sectional compromise, the orchestrator of the great Missouri Compromise of 1820 and the Compromise of 1850.

While Clay was an opponent of slavery, he was truly a *moderate* one. He had served for a very long time as president of the cautious American Colonization Society, for which reason he was often denounced by abolitionist militants.

After a long and illustrious career, Clay died in 1852. Lincoln's eulogy, delivered in Springfield, demonstrates the steady influence that Clay's anti-slavery precepts continued to exert upon his thought. Since the days of the Missouri Compromise, Lincoln observed, Americans had rightly regarded Henry Clay as "*the* man" in periods of national crisis, and especially in crises over slavery.

Clay had saved his country on several occasions, said Lincoln, and he hoped to see America flourish more and more as a land of universal freedom. Clay supported the eventual abolition of slavery, and he did so throughout his life as a matter of fundamental conviction, according to Lincoln. "He was, on principle and feeling, opposed to slavery," Lincoln observed. "The very earliest, and one of the latest public efforts of his life . . . were both made in favor of gradual emancipation of slaves in Kentucky. He did not perceive, that on a question of human right, the negroes were to be excepted from the human race."

Yet Clay was also a gradualist who thought that the two "extremes" in the great dispute over slavery were both misguided. Clay opposed the sorts of abolitionists, Lincoln said, "who would shiver into fragments the Union of these states; tear to tatters its now venerated constitution; and even burn the last copy of the Bible, rather than slavery should continue a single hour. . . ." Such people, said Lincoln, "have received, and are receiving their just execration. . . ."

But Clay, added Lincoln, was also opposed to the other extreme in the slavery debate, the Southern militants who, "for the sake of perpetuating slavery, are beginning to assail and to ridicule the white-man's charter of freedom—the declaration that 'all men are created free and equal.'"

Clay fervently hoped to resolve the problem of slavery through colonization, and Lincoln went on to commend this vision, citing images from Scripture as he did so:

> Pharaoh's country was cursed with plagues, and his hosts were drowned in the Red Sea for striving to retain a captive people who had already served them more than four hundred years. May like disasters never befall us! If as the friends of colonization hope, the present and coming generations of our countrymen shall . . . succeed in freeing our land from the dangerous presence of slavery; and, at the same time, in restoring a captive people to their long-lost fatherland, with bright prospects for the future; and this too, so gradually, that neither races nor individuals shall have suffered by the change, it will indeed be a glorious consummation. And if, to such a consummation, the efforts of Mr.

Clay shall have contributed . . . none of his labors will have been more valuable
to his country. . . .[35]

It is striking to observe at this point the degree to which passages
such as the above appear to vindicate all of the conventional views about
Lincoln as a moderate Unionist, a man who had pledged himself to the
rule of sweet reason and its corollary ethics of compromise, a man who
scorned both extremes in the American slavery dispute, and who advocated mild and gradual measures to resolve the problem over time.
Here, if anywhere, the evidence presents us with a very clear portrait
of the Lincoln who is currently praised (or attacked) for his steady
ways of "moderation."

Look closely at the picture while it lasts. For the Lincoln who had
eulogized Henry Clay was about to change his precepts forever.

An event just beyond the historical horizon as he eulogized his hero,
an event that would burst upon the nation only two years later—an
event so completely disgusting to Lincoln as to catalyze his inner potential through the force of irrepressible outrage—was about to cause
Lincoln to transform himself into a very different kind of politician.

He would swiftly abandon the principles of Clay and embrace, in effect, the more determined politics of Zachary Taylor as he launched a
new phase of his career, a phase that would quickly propel him to the
head of the Free-Soil movement and beyond, to his presidential destiny.

This was the Lincoln who would start to denounce any further appeasement on slavery. This was the Lincoln who prepared to use federal force in the struggle.

This was the Lincoln who avowed, as the crisis of secession was
approaching, that "the tug" between the advocates and foes of American slavery expansion should come, and "better now than later." This
was the Lincoln who would cast aside doubts and push his gifts to the
"utmost stretch"—not to dominate his country like Napoleon or
Caesar, but to realize the hopes of its Founders.

He aspired to be America's executive commander of the free in their
greatest ordeal. And he was only beginning to discover the extent of
his powers.

TWO

Lincoln and Free Soil, 1854–1858

LINCOLN'S SURGE into national prominence began with a series of speeches that he gave in the autumn of 1854. By the end of the decade, he emerged as a forceful new leader of the Free-Soil movement and the new Republican Party. It started with his angry reaction to a cataclysmic development in the early part of 1854.

After months of impassioned debate, Congress voted to repeal the Missouri Compromise of 1820. What this meant for the ongoing sectional struggle over slavery remained to be seen. But for people like Abraham Lincoln, what it meant was almost unbelievable. It meant that all the unorganized lands that still remained in the Louisiana Territory would be opened again to slavery.

The move resulted in a wave of anger and loathing that electrified the Free-Soil movement. For Lincoln, the repeal of the Missouri Compromise was nothing short of an obscenity. And it was largely the work of an old political rival, Stephen A. Douglas.

The advocates of slavery had been taking the offensive since 1852. They were clearly emboldened by the fact that a pro-slavery democrat had won the presidency in that year. He was a "northern man of southern principles," Franklin Pierce of New Hampshire. To a certain extent, the Democrats had won because the Whigs were so bitterly divided in regard to the Compromise of 1850. While the Democratic Party was also divided into Free-Soil and pro-slavery factions, the old belief in Manifest Destiny—the belief that the expansion of American territory would unify whites, both North and South, as they joined together in the great adventure of building the "Empire of

Liberty"—died hard in the Democratic Party, notwithstanding the fact that its use by the Polk administration had intensified the slavery dispute instead of quieting it.

In 1850, Governor John A. Quitman of Mississippi tried to help a Venezuelan soldier of fortune named Narciso Lopez in fomenting a revolt by the Cuban people against their imperial overlord, Spain. Lopez, Quitman, and others were indicted by the federal government (under the Fillmore administration) for violating American neutrality laws. Quitman resigned as governor to defend himself against the charges.[1]

No sooner had Pierce won the presidency, however, than Quitman was at it again: he tried to organize an American "filibustering" expedition that would "liberate" Cuba and annex it to the Union as a slave state. Other "filibusterers"—a Spanish-derived term for pirates or desperadoes—began to call for a second Mexican War to create more expansion room for slavery. In 1853, a Tennessean named William Walker invaded Mexico with a band of followers. But the Mexicans overpowered his forces and ejected him.

In 1854, under the leadership of a Virginian named George Bickley, a secret organization called the "Knights of the Golden Circle" was founded in Kentucky. Its members dreamed of a "Golden Circle" of rule by the white master race, a tropical empire for slavery that would take in the whole Caribbean rim, including upper South America.[2]

Throughout the 1850s, this "filibustering" spirit generated one provocation after another in Latin America. Senator Albert Gallatin Brown of Mississippi pushed for annexation of Cuba along with additional conquests in Mexico and Central America. He wanted "Cuba . . . and one or two other Mexican States; and I want them all for the same reason—for the planting or spreading of slavery."[3]

In 1854, at the request of Pierce's secretary of state, three diplomats, Pierre Soulé of Louisiana, John Y. Mason of Virginia, and James Buchanan of Pennsylvania—another "northern man of southern principles," as well as the next man to occupy the White House—met in Ostend, Belgium to confer about the Cuba "issue." Their aim was to trigger a sequence of events that would lead to American seizure of the island. They proclaimed, in their soon-to-be notorious "Ostend Manifesto," that if Spain refused to sell Cuba, Americans would be perfectly justified in taking it over.

These attempts to expand the slavery system through additional sei-
zures of territory were prompted by the widespread desire in the slave-
holding states to "keep up" with the free-state bloc in numerical power.
But the need to maintain the Southern "Cordon Sanitaire" was also
important. Congressman Thomas L. Clingman of North Carolina said
that Northerners were surely too intelligent to think "that humanity,
either to the slave or the master, requires that they should be pent up
within a territory which after a time will be insufficient for their subsistence, and where they must perish from want, or from collision that
would occur between the races."[4]

Collision that would occur between the races: the old Southern fear
of slave insurrections was as powerful a theme in the 1850s as it was in
previous decades. According to pro-slavery theorists, the expansion of
slavery amounted to the operation of a salutary pressure valve that would
siphon off the "excess" black population in the interest of public safety.
The fear was that the blacks would outnumber the whites and endan-
ger white supremacist control.

So the advocates of American slavery were pushing more fervently
than ever in the early 1850s to expand their system. They did it without apology. They did it, indeed, with an air of self-conscious bravado.
This was the context of sectional politics in which Senator Stephen A.
Douglas of Illinois ignited a firestorm in 1854.

Like many Americans, Douglas was advocating the construction of
a transcontinental railroad to hasten the flow of people and goods between the new state of California and the rest of America. Moreover,
Douglas was committed to a northerly route that would extend due
west from Chicago, his state's greatest city. It seemed imperative to
Douglas that the western lands along this route be settled and admitted to the Union quickly.

In 1853, at the behest of Douglas, the Pierce administration took
steps to remove all the Indian peoples who were living in Nebraska, a
territorial subdivision of the Louisiana Territory. Nebraska lay immediately north and west of the slave state of Missouri.

After Indian removal was completed, the next precondition for construction of the railroad was the preparation of Nebraska for statehood.
To this end, Douglas crafted and introduced legislation that was passed
by the House of Representatives in February 1853. But then the slave
state leaders objected when the measure was sent to the Senate.

Because of the Missouri Compromise, they reminded Douglas and his supporters, the territory of Nebraska was forbidden to slavery. Nebraska lay beyond the great dividing line that ran across the Louisiana Purchase, the dividing line that began at the southern border of Missouri and forbade the introduction of slavery both to the north and west of the state.

Senator David Atchison of Missouri declared that he would sooner see Nebraska "sink in hell" than he would ever consent to the creation of any more free states near Missouri. Most of the Senators from slaveholding states took a similar position.

Then, pro-slavery leaders began to see a more interesting angle in the issue of Nebraska statehood. They began to see a chance to convert their initially defensive reaction to Douglas's bill into a new and decisive opportunity to launch a pro-slavery offensive. Led by David Atchison of Missouri, Robert M.T. Hunter of Virginia, Andrew Butler of South Carolina, and others, the slave-state bloc leaders saw a chance in Douglas's predicament to open another geographical front for the expansion of slavery. They decided to hold the Nebraska bill hostage until Douglas consented to repeal the old dividing line established in the Missouri Compromise.

By the end of 1853, Stephen Douglas began to come around. And on January 4, 1854, he introduced legislation to create a new Nebraska policy. His bill, which he introduced on January 4, consigned the slavery issue in Nebraska to the principles of "Popular Sovereignty." His bill stipulated that Congress would vote on Nebraska statehood "with or without slavery as her constitution may prescribe."

But this tremendous concession was still not enough for pro-slavery leaders. Senator Archibald Dixon of Kentucky introduced an amendment to the Nebraska bill that explicitly repealed the section of the Missouri Compromise (the Thomas Proviso) that established the anti-slavery dividing line.

Douglas capitulated: on January 23, 1854, he revised his Nebraska bill to incorporate the Dixon amendment. He also consented to divide Nebraska into northern and southern segments. The northern portion would retain the name of Nebraska while the southern portion would bear the name of Kansas.

And since Kansas was situated right next door to Missouri, it was widely presumed at the time that it would enter the Union as a slave state, just like its older neighbor to the east. For whatever it was worth,

Douglas struggled to remind his constituents that settlers in Kansas and Nebraska would certainly decide the matter for themselves.

The Free-Soil movement was livid. *An Appeal of the Independent Democrats*, written by Salmon P. Chase and Joshua R. Giddings, accused Stephen Douglas of a "gross violation of a sacred pledge" in repealing the Missouri Compromise. Nonetheless, with crucial support from President Pierce, the Kansas-Nebraska Bill was passed by Congress in May 1854 and signed into law. In theory, all the unorganized lands in the Louisiana Territory were open to slavery. No one could be sure of where the owners of slaves might settle.

All through the summer of 1854, the backlash against this series of events began to shake the foundations of the two-party system in the North. Free-Soil Democrats and Conscience Whigs began abandoning their parties and joining together in hopes of creating a "fusion" movement that would put the Free-Soil issue at the center of its national agenda. The new Republican Party emerged rather quickly as the clear frontrunner in the movement.

As anti-slavery leaders looked back upon the shattering events of that spring, they were aghast: was there nothing too audacious for the leaders of the slave-state bloc to foist upon the nation? At this critical juncture, a provocative book was published in Virginia. While its audience was limited at first to the regional vicinity, it was triggering reactions by the end of the year from as far away as New York City, where Horace Greeley, editor of the *New York Tribune*, condemned it.[5]

The book was entitled *Sociology for the South*, and its author was a Virginia planter named George Fitzhugh. Ever since the forthright defense of slavery by John C. Calhoun, pro-slavery literature in the United States was common. What set this new book apart from the others, however, was its astonishing radicalism.

Fitzhugh argued that slavery was such an obviously wise and justified social institution that its benefits ought to extend across the race line. Indirectly, he seemed to be recommending the enslavement of "inferior" whites.

Fitzhugh took direct aim at America's iconic fountainhead of anti-slavery ideals, his fellow Virginian Thomas Jefferson. With sarcastic verve, he took on the man who had stated in the final year of his life, "the mass of mankind has not been born with saddles on their backs, nor a favored few booted and spurred, ready to ride them legitimately by the grace of God."

Quite wrong, said Fitzhugh, for precisely the reverse was true. It was a clear and self-evident truth, he insisted, that inferior people are suited by their nature to the status of dependent livestock: "It would be nearer the truth to say," he continued with relish, "that some were born with saddles on their backs, and others booted and spurred to ride them; and the riding does them good." "Slavery," he continued, "is the natural and normal condition of the working man, whether white or black."[6]

And there it was: the spectre that had energized the leaders of the Free-Soil movement since the early 1840s, the threat that American slavery would gradually erode the liberty of whites just as surely as it stole away the liberties of blacks.

The Fitzhugh book began to penetrate the North about the same time that Senator Stephen Douglas came back to Chicago, Illinois, to explain himself to his constituents, to mend some fences if he could. But he was greeted at home with rage. As he looked out the window of his train, he saw his own burning effigy in cities across the state.

When he arrived in Chicago, he lost his temper and cursed at a hostile crowd. Afterward, he was hounded by "Anti-Nebraska" speakers who followed him, pelting him with ridicule and vilifying the Kansas-Nebraska Act.

In a series of speeches throughout Illinois, Douglas answered his Free-Soil critics. His application of the principle of Popular Sovereignty to Kansas and Nebraska, he said, was merely an extension of the Compromise of 1850, which adopted the very same policy in all of the newly acquired lands between Texas and California. Besides, he boasted, the principle of letting the people in every new territory choose for themselves by majority vote about the presence of slavery was nothing less than American democracy at work. And the principle of letting American whites decide the fate of American blacks was also quite natural and wholesome, he said.

In any case, he contended, the chance that slavery would root itself in Kansas and Nebraska was negligible. The climate and soil of the plains, he theorized, were clearly unsuited to slavery.

Some of his listeners began to be convinced by these nimble arguments. But others, like Lincoln, were even more enraged at Douglas than before.

For Lincoln, these weeks and months became the great turning point of his career. Not only the developments themselves but also the seductive perversities of Douglas caused Lincoln to abandon any previous restraints or inhibitions in asserting his Free-Soil convictions.

But Lincoln did not choose to join the new Republican Party right away. He was not at all certain that the situation of the old Whig Party was hopeless. What he did, however, was to take to the stump against Douglas in the autumn months of 1854.

In the city of Bloomington, Illinois, he accosted Douglas in mid-to-late September. But the angry Douglas refused to debate him. So Lincoln gave speeches by himself on September 12 and September 26. These two speeches in Bloomington were published only in summary form.

Then Lincoln followed Douglas to Springfield. On October 3, as Douglas gave his usual remarks of prepared self-justification, Lincoln paced back and forth in the hall. He then announced to the crowd that he would answer Douglas point for point on the very next day and in the very same location. Like the Bloomington speeches, the text of his October 4, Springfield address has survived only in summary. But when he gave the same speech on October 16, in Peoria, newspapers published it in full.

His "Peoria Speech," as we have known it ever since, was both a legal brief against Douglas and a charismatic statement of ideals. It was one of Lincoln's earliest attempts to get an audience aroused not only by the menace of slavery toward whites but also by its subjugation of blacks.

By pre-arrangement, Lincoln and Douglas gave sequential speeches that amounted to a veritable debate. Douglas was the first to speak. Then Lincoln followed up with some tactical ploys that were aimed at both sides of his audience. His use of wry humor in these opening remarks went beyond mere forensic technique. It exemplified a shrewd psychological strategy. It is therefore worth sharing at length:

> I do not arise to speak now, if I can stipulate with the audience to meet me here at half past 6 or at 7 o'clock. It is now several minutes past five, and Judge Douglas [a reference to Douglas's earlier service on the Illinois Supreme Court] has spoken over three hours. . . . Now every one of you who can remain that long, can just as well get his supper, meet me at seven, and remain one hour or two later. The Judge has already informed you that he is to have an hour to reply to me. I doubt not but you have been a little surprised to learn that I have consented to give one of his high reputation and known ability, this advantage of me. Indeed, my consenting to it, though reluctant, was not wholly unselfish; for I suspected if it were understood, that the Judge was entirely done, you democrats would leave, and not hear me; but by giving him the close, I felt confident you would stay for the fun of hearing him skin me.[7]

Quite a package: self-deprecating humor, concern for the comfort of his audience, an open confession of a very sly purpose, all delivered in a manner that would soften his opponents' hostility while treating his friends to bonhomie.

When the audience gathered once again that evening, his tone became different. With razor-sharp analysis, he passionately attacked every one of his opponent's contentions with regard to the subject of slavery.

For instance, he took up the issue of the Compromise of 1850 as compared to the Kansas-Nebraska Act. Did the fact that the 1850 Compromise applied the principle of Popular Sovereignty to lands between Texas and California mean, as Douglas asserted, that Congress had somehow given that principle its blessing in every open territory? Ridiculous, Lincoln said; the Compromise of 1850 was merely an expedient hodge-podge of balancing elements, a deal that was struck at an urgent point of tension in the ongoing struggle over slavery.

"I insist," he said, that the Popular Sovereignty provision of the Compromise of 1850 was "made for Utah and New Mexico, and for no other place whatsoever. It had no more direct reference to Nebraska than it had to the territories of the moon. . . . The North consented to this provision, not because they considered it right in itself; but because they were compensated—paid for it. They, at the same time, got California into the Union as a free State. . . . Also, they got the slave trade abolished in the District of Columbia."[8]

But what of Douglas's larger contention that the principle of Popular Sovereignty amounted to a "sacred" distillation of American democracy by giving "the people" of every new territory—specifically the white people, of course—full power to decide about the slavery issue for themselves? In Lincoln's opinion, this assertion was wrong to the point of indecency.

That Douglas even dared to offer this argument, Lincoln said, "shows that the Judge has no very vivid impression that the negro is a human; and consequently has no idea that there can be any moral question in legislating about him. In his view, the question of whether a new country shall be slave or free, is a matter of as utter indifference, as it is whether his neighbor shall plant his farm with tobacco, or stock it with horned cattle."[9]

Citing Douglas's frequent use of white supremacist slogans, Lincoln challenged his audience, including his very own supporters, to reject white supremacist thinking when it came to the fundamentals of freedom. "Judge Douglas," he said, "frequently . . . paraphrases our argument by saying 'The white people of Nebraska are good enough to govern themselves, *but they are not good enough to govern a few miserable negroes!!'* Well," said Lincoln, "I doubt not that the people of Nebraska are, and will continue to be as good as the average of people elsewhere. I do not say the contrary. What I do say is, that no man is good enough to govern another man, *without that other's consent.* I say this is the leading principle—the sheet anchor of American republicanism."[10]

Lincoln pressed the argument further, using logic and analogies to hammer home a point that many racists would never concede, the point that blacks should be regarded as human, and not subhuman:

> Equal justice to the south, it is said, requires us to consent to the extending of slavery to new countries. That is to say, inasmuch as you do not object to my taking my hog to Nebraska, therefore I must not object to you taking your slave. Now, I admit this is perfectly logical, if there is no difference beween hogs and negroes. But while you thus require me to deny the humanity of the negro, I wish to ask whether you of the south yourselves, have ever been willing to do as much?[11]

Every slave owner who ever freed some or all of his human "property" was clearly unable to accept the proposition that blacks were mere beasts of burden. "There are in the United States and territories," Lincoln pointed out, "433,643 free blacks." How could such a situation exist if black Americans were little more than livestock? "How comes this vast amount of property to be running around without owners," Lincoln asked. "We do not see free horses or free cattle running at large. How is this? All these free blacks are the descendants of slaves, or have been slaves themselves, and they would be slaves now, but for SOMETHING which has operated on their white owners, inducing them, at vast pecuniary sacrifices, to liberate them."

Lincoln pressed the point harder: "What is that SOMETHING? Is there any mistaking it? In all these cases it is your sense of justice, and human sympathy, continually telling you, that the poor negro has some natural right to himself—that those who deny it, and make mere merchandise of him, deserve kickings, contempt and death."[12]

And clearly, said Lincoln, "if the negro *is* a man," is it not indecent and grotesque "to say that he too shall not govern *himself*? . . . If the negro is a *man*, why then my ancient faith teaches me that 'all men are created equal'. . . ."[13]

But what of Douglas's contention that American slavery would stay away from Kansas and Nebraska due to inauspicious conditions—that slavery was such a distinctive feature of the very Deep South that it was laughable to think that the system would flourish on the Great Plains?

Wrong again, said Lincoln, and American experience proved it. Experience showed that the American system of slavery would root itself in any locale in which involuntary labor could be put to any use, and where public opinion would condone it. "A glance at the map," Lincoln said, "shows that there are five slave states—Delaware, Maryland, Virginia, Kentucky, and Missouri—and also the District of Columbia, all north of the Missouri Compromise line," at the same latitude or even further north than Kansas.

So what was to keep the institution of slavery from coming into Kansas from Missouri, the state next door? "Missouri adjoins these territories," Lincoln observed, "by her entire western boundary, and slavery is already within every one of her western counties. . . . Slavery pressed entirely up to the old western boundary of the State, and when, rather recently, a part of that boundary, at the north-west was moved a little farther west, slavery followed on quite up to the new line. Now, when the restriction is removed, what is to prevent it from going still further? Climate will not. No peculiarity of the country will. . . ."[14]

Indeed, Lincoln asked his midwestern audience, what kind of geographical difference kept slavery away from Illinois, when the state of Missouri lay directly to the west of it, just across the Mississippi River? "What was it," he asked, "that made the difference between Illinois and Missouri? They lie side by side, the Mississippi river only dividing them." One thing only, he contended, had prevented the institution of slavery from coming right into Illinois: the prior prohibition put in place by the founding generation in the Northwest Ordinance of 1787.

The founding generation, Lincoln said, had done its best to keep slavery contained. Most of the Founding Fathers had known that the institution was wrong, but they could not get rid of it at once. So they blocked it and hemmed it in; they even shunned the very name of slavery, as if to avoid the rhetorical pollution of the nation's great charter of law with the mention of an unclean thing. "At the framing and adoption of the constitution," Lincoln said, the Founding Fathers "forebore so much as to mention the word 'slave' or 'slavery' in the whole instrument. In the provision for the recovery of fugitives, the slave is spoken of as a 'PERSON HELD TO SERVICE OR LABOR'. . . . Thus, the thing is hid away, in the constitution, just as an afflicted man hides away a wen or a cancer, which he dares not cut to the bone at once, lest he bleed to death; with the promise, nevertheless, that the cutting may begin at the end of a given time."[15]

The "cutting," however, was opposed in the South, and so slavery had spread, notwithstanding the fact that the greatest of the Founding Fathers had wanted to contain and shrink it over time.

And now, politicians like Stephen Douglas were telling the American people that they ought to be indifferent to the spread of unfreedom, that the fate of American blacks did not matter. "This *declared* indifference," Lincoln said, was nothing less than a thinly veiled zeal for slavery.[16] "Nearly eighty years ago we began by declaring that all men are created equal; but now . . . we have run down to the other declaration that for SOME men to enslave OTHERS is a 'sacred right of self-government.'" Unfreedom was on the rise, and people like Douglas were helping it along. "Nebraska brings it forth, places it on the high road to extension and perpetuity; and, with a pat on its back, says to it, 'Go and God speed you.'"[17]

But the forces of freedom and slavery were too fundamentally at war for Senator Stephen Douglas or anyone like him to keep them from collision. "Slavery," said Lincoln, "is founded in the selfishness of man's nature—opposition to it in his love of justice. These principles are an eternal antagonism. . . . Repeal the Missouri Compromise—repeal all compromises—repeal the declaration of independence—repeal all past history, you still cannot repeal human nature. It still will be the abundance of man's heart, that slavery extension is wrong; and out of the abundance of his heart, his mouth will continue to speak."[18]

And his hands would continue to act in response to his heart. Lincoln predicted that warfare and bloodshed would probably break out in Kansas. The mechanics of the Kansas-Nebraska Act made this prospect nearly inevitable. "The people are to decide the question of slavery for themselves," Lincoln acknowledged, but the questions as to "WHEN they are to decide; or HOW they are to decide; or whether, when the question is once decided, it is to remain so . . . the law does not say. Is it to be decided by the first dozen settlers who arrive there? Or is it to await the arrival of a hundred? Is it to be decided by a vote of the people? Or a vote of the legislature? Or, indeed, by a vote of any sort?"

The situation was made to order for a violent showdown, he predicted: "Some Yankees are sending emigrants to Nebraska, to exclude slavery from it; and, so far as I can judge, they expect the question to be decided by voting, in some way or other. But the Missourians are awake too. They are within a stone's throw of the contested ground. . . . They resolve . . . that abolitionists shall be hung, or driven away. Through all this, bowie-knives and six-shooters are seen plainly enough."[19]

Maybe peaceful measures would somehow avert the threat of violence, Lincoln mused. But for this to happen, the leaders of America's Free-Soil movement had to summon forth the spirit to oppose Stephen Douglas and his politics of sleazy "indifference" on the subject of slavery. And surely they would do so.

Be not complacent, Lincoln warned the supporters of Douglas, regarding the temporary disarray of the "Anti-Nebraska" movement. Douglas "should remember that he took us by surprise—astounded us—by this measure. We were thunderstruck and stunned; and we reeled and fell in utter confusion. But we rose each fighting, grasping whatever he could first reach—a scythe—a pitchfork—a chopping axe, or a butcher's cleaver. We struck in the direction of the sound; and we are rapidly closing in upon him."[20]

Such was the "Peoria Speech," the most vivid demonstration of the change in the political outlook of Lincoln that began in 1854. It heralded the fiery orations that would blaze his path to the White House. And it established the moral fundamentals of his whole political creed.

But in the view of certain latter-day detractors, the Peoria Speech was something else: it was clear and unambiguous proof of Lincoln's racism.

Why? Because Lincoln demurred about extending civil rights to former slaves after slavery had ended. This is the offending passage:

> If all earthly power were given me, I should not know what to do, as to the existing institution [of slavery]. My first impulse would be to free all the slaves, and send them to Liberia,—to their own native land. But a moment's reflection would convince me, that whatever of high hope, (as I think there is) there may be in this, in the long run, its sudden execution is impossible. If they were all landed there in a day, they would all perish in the next ten days; and there are not surplus shipping and surplus money enough in the world to carry them there in many times ten days. What then? Free them all, and keep them among us as underlings? Is it quite certain that this betters their condition? I think I would not hold one in slavery, at any rate; yet the point is not clear enough for me to denounce people upon. What next? Free them, and make them politi-

cally and socially, our equals? My own feelings will not admit of this; and if mine would, we well know that those of the great mass of white people will not. Whether this feeling accords with justice and sound judgment, is not the sole question, if indeed, it is any part of it. A universal feeling, whether well or ill-founded, can not be safely disregarded.[21]

What are we to make of such words as applied to the issue of black civil rights? "My own feelings," Lincoln said, "will not admit of this." What "feelings" did he mean in particular?

The conventional wisdom these days is that Lincoln shared many of the bigoted notions that were common in nineteenth-century America. Possibly, he did. He proclaimed, for instance, just a few years later—if indeed we can be sure that he was telling the truth and not fending off racist attacks by Douglas with expedient verbiage—that he disapproved of racial intermarriage.

Perhaps so. Or perhaps, for the moment, he decided to surrender to the passions of his white supremacist audience to nullify the arguments of Douglas on race and thus prevail in the fight against slavery. Douglas, after all, was a virulent racist, and his snide denigrations of blacks were delivered with gusto, much to his supporters' delight.

"I do not believe that the Almighty ever intended the Negro to be the equal of the white man," Douglas told his supporters on one occasion. "If he did, he has been a long time demonstrating the fact. (Cheers) For thousands of years, the negro has been a race upon the earth, and during all that time, in all latitudes and climates, wherever he has wandered or been taken, he has been inferior to the race which he has there met. He belongs to an inferior race, and must always occupy an inferior position."[22]

White supremacy attitudes were rampant in this milieu. Free blacks had been barred under Illinois law from setting foot in the state, and there was even a law on the books against racial intermarriage. Historian James M. McPherson has confirmed that Illinois was "one of the most race-conscious of the free states" in the 1850s.[23] William Lee Miller is a bit more severe: in Miller's opinion, Illinois was "probably the most racially prejudiced free state in the Union" during this period.[24] Such was the political atmosphere in which Lincoln had to work.

Why did Lincoln, if he were nothing but a racist politician, argue so fervently that blacks were fully human and their feelings had the utmost importance? Why shoulder such a burden at all when the easiest way for him to attack Stephen Douglas in front of an audience composed of a great many other white supremacists was perfectly obvious? The most crowd-pleasing move would be to sound the hue-and-cry that kept resounding in the Free-Soil movement: the tried-and-true message that the slavery system was a threat to all working-class *whites*.

Why on earth would a racist politician try to tell a white audience that blacks and their feelings really mattered? Why invoke "human sympathy" for every "poor negro" who desired the "right to himself?" Lincoln did this again and again.

Lincoln said that black Americans possessed the basic right to freedom. He said his personal preference on the issue of slavery was full emancipation, over time if conditions should require it. When it came to political and social equality, his feelings, he said, did not "admit of this." He did not say *why* this was the case. Yet he added that when and if his feelings *should* "admit of it," he feared that "universal" feelings, which could never be safely ignored, would oppose him overwhelmingly.

Harry V. Jaffa has observed of this speech that while Lincoln said his feelings were unable to support the proposition of black civil rights, "he immediately introduced, as a hypothetical possibility, that his own feelings might not be against it. Why? The sentence, taken as a whole, is an equivocation."[25]

It was hardly white supremacist chatter by a bigot. It seemed to be the struggle of a man who knew perfectly well that his principles of universal freedom led in practice beyond emancipation.

But it was also the talk of a man who knew equally well that if he came out openly for black civil rights because of principles that overrode "feeling"—if he contended that the widespread visceral dynamics of racial aversion were stupid, unworthy, and vile—the white supremacists would jeer him off the stage.

Lincoln's present-day detractors say his anti-slavery politics fail to measure up to the morally uncompromising stand of the boldest abolitionists, those who consistently supported civil rights for all Americans. But abolitionists *by themselves* could not summon the power to eliminate so deeply entrenched an institution as slavery.

The summoning of power requires strategy as well as ideals. This leads to the frequently thankless political task of balancing the lesser evils with the greater.

What alternative really existed to the power manipulations of Lincoln and his fellow politicians? What strategy to overcome the South—a region that was armed to the teeth with militias, and weapons, and first-rate military schools, a region that suppressed the abolitionists and made their movement *illegal* under many state laws—did the morally advanced abolitionists offer to the slaves?

The most forceful of them—John Brown, for example—tried to start the kind of war between the races that the slaveholders feared the most. But what chances did a fragmented slave insurrection really have? Consider a comparison: when *political* action caused the Union to split, it took four long years for the powerful North to beat the South in the Civil War, and the South came very close to winning on a number of occasions.

This is not to dismiss the abolitionists, whose work was both vital and heroic.[26] But they could simply not destroy the power of slavery without assistance. It took a great *coalition* of power that was centered in the Northern states.

The inescapable fact is that the power of the North could be channeled in one way alone: through the work of politics. And any working politician who ignored the force of white supremacy, either within or beyond his own political base, was too naïve for the work that lay before him.

For the rest of their political rivalry, Douglas would attempt to bait Lincoln with the charge that he favored the "mongrelization" of the races. Lincoln sensed this intention as he faced Stephen Douglas in October 1854. He would face it again, and from a great many others, in the years of campaigning ahead of him. He would face it right down to the very last week of his life when he supported black voting rights explicitly—for which John Wilkes Booth would shoot him dead.

IN THE NEXT FEW YEARS, Lincoln's reputation spread as he continued to excoriate Douglas. And his angry response to an outrageous judicial decision kept his name in the public eye.

As political events grew worse for the principles he championed, Lincoln's mood in the final months of 1854 became bitter. He tried to run for the Senate, where he hoped to undo the work of Douglas. Since the Constitution still provided for the election of Senators by the legislatures of the states, he worked the back-room politics of Springfield. He came close, but the seat in the United States Senate eluded him.[27]

Concurrently, the leaders of the slave-state bloc were on the move. In the middle of 1855, the Tennessean William Walker and his followers, who called him the "grey-eyed man of destiny," embarked for Nicaragua. Intervening in a civil war, they seized control of the country. After instituting slavery, they ran Nicaragua despotically for several years.[28]

Meanwhile, settlers had poured across the border into Kansas from Missouri, just as Lincoln had warned. Early in 1855, they elected a territorial legislature. Some of these settlers were long-term residents, but others were "border ruffians," Missourians who crossed the border into Kansas, cast illegal votes, and then returned to their homes in Missouri.

The legislature passed some pro-slavery laws that were draconian. Any aid to a fugitive slave in the territory of Kansas would be punished by death. Abolitionist speeches would be felonies.

Anti-slavery settlers poured into Kansas as well, and by the autumn of 1855 a civil war had broken out. That summer, Lincoln told a politician in Kentucky he had given up hope for any peaceful resolution of America's slavery crisis. "There is no peaceful extinction of slavery in prospect for us," he said.[29]

He asked another correspondent in Kentucky to consider how Northerners "crucify their feelings" on slavery. He said that he hated the existing institution as much as he hated its extension to the west. The fate of fugitive slaves, above all, made him miserable: "I hate to see the poor creatures hunted down, and caught," Lincoln wrote, "and carried back to their stripes, and unrewarded toils; but I bite my lip, and keep quiet." Attacks against the Fugitive Slave Law were probably hopeless.

He was deeply pessimistic in the short run. "Kansas," he said, "will form a Slave constitution, and, with it, will ask to be admitted to the Union." And though Lincoln and his friends would oppose such a move, "we may be beaten," he admitted.[30]

In the final months of 1855, the Free-Soilers decided to establish a legitimate territorial legislature in Kansas. All the credible evidence shows that these settlers were in the majority.[31] But the Pierce administration, predictably, supported the old pro-slavery legislature.

The fighting in Kansas reached a climax in 1856. Artillery barrages were directed at Lawrence, a Free-Soil settlement. On May 21, seven hundred pro-slavery men attacked the town, burning buildings and wreaking havoc. The anti-slavery zealot John Brown led a raid of retaliation with help from his sons and some angry Free-Soilers. They attacked Pottawatomie Creek, where they split the skulls of pro-slavery victims and slashed them to death with swords. All of these events took place on the eve of the 1856 presidential election.

The Democrats spurned both their controversial incumbent, Pierce, and the controversial Stephen A. Douglas, who had long since begun to entertain presidential ambitions. Instead, they nominated Pennsylvania's James Buchanan—one of the Ostend Manifesto's framers. In spite of this latter notoriety, Buchanan was perceived to be "safe" because he was conveniently out of the country in Britain when the Kansas-Nebraska drama began to unfold. But he was just as sympathetic to the South as his Democratic predecessor Pierce.

The Republicans were just as decisively anti-slavery. Lincoln at last made the move to the Republican Party; the whole structure of the old Whig Party was a shambles and the Whigs had all but ceased to exist. He gave the keynote speech at the Bloomington Convention that established the Republican Party in the state of Illinois.

John C. Frémont, an explorer and military hero who endorsed the cause of free soil, was nominated by the Republicans. The new Republican Party did reasonably well, in light of the facts that it was only two years old and its first campaign was unfortunately blunted by a third-party presence: the short-lived American Party whose stock-in-trade was its resistance to the influence in politics of Catholics and non-Anglo-Saxons. It drew off some of the white working-class vote that would have supported free-soil policies.

Lincoln stumped Illinois and other midwestern states for Frémont, responding to some shrill pro-slavery warnings that a Frémont victory would trigger the secession of the slave states. Lincoln ridiculed Buchanan as an agent of the South, like Pierce, Douglas, and the rest of the Northern politicians whose political self-damnation had reduced them to lackeys of the slave-holding interests.

Southern strategy, Lincoln claimed, was to operate by proxy using Northern political agents whenever it was feasible. In notes for a campaign speech, he addressed this issue with sarcastic anger. "If a Southern man aspires to be president," he wrote, "they choke him down instantly, in order that the glittering prize of the presidency, may be held up, on Southern terms, to the greedy eyes of Northern ambition. . . . The democratic party, in 1844, elected a Southern president. Since then, they have neither had a Southern candidate for *election*, or *nomination*. Their Conventions of 1848, 1852 and 1856, have been struggles exclusively among *Northern* men, each vieing [*sic*] to out-bid the other for the Southern vote—the South standing calmly by to finally cry going, going, gone to the highest bidder; and, at the same time, to make its power more distinctly seen, and thereby to secure a still higher bid at the next succeeding struggle."[32]

If the offer of political rewards should ever fail them, the leaders of the South would use blackmail, he said, to maintain their domination of the North. The form of this blackmail was obvious: the threat of secession. But if Frémont should win and the Free-Soil movement should prevail, Lincoln vowed, any threat of secession would be stamped out swiftly and sternly. Overwhelming force would be used. He warned the "fire-eating" leaders of the South who had started to advocate a new Southern nation that the Union "won't be dissolved. We don't want to dissolve it, and if you attempt it, *we won't let you*. With the purse and the sword, the army and navy and treasury in our hands and at our command, you *couldn't do it*. This Government would be very weak, indeed, if a majority, with a disciplined army and navy, and a well-filled treasury, could not preserve itself, when attacked by an unarmed, undisciplined, unorganized minority. All this talk about the dissolution of the Union is humbug—nothing but folly. *We* WON'T dissolve the Union, and *you* SHAN'T."[33]

This was confident defiance of the enemy, the talk of a man who was roused to a very high pitch by the heat of the campaign. Yet Buchanan won the election.

Additional reasons for gloom had arisen from the white supremacist attitudes that Lincoln encountered that year while campaigning. Even though his speeches in the 1856 campaign drew thunderous applause from his fellow Republicans, Lincoln had been booed and jeered on the hustings by Democrats and bigots when he argued that blacks deserved freedom.

These events, however, were trifling compared to a major new disaster for the Free-Soil movement that was brewing in the federal judiciary, one so wretched that it surpassed the worst crimes of the Nebraska-Kansas crisis.

A slave from Missouri, Dred Scott, had been seeking his freedom in court. He claimed that his master unwittingly gave him his freedom when he took him to places where slavery was barred under law. In the

1830s, when his master had lived in Illinois, he had taken Scott along as his servant. Afterward, his master had taken him into the territory of Wisconsin, well above the anti-slavery dividing line of the Missouri Compromise.[34]

The Dred Scott case had gone through several appeals to the United States Supreme Court. The arguments began on February 11, 1856. Of the nine Supreme Court justices, five were pro-slavery Democrats.

The significance of this case went far beyond the status of Scott (and his wife, who had signed on as co-plaintiff). The issues of the case could set precedents determining some fundamental questions of law. Could slaves, for example, bring lawsuits? Did residence, if only for a time, in any of the free states or territories liberate "sojourning" slaves? How far did the power of Congress extend when it came to the regulation of slavery in federal territories?

At first glance, the power of Congress appeared to be obvious. In clear and extremely open-ended language, the Constitution (Article IV, Section 3) gave Congress the "Power to dispose of and make all needful Rules and Regulations respecting the Territory" of the United States before statehood was granted to a territory.

Since the 1840s, however, the issue had been clouded by interpretation. Two reverse-logic schools of thought—one of them pro-slavery and one of them anti-slavery—maintained that the above-cited language was forever superceded by the language of the Constitution's Fifth Amendment, which states, in part, "No person shall be . . . deprived of life, liberty, or property, without due process of law. . . ."

John C. Calhoun had invoked the Fifth Amendment as he argued that congressional attempts to prevent the owners of slaves from bringing their slaves into federal territories amounted to depriving them of their property without due process.[35]

Salmon P. Chase, however, had developed an opposite interpretation: if Congress should *permit* slave owners to bring their slaves into federal lands, he argued, it would thus deprive the *slaves* of their *liberty* without due process, since slavery was merely a *state*-sanctioned institution.[36]

All of these issues were intrinsic to the Dred Scott case. The Supreme Court delayed its decision as election year events played out. In his final message to Congress, President Pierce endorsed the imminent decision and urged all American citizens to obey it.

The Supreme Court's decision was about to be issued as President-elect Buchanan took the oath of office and delivered his Inaugural Address in 1857. He announced in his speech that the Supreme Court would issue a ruling very shortly that would settle the issue of slavery in the territories once and for all. Like Pierce, he urged the public to accept this decision, whatever it turned out to be. He did not, however, tell the public that he and two justices were busily engaged in a detailed and secret correspondence about the decision.[37]

On March 6, 1857, the Supreme Court issued its ruling. It was not unanimous. Every justice wrote a separate opinion, and those in the majority differed in a number of respects. But an overall majority decision was written by Chief Justice Roger Brooke Taney.

Taney said that this particular case should not have been in court at all: Scott, he observed, was quite obviously black, and blacks, proclaimed Taney, were "inferior . . . beings," who had absolutely "no rights . . . the white man was bound to respect." At the time the Constitution was written, said Taney, this view was universal.

In any case, Taney continued, Scott's sojourn in Illinois did nothing to free him, since precedents of interstate comity required that the laws of Missouri should govern his status on trips beyond the boundaries of the state.

Finally, Scott's sojourn in Wisconsin did nothing to free him, since Congress had *never* had the power—at least since the Fifth Amendment's ratification—to prohibit the owners of slaves from transporting their property wherever they wished in the federal domain.

In other words, long before Congress had chosen to repeal the Missouri Compromise, the Compromise was void since its contents violated the Fifth Amendment of the Constitution (as John C. Calhoun had construed it). Thus, by extension, the goals of the Republican Party and the Free-Soil movement were illegal. There was nothing any Congress could do to prevent the institution of slavery from spreading just as far and as wide in any federal lands as the owners of slaves could take it, said the justices who voted with Taney.

Furthermore, Taney contended, "if Congress itself cannot do this—if it is beyond the powers conferred on the Federal Government—it will be admitted, we presume, that it could not authorize a Territorial Government to exercise them."[38] This pronouncement was directly germane to the doctrine of Popular Sovereignty. If the territorial legislatures lacked jurisdiction on the slavery question, then how could the wishes of the territorial settlers be addressed?

The justices in the minority dissented as vigorously as they could. Justices John McLean and Benjamin Curtis, in particular, disputed Taney's version of history. Curtis showed that when the Constitution was drafted in 1787, several states allowed blacks the rights of citizenship; he added that the Constitution, in Article IV, Section 2, guarantees that "the Citizens of each State shall be entitled to all Privileges and Immunities of Citizens of the several States." So much for the argument that blacks were universally regarded as beings of an inferior order when the Constitution was written.

As to the Fifth Amendment, insofar as it figured in Taney's opinion, McLean and Curtis denounced the Court's decision as simplistic. They denied that exclusion of slavery from federal territories amounted to an actual deprivation of property or an abridgement of due process. In any case, Curtis contended, since Taney had argued that the case was improperly in court, the matter should have ended right there: the case should have been dismissed. Consequently, he said, the more sweeping pronouncement of the Court upon larger constitutional issues amounted to an *obiter dictum*, a comment in passing, of no legal force at all.

But the Dred Scott ruling held. White supremacists welcomed it, and Democrats demanded that Republicans obey it at the risk of being branded as outlaws if they did not. The Republicans—those who were told between the lines that their party might just as well disband, since the Free-Soil program at the center of its organizational mission was unconstitutional—denounced Taney as a viper and the Dred Scott decision as a virulent pack of lies.

They said its arguments were farcical and twisted. But they struggled to avoid the charge of lawlessness as they groped for some way to resist it. Many promised to abide by the Dred Scott decision in a minimal way, along the lines that Justice Curtis sketched out: by acknowledging the fact that Dred Scott was still a slave under law, while declaring that the larger constitutional pronouncements of the Court were not binding.

Stephen Douglas was in a very different sort of quandary. The decision placed his politics in serious jeopardy. The denial of Congress's power to bar slavery in federal territories was one thing—but the further denial of this power to the legislatures of the territories seemed fatal to the politics of Douglas. He had after all assured his supporters that whites would have a choice in the matter. But the logic of the Dred Scott decision raised serious doubts about his program.

And events in Kansas eroded his position even further in 1857. In February, the dubiously elected territorial legislature called a constitutional convention for Kansas. But the resulting constitution would not be presented to the voters for ratification.

The viability of Popular Sovereignty was slipping away, and for many of the reasons that Lincoln had predicted in 1854. He would naturally pounce upon the issue at the first opportunity, especially to counter Douglas in his reelection campaign of 1858.

Douglas pondered his reelection chances and foresaw his own vulnerabilities. So he decided to make a big speech to the voters, a speech that would give him a chance to react to the Dred Scott decision, to defend the vitality of Popular Sovereignty, and, most importantly of all, to taunt the Republicans with the issue of race. He spoke to his constituents in Springfield on June 7, 1857.

He acknowledged that the Dred Scott decision gave him pause the first time he read it. But he insisted that the principles of Popular Sovereignty were viable. If white settlers were bound and determined to keep slavery out of a territory, Douglas reasoned, the way to accomplish such a goal was easy: just refrain from either passing or enforcing the "police regulations and local legislation" that slaveholders always demanded before they would put their slave property at risk in an open territory. Then Douglas fell back upon the demagoguery of race.

He agreed with Taney's contention that blacks were regarded as inferior beings at the time of America's founding. He said political and social equality was intended for equals only, and blacks were not equal to whites.

Douglas viewed the Declaration of Independence in minimal terms: He said that it was merely an instrument by which to gain colonial freedom from Britain. In historical context, he argued, the statement that "all men are created equal" was simply shorthand for arguing that British Americans were equal to the British themselves. It was *not* a declaration, he insisted, that applied to inferior races.

He said Republicans were secret abolitionists or worse; he said they wanted the "amalgamation" of the races through black and white intermarriage. And he warned against indulging the Negro-loving affinities of "Black Republicans."

Upon the invitation of some Illinois Republicans, Lincoln answered Douglas on June 26, in Springfield. Excoriating the Dred Scott decision, Lincoln challenged its assertion that the Founding generation viewed blacks as "inferior beings." He cited all of the evidence amassed by Justice Curtis to demonstrate that blacks were in many ways far better off in the days of the early Republic than they were in the 1850s.

"In those days," he pointed out, "Legislatures held the unquestioned power to abolish slavery in their respective States; but now it is becoming quite fashionable for State Constitutions to withhold that power from the Legislatures. In those days, by common consent, the spread of the black man's bondage to new countries was prohibited; but now, Congress decides that it *will* not continue the prohibition, and the Supreme Court decides that it *could* not if it would. In those days, our Declaration of Independence was held sacred by all, and thought to include all; but now, to aid in making the bondage of the negro universal and eternal, it is assailed, and sneered at, and construed, and hawked at, and torn, till, if its framers could rise from their graves, they could not at all recognize it."[39]

Lincoln tried his very best to get his audience to empathize with slaves. He used picturesque imagery—the image, for example, of a man in a cage—to make his audience suffer as they listened. "All the powers of earth seem rapidly combining" against the slave in the United States, Lincoln said. "They have him in his prison house; they have searched his person, and left no prying instrument with him. One after another they have closed the heavy iron doors upon him, and now they have him, as it were, bolted in with a lock of a hundred keys, which can never be unlocked without the concurrence of every key; the keys are in the hands of a hundred different men, and they [have] scattered in a hundred different and distant places; and they stand musing as to what invention, in all the dominions of mind and matter, can be produced to make the impossibility of his escape more complete than it is."[40]

Stephen Douglas, said Lincoln, cared nothing for the suffering of slaves. He coldly assisted in expanding the vile institution that oppressed them. He was reckless and callous as he tried to deflect the public's anger by pandering to racial aversions; he sought to cover his tracks and change the subject politically by stirring up the "natural disgust in the minds of nearly all white people, to the idea of an indiscriminate amalgamation of the white and black races [racial intermarriage]." Douglas, said Lincoln, "evidently is basing his chief hope, upon the chances of being able to appropriate the benefit of this disgust" and thus beguile a white supremacist public:

> If he can, by much drumming and repeating, fasten the odium of that idea [racial "amalgamation"] upon his adversaries, he thinks he can struggle through the storm. He therefore clings to this hope, as a drowning man to the last plank. . . . He finds the Republicans insisting that the Declaration of Independence includes ALL men, black as well as white; and forthwith he boldly denies that it includes negroes at all, and proceeds to argue gravely that all who contend it does, do so only because they want to vote, and eat, and sleep, and marry with negroes! . . . Now I protest against the counterfeit logic which concludes that, because I do not want a black woman for a *slave* I must necessarily want her for a *wife*. I need not have her for either, I can just leave her alone. In some respects she certainly is not my equal; but in her natural right to eat the bread she earns with her own hands without asking leave of anyone else, she is my equal, and the equal of all others.[41]

"She is my equal," Lincoln said, in her right to freedom. Yet "in some respects she certainly is not my equal," Lincoln stated.

Here again, Lincoln's documented words provide his critics with evidence of bigotry. Indeed, there is more: in explicit terms, Lincoln put his opposition to racial intermarriage on the record in his Springfield speech.

It bears noting, however, that he crafted this statement on racial intermarriage in a way that came very close to satirizing white supremacist fears. He approached the point of tongue-in-cheek humor when he said there were fortunately "white men enough to marry all the white women, and black men enough to marry all the black women; and so let them be married. . . . On this point we fully agree with the Judge."[42]

Like Gilbert and Sullivan's Mikado, he strove to turn this evil into humor that was relatively harmless. Whereas Douglas warned against "mongrelization," Lincoln calmed and amused his touchy audience with visions of benign mass weddings.

Where does that put Lincoln? Did he oppose the "mixing" of the races? Lincoln uttered one sentence in his Springfield address that appears to support this view. "Judge Douglas," he said, "is especially horrified at the thought of the mixing of the blood by the white and black races: agreed for once—a thousand times agreed."[43]

Yet the statement in question makes very little sense if we compare it to Lincoln's *behavior*. Here, after all, was a man who alleged that he was "horrified" by the thought of racial intermarriage. But then he *joked* about the subject, and he sought to make light of it whenever Douglas raised the issue.

So again, we face the issue of candor: Was Lincoln really telling the truth? Did he really find the concept of racial intermarriage disgusting? Or did he deem it *unwise* to depart from the conventional views when the "near universal disgust" among whites with regard to this subject would distract them from the evil of slavery if Douglas succeeded in changing the subject from slavery to interracial sex? Were Lincoln's words a statement of *principle*? Or was he making expedient concessions?

Before we jump to any quick conclusions—if we can put the above-cited statements by Lincoln to the side, at least momentarily—it behooves us to read a very different statement by Lincoln in the course of the very same speech.

Lincoln used this occasion to unfold a great vision for America: the vision that America's equality principle should spread and expand its inner meaning over time to ever greater heights of moral fulfillment.

He began by refuting the perverse illogic that was used by Taney and Douglas when they spoke about the issue of "original intent" as it related to racial equality. Lincoln said: "Chief Justice Taney admits that the language of the Declaration is broad enough to include the whole human family, but he and Judge Douglas argue that the authors of that instrument did not intend to include negroes, by the fact that they did not at once, actually place them on an equality with the whites. Now this grave argument comes to just nothing at all, by the other fact, that they did not at once, *or ever afterwards*, actually place all white people on an equality with one another."

So what was the innermost meaning of the Declaration of Independence? Lincoln quickly asserted that the signers of the document intended "to include *all* men, but they did not intend to declare all men equal *in all respects*. They did not mean to say all were equal in color, size, intellect, moral developments, or social capacity. They defined with tolerable distinctness, in what respects they did consider all men created equal—equal in 'certain inalienable rights, among which are life, liberty, and the pursuit of happiness.' This they said, and this they meant."

They did *not* assert "the obvious untruth, that all were then actually enjoying that equality, nor yet, that they were about to confer it immediately upon them," said Lincoln. "In fact they had no power to confer such a boon. They meant simply to declare the *right*, so that the *enforcement* of it might follow as fast as circumstances should permit. They meant to set up a standard maxim for free society, which should be familiar to all, and revered by all; constantly looked to, constantly labored for, and even though never perfectly attained, constantly approximated, and thereby constantly spreading and deepening its influence, and augmenting the happiness and value of life to all people of all colors everywhere."[44]

How can we reconcile this eloquent manifesto with equivocal statements by Lincoln on the subject of race? In what manner did his wish to see a constant expansion of the "the happiness and value of life" for "all people everywhere" relate to his words about a hypothetical female black who was not to be regarded as his equal *in every respect*? Did the statement really mean what it implied? Or, was Lincoln playing games with his audience?

It all depends upon the meaning (or the multiple meanings) of "equal" as he used the term. Did he mean, in effect, that the hypothetical female black was less *worthy* than he? Or did he mean, without spelling it out, that she lacked the same *qualifications* (at the moment) for citizenship?

"Equal" could be used in three senses: to denote an "equality" in *abstract rights* such as freedom or liberty itself; an "equality" of *talent*, an issue of the sort that preoccupied gut-level racists; or an "equality" of *status* or *condition*, as when Lincoln referred to the Founders and the issue of their power to "place" certain people "on an equality" in terms of social standing. Which of these different definitions was Lincoln employing at any given time? Consider this problem in regard to the issue of voting.

Many of the states had put voting restrictions in place for *adult white males*. Even some Northern states had set property requirements for voting, and a few of them subjected their voters to literacy tests. Connecticut and Massachusetts, for example, had established such tests in the 1850s.[45]

It bears noting that when Lincoln came around to supporting black voting rights (in 1864), he intended to *phase in* the delicate reform so that whites would stay calm about the change and accept it peacefully. To that end, he proposed to give the vote to certain blacks who had impressive *credentials*—who were "equal" to the challenges of voting.

In the political culture of today, a great deal of this sounds absurd. Many take it for granted that American adults (with a few exceptions such as felons) are entitled automatically to vote. But this state of affairs has resulted from a long revolution in constitutional law. The Fifteenth Amendment to the Constitution, which Republicans drafted at the high tide of Reconstruction in 1869, was one of the first great national milestones in this revolution.

An amendment such as this was unthinkable before the Civil War. So we return to the middle of 1857, and the issue of "equality" vis-à-vis Lincoln and the female black. If she were not at the moment his "equal" either in her *power* or her *qualifications*, she could nonetheless *become* his equal over time. Lincoln, after all, had said America's Founders lacked the *power to confer* certain rights, notwithstanding the fact that a few of these rights were inherent—indeed, inalienable—in the human condition.

For which reason the rights would have to be *conferred* just "as fast as circumstances should permit." The first of the rights to be conferred was the right to be free. Then some other basic rights could be added in the fullness of time.

Some observers are impatient with attempts such as this to distinguish Lincoln's views on the subject of race from the bigotry of Douglas. It is easy enough to view Lincoln in a very bad light by our contemporary standards. It is possible to say that he was little more than a racist, and leave it at that.[46]

It is equally possible that Lincoln made concessions to the phobias and biases of mainstream America—on racial intermarriage, for example—in a defense against the crude demagoguery of Douglas. But he limited each of these concessions through the use of qualifying language, or else through the medium of clever ambiguities, the sort of thing he learned as a lawyer to concoct in tight situations.

He made statements on the subject of race that in many ways *sounded* like the sort of thing his audience demanded to hear. But these statements were often ambiguous. And perhaps that was Lincoln's intention. The very same Lincoln who could scrutinize a text for any secrets its author had encrypted—and he would demonstrate the art as he extracted hidden meanings or intentions from the Dred Scott decision—had the skill to encode special caveat provisions of his own.

He could craft a written speech in such a way that it contained *alternative* meanings. No less an observer than Stephen Douglas said that Lincoln excelled in this art. He paid Lincoln the backhanded compliment of crediting him with a "fertile genius in devising language to conceal his thoughts."[47]

Again, take the outwardly racist formulation on the female slave: "in some respects she certainly is not my equal." Plain language, it would seem—but murky enough if we subject it to a probing analysis. In *which* respects was Lincoln contending that the woman was "not his equal?"

And what *meaning* did he give the word "equal?" Was it "equal" in the sense of her *ability?* Or was it "equal" in the sense of *social standing?* Lincoln left this important matter vague, and perhaps deliberately.

We often chafe at ambiguities when issues such as this are on the line. We want to know the full truth about Lincoln's racial views, since the issue is central to his legacy. An easy resolution is impossible. But there remain some interesting clues about his racial feelings.

Some of them consist of memoranda that were written by Lincoln. In 1854, Lincoln jotted down the following reflections as he grappled with the arguments propounded by the advocates of slavery: "If A. can prove, however conclusively, that he may, of right, enslave B.," Lincoln reasoned, "why may not B. snatch the same argument, and prove equally, that he may enslave A?—You say A. is white, and B. is black. It is *color*, then; the lighter, having the right to enslave the darker? Take care. By this rule, you are to be the slave to the first man you meet, with a fairer skin than your own. You do not mean *color* exactly?—You mean the whites are *intellectually* the superior of the blacks, and, therefore, have the right to enslave them? Take care again. By this rule, you are to be slave to the first man you meet, with an intellect superior to your own."[48]

In other words, traits are diffused in such a very broad range across the races that the issue of racial identity is frequently pointless in individual instances. *Individual* traits are all-important, Lincoln seemed to be saying.

On another occasion, in 1858, Lincoln searched his soul in response to the incessant racial demagoguery of Douglas. What Lincoln told himself on this occasion was simple and clear: *he did not really know* whether blacks were inferior to whites in any crucial respect. In other words, he faced the issue honestly in private and without preconceptions. A most curious thing, by the way, for any knee-jerk racist to do.

But his instinct, regardless of the facts about the matter, was to err on the side of magnanimity. If, for the sake of the argument, he wrote, one hypothesized black inferiority, the ethical response, and indeed

the only decent response, was an attitude of kindliness and not ma-
levolence: "*Suppose* [my emphasis] it is true, that the negro is inferior
to the white, in the gifts of nature; is it not the exact reverse [of] justice
that the white should, for that reason, take from the negro, any part of
the little which has been given him? '*Give* to him that is needy' is the
christian rule of charity; but 'Take from him that is needy' is the rule
of slavery."[49]

But the racist hypothesis was nothing but a vague conjecture. In the
Civil War years, Lincoln made this point to a white supremacist who
sent him a telegram of pushy admonitions that whites were the "first-
class" people of America and blacks were merely "second-class" detri-
tus. The method chosen by Lincoln to respond to this particular critic
was the method of tongue-in-cheek ridicule.

He had a secretary write to the critic and ask him to identify his own
race distinctly—white or black (as if Lincoln didn't know the answer)—
so the President could understand his point of view with maximum
clarity. But "in either case," Lincoln's secretary told the critic, the president believes "you cannot be regarded as an impartial judge. It may be
that you belong to a third or fourth class of *yellow* or *red* men, in which
case the impartiality of your judgment would be more apparent."[50]

Another clue to Lincoln's feelings on race can be found in the memoirs of blacks who encountered him in person. They, above all, were in
an excellent position to *sense* and to *feel* his racial attitudes. Frederick
Douglass, the black abolitionist, was in such a position.

Though Douglass concluded in a speech before a largely black audience in 1876 (presumably on the basis of Lincoln's public statements
in the 1850s) that Lincoln "was a white man and shared toward the
colored race the prejudices common to his countrymen," he reached a
very different conclusion in the summer of 1865—when the memory
of Lincoln was vivid.[51] Douglass stated that Lincoln was "emphatically
the black mans [*sic*] President: the first to show any respect for their
rights as men."[52]

Moreover, Douglass stated on a number of occasions that whenever
he had called upon Lincoln, he encountered no hint of racial tension.
"I was never more quickly or more completely put at ease in the presence
of a great man," Douglass stated, "than in that of Abraham Lincoln. . . .
In his company I was never in any way reminded of my humble origin,
or of my unpopular color."[53]

He recalled a particular visit to the White House early in 1865. Lincoln recognized him as he approached, and then, said Douglass, "he exclaimed, so that all around could hear him, 'Here comes my friend Douglass.' Taking me by the hand, he said, 'I am glad to see you.'"[54]

Historian David Grimsted has argued that Lincoln was struggling with a "self-admitted racism." In the course of this struggle, he would not allow his prejudice to "cloud his sense of blacks' full humanity." If such a theory is correct, then Lincoln's struggle, as Grimsted suggests, "has something of the transcending dignity of Huck Finn's."[55]

But there remains the possibility that *no* real prejudice existed in the mind of Lincoln. It is possible that Lincoln, under pressure and confronting a militantly white supremacist electorate, pretended to feelings he did not really have on the subject of race.

Whatever his innermost feelings on race, Lincoln's overall intention in the 1850s was apparent to all: to make whites disgusted with slavery, as much for its oppression of blacks as for its ancillary menace to themselves.

As events played out in the summer and autumn months of 1857, Lincoln made it clear that he intended to challenge Stephen Douglas for his seat in the United States Senate. Meanwhile, surprising events in Kansas drove a wedge between Douglas and Buchanan.

Because of widespread electoral fraud in Kansas, Free-Soilers decided to boycott the gerrymandered election for delegates to serve in the territory's constitutional convention. The convention, which met at Lecompton in September, wrote a slave-state constitution.

But Buchanan's new territorial governor, Robert J. Walker (a Mississippian), insisted that this constitution be submitted to the voters of Kansas in a referendum to be held in December. Furthermore, he guaranteed an honest election in October when the members of the territorial legislature had to face the voters. Because of Walker's oversight, the Free-Soilers gained a majority in the legislature.

After the October election, the pro-slavery convention reacted with a blatant and arrogant gambit to rig the referendum on the constitution. They decided to submit *two* options to the voters: (1) the draft constitution containing an unlimited slavery provision; (2) the same constitution with a special alternative provision that barred any future importation of slaves while permitting the slave-holding settlers of Kansas to keep the slaves they owned already, along with their progeny.

Either way, the institution of slavery would to some extent be legalized in Kansas. Either way, the slave-holding interests would win. Once again, the Free-Soilers in Kansas cried foul and they sat out the trick referendum, which was held in December. So the slave-state "Lecompton Constitution" was approved with the wide-open slavery provision.

But then the Free-Soil legislature called for a new and honest referendum: one in which the voters of Kansas would be given the option of rejecting the entire constitution if they wished to do so. They did so in January 1858.

And yet President Buchanan maintained that the first referendum was valid. He sent the Lecompton Constitution to Congress and proposed that Kansas be admitted to the Union as a slave state right away. Whereupon, Stephen Douglas broke relations with James Buchanan and declared an open war with his own party's leader in the White House.

The "Lecompton fraud" was a very real threat to Stephen Douglas. For if Popular Sovereignty, Douglas's rallying cry, appeared to be a sham, then he would probably fail in his upcoming bid for reelection to the Senate, and his presidential hopes would be destroyed. So he battled to the death against Buchanan and his "Buchaneers," as the Republicans watched in amazement.

The Douglas-Buchanan fight was so spectacular that certain Republican leaders and opinion makers (political journalist Horace Greeley, for example, and Senator William H. Seward) urged their Illinois counterparts to throw their full support behind Douglas in his reelection struggle.

Lincoln worried that Douglas and his politics of Popular Sovereignty would hijack the Free-Soil movement and ruin it, at least in Illinois. But he consoled himself when the United States House of Representatives rejected the Lecompton Constitution for Kansas in April 1858.

All the while, he was brooding on an issue that the Dred Scott case had left dangling. The Supreme Court had declared that the right of American whites to own slaves was constitutionally sacred. It denied that Congress or the territorial legislatures had power to prevent the spread of slavery in federal lands. But what about the power of the *states*?

What could stop Roger Taney or another Chief Justice from issuing a ruling sometime in the future claiming that *states* were just as impotent as Congress in regulating slavery? If Congress lacked the power to prevent the spread of slavery, then how could any state claim the power?

Maybe this was the last secret weapon of the South, the final trump card for slavery expansion, the endgame of Southern domination that its leaders had been planning all along. Perhaps the next outrageous surprise from the South would be a ruling by Taney that would open the floodgates for slavery expansion in the North. Was it possible?

IT WAS POSSIBLE INDEED: and the issue gave Lincoln the conceptual basis for his formal challenge to Douglas. In the course of the 1858 election campaign, his debates and confrontations with Douglas gained national attention: indeed, by the end of the year, his political prospects were national.

Lincoln's genuine alarm about the prospect of slavery invading the North was related to his sense of a slaveholders' scheme. The new *modus operandi* of the schemers was to take Free-Soilers *by surprise* in an escalating manner.

When the Compromise of 1850 was adopted, the Free-Soil strategists expected that the next great sectional battle would occur in New Mexico territory. Then, surprise—the whole slavery issue was reopened to the East, and all the federal lands that had for years been off-limits to slavery were suddenly at risk. The great rollback of Free-Soil power had begun: the battle had erupted in Kansas, and the outcome would determine the fate of all the other open federal lands.

Then, surprise—the Dred Scott decision changed the rules of the game and made the politics of Kansas almost moot. The slavery system could extend freely west, and there was nothing any Free-Soil majority could do that would prevent it, said Chief Justice Taney.

The fact that Dred Scott had lived in an area cordoned off from slavery—not as a *fugitive slave* but rather as a servant attending his master—gave Taney no discomfort whatsoever. Scott's presence in Wisconsin Territory did nothing to free him, since the rights of private property were sacred. In the aftermath of this ruling almost everyone seemed to be focused on its stark *territorial* component.

Perhaps another big surprise was now in store. For the presence of Scott in *the state of Illinois* had done nothing to liberate him either. And the logic of Taney was the same. Dred Scott, said Taney, was a slave "sojourner" whose status outside of his owner's home state would be controlled by the laws of that state.

Lincoln thought about the issue in the early months of 1858, and then it hit him: what could stop the Southern owners of slaves from bringing *thousands* of their slaves into the North on the very same basis?[56]

In a fragment of an undelivered speech, Lincoln gathered some preliminary thoughts about the fact that the "bringing of Dred Scott into Illinois by his master, and holding him there for a long time as a slave, did not operate his emancipation." This point, said Lincoln, was in all probability established by the Taney Court for some intended use in the future. It was "not to be pressed immediately; but if acquiesced in for a while, then to sustain the logical conclusion that what Dred Scott's master might lawfully do with Dred in the free State of Illinois, every other master may lawfully do with any other one or one hundred slaves in Illinois, or in any other free State."[57]

It would be easy: just rent them out to businessmen whose workers went out on strike. Slave "sojourners" would remain enslaved. There was nothing that the laws of any Northern state could do to free them, or even to remove them. The rights of private property were sacred, said Taney, and the Constitution—as interpreted by him along the lines that Calhoun recommended—was supreme.

This was the threat that Lincoln gradually perceived, and it should not be dismissed or shrugged away. As Harry V. Jaffa has observed, "There is no reason to suppose that, should slavery in the mines, foundries, factories, and fields of the free states have proved advantageous to powerful groups therein, new systems of discipline might not have been invented to make the exploitation of slave labor highly profitable there."[58]

Lincoln pondered these matters with increasing private rage as he wrote the big speech that he was planning to deliver in June. He was writing this speech for the Republican convention that would nominate him for the position of United States senator. He had worked through the spring with Republican leaders in the state (men such as Norman Judd, who chaired the Republican State Central Committee) to get the Senate nomination locked up before the convention.[59] He had fought against naifs who saw in Douglas a heroic contender against the "Buchaneers."

This was nonsense, Lincoln insisted. Douglas was waging the fight of his life because his policies exploded in his face. He had hoped to get ahead by appeasing the South and by lulling the opponents of slavery with Popular Sovereignty. But Buchanan was about to spoil everything by pushing the Lecompton Constitution too hard: the attempted rape of Kansas was sufficiently blatant to deprive Stephen Douglas of his very last shred of credibility.

So his schism with Buchanan was sensible. But it was hardly an act to be rewarded by Free-Soil Republicans. Douglas was a rogue, and if Republicans should "drop their own organization, fall into rank behind him, and form a great free-State Democratic Party," Lincoln warned, they would reap the grim results of such stupidity. "If they so fall in with Judge Douglas, and Kansas shall be secured as a free State," Lincoln wrote, "will not the Republicans stand ready, haltered and harnessed, to be handed over by him to the regular Democracy, to filibuster indefinitely for additional slave territory,—to carry slavery into all the States, as well as Territories, under the Dred Scott decision, construed and enlarged from time to time, according to the demands of the regular slave Democracy,—and to assist in reviving the African slave-trade in order that all may buy negroes where they can be bought the cheapest. . . ?"[60]

A revival of the African slave trade? Why not? Why not go farther and imagine the entire Western Hemisphere converted to a bastion for a tyranny of global dimensions? The pro-slavery movement was sufficiently shameless that nothing of the sort could be precluded.

It was all a matter of conviction, Lincoln said, and of conviction augmented by power. Those whose convictions held that slavery was right would keep pushing their repulsive system. And the push would go on until those whose convictions told them slavery was wrong could get the power to push the other way.

And when push came to shove, Lincoln said in the speech that he delivered in Springfield on June 16, the country's future would be settled one way—and one way alone. He cited Scripture in the famous invocation:

> "A house divided against itself cannot stand."
> I believe this government cannot endure, permanently half *slave* and half *free*.
> I do not expect the Union to be *dissolved*—I do not expect the house to *fall*—but I do expect it will cease to be divided. It will become *all* one thing, or *all* the other. Either the *opponents* of slavery, will arrest the further spread of it, and place it where the public mind shall rest in the belief that it is in course of ultimate extinction; or its *advocates* will push it forward, till it shall become alike lawful in *all* the States, *old* as well as *new*—*North* as well as *South*.
> Have we no *tendency* to the latter condition?[61]

The tendency toward slavery expansion was dominant, Lincoln said, and this was hardly an accident—hardly a fortuitous convergence of events or impersonal forces. It was nothing less than a *scheme* that was deliberate, willful, and shameless.

Stephen Douglas had helped the scheme along by opening the federal lands in the West to the spread of slavery. He helped it along by telling whites not to care, and that the fate of black slaves didn't matter. Franklin Pierce had provided some crucial leverage by using and abusing his presidential office to manipulate events in Kansas. James Buchanan had done the same thing.

Both Pierce and Buchanan paved the way for the Dred Scott decision by telling the public to obey it before it was even issued. Then Taney followed up with his judicial revolt against the Founding Fathers and their legacy.

And this was where matters then stood, Lincoln said, as he summarized the recent historical events in terms of *power* for the advocates of slavery. They perverted the law to gain power, he said, and their method was to build a political structure of enslavement through the following precedents of law:

> First, that no negro slave, imported as such from Africa, and no descendant of such slave can ever be a *citizen* of any State. . . .
> Secondly, that "subject to the Constitution of the United States," neither *Congress* nor a *Territorial Legislature* can exclude slavery from any United States Territory. . . .
> Thirdly, that whether the holding [of] a negro in actual slavery in a free State, makes him free, as against the holder, the United States courts will not decide, but will leave to be decided by the courts of any slave State the negro may be forced into by the master.
> This point is made, not to be pressed *immediately*; but, if acquiesced in for a while, and apparently *indorsed* [sic] by the people at an election, *then* to sustain the logical conclusion that what Dred Scott's master might lawfully do with Dred Scott, in the free State of Illinois, every other master may lawfully do with any other *one*, or one *thousand* slaves, in Illinois, or in any other free State.[62]

All the while, Stephen Douglas played a role in this despicable drama by urging white Americans to turn their thoughts away from the subject. He urged whites to "live and let live" when it came to the ownership of Negroes. He meant to lull the Northern public—including the Northern anti-slavery public—into quiet but maleficent sleep. "We shall *lie down* pleasantly dreaming that the people of *Mississippi* are on the verge of making their State *free*," said Lincoln, and then "we shall *awake* to the *reality*, instead, that the Supreme Court has made *Illinois* a slave State."[63]

It could happen in the blink of an eye. And the preparations had begun as far back as the Kansas-Nebraska Act. In a little-noticed passage of the act, Lincoln said, the law stated that "the people of a *State* as well as *Territory*, were to be left '*perfectly free*'" to decide about the issue of slavery, "'*subject only to the Constitution.*'"

But why, Lincoln asked, had there been mention of a *state* in the Nebraska legislation? "Why mention a *State*? They were legislating for *territories*, and not *for* or *about* States. Certainly the people of a State *are* and *ought to be* subject to the Constitution of the United States; but why is mention of this *lugged* into this merely *territorial* law? Why are the people of a *territory* and the people of a *state* therein *lumped* together, and their relation to the Constitution therein treated as being *precisely* the same?"[64]

The reason, said Lincoln, was to open up a path for a new interpretation—the Calhoun school-of-thought interpretation—of the United States Constitution in defining the *powers of a state*. "Put *that* and *that* together, and we have another nice little niche, which we may, ere long, see filled with another Supreme Court decision, declaring that the Constitution of the United States does not permit a *state* to exclude slavery from its limits."[65]

It was all a coordinated plan, Lincoln argued, a conspiracy to shrink away the power of the anti-slavery movement. The principal conspirators—Douglas, Pierce, Taney, and Buchanan—had been working from a kind of a strategic blueprint, a political schematic for gradually constructing a national edifice of slavery.

As if they were laborers, he called them by their first names—Stephen and Franklin and Roger and James—as he worked the Republican crowd at the Springfield convention. His logic was tinged with sarcastic anger as he argued that the busy machinations of the Democratic crew had been coordinated from the beginning. "We cannot absolutely *know* that all these exact adaptations are the result of preconcert," Lincoln admitted. "But when we see a lot of framed timbers, different portions of which we know have been gotten out at different times and places by different workmen—Stephen, Franklin, Roger, and James, for instance—and when we see these timbers joined together, and see they exactly make the frame of a house or mill, all the tenons and mortices exactly fitting, and all the lengths and proportions of the different pieces exactly adapted to their respective places, and not a piece too many or too few—not omitting even scaffolding—or, if a single piece be lacking, we can see the place in the frame exactly fitted and prepared to yet bring such piece in—in *such* a case, we find it impossible to not *believe* that Stephen and Franklin and Roger and James all understood one another from the beginning, and all worked upon a common *plan* or *draft* drawn up before the first lick was struck."[66]

But the edifice of slavery was still unfinished, and Republican crusaders could destroy the ugly thing if they rose to their challenge in time. "Two years ago the Republicans of the nation mustered over thirteen hundred thousand strong," Lincoln said, making reference to the 1856 election. This was done "under the single impulse of resistance to a common danger, with every external circumstance against us. Of *strange*, *discordant*, and even, *hostile* elements, we gathered from the four winds, and *formed* and fought the battle through, under the hot fire of a disciplined, proud, and pampered enemy. Did we brave all *then*, to falter now?—*now*—when that same enemy is *wavering*, dissevered and belligerent?"[67]

This "House Divided" speech—so completely the reverse in its feelings and intentions from the notions that "sound-bite" summaries suggest—was the prelude to Lincoln's great speech in Chicago the following month, the speech from the balcony of the Tremont House hotel.

As he readied his challenge to Douglas, Lincoln hoped to see the day when he could use his new position in the Senate to reverse the course of slavery expansion. The following reflections leave very little doubt that Lincoln hoped to usher in a long phaseout of slavery, one that was modeled as closely as possible on Britain's great achievement of the 1830s. "I have not allowed myself to forget," he wrote, "that the abolition of the Slave-trade by Great Brittain [*sic*], was agitated a hundred years before it was a final success; that the measure had its open fire-eating opponents; its stealthy 'don't care' opponents; its dollar and cent opponents; its inferior race opponents; its negro equality opponents; and its religion and good order opponents; that all these opponents got offices, and their adversaries got none." Nonetheless, he continued,

> I have also remembered that though they blazed, like tallow-candles for a century, at last they flickered in the socket, died out, stank in the dark for a brief

season, and were remembered no more, even by the smell. School-boys know that Wilbe[r]force, and Granville Sharpe, helped that cause forward; but who can now name a single man who labored to retard it? Remembering these things I can not but regard it as possible that the higher object of this contest may not be completely attained within the term of my natural life. But I can not doubt either that it will come in due time. Even in this view, I am proud, in my passing speck of time, to contribute an humble mite to that glorious consummation. . . .[68]

Douglas—one of those men who were currently blazing like candles but whose fate was to flicker out and stink in the dark for a time— charged that Lincoln was calling for a war between the sections in his "House Divided" speech. He said that Popular Sovereignty worked— indeed, he even claimed paramount credit for defeating the Lecompton Constitution. And he told his constituents again and again that a vote for Lincoln was a vote for mongrelization.

He did it in his kick-off address in Chicago, delivered from a window balcony at Tremont House hotel. On the very next evening, however, Lincoln occupied the very same balcony. As we heard in chapter one, he roused the crowd with passionate oratory, striking back hard at Douglas. It was Douglas, after all, said Lincoln, who had opened up Kansas to slavery. It was Douglas who said he didn't care whether slavery spread. He parted company with James Buchanan over matters of *procedure*.

But it was Republican anti-slavery men who had done the real work to stop slavery expansion in Kansas. It was anti-slavery Republicans who stopped the Lecompton fraud in the House of Representatives. Douglas and his Democratic allies furnished "some twenty votes," said Lincoln, "and the Republicans furnished *ninety odd*. [Loud applause] Now who was it who did the work?"[69]

Lincoln denied Douglas's charge that he was fomenting war between the sections. His "House Divided" speech, he observed, was a *prediction* that America's struggle over slavery would resolve itself in one way alone: "If you will carefully read that passage over," he said, "I did not say that I was in favor of anything in it. I only said what I expected to take place. . . . I did not even say that I desired that slavery should be put in course of ultimate extinction."[70]

But now, said Lincoln, since Douglas forced the question, he was ready to declare that the extinction of slavery was precisely what he *did* wish to see: "I do say so now, however [great applause] so there need be no longer any difficulty about that. It may be written down . . . [Applause and laughter]."[71]

Still, said Lincoln, he had never proposed any short-term action that would interfere with slavery in states that permitted it: "I believe there is no right, and ought to be no inclination on the part of the people of the free States to enter into the slave States, and interfere with the question of slavery at all."[72] Instead, Lincoln wanted the *containment* of slavery, so that others could extinguish its evil in the future.

But when Taney, Pierce, Buchanan, and Douglas tried to force the *expansion* of slavery, Lincoln said that he would fight them to the end, to the point of ignoring the Dred Scott decision. He would not so much *resist* the decision as ignore it completely. "If I were in Congress," he proclaimed, "and a vote should come up on a question whether slavery should be prohibited in a new territory, in spite of that Dred Scott decision, I would vote that it should. [Applause; 'good for you;' 'we hope to see it;' 'that's right.']"[73]

Lincoln worked this audience in ways that we have seen already; he invoked the recent pageant of the Fourth of July as he spoke to the descendants of people who had come from all over Europe, telling them that they and their kind were quite right to feel kinship with America's Founding Fathers. It was a kinship based upon a principle transcending ethnicity and race; people like themselves had "a right to claim it as though they were blood of the blood, and flesh of the flesh of the men who wrote that Declaration, (loud and long continued applause) and so they are."[74] He continued:

> Now, sirs, for the purpose of squaring things with this idea of "don't care if slavery is voted up or down," for sustaining the Dred Scott decision [A voice— "Hit him again"], for holding that the Declaration of Independence did not mean anything at all, we have Judge Douglas giving his exposition of what the Declaration of Independence means, and we have him saying that the people of America are equal to the people of England. According to his construction, you Germans are not connected with it. Now I ask in all soberness, if all these things, if indulged in, if ratified, if confirmed and endorsed, if taught to our children, and repeated to them, do not tend to rub out the sentiment of liberty in this country, and to transform this Government into a government of some other form. Those arguments that are made, that the inferior race are to be treated with as much allowance as they are capable of enjoying; that as much is to be done for them as their condition will allow. What are these arguments? They are the arguments that kings have made for enslaving the people in all ages of the world.[75]

We have heard the climax of the speech:

> I should like to know if taking this old Declaration of Independence, which
> declares that all men are equal upon principle and making exceptions to it where
> will it stop. If one man says it does not mean a negro, why not another say it
> does not mean some other man? If that declaration is not the truth, let us get
> the Statute book, in which we find it and tear it out![76]

As he concluded, Lincoln urged his supporters to "discard all this quibbling about this man and the other man—this race and that race and
the other race being inferior, and therefore they must be placed in an
inferior position. . . . Let us discard all these things, and unite as one
people. . . ."[77]

But Douglas meant to sabotage Lincoln on race, and he continued
to agitate the issue by dwelling on interracial sex. So Lincoln crafted a
lawyer-like position that he hoped would be of use throughout the
weeks and months of campaigning. He tried it out on a Springfield
audience a week after issuing his plea in Chicago.

"Last night," he said, "Judge Douglas tormented himself with hor-
rors about my disposition to makes negroes perfectly equal with white
men in social and political relations. He did not stop to show that I
have said any such thing, or that it legitimately follows from any thing
I have said, but he rushes in with his assertions." Lincoln carefully
avoided *denying* that he wished to make blacks and whites socially and
politically equal; he just denied that he had actually *said* he wished to
make them equal.

He further tiptoed along the boundary of racial prejudice with more
careful language that echoed his earlier remarks about a "Negro wife":
"Certainly the negro is not our equal in color—perhaps not in other
respects; still, in the right to put into his mouth the bread that his own
hands have earned, he is the equal of every other man, white or black.
. . . All I ask for the negro is that if you do not like him, let him alone."[78]

To counter the racial demagoguery of Douglas, Lincoln temporized—
though on close inspection his formulations conceded very little. "Certainly the negro is not our equal in color," Lincoln said, and "perhaps
not in other respects." The only difference that was definite—Lincoln
used the word "certainly"—was difference in *color*.

But if blacks and whites were "unequal" in color—that is, they had
different amounts of pigmentation—this form of "inequality" was noth-

ing but a matter of taste with regard to the physical appearance of others. If one happened not to like the appearance of others, one could obviously leave them alone.

Though other forms of racial "inequality" *might* exist (Lincoln pointedly used the word "perhaps"), none had been *proven*. The only thing that could be proven on the subject of race was that blacks were the equals of whites when it came to their liberty.

Would the strategy work? The question had become more urgent since the speech in Chicago. Lincoln had challenged Stephen Douglas to a series of debates that would carry their struggle into every major section of the state. And this included southern Illinois ("Egypt," as its natives dubbed it), where the sentiments of white supremacy were near universal.

Though Illinois voters lacked the power to elect their senators, they did vote for the members of the state legislature, who in turn voted for the senators. The Lincoln-Douglas debates made the senatorial choice the big issue in the statewide elections.

The first debate took place on August 21, 1858, in Ottawa, in northern Illinois. Over twelve thousand people had jammed the public square to hear Lincoln and Douglas debate. Republican sentiment prevailed in this town, but Douglas used the occasion for all it was worth to get Lincoln on the record in a number of ways that would damage his chances in "Egypt," where white supremacy was stronger.

Douglas started with assertions that America's "divided House" could stand forever in a state of division. He said the Founding Fathers had intended this state of affairs. In their wisdom, said Douglas, the Founders left the people to decide about the issue for themselves—state by state. The Founding Fathers, in effect, were thus the earliest practitioners and advocates of Popular Sovereignty.

Then Douglas launched into his white supremacy routine. He began with some questions for the audience. "I ask you," said Douglas, "are you in favor of conferring upon the negro the rights and privileges of citizenship? ('No, no.') Do you desire to strike out of our State Constitution that clause which keeps slaves and free negroes out of the State, and allow the free negroes to flow in, ('never') and cover your prairies with black settlements? Do you desire to turn this beautiful State into a free negro colony, ('no, no') in order that when Missouri abolishes slavery she can send one hundred thousand emancipated slaves

into Illinois, to become citizens and voters, on an equality with yourselves? ('Never,' 'no.') If you desire negro citizenship . . . then support
Mr. Lincoln and the Black Republican party. . . . For one, I am opposed to negro citizenship in any and every form. (Cheers.) I believe
this government was made on the white basis. ('Good.') I believe it was
made by white men, for the benefit of white men and their posterity
for ever. . . ."[79]

Then he twisted the knife a bit more: "I do not question Mr. Lincoln's
conscientious belief that the negro was made his equal, and hence is
his brother, (laughter) but for my own part, I do not regard the negro
as my equal, and positively deny that he is my brother or any kin to me
whatever. ('Never.' 'Hit him again,' and cheers)."[80]

Douglas challenged Lincoln to reply to a series of questions regarding the Republican Party's doctrines—did Lincoln, for example, stand
pledged to prevent the admission of any more slave states to the Union,
"even if the people want them?" Did Lincoln stand pledged to bar
slavery from all the open territories of the United States? Did he oppose the acquisition of any more American territory unless it was forbidden to slavery?

"I ask Abraham Lincoln to answer these questions," said Douglas,
"in order that when I trot him down to lower Egypt I may put the same
questions to him. (Enthusiastic applause.) My principles are the same
everywhere. (Cheers, and 'hark.') I can proclaim them alike in the
North, the South, the East, and the West. . . . I desire to know whether
Mr. Lincoln's principles will bear transplanting from Ottawa to
Jonesboro."[81]

Lincoln was on the defensive. He avoided quick answers to the questions, and he tried to defuse the racial issue by employing some new
formulations—carefully composed, with all the qualifying language he
could manage—that would sound good enough when he was forced to
"trot down" to "lower Egypt": "I have no purpose to introduce political and social equality between the white and the black races," he said.
"There is a physical difference between the two, which in my judgment will probably forever forbid their living together upon the footing of perfect equality, and inasmuch as it becomes a necessity that
there must be a difference [in the power positions of the races], I, as
well as Judge Douglas, am in favor of the race to which I belong, having the superior position."[82]

A tricky disclaimer: though it *sounded* like a racist manifesto, Lincoln carefully restricted its moral implications, as a critical analysis reveals. Lincoln said that he had *no intention at the moment* ("no purpose") of pursuing full equality for blacks *in light of the existing political reality*: the reality that blacks and whites were so deeply divided due to hatred arising from their "physical difference" that the politics of racial equality were probably impossible, at least in America. All attempts to place the races on the "footing" of perfect equality would probably fail, for political reasons.

If, therefore, a choice should ever have to be made between subjection and domination—then Lincoln, for obvious reasons, would not choose subjection.[83]

But the choice between subjection and total domination was gratuitous, in Lincoln's estimation. Lincoln firmly denied that any such choice was predestined when it came to the issue of *freedom*.

Lincoln then struck back at Douglas on the issue of Popular Sovereignty vis-à-vis the Dred Scott decision. He demanded to know the real meaning of Popular Sovereignty: "Is it the right of the people to have Slavery or not have it, as they see fit, in the territories? . . . My understanding is that Popular Sovereignty . . . does allow the people of a Territory to have Slavery if they want to, but does not allow them *not* to have it if they *do not* want it. [Applause and laughter.]" According to the Dred Scott decision, he said, if a single settler should make up his mind to hold slaves, then the rest of the settlers would have "no way of keeping that one man from holding them."[84]

He then returned to his charge from the House Divided Speech: Douglas was complicit with Pierce, Buchanan, and Taney in extending the reach of the slavery system with intentions of making it national. He reminded his listeners that Douglas had placed the word "state" in the Kansas-Nebraska Bill, for what reason one could gradually infer: "I have always been puzzled to know what business the word 'State' had in that connection. Judge Douglas knows. *He put it there.* . . . This law they were passing was not about States, and was not making provisions for States." But after "seeing the Dred Scott decision, which holds that the people cannot exclude slavery from a *Territory*, if another Dred Scott decision shall come, holding that they cannot exclude it from a *State*, we shall discover that when the word was originally put there, it was in view of something which was to come in due time. . . ."[85]

And Douglas, said Lincoln, was a cheerleader *par excellence* for the Dred Scott decision—even though it gutted his supposedly sacred principles of Popular Sovereignty. So what were his real convictions? "This man," said Lincoln, "sticks to a decision which forbids the people of a Territory from excluding slavery, and he does so not because he says it is right in itself—he does not give any opinion on that—but because it has been *decided by the court....*"[86]

Yet this same Stephen Douglas held Supreme Court opinions in contempt when his interests had demanded it. Decades earlier, Lincoln pointed out, both Douglas and his Democratic colleagues refused to go along with a Supreme Court ruling on the charter of a National Bank. But now, they insisted that the Dred Scott decision was sacrosanct, a holy pronouncement.

Douglas, in the course of his rebuttal, called immediate attention to the fact that Lincoln failed to respond to his questions, which he called "interrogatories." For his own part, Douglas shrugged away the charges that Lincoln had made with respect to what Douglas called "that nonsense about Stephen, and Franklin, and Roger, and Bob, and James." The conspiracy charges were hardly worth rebutting, said Douglas. It was all a mere political conceit by Lincoln, a ploy to call attention to himself:

> He studied that out, prepared that one sentence with the greatest care, committed it to memory, and put it in his first Springfield speech, and now he carries that speech around and reads that sentence to show how pretty it is. (Laughter.) His vanity is wounded because I will not go into that beautiful figure of his about the building of a house. (Renewed laughter.) All I have to say is, that I am not green enough to let him make a charge which he acknowledges he does not know to be true, and then take up my time in answering it, when I know it to be false and nobody else knows it to be true.... Let him prove it if he can.[87]

As to the insertion of "state" into the language of the Kansas-Nebraska Act, Douglas claimed that his intentions were innocuous: "Mr. Lincoln wants to know why the word 'state,' as well as 'territory,' was put into the Nebraska Bill! I will tell him. It was put there to meet just such false arguments as he had been adducing. (Laughter.) That first, not only the people of the territories should do as they pleased, but that when they come to be admitted as States, they should come into the Union with or without slavery, as the people determined. I meant to knock in the head this Abolition doctrine of Mr. Lincoln's, that there shall be no more slave States, even if the people want them. (Tremendous applause.)"[88]

In the aftermath of the Ottawa debate, Lincoln urgently sought the advice of his fellow Republicans. He met with Norman Judd and the members of the Republican State Central Committee. He met with Joseph Medill of the *Chicago Tribune*, who advised him to hit back at Douglas with embarrassing questions of his own.

He did so at Freeport, in northern Illinois, where some fifteen thousand people turned out for the second of the Lincoln-Douglas debates on August 27. Lincoln struck back at Douglas by proclaiming he would gladly "answer any of the interrogatories" Douglas had framed "upon condition that he will answer questions from me not exceeding the same number." Lincoln paused for the effects of one-upmanship: "I give him an opportunity to respond. The Judge remains silent. I now say to you that I will answer his interrogatories, whether he answers mine or not; [applause] and that after I have done so, I shall propound mine to him."[89]

Lincoln's answers took advantage of the way in which Douglas posed the questions: he had asked whether Lincoln at the time "stood pledged" to key Republican doctrines. One should bear this distinctly in mind in making sense of Lincoln's responses; the mere fact that he denied being "pledged" to certain goals *at the moment* meant nothing when it came to his possible actions in the *future*: it never stopped him from embracing the very same goals later on, when conditions had improved. Here are a few of his answers: "I do not now, nor ever did, stand pledged against the admission of any more slave States into the Union. . . . I do not stand to-day pledged to the abolition of slavery in the District of Columbia. . . . I do not stand pledged to the prohibition of the slave trade between the different States."[90]

One of his answers, however, was a pledge he meant everyone to hear: "I am impliedly, if not expressly, pledged to a belief in the *right* and *duty* of Congress to prohibit slavery in all the United States Territories. [Great applause]"[91]

He pointed out quickly that his answers to Douglas were deliberately legalistic: "Now my friends, it will be perceived upon an examination of these questions and answers, that so far I have only answered that I was not *pledged* to this, that or the other. The Judge has not framed his interrogatories to ask me anything more than this, and I have answered in strict accordance with the interrogatories. . . . But I am not disposed to hang upon the exact form of the interrogatory. I am rather disposed to take up at least some of these questions, and state what I really think upon them."[92]

Lincoln stated his belief that if Congress kept slavery from federal lands it was extremely unlikely the settlers there would write slave-state constitutions. Hence the issue of whether he was "pledged" to oppose the admission of any more slave states was probably moot if his policies prevailed.

Then he turned to his personal *wishes*. Even though he had never been "pledged" to abolishing slavery in Washington, D.C., he announced that he heartily endorsed the idea, with a few stipulations: "I should be exceedingly glad to see slavery abolished in the District of Columbia. [Cries of 'good, good.'] . . . Yet as a member of Congress, I should not with my present views, be in favor of *endeavoring* to abolish slavery in the District of Columbia, unless it would be upon these conditions. *First*, that the abolition should be gradual. *Second*, that it should be on a vote of the majority of qualified voters in the District, and *third*, that compensation should be made to unwilling owners."[93]

It should be noted that the very same principles Lincoln set forth in this speech for abolition in the nation's capital—gradual emancipation, with full compensation to the owners—were an embryonic version of the principles he sought to apply later on across the country.

Then Lincoln asked Douglas to respond to some questions of his own. "Can the people of a United States Territory, in any lawful way, against the wish of any citizen of the United States, exclude slavery from its limits prior to the formation of a State Constitution," he inquired. Then he asked a more painful question: "If the Supreme Court of the United States shall decide that States can not exclude slavery from their limits, are you in favor of acquiescing in, adopting and following such decision as a rule of political action?"[94]

Douglas answered these questions energetically. As Lincoln had heard him proclaim many times, he exclaimed, it was his settled opinion that "the people of a territory can, by lawful means, exclude slavery from their limits . . . for the reason that slavery cannot exist a day or an hour anywhere, unless it is supported by local police regulations." Hence "if the people are opposed to slavery they will elect representatives" to their territorial legislature "who will by unfriendly legislation effectually prevent the introduction of it in their midst."[95]

As to a Supreme Court decision overturning all the free-state constitutions, Douglas said, "I am amazed that Lincoln should ask such a question. . . . He casts an imputation upon the Supreme Court of the United States by supposing that they would violate the Constitution of the United States. I tell him that such a thing is not possible. (Cheers.) It would be an act of moral treason that no man on the bench would ever descend to."[96]

Then Douglas reverted to his warnings about racial equality. "The last time I came here to make a speech," he intoned, "while talking from the stand to you, people of Freeport, as I am doing to-day, I saw a carriage and a magnificent one it was, drive up and take a position outside the crowd; a beautiful young lady was sitting on the box seat, whilst Fred. Douglass and her mother reclined inside, and the owner of the carriage acted as driver. (Laughter, cheers, cries of right, what have you to say against it, &c.) I saw this in your own town. ('What of it.') All I have to say of it is this, that if you, Black Republicans, think that the negro ought to be on a social equality with your wives and daughters, and ride in a carriage with your wife, whilst you drive the team, you have a perfect right to do so."[97]

This was a Republican crowd, and Douglas knew it perfectly well. He was baiting both Lincoln and the crowd not so much for its immediate effect as for its use later on in the campaign—so he could brag about speaking in the very same language all over the state as he dished out his bigoted opinions. He would strive to contrast his own forthright behavior with the difference in tone that he expected from Lincoln when the two of them went down to "Egypt."

In mid-September, the scene of the debates began to shift in Douglas's favor: it shifted to the South. On September 15, the third Lincoln-Douglas debate was held in Jonesboro, Illinois. Douglas used the same anecdote that rattled the crowd at Freeport. But the reactions in southern Illinois were very different.

"In the extreme northern counties," Douglas said, "they brought out men to canvass the State whose complexion suited their political creed, and hence Fred Douglass, the negro, was to be found there. . . . Why, they brought Fred Douglass to Freeport when I was addressing a meeting there in a carriage driven by the white owner, the negro sitting inside with the white lady and her daughter. (Shame.) When I got through canvassing the northern counties that year [1854] and progressed as far south as Springfield, I was met and opposed in discussion by Lincoln,

Lovejoy, Trumbull, and Sidney Breese, who were on one side. (Laughter.) Father Giddings, the high priest of abolitionism, had just been there, and Chase came about the time I left. ('Why didn't you shoot him?') I did take a running shot at them, but as I was single-handed against the white, black and mixed drove, I had to use a short gun and fire into the crowd instead of taking them off singly with a rifle. (Great laughter and cheers.)"[98]

Douglas then presented all his standard declarations of white supremacy; he said that "I hold that a negro is not and never ought to be a citizen of the United States. (Good, good, and tremendous cheers.) . . . I do not believe that the Almighty made the negro capable of self-government."[99] As to the Declaration of Independence, "in my opinion the signers of the Declaration had no reference to the negro whatever when they declared all men to be created equal. They desired to express by that phrase, white men, men of European birth and European descent, and had no reference either to the negro, the savage Indians, the Fejee, the Malay, or any other inferior and degraded race. . . ."[100]

Lincoln decided not to rise to this bait "down in Egypt." Instead, he used folksy humor in an effort to change the subject—he sought to shift attention to himself. He made sport of his opponent's attempt to depict him as fearful of the voters in Egypt; Douglas let it be known that "I would not come to Egypt unless he forced me—that I could not be got down here, unless he, giant-like, had hauled me down here. [Laughter.] . . . Judge Douglas, when he made that statement must have been crazy, and wholly out of his sober senses, or else he would have known that when he got me down here—that promise—that windy promise—of his powers to annihilate me, wouldn't amount to anything. Now, how little do I look like being carried away trembling? . . . Did the Judge talk of trotting me down to Egypt to scare me to death? Why, I know this people better than he does. I was raised just a little east of here. I am a part of this people. But the Judge was raised further north, and perhaps he has some horrid idea of what this people might be induced to do. [Roars of laughter and cheers.]"[101]

Lincoln avoided the subject of race as he launched new attacks against Douglas's positions, especially the doctrine that settlers could stop the spread of slavery in federal lands by "unfriendly" legislation. Lincoln said the proposition "that slavery cannot enter a new country without police regulations is historically false." How else could one account for the fact that Dred Scott had been taken into lands that were forbidden to slavery?

Besides, said Lincoln, if the views of Roger Taney set the tone for interpreting the Constitution, consider the effect this would have upon the territorial legislatures: "I will ask you my friends, if you were elected members of the Legislature, what would be the first thing you would have to do before entering upon your duties? *Swear to support the Constitution of the United States.* . . . How could you, having sworn to support the Constitution, and believing it guaranteed the right to hold slaves in the Territories, assist in legislation *intended to defeat that right?* . . . Not only so, but if you were to do so, how long would it take the courts to hold your votes unconstitutional and void? Not a moment."[102]

So far so good: notwithstanding the race-baiting tactics of Douglas, the Jonesboro clash was bereft of any lurid confrontations on the racial issue. But Douglas kept taunting both Lincoln and his fellow Republicans to get a rise on the subject. He told the crowd that Lincoln's "party in the northern part of the State hold to that abolition platform, and . . . if they do not in the south and in the centre they present the extraordinary spectacle of a house divided against itself. . . ."[103]

Douglas said the very same thing in his next debate with Lincoln on September 18, in Charleston, central Illinois. Douglas charged that the Republicans deliberately altered their rhetoric and principles in different parts of the state: "Their principles in the North are jet black, (laughter), in the centre they are in color a decent mulatto, (renewed laughter), and in lower Egypt they are almost white. (Shouts of laughter.)"[104]

Lincoln countered Douglas with a strong outpouring of ridicule. He began by restating his racial formulations from their very first debate in Ottawa. He challenged "every fair-minded man" to read his printed speeches from the Ottawa and Freeport debates and then compare them to what he said in Charleston that very day: "*I dare him to point out any difference between my printed speeches north and south.*"[105]

But there *were* great differences in *tone* between his "speeches north and south." The great plea in Chicago for cessation of racial animosities, the plea to discard racial consciousness entirely and stop the incessant "quibbling about this man and the other man—this race and that race and the other race being inferior," could not be used among voters in southern or central Illinois if Lincoln wanted to drive Stephen Douglas from office in 1858.

Politics had forced the racial issue on Lincoln. And there were limits to the number of times he could get away with changing the subject. So Lincoln seized upon the issue in the Charleston debate and turned it back upon Douglas in a manner that he hoped would make his enemy look like a fool.

Once again, he took aim at the phobia of racial intermarriage, and he treated it in ways that made his audience laugh it off. He observed that racial intermarriage was illegal in the state of Illinois. Even so, "I have never had the least apprehension," he said, "that I or my friends would marry negroes if there was no law to keep them from it."

But Judge Douglas kept bringing up the issue. Very well: since it seemed to preoccupy the mind of Stephen Douglas, it would probably be best if he retired from the Senate to devote his full energies to supervising Illinois mores. "I do not understand [that] there is any place where an alteration of the social and political relations of the negro and the white man can be made except in the State Legislature," Lincoln said, and most certainly "not in the Congress of the United States." Inasmuch "as Judge Douglas seems to be in constant horror that some such danger is rapidly approaching, I propose as the best means to prevent it that the Judge be kept at home and placed in the State Legislature to fight the measure. [Uproarious laughter and applause.] I do not propose dwelling any longer at this time on the subject."[106]

Douglas, of course, chose to dwell upon the subject continually. His speeches in the Charleston debate contained the regular nasty fare: snide quips about Frederick Douglass in the coach at Freeport, warnings about the insidious measures that whites could expect the Republicans to foist upon the people, and allusions to the interest that "the colored brethren felt in the success of their brother Abe."[107]

On October 7, the debates between Lincoln and Douglas moved north to the city of Galesburg. Douglas was slightly more civil. He asked the audience to think about the dire implications if a Lincoln-type "House Divided" doctrine had prevailed at the founding of the nation: "When this government was made," he said, "there were twelve slaveholding States and one free State in this Union. . . . Suppose Mr. Lincoln himself had been a member of the convention which framed the constitution, and that he had risen in that august body, and addressing the father of his country, had said as he did at Springfield: A house divided against itself cannot stand. . . ." If the issue had been forced at the Constitutional Convention, said Douglas, the "House

Divided" doctrine would have caused the twelve slave states to over-whelm the isolated free state:

> Would not the twelve slaveholding States have outvoted the one free State, and under his doctrine have fastened slavery by an irrevocable constitutional provi-sion upon every inch of the American Republic? Thus you see that the doctrine he now advocates, if proclaimed at the beginning of the government, would have established slavery everywhere throughout the American continent, and are you willing, now that we have the majority section, to exercise a power which we never would have submitted to when we were in the minority?[108]

This was clever, said Lincoln, but the tricks of Stephen Douglas all flowed from his stark amorality. For he would never say that slavery was *wrong*.

And that was the difference, not only in the choice between Lincoln and Douglas but also in the choice between their two parties: "Every-thing that emanates from him or his coadjutors in their course of policy, carefully excludes the thought that there is anything wrong with Sla-very," Lincoln pointed out.[109]

And that was the reason why the Dred Scott decision, if accepted as the binding law of the land, was positioning the South to export its great evil to the North:

> The essence of the Dred Scott case is compressed into the sentence which I will now read . . . "The right of property in a slave is distinctly and expressly affirmed in the Constitution!" What is it to be "affirmed" in the Constitution? Made firm in the Constitution—so made that it cannot be separated from the Constitution without breaking the Constitution—durable as the Constitution, and part of the Constitution. Now, remembering the provision of the Consti-tution which I have read, affirming that the instrument is the supreme law of the land; that the Judges of every State shall be bound by it, any law or Consti-tution of any State to the contrary notwithstanding; that the right of property in a slave is affirmed in that Constitution, is made, formed into and cannot be separated from it without breaking it; durable as the instrument; part of the instrument;—what follows . . . ?[110]

What followed was the overthrow of Northern institutions, just as soon as the electorate was ready.

Stephen Douglas was working night and day to prepare Northern public opinion. He told the Northern public not to *care* about blacks and that reducing a slave to the status of a beast of the field was in no way morally *wrong*. He told them that any community of whites who wished to have the institution of slavery should certainly have it. He told them to obey the decisions of Taney and his court without worrying about the *rightness* of such decisions.

Douglas's adherence to the Dred Scott decision, said Lincoln, "commits him to the next decision, whenever it comes, as being as obligatory as this one, since he . . . won't inquire whether this opinion is right or wrong. So he takes the next one without inquiring whether *it* is right or wrong. [Applause.] He teaches men this doctrine, and in so doing prepares the public mind to take the next decision when it comes, without any inquiry."[111]

Perhaps, said Lincoln, this was not what Stephen Douglas intended, but "I call upon your minds to inquire, if you were going to get the best instrument you could, and then set it to work in the most ingenious way, to prepare the public mind for this movement, operating in the free States, where there is now an abhorrence of the institution of Slavery, could you find an instrument so capable of doing it as Judge Douglas? or one employed in so apt a way to do it? [Great cheering. Cries of 'Hit him again,' 'That's the doctrine.']"[112]

The campaign was drawing to an end. On October 13, the penultimate debate occurred in Quincy, a town in the south-central portion of the state. Douglas challenged Lincoln to present a good Republican way in which America's people could unite along *peaceful* lines. Precisely *how*, he asked, would Lincoln put slavery on course for an ultimate extinction in the states that already permitted it? "How can he extinguish it in Kentucky, in Virginia, in all the slave States by his policy, if he will not pursue a policy which will interfere with it in the States where it exists?"[113]

This was a very good question, but Lincoln passed over it in silence. Furthermore, asked Douglas, how did Lincoln envision overturning the Dred Scott decision? "By what tribunal will he reverse it? Will he

Abraham Lincoln as he looked a few weeks before his final debate with Stephen Douglas in 1858. Photograph by Calvin Jackson. (Library of Congress, Meserve Collection #12)

appeal to a mob? Does he intend to appeal to violence, to Lynch law? Will he stir up strife and rebellion in the land and overthrow the Court by violence?"[114]

Lincoln was fomenting war between the states, Douglas said, and the voters should prevent him from succeeding in his plans. "Let each State mind its own business and let its neighbors alone, and there will be no trouble on this question. If we will stand by that principle, then Mr. Lincoln will find that this republic can exist forever divided into free and slave States. . . ."[115]

Lincoln replied: "I wish to return Judge Douglas my profound thanks for his public annunciation here to-day, to be put on record, that his system of policy in regard to the institution of slavery *contemplates that it shall last forever*. [Great cheers, and cries of 'Hit him again.']"[116]

As to reversing the Dred Scott decision, Lincoln ridiculed Douglas by reminding him of all the many times in the past when he had over-turned decisions of the courts: "He is desirous of knowing how we are going to reverse the Dred Scott decision. Judge Douglas ought to know how. Did not he and his political friends find a way to reverse the decision of that same Court in favor of the constitutionality of the National Bank? [Cheers and laughter.] . . . And let me ask you, didn't Judge Douglas find a way to reverse the decision of our [Illinois] Su-preme Court, when it decided that Carlin's old father—old Governor Carlin—had not the constitutional power to remove a Secretary of State? [Great cheering and laughter.] Did he not appeal to the 'MOBS' as he calls them? Did he not make speeches in the lobby to show how villainous that decision was, and how it ought to be overthrown? Did he not succeed too in getting an act passed by the Legislature to have it overthrown? And didn't he himself sit down on the bench as one of the five added judges, who were to overslaugh the four old ones—getting his name of 'Judge' in that way and no other? [Thundering cheers and laughter.]"[117]

In the final debate held in Alton, Illinois, down in "Egypt"—the very same place in which Elijah Lovejoy had been murdered almost twenty years earlier—Lincoln decried the Democrats' tendency to "de-humanize the negro—to take away from him the right of ever striving to be a man. I combat it as being one of the thousand things constantly done in these days to prepare the public mind to make property, and nothing but property of the *negro in all the States of this Union*."[118]

Lincoln was confident of victory, so long as the Illinois Democrats refrained from any frauds or hoaxes at the polls.[119] The Illinois electorate voted on November 7. Lincoln's candidates for the legislature got approximately 125,000 votes to 121,000 for the candidates pledged to Douglas.[120]

But that was not enough. Because Douglas had carried more *counties* statewide, the Democratic Party retained its existing control of the legislature.[121] The reelection of Stephen Douglas was thereby assured.

Lincoln's supporters were distraught. And Lincoln was depressed, but he tried to view the matter philosophically. "I am glad that I made the late race," he told supporters on a wistful note. "It gave me a hearing on the great and durable question of the age, which I could have had in no other way; and though I now sink out of view, and shall be forgotten, I believe that I have made some marks which will tell for the cause of liberty long after I am gone."[122]

His spirits would revive soon enough. To one supporter he wrote: "I hope and believe that the seed has been sown that will yet produce fruit. . . . Douglas managed to be supported both as the best means to *break down* and to *uphold* the slave power. No ingenuity can long keep those opposing elements in harmony. Another explosion will come before a great while."[123]

In fact, the Kansas-Nebraska and Dred Scott issues had inflicted great damage on the presidential prospects of Douglas. And the 1858 debates would make the name of Lincoln better known far beyond Illinois. His speeches were eventually reprinted all over the country in books and political pamphlets.

To another supporter he imparted an impish consolation: "I believe . . . [that] you are 'feeling like h—ll yet.' Quit that. You will soon feel better. Another 'blow-up' is coming; and we shall have fun again."[124]

But it was something very different that Lincoln and his followers would have when the blowup occurred. They would have a great war between the states, just as Douglas, perverse and bombastic though he was, had predicted so forcefully to Lincoln.

And with war, Lincoln gradually learned something new about his talents as a strategist. He knew better than most of his generals the way to destroy the power of the South. And this would lead to the destruction of the slavery system much faster than he ever thought possible—if he won.

THREE

Lincoln and Slavery: Containment, 1859–1861

L INCOLN CAPTURED THE WHITE HOUSE in spite of his defeat for a
Senate seat in 1858. And his politics quickly unleashed a secessionist movement in the South.

American politics were nothing short of explosive in 1860.
For if Republicans won a clean sweep—if they managed to secure the
White House and take control of Congress as well—the slave-holding
interest would be jeopardized.

The expansion of slavery was halted in Kansas by the U.S. House of
Representatives in 1858. The free-state majority was growing, and the
Northern population was surpassing the Southern by a greater margin
every year. Republican strategists determined early on that if they could
take just the *Northern* states that had been lost to Buchanan in 1856,
they would win the presidential election of 1860 decisively.

The power of the presidency had been vested since 1852 in the hands
of pro-slavery leaders who endeavored to "save the Union" by appeasing slave-holding interest. As late as 1859, Buchanan's party was still
continuing its near-relentless push for the expansion of slavery. He
had reopened the issue of Cuban annexation and had attempted to
bribe the government of Spain into acquiescence.[1] Meanwhile, pro-
slavery leaders created a brand-new lobbying group to force repeal of
the old Jeffersonian-era prohibition on the importation of slaves from
Africa. The new "African Labor Supply Organization" was launched
in 1859.[2]

In the early months of that year, some Republican friends began
suggesting to Lincoln that he think about a race for the White House.

At first, Lincoln dismissed the presidential possibility. After all, some impressive Republicans of national stature had already assembled in the wings for the 1860 nomination struggle: Salmon P. Chase of Ohio, for example, and William H. Seward of New York. Both of them had been leaders of the Free-Soil movement for a great many years before Lincoln was known by voters beyond Illinois.

And the prominence of Seward had increased dramatically. In the very same year that Lincoln's "House Divided" speech had gained national attention, Seward made a similar and widely publicized speech about America's "irrepressible conflict" over slavery.

Yet before long, Lincoln took a fresh view of his political future. He began to imagine himself as an *executive* leader instead of a mere parliamentary figure. As historian Don E. Fehrenbacher has observed, "a change gradually came over Lincoln in 1859; this was his year of self-discovery."[3]

Lincoln kept criticizing Stephen Douglas in a way that made the latter's presidential ambitions an occasion for advancing his own. Fehrenbacher has argued that throughout the 1850s Douglas was "unquestionably . . . the most vibrant and controversial public figure of his time." Accordingly, "Lincoln achieved prominence without election to office by making a career of opposing the famous Little Giant. His speeches throughout [the 1850s] constituted one long running rebuttal to what Douglas said and what Douglas did. And when the latter was compelled in 1858 to acknowledge him formally as a rival, Lincoln at last began to acquire a national reputation. Indeed, it is no great exaggeration to say that Douglas for a number of years was unwittingly engaged in clearing Lincoln's path to the White House."[4]

By 1859, Douglas's political position was increasingly fragile. His attempts to reinvigorate his doctrine of Popular Sovereignty caused trouble for his presidential chances in the South. In the eyes of a significant number of Southerners, Douglas was far too entangled with the Free-Soil movement. His resistance to Buchanan's Lecompton policy had impeded the accession of Kansas as a slave state.

And his attempt to assure his constituents that settlers could halt the spread of slavery by means of "unfriendly" territorial laws prompted several pro-slavery leaders to demand the enactment of a territorial slave code—a code to be created by Congress and enforced by the federal government. But Douglas's stated philosophy of federal non-interference with slavery in federal territories made such a code an impossible pill for him to swallow.

In December 1858, Lincoln wrote to a political ally, Senator Lyman Trumbull of Illinois, in regard to Douglas's predicament, along with its flip-side threat to the Republicans. If Douglas, whom Lincoln regarded as the South's greatest hope, were ironically rejected by an overwrought South, he could still win the White House with Northern electoral votes by seducing the Republican Party. "Since you left," Lincoln wrote, "Douglas has gone South, making characteristic speeches, and seeking to re-instate himself in that section. The majority of the democratic politicians of the nation mean to kill him; but I doubt whether they will adopt the aptest way to do it."

Lincoln said that the best course of action for the Democratic enemies of Douglas would be "to present him with no new test, let him into the Charleston Convention [in 1860], and then outvote him, and nominate another. In that case, he will have no pretext for bolting the nomination, and will be as powerless as they can wish. On the other hand, if they push a Slave code upon him, as a test, he will bolt at once, turn upon us, as in the case of Lecompton, and claim that all Northern men shall make common cause in electing him President as the best means of breaking down the Slave power. In that case, the democratic party go into a minority inevitably; and the struggle in the whole North will be, as it was in Illinois last summer and fall, whether the Republican party can maintain its identity, or be broken up to form the tail of Douglas's new kite."[5]

In 1859, Lincoln sent out warnings to his fellow Republicans—warnings of the trickery of Douglas. If Republicans were ever seduced by the "Little Giant," Lincoln said, the Republican Party would be ruined and its cause would be set back, perhaps for a whole generation. On March 1, 1859, Lincoln told a Republican rally in Chicago that "if we, the Republicans of this State, had made Judge Douglas our candidate for the Senate of the United States last year and had elected him, there would to-day be no Republican Party in this Union." While the "principles around which we have rallied and organized would live" and "reproduce" in "another party in the future . . . in the meantime all the labor that has been done to build up the present Republican party would be entirely lost, and perhaps twenty years of time" would elapse "before we would again have formed around that principle" of containing slavery.[6]

In April, he wrote to the organizers of a Jefferson birthday celebration in Boston and warned that the great Jeffersonian maxims of liberty were slowly succumbing to the kinds of politicians who were really "the van-guard—the miners, and sappers—of returning despotism."

"It is now no child's play to save the principles of Jefferson from total overthrow in this nation," Lincoln wrote. "They are denied, and evaded, with no small show of success. One dashingly calls them 'glittering generalities'; another bluntly calls them 'self-evident lies'; and still others insidiously argue that they apply only to 'superior races.'" But since "this is a world of compensations," Lincoln argued, "he who would *be* no slave, must consent to *have* no slave. Those who deny freedom to others, deserve it not for themselves; and, under a just God, can not long retain it. All honor to Jefferson—to the man who . . . had the coolness, forecast, and capacity to introduce into a merely revolutionary document, an abstract truth, and so to embalm it there, that to-day, and in all coming days, it shall be a rebuke and a stumbling block to the very harbingers of re-appearing tyrany [*sic*] and oppression."[7]

In July, he warned Schuyler Colfax, a Republican Congressman from Ohio, that there were "three substantial objections" to Republican dalliance with Douglas and Popular Sovereignty: "First, no party can command respect which sustains this year, what it opposed last. Second, Douglas, (who is the most dangerous enemy of liberty, because the most insidious one) would have little support in the North, and by consequence, no capital to trade on in the South, if it were not for our friends thus magnifying him and his humbug. But lastly, and chiefly, Douglas's popular sovereignty, accepted by the public mind, as a just principle, nationalizes slavery, and revives the African Slave-trade, inevitably. . . ." After all, Lincoln reasoned, "taking slaves into new territories, and buying slaves in Africa, are identical things—identical *rights* or identical *wrongs*—and the argument which establishes one will establish the other. Try a thousand years for a sound reason why congress shall not hinder the people of Kansas from having slaves, and when you have found it, it will be an equally good one why congress should not hinder the people of Georgia from importing slaves from Africa."[8]

As Lincoln strove to counteract Republican apostasy, he also warned Republicans to limit themselves to the doctrine of slavery containment and avoid the more divisive proposals and platforms on the subject of slavery. Divisions over issues like repeal of the Fugitive Slave Law,

Lincoln said, could "explode" the Republican Party and play into the hands of the Democrats. In July, he told Schuyler Colfax that "the point of danger is the temptation in different localities to 'platform' there for something which will be popular just there, but which, nevertheless, will be a firebrand elsewhere, and especially in a National convention."[9]

Above all, the free-soil principle had to be championed. In a letter that he wrote to Republican Senator Thomas Corwin of Ohio on October 9, 1859—a long-lost letter that was purchased by a manuscript dealer in 2004—Lincoln stated that Republicans "must have . . . a man who recognizes that Slavery issue as being the living issue of the day; who does not hesitate to declare slavery a wrong, nor to deal with it as such; who believes in the power, and duty of Congress to prevent the spread of it."[10]

In all of these speeches and letters, which so shrewdly analyzed the political calculus on a national scale, Lincoln sought to advise the Republicans in ways that implicitly suggested his fitness to *lead* the Republican Party. As Fehrenbacher has observed, by the autumn of 1859, Lincoln "was fast becoming, without acknowledging it, a presidential candidate in earnest."[11]

As a candidate, he familiarized himself with the electoral college and its crucial arithmetic for presidential victory in 1860. Republicans would have to win all or most of the lower Northern states that were lost to Buchanan in 1856 if they meant to win the presidency. This included Lincoln's own state of Illinois. Whomever the Republicans should nominate in 1860 would have to be "centrist" enough to attract the swing votes in all of the lower Northern border states.

Lincoln began a series of speaking engagements in the middle of August 1859. The tour was designed to show Republicans that Lincoln— a favorite son of the swing-state Illinois—had the qualities the party would need to win the White House. A charismatic leader for the principles of free soil, he nonetheless appeared to be "moderate" compared to both Seward and Chase. Moreover, he had out-polled Douglas in the 1858 senatorial race, notwithstanding the latter's reelection by a state legislature dominated by his party.

In preliminary notes for some mid-September speeches, Lincoln set forth the themes that he intended to develop in his swing through the border-state cities north of the Ohio River. The most fundamental theme was the danger of Douglas's white supremacist appeal.

If Douglas convinced Northern whites to view blacks as subhuman, said Lincoln, it was only a matter of time before the South would try to use the doctrine of Popular Sovereignty to overturn the free-state system in the North. Lincoln cited recent statements by Douglas that appeared to classify blacks as a different species. "At Memphis," Lincoln wrote, "Douglas told his audience that he was for the negro against the crocodile, but for the white man against the negro. This was not a sudden thought spontaneously thrown off at Memphis. He said the same thing many times in Illinois last summer and autumn, though I am not sure it was reported then. It is a carefully framed illustration of the estimate he places on the negro and the manner in which he would have him dealt with. It is a sort of proposition in proportion. '*As* the negro is to the crocodile, *so* the white man is to the negro.' As the negro ought to treat the crocodile as a beast, so the white man ought to treat the negro as a beast."[12]

The corollary to this crude suggestion of black inhumanity was simple. It was the proposition that the legal status of blacks should be determined by majority votes of all the whites in every territory or state. This, said Lincoln—in phonetic imitation of his rival's bombastic manner—was the substance of that "gur-reat pur-rinciple" that Douglas called Popular Sovereignty.[13]

Republicans should never succumb to such poison, Lincoln warned: "Republicans believe that slavery is wrong," he said, "and they insist, and will continue to insist upon a national policy which recognizes it, and deals with it, *as a wrong*. There *can* be no letting down about this."[14]

As the Illinois Republicans had warded off Douglas in 1858 by nominating Lincoln, the fight should be extended, Lincoln said. Though "Douglas is back in the Senate in spite of us," Lincoln observed, "we are *clear* of *him*, and *his* principles; and, we are uncrippled and ready to fight both him and them straight along till they shall finally be 'closed out.' Had we followed the advice [of people like Seward and Greeley, who had urged Illinois Republicans to re-elect Douglas] there would now be no Republican party in Illinois, and none, to speak of, anywhere else. The whole thing would now be floundering along after Douglas, upon the Dred Scott and crocodile theory. It would have been the grandest '*haul*' for slavery, ever yet made."[15]

The Republicans' duties were clear, Lincoln wrote: "We must, by a national policy, prevent the spread of slavery into new territories, or free states, because the constitution does not forbid us, and the general welfare does demand such prevention. We must prevent the revival of the African slave trade, because the constitution does not forbid us, and the general welfare does require the prevention. We must prevent these things being done by either *congresses* or *courts*. The people—the people—are the rightful masters of both congresses, and courts—not to overthrow the constitution, but to overthrow the *men* who pervert it."[16]

Lincoln's opening speech in the campaign was an address he had delivered in August on a trip to Council Bluffs, Iowa. Only newspaper summaries of this speech survive. But the speech that Lincoln gave on September 16, in Columbus, Ohio, was reported verbatim.

He began with a statement designed to show his "moderate" credentials in the swing states. The "chief and real purpose of the Republican party," Lincoln asserted, "is eminently conservative. It proposes nothing save and except to restore this government to its original tone in regard to this element of slavery," in other words to roll back the drive for the expansion of slavery and bring back a policy that looked to its termination.[17]

But then, Lincoln's "moderate" stance gave way to a manner very close to his 1858 fervor. Lincoln warned that the schemers pushing slavery expansion were active. While their endgame strategy was still in abeyance, their short-term tactics were as stealthy as they were effective. "The chief danger to this purpose of the Republican party," Lincoln said, "is not just now the revival of the African slave trade, or the passage of a Congressional slave code, or the declaring of a second Dred Scott decision, making slavery lawful in all the States. These are not pressing us just now. . . . The authors of these measures know that we are too strong for them; but they will be upon us in due time, and we will be grappling with them hand to hand, if they are not now headed off. They are not now the chief danger to the purpose of the Republican organization; but the most imminent danger that now threatens that purpose is that insidious Douglas Popular Sovereignty."[18]

Lincoln turned his attention to an article that Douglas had written, a piece that was hot off the press in the September 1859 issue of *Harper's Magazine*. It provided the occasion for Douglas to revise his claims about Popular Sovereignty.[19]

While playing down the issue as much as he could, Douglas modified his earlier boasts that under Popular Sovereignty the legislatures of the territories could bar the institution of slavery by means of "unfriendly legislation." Instead, Douglas limited himself to the assertion that territories could *control* the institution of slavery as regulated property.

Lincoln ridiculed this article in several ways. He began by stating that its author "has had a good deal of trouble with his popular sovereignty. His explanations explanatory of explanations explained are interminable. [Laughter]"[20]

After paraphrasing Douglas's claims about the Founding Fathers, Lincoln asked how Douglas could possibly ignore what the anti-slavery Founders had accomplished in the Northwest Ordinance of 1787, which successfully stopped the institution of slavery from spreading right into Ohio and the states next door. "Under that ordinance we live," Lincoln argued. "First here in Ohio you were a territory, then an enabling act was passed authorizing you to form a constitution and State government, provided it was . . . not in conflict with the ordinance of '87."

Lincoln pointed out that "the Constitution of the United States was in process of being framed when that ordinance was made by the Congress of the Confederation; and one of the first acts of Congress itself under the new Constitution itself was to give force to that ordinance by putting power to carry it out into the hands of the new officers under the Constitution." Lincoln then observed that "Indiana once or twice, if not Ohio, petitioned the general government for the privilege of suspending that provision and allowing them to have slaves. A report made by Mr. Randolph [Edmund J. Randolph] of Virginia, himself a slaveholder, was directly against it, and the action was to refuse them the privilege of violating the ordinance of '87."[21]

Having demonstrated the degree of anti-slavery feelings among the Founders, Lincoln turned to the counter-revolution that Roger Taney and his fellow pro-slavery schemers were trying to initiate.

"The Dred Scott decision expressly gives every citizen of the United States a right to carry his slaves into the United States' Territories," Lincoln said, reiterating his critique of the Scott ruling.[22]

Yet Douglas kept claiming that a territorial legislature could fulfill the wishes of an anti-slavery majority. This was nonsense, Lincoln contended: "When all the trash, the words, the collateral matter was cleared away from it; all the chaff was fanned out of it," Douglas's claim was "a bare absurdity—*no less than a thing may be lawfully driven away from where it has a lawful right to be.* [Cheers and laughter.] Clear away all the verbiage, and that is the naked truth of his proposition."[23]

Observe, Lincoln said, that the nimble Douglas "does not say any longer that the people [can] exclude slavery. . . . What he says now is different in language, and we will consider whether it is not different in sense too. It is now that the Dred Scott decision, or rather the Constitution under that decision, does not carry slavery into the Territories beyond the power of the people in the territories *to control it as other property*."[24] Lincoln made sport of this language with a lengthy barnyard analogy:

> Driving a horse out of this lot, is too plain a proposition to be mistaken about; it is putting him on the other side of the fence. [Laughter] Or it might be a sort of exclusion of him from the lot if you were to kill him and let the worms devour him; but neither of these things is the same as "controlling him as other property." That would be to feed him, pamper him, to ride him, to use and abuse him, to make the most money out of him "as other property"; but, please you, what do the men who are in favor of slavery want more than this? [Laughter and applause] . . . I know the Judge sometimes squints at the argument that in controlling [slavery] as other property by unfriendly legislation they may control it to death, as you might in the case of a horse, perhaps, feed him so lightly and ride him so much that he would die. [Cheers and laughter] . . . But I undertake to give the opinion, at least, that if the territories attempt by any direct legislation to drive the man with his slave out of the territory, or to decide that his slave is free because of his being taken in there, or to tax him to such an extent that he cannot keep him there, the Supreme Court will unhesitatingly decide all such legislation unconstitutional, as long as that Supreme Court is constructed as the Dred Scott Supreme Court is.[25]

But such issues were *secondary*, argued Lincoln, to the ugly contention of Douglas that the fate of black slaves should be regarded by whites as a matter of very little importance. He warned that "if this principle is established, that there is no wrong in slavery, and whoever wants it has a right to have it, is a matter of dollars and cents, a sort of question as to how they shall deal with brutes, that between us and the negro here there is no sort of question, but that at the South the question is between the negro and the crocodile. . . . where this doctrine prevails, the miners and sappers will have formed public opinion for the slave trade. They will be ready for Jeff. Davis and Stephens and other leaders of that company, to sound the bugle for the revival of the slave trade, for the second Dred Scott decision, for the flood of slavery to be poured over the free States, while we shall be here tied down and helpless and run over like sheep."[26]

Just look at the erosion, said Lincoln, in the state of Northern public opinion since the Kansas-Nebraska Act and the launching of

Douglas's quest for the presidency: "Did you ever five years ago, hear of anybody in the world saying that the negro had no share in the Declaration of National Independence; that it did not mean negroes at all; and when 'all men' were spoken of negroes were not included? . . . I have been unable at any time to find a man in an audience who would declare that he had ever known any body saying so five years ago. But last year there was not a Douglas popular sovereign in Illinois who did not say it."[27]

How far, asked Lincoln, had this sinister change in opinion proceeded in Ohio? Surely many a man in Ohio "declares his firm belief that the Declaration of Independence did not mean negroes at all," said Lincoln, but how many of them had believed such a thing only five years earlier? Something fundamental had changed. "If you think that now," he observed, "and did not think it then, the next thing that strikes me is to remark that there has been a *change* wrought in you (laughter and applause), and a very significant change it was, being no less than changing the negro, in your estimation, from the rank of a man to that of a brute. They are taking him down, and placing him, when spoken of, among reptiles and crocodiles, as Judge Douglas himself expresses it. . . . I ask you to note that fact, and the like of which is to follow, to be plastered on, layer after layer, until very soon you are prepared to deal with the negro everywhere as with the brute. If public sentiment has not been debauched already to this point, a new turn of the screw in that direction is all that is wanting; and this is constantly being done by the teachers of this insidious popular sovereignty."[28]

On the very next day after giving this speech in Columbus, Lincoln gave another speech in Cincinnati. "I should not wonder," Lincoln ventured to say, "that there are some Kentuckians about this audience; we are close to Kentucky; and . . . we are on elevated ground, and by speaking distinctly, I should not wonder if some of the Kentuckians would hear me on the other side of the river. [Laughter.]"[29]

He told the residents of slave-state Kentucky that they ought to view Douglas as their perfect presidential candidate. Regardless of Southern discontent with some of the positions that Douglas had taken, Lincoln told the Kentuckians to look at the larger picture: "he is as sincerely for you, and more wisely for you, than you are for yourselves." He followed up with pointed questions: "What do you want more than anything else to make successful your views on Slavery, to advance the outspread of it, and to secure and perpetuate the nationality of it? . . .

What is indispensable to you? Why! if I may be allowed to answer the question, it is to retain a hold upon the North—it is to retain support and strength from the Free States. If you can get this support and strength from the Free States, you can succeed. If you do not get this support and strength from the Free States, you are in the minority, and you are beaten at once."[30]

Lincoln told the Kentuckians that Douglas was their very best advocate because he was *sneaky*: "I lay down the proposition that Douglas is not only the man that promises you in advance a hold upon the North, and support in the North, but that he constantly moulds public opinion to your ends . . . and if there are a few things in which he seems to be against you—a few things which he says that appear to be against you, and a few that he forbears to say which you would like to have him say—you ought to remember that the saying of the one, or the forbearing to say the other, would loose his hold upon the North, and, by consequence, would lose his capacity to serve you. (A Voice, 'That is so.')"[31]

For example, Douglas refused to state clearly his belief about the rightness or wrongness of slavery. Many Southerners were angered by this, and they demanded that Douglas endorse "the Southern way of life."

But he served Southern interests far better, said Lincoln, by evading and dodging the issue: "Upon this subject of moulding public opinion, I call your attention to the fact . . . that the Judge never says your institution of Slavery is wrong; he never says it is right, to be sure, but he never says it is wrong. [Laughter] . . . He leaves himself at perfect liberty to do all in your favor which he would be hindered from doing if he were to declare the thing to be wrong. . . . This you ought to set down to his credit. [Laughter.] . . . He said upon the floor of the United States Senate . . . that he does not care whether Slavery is 'voted up or voted down.' This again shows you, or ought to show you, if you would reason upon it, that he does not believe it to be wrong, for . . . no man can logically say that he cares not whether a thing goes up or goes down, which to him appears to be wrong. You therefore have a demonstration in this, that to Douglas' mind your favorite institution which you would have spread out, and made perpetual, is no wrong."[32]

Lincoln finally abandoned this tone and spoke directly to the men of Ohio, but not without a final sally at his absent but handy Kentuckians. He advised them about their own prospects in resisting the

Free-Soil movement. "You will surely be beaten," he said, "if you do not take him [Douglas]. We, the Republicans and others forming the Opposition of this country, intend to 'stand by our guns,' to be patient and firm, and in the long run to beat you whether you take him or not. [Applause.] We know that before we fairly beat you, we have to beat you both together. We know that you are 'all of a feather,' [loud applause,] and that we have to beat you altogether, and we expect to do it. [Applause.]"[33]

Yet Lincoln was careful to qualify the taunts with some assurances of fair treatment. "When we do as we say, beat you," he told the Kentuckians, "you perhaps want to know what we will do with you. [Laughter] . . . We mean to treat you as near as we possibly can, like Washington, Jefferson and Madison treated you. [Cheers] We mean to leave you alone, and in no way to interfere with your institution; to abide by all and every compromise of the constitution. . . . We mean to recognize and bear in mind that you have as good hearts in your bosoms as other people. . . ."[34]

But if Northern magnanimity were not reciprocated by the South— if Southern militants attempted to break up the Union if the Free-Soil movement prevailed—then the South would be totally defeated. "I have told you what we mean to do," Lincoln said, and "I want to know, now, when that thing takes place, what you mean to do. I often hear it intimated that you mean to divide the Union whenever a Republican, or anything like it, is elected President of the United States. [A voice, 'That is so.'] 'That is so,' one of them says. I wonder if he is a Kentuckian? [A voice, 'He is a Douglas man.'] Well, then, I want to know what you are going to do with your half of it? [Applause and laughter] Are you going to split the Ohio down through, and push your half off a piece? Or are you going to keep it right alongside of us outrageous fellows? Or are you going to build up a wall some way between your country and ours, by which that movable property of yours can't come over here any more, to the danger of your losing it?"

Lincoln said that if the Union was successfully divided, and the people of the North "cease to be under obligations to do anything for you, how much better off do you think you will be? Will you make war upon us and kill us all? Why, gentlemen, I think you are as gallant and as brave men as live . . . but, man for man, you are not better than we are, and there are not so many of you as there are of us. [Loud cheering.]"[35] It bears noting, of course, that Lincoln continued to regard the secession talk at this point as essentially bluff.

Two days after his Cincinnati speech, Lincoln went to Indiana to address a crowd in Indianapolis. Then he traveled to Milwaukee to address the Wisconsin State Agricultural Society. He talked about the virtues of the free labor system: "the just and generous, and prosperous system, which opens the way for all."[36]

Just after he gave these speeches, some electrifying news arrived: on October 16, John Brown and his supporters seized the federal arsenal at Harpers Ferry, Virginia, in a bid to initiate a full-scale slave revolt. After Brown was arrested and tried for treason, all over the South arose a chorus of militant voices condemning "Black Republicans" and warning that the Union would break if the voters elected a Republican president in 1860.

Lincoln answered these threats in December, when he traveled to Kansas. He made this pilgrimage to praise the Free-Soilers and to celebrate the imminent admission of Kansas to statehood. At Leavenworth, he aimed some remarks at Southern militants, much as he had done in Cincinnati when he talked to pro-slavery Kentuckians *in absentia*. He spoke of their threats to dissolve the Union: "Your own statement of it is, that if the Black Republicans elect a President, you won't stand it. You will break up the Union. That will be your act, not ours. . . ."[37]

He bade Southern militants reflect upon the way in which Republicans put up with the likes of Buchanan and Pierce without trying to break up the Union. "While you elect [the] President," he argued, "we submit, neither breaking nor attempting to break up the Union. If we shall constitutionally elect a President, it will be our duty to see that you submit. Old John Brown has just been executed for treason against a state. We cannot object, even though he agreed with us in thinking slavery wrong. That cannot excuse violence, bloodshed, and treason. It could avail him nothing that he might think himself right. So, if constitutionally we elect a President, and therefore you undertake to destroy the Union, it will be our duty to deal with you as old John Brown has been dealt with."[38]

Lincoln could afford to talk tough about secession in December, 1859. Southern anger over Harpers Ferry was directed less at Lincoln than it was at his Republican rival, William H. Seward. Seward's "irrepressible conflict" slogan appeared to be a call to arms—an incitement to abolitionist militants like John Brown.

Lincoln's managers were quick to make the most of this. They argued that the "radical" tone of Seward's speech made the nomination of Lincoln advisable in light of the importance of the lower-Northern swing votes. They said much the same thing about Chase, who had fought against the Fugitive Slave Law.

Lincoln's managers were largely self-appointed. They included such Illinois Republican movers and shakers as David Davis, Norman Judd, Jesse Fell, and more than half a dozen others. In December, as Lincoln was speaking in Kansas, Judd struck a blow for his nomination chances. Judd nonchalantly suggested at a meeting of the Republican National Committee that the 1860 Republican convention be held in Chicago, a "neutral" location for the nomination struggle. The Committee agreed— so the Republican convention would be held in Lincoln's own state.

Meanwhile, Lincoln took advantage of a speaking offer from New York. Several months before, he had received an invitation from illustrious clergyman Henry Ward Beecher to speak at the famous Plymouth Church in Brooklyn. The location for the speech was then changed to the Cooper Institute (or "Cooper Union") in downtown New York City.

Here was Lincoln's chance to the show Republican leaders— and to show them in Seward's home state—that he was fit to lead the Republican Party. Moreover, as Lincoln scholar Harold Holzer has observed, this speech, if successful, might complete the transformation of Lincoln "from a regional phenomenon to a national figure. Lincoln knew it, and rose to the occasion."[39] He traveled to New York in late February 1860.

Lincoln in New York City just before his Cooper Institute address in 1860. Photograph by Matthew Brady. (Library of Congress, Meserve Collection #20)

Seward's local enemies pounced upon the chance to boost Lincoln to the detriment of Seward. They set up a gala reception for Lincoln at Astor House and got an audience of over a thousand to travel to hear Lincoln speak on the night of February 27.

Lincoln's Cooper Institute address was a turning point in his quest for the Republican nomination. The major point of his address was to link the Republican program to the Founding Fathers and their anti-slavery legacy.

He devoted the first portion of the speech to historical evidence, beginning with the thirty-nine men who had signed the Constitution in 1787. Most of these men, he argued, took part in creating or supporting the creation of policies designed to prevent the spread of slavery.

He showed that three of the thirty-nine had voted for the bill in the Confederation Congress that was introduced by Jefferson in 1784: the bill that would have banned the institution of slavery from any Western territory. Two more of the thirty-nine, he said, had voted in Congress later on for the anti-slavery Northwest Ordinance of 1787.

In 1789, when the Federal Congress convened under the newly-ratified Constitution, "an act was passed to enforce the Ordinance of '87, including the prohibition of slavery in the Northwestern Territory. The bill for this act was reported by one of the 'thirty-nine,' Thomas Fitzsimmons, then a member of the House of Representatives from Pennsylvania. It went through all its stages without a word of opposition, and finally passed both branches without yeas or nays, which is equivalent to an unanimous passage. In this Congress there were sixteen of the thirty-nine fathers who framed the original Constitution."[40]

Moreover, "George Washington, another of the 'thirty-nine,' was then President of the United States, and, as such, approved and signed the bill; thus completing its validity as a law, and thus showing that, in his understanding, no line dividing local from federal authority, nor anything in the Constitution, forbade the Federal Government, to control as to slavery in federal territory."[41]

Then Lincoln took aim at Roger Taney and his use of the Fifth Amendment in the Dred Scott decision. He also took aim at the analogous use of the Tenth Amendment (which states that "the powers not delegated to the United States by the Constitution . . . are reserved to the States respectively, or to the people").

Both of these amendments, Lincoln pointed out, had been passed by the very same people who had done what Roger Taney was calling outrageous and unconstitutional. "Now it so happens," he observed, "that these amendments were framed by the first Congress which sat under the Constitution—the identical Congress which passed the act already mentioned, enforcing the prohibition of slavery in the North-western Territory. Not only was it the same Congress, but they were the identical, same individual men who, at the same session, had under consideration, and in progress toward maturity, these Constitutional amendments, and this act prohibiting slavery in all the territory the nation then owned. The Constitutional amendments were introduced before, and passed after the act enforcing the Ordinance of '87, so that, during the whole pendency of the act to enforce the Ordinance, the Constitutional amendments were also pending."

In light of these facts, Lincoln argued, "is it not a little presumptuous in any one at this day to affirm that the two things which that Congress deliberately framed, and carried to maturity at the same time, are absolutely inconsistent with each other?"[42] Clearly, he said, a great number of the framers of the Constitution had supported the premise of the Free-Soil movement and believed it constitutional.

As he finished expounding this theme, Lincoln chose once again to lecture "fire-eating" Southerners in ways that would please a Northern audience. He reminded the South that George Washington had hoped for the eventual extinction of slavery: "Some of you delight to flaunt in our faces the warning against sectional parties given by Washington in his Farewell Address. Less than eight years before Washington gave that warning, he had, as President of the United States, approved and signed an act of Congress, enforcing the prohibition of slavery in the Northwestern Territory . . . and about one year after he had penned it [the warning] he wrote La Fayette that he considered the prohibition a wise measure, expressing in that same connection his hope that we should at some time have a confederacy of free states."

"Bearing this in mind," Lincoln said, "and seeing that sectionalism has since arisen upon this same subject, is that warning a weapon in your hands against us, or in our hands against you? Could Washington himself speak, would he cast the blame of that sectionalism upon us, who sustain his policy, or upon you who repudiate it?"[43]

Turning to current events, Lincoln talked about Harpers Ferry. "You charge that we stir up insurrections among your slaves," he said. "We deny it; and what is your proof? Harpers Ferry! John Brown! John

Brown was no Republican; and you have failed to implicate a single Republican in his Harpers Ferry enterprise. If any member of our party is guilty in that matter, you know it or you do not know it. If you do know it, you are inexcusable for not designating the man and proving the fact. If you do not know it, you are inexcusable for asserting it."[44]

Lincoln chided Southern militants for warning they would break up the Union "unless you be allowed to construe and enforce the Constitution as you please, on all points in dispute between you and us. You will rule or ruin in all events."[45] Indeed, "you will not abide the election of a Republican President! In that supposed event, you say, you will destroy the Union; and then, you say, the great crime of having destroyed it will be upon us! That is cool. A highwayman holds a pistol to my ear, and mutters through his teeth, 'Stand and deliver, or I shall kill you, and then you will be a murderer!'"[46]

Lincoln finished this speech with a clarion call to the Republicans. He told them that the South would never be satisfied with anything less than Republican capitulation. What on earth would convince Southern militants that "black Republicans" deserved a fair hearing? Lincoln said: we must "cease to call slavery wrong, and join them in calling it right. . . . Silence will not be tolerated—we must place ourselves avowedly with them. . . . We must arrest and return their fugitive slaves with greedy pleasure. We must pull down our Free State constitutions. The whole atmosphere must be disinfected from all taint of opposition to slavery, before they will cease to believe that all their troubles proceed from us."[47]

All this, said Lincoln, "we could readily grant" if we thought that slavery was right. And yet "thinking it wrong, as we do, can we yield to them? . . . If our sense of duty forbids this," he said, "let us stand by our duty. . . ."

> Let us be diverted by none of those sophistical contrivances wherewith we are so industriously plied and belabored—contrivances such as groping for some middle ground between the right and the wrong, vain as the search for a man who should be neither a living man nor a dead man—such as a policy of "don't care" on a question about which all true men do care—such as Union appeals beseeching true Union men to yield to Disunionists, reversing the divine rule, and calling, not the sinners, but the righteous to repentance—such as invocations to Washington, imploring men to unsay what Washington said, and undo what Washington did.
>
> Neither let us be slandered from our duty by false accusations against us, nor frightened from it by menaces of destruction to the Government nor of

dungeons to ourselves. LET US HAVE THE FAITH THAT RIGHT MAKES MIGHT, AND IN THAT FAITH, LET US, TO THE END, DARE TO DO OUR DUTY AS WE UNDERSTAND IT.[48]

Lincoln's audience rose to a standing ovation as he finished: cheer upon cheer rang out through the hall as people waved their hats and Lincoln bowed. Newspapers published the speech the next day, and more speaking invitations began to pour in from other cities. Consequently, in the weeks that followed, Lincoln spoke in Rhode Island, New Hampshire, and Connecticut.

Since the anti-slavery movement was strong in New England, Lincoln's moderate stance required appeals for abolitionist prudence. He used a new metaphor in some of the speeches: to convince anti-slavery militants to limit their goals to free soil—to eschew the more radical short-term goals that lacked a firm constitutional basis and would lead to political defeat—he likened slavery to a poisonous serpent that threatened his children.

> If I saw a venomous snake crawling in the road, any man might say I might seize the nearest stick and kill it; but if I found that snake in bed with my children, that would be another question. [Laughter.] I might hurt the children more than the snake, and it might bite them. [Applause.] Much more, if I found it in bed with my neighbor's children, and I had bound myself by a solemn compact not to meddle with his children under any circumstances, it would become me to let that particular mode of getting rid of the gentleman alone. [Great laughter.] But if there was a bed newly made up, to which the children were to be taken, and it was proposed to take a batch of young snakes and put them there with them, I take it no man in the world would say there was any question how I ought to decide! [Prolonged applause and cheers.] That is just the case! The new Territories are the newly made bed to which our children are to go, and it lies with the nation to say whether they shall have snakes mixed up with them or not.[49]

As Lincoln built up his national following, Douglas prepared for the Democratic National Convention that was scheduled for April in Charleston, South Carolina. The results of that convention would ruin the Democrats' chances in 1860.

A two-thirds vote was required for the Democratic nomination; Douglas failed to get it. But he controlled a simple majority of delegates. And by this simple majority, his delegates voted down the territorial slave-code plank that Southern delegates demanded for the Democratic Party platform. Whereupon, the delegates from seven Southern states walked out: no one had been nominated.

The "fire-eating" Southerner who orchestrated this move was William Lowndes Yancey of Alabama. Yancey had berated Douglas from the podium. He condemned the unwillingness of Douglas to side with the "legitimate" rights of the South in unequivocal terms: "If you had taken the position directly that slavery was right," Yancey thundered, "you could have triumphed, and anti-slavery would now be dead in your midst."[50] Yancey had worked out a prearranged plan—the "Alabama Platform," they called it—for a Southern walk-out if Douglas and his delegates defeated the slave-code plank. The Democrats agreed to re-assemble that June for another convention in Baltimore.

The Republican convention was scheduled for May. Seward was still the front-runner. Lincoln confided to a friend that his strategy was watchful waiting. "My name is new in the field," he admitted, "and I suppose I am not the *first* choice of a very great many. Our policy, then, is to give no offense to others—leave them in a mood to come to us, if they shall be compelled to give up their first love."[51] He also confided to an ally that "the taste *is* in my mouth a little."[52]

Once Lincoln had secured the support of the Illinois delegation, his managers set up his convention headquarters at Tremont House hotel. As Fehrenbacher has observed, "when they arrived on the scene and sounded out certain key delegations, the Lincoln men discovered that their prospects were brighter than anyone had dreamed."[53] And when the first ballot started, "it became apparent that Seward was weaker and Lincoln stronger than anyone had expected."[54]

His managers counseled him to keep a level head. One of them wrote to him as follows: "Things are working; keep a good nerve—be not surprised at any result—but I tell you that your chances are not the worst. . . . We are dealing tenderly with delegates, taking them in detail, and making no fuss. Be not too expectant, but rely upon our discretion. Again I say brace your nerves for any result."[55]

Seward failed to gain the Republican nomination on the first ballot. His support became weaker on the second. A massive shift to Lincoln began to take place, and the mood of the convention, in Fehrenbacher's opinion, revealed "a hard-headed decision that the leading candidate could not win and must give way to someone who could. Yet in nominating the more 'available' Lincoln, the Republicans did not compromise themselves or their principles. In fact, without fully realizing it, they had selected a man whose moral fibre was tougher than Seward's."[56]

Along the range of "conservative" to "moderate" to "radical" Republicans, Lincoln was closest to the Radicals in spite of all the "moderate" stances that his short-term strategy required. As historian Eric Foner has pointed out, "at the time of his nomination, Lincoln's political outlook more closely resembled that of the radicals than of the conservatives in his party." Though his short-term stance required a promise of non-interference with slavery in existing slave slaves, "his ultimate goal was not merely the non-extension of slavery . . . but its 'ultimate extinction.'"[57]

In June, Lincoln's chances of winning the election increased because the Democrats' schism got worse. Some of the seceders from the Charleston convention refused to go to Baltimore and tangle with the Douglas men. This group of pro-slavery seceders met in Richmond while another group of fire-eating Southerners went to Baltimore. When they got there, the chairman of the Democratic Party Convention ruled that a majority of two-thirds *present* could select the nominee. Douglas was quickly selected.

Once again, the Southern militants bolted: they regrouped in a rump convention, passed a platform demanding a tough territorial slave code, and nominated John C. Breckinridge of Kentucky. Their colleagues in Richmond approved. And so the Democratic Party split in two. To make matters trickier, a new "Constitutional Union Party" was created by some former Whigs who proceeded to nominate John Bell of Tennessee.

Lincoln, following a time-honored code for presidential elections, declined to make speeches that summer or fall.

But Douglas, approaching desperation, tried to barnstorm the country.

It did him little good, for the voters of the deep South were stampeding to Breckinridge. All over the South, predictions of Northern aggression, of slave insurrections, of war between the races made voters view Lincoln's election as a veritable doomsday event. In most Southern states the name of Lincoln would be kept off the ballot.

Lincoln listened to advisers who told him that the threat of disunion from the South was probably bluster. In August, he wrote that "the people of the South have too much of good sense, and good temper, to attempt the ruin of the government, rather than see it administered as it was administered by the men who made it. At least, so I hope and believe."[58]

The Republicans were sweeping the North. All over the region Republican "Wide-Awake" clubs were parading through the streets by torchlight. "A Political Earthquake—THE PRAIRIES ON FIRE FOR LINCOLN," cried Republican editors and pundits.[59] It was more than propaganda: in October, the Republicans captured state offices in two of the lower-Northern states that would be crucial in the electoral college. Douglas was doomed.

The alternately proud and self-effacing manners of the "two-faced" Lincoln: an 1860 cartoon by an unknown artist. (Library of Congress)

Certificate of membership in the 1860 Republican "Wide-Awake" marching club—"wide awake" to the tricky machinations of the pro-slavery Democrats. (Library of Congress)

A pro-Lincoln cartoon that was published by Currier & Ives in the election of 1860: wearing "Wide-Awake" garb, Lincoln proudly declares that he will not be caught napping by his various opponents, including the incumbent president, Buchanan. This print has been attributed to artist Louis Maurer. (Library of Congress)

An anti-Lincoln cartoon that was published by Currier & Ives in the election of 1860: Republican editor Horace Greeley tries to play down the anti-slavery content of Lincoln's platform. But the racist skeptic can nonetheless perceive the grinning "nigger in the woodpile." The print has been attributed to Louis Maurer. (Library of Congress)

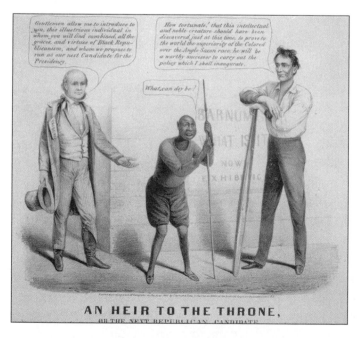

Another racist cartoon attacking Lincoln that was published by Currier & Ives in 1860. The artist portrayed the most likely Republican successor to Lincoln if the latter should capture the White House: a deformed black man who had been recently featured at P. T. Barnum's Museum as the "What-is-it." The print has been attributed to Louis Maurer. (Library of Congress)

THE REPUBLICAN PARTY GOING TO THE RIGHT HOUSE.

One more anti-Lincoln cartoon from the presses of Currier & Ives in 1860. The artist shows Lincoln on his way to an insane asylum with his various followers, including a black who mutters, "De white man hab no rights dat cullud pussons am bound to spect. . . ." The print has been attributed to Louis Maurer. (Library of Congress)

He went South, making speeches that would put him on record as a Unionist. He urged Southerners to keep their cool and reject secession. On November 6, Lincoln carried every Northern state except New Jersey. He won 173 electoral votes compared to 72 for Breckinridge, 39 for Bell, and just 12 for Douglas.

Abraham Lincoln had become the highest magistrate in the land. He would soon have the power—the enormous power—to start controlling the evil of slavery.

He would clamp a firm lid upon the South. The Southern black population would continue to grow and yet the "safety valve" would start to close. And how long would it take for the fear of revolution to persuade Southern leaders to reform? Thirty years? Forty?

Southern militants determined not to wait. Fire-eating South Carolinians demanded a secession convention in December. The convention made its logic very clear:

We affirm that . . . [the] ends for which this Government was instituted have been defeated, and the Government itself has been destructive of them by the action of the non-slaveholding States. Those States have . . . denounced as sinful the institution of Slavery; they have permitted the open establishment among them of societies, whose avowed object is to disturb the peace of and eloin [*sic*] the property of the citizens of other States. They have encouraged and assisted thousands of our slaves to leave their homes; and those who remain have been incited by emissaries, books, and pictures, to servile insurrection. . . .

On the 4th of March next . . . [a sectional] party will take possession of the Government. It has announced that the South shall be excluded from the common territory, that the Judicial tribunal shall be made sectional, and that a war must be waged against Slavery until it shall cease throughout the United States.

Their preference was to leave at once: "We, therefore, the people of South Carolina, by our delegates in Convention assembled, appealing to the Supreme Judge of the world for the rectitude of our intentions, have solemnly declared that the Union heretofore existing between this State and the other States of North America is dissolved, and that the State of South Carolina has resumed her position among the Nations of the world. . . ."[60]

The election of President Lincoln had broken up the Union.

LINCOLN ROSE TO THE CHALLENGE when secession broke out: he refused to back down on his policies. And he resisted all attempts at appeasement.

As the South Carolina convention did its work—and as other secession conventions started meeting— congressional leaders took action. Both the House and the Senate formed special committees to explore the possibility of measures to avert secession.

Senator John J. Crittenden of Kentucky suggested a series of constitutional amendments. One would revive and extend the Missouri Compromise line: slavery could spread in all the territories "now held, or hereafter acquired" by the United States below the latitude of 36° 30'.

Other amendments would have bolstered the Fugitive Slave Law, indemnified the owners of runaway slaves, and protected the interstate slave trade. The capstone amendment would forbid any future attempts by Congress to abolish slavery. These amendments would be unamendable.

Lincoln lashed out quickly at the deal. He dashed off letters marked "Private & confidential" to congressional Republicans. "Entertain no proposition for a compromise in regard to the *extension* of slavery," he told one of them. "The instant you do, they have us under again; all our labor is lost, and sooner or later must be done over. . . . Have none of it. The tug has to come & better now than later."[61]

He told another Republican to spread the word that there was "no possible compromise" on slavery extension. Extend the Missouri Compromise line, he warned, and "immediately filibustering and extending slavery recommences. On that point hold firm, as with a chain of steel."[62]

He told Senator Lyman Trumbull that "if any of our friends do prove false, and fix up a compromise on the territorial question, I am for fighting again—that is all."[63] As to the amendment to prevent abolition legislation in Congress, Lincoln was silent. After all, his plans for the ultimate extinction of slavery appeared to envision a *voluntary*, compensated phaseout rather than compulsion.

He did, however, tell an emissary of the lame-duck President Buchanan that he found the idea of constitutional amendments distasteful. "I do not desire any amendment of the Constitution," he said. Nonetheless, as he was willing to acknowledge "that questions of such amendment rightfully belong to the American People, I should not feel justified, or inclined, to withhold from them, if I could, a fair opportunity of expressing their will thereon."[64]

Buchanan urged Lincoln to agree to some plan that would slow the drive for secession. Lincoln drafted a statement supporting "the maintenance inviolate of the rights of the States" and condemning "the lawless invasion, by armed force, of the soil of any State or Territory, no matter under what pretext."

But this was as far as he would go in December 1860. "I am greatly averse to writing anything for the public at this time," he stated, "and I consent to the publication of this, only upon the condition that six of the twelve United States Senators for the States of Georgia, Alabama, Mississippi, Louisiana, Florida, and Texas [all of which had summoned secession conventions] shall sign their names to what is written on this sheet below my name, and allow the whole to be published together."[65] Below his signature, Lincoln wrote the following: "We recommend to the people of the States we represent respectively, to suspend all action for dismemberment of the Union, at least, until some act, deemed to be violative of our rights, shall be done by the incoming administration."[66]

He was angry. He asked a Southerner who pleaded for concessions whether people expected him to grovel for the fire-eating militants: "Is it desired that I shall shift the ground upon which I have been elected? I can not do it. . . . It would make me appear as if I repented for the crime of having been elected, and was anxious to apologize and beg forgiveness."[67]

He was firm about secession as well. In mid-December he wrote to Thurlow Weed, a Republican leader in New York as well as an erstwhile Seward supporter, telling him that "no state can, in any way lawfully, get out of the Union, without the consent of the others" and that "it is the duty of the President, and other government functionaries to run the machine as it is."[68]

He instructed a political ally, Elihu Washburne, to "present my respects to General [Winfield Scott, the general in chief of the United States Army], and tell him, confidentially, I shall be obliged to him to be as well prepared as he can to either *hold*, or *retake*" any federal forts that secessionists might attack and to be ready to swing into action "after the inaugeration [*sic*]."[69]

As Republicans voted down the Crittenden Compromise, secessionist fervor was sweeping through the lower South. South Carolina's convention proclaimed secession on December 20. The following states joined the exodus: Mississippi on January 9, Florida on January 10, Alabama on January 11, Georgia on January 19, Louisiana on January 26, and Texas on February 1.

In the city of Montgomery, Alabama, on February 4, commissioners from all of these states came together to draft a preliminary constitution for a confederacy of slave states and to elect provisional officers. Jefferson Davis of Mississippi was elected provisional president of the Confederate States of America.

The leaders of upper-Southern states like Virginia, Tennessee, and North Carolina were divided about joining the Confederacy. So were the leaders of the border slave states like Maryland, Kentucky, and Missouri. Unionists in the Virginia legislature called for a "peace convention" of all the states to meet in Washington, D.C., on February 4. The convention was held, and yet the seven self-proclaimed Confederate states ignored it.

William H. Seward, whom Lincoln had invited to be secretary of state—Seward, whom the militant South had regarded as a war-crazed abolitionist—began to show his true colors by advising Lincoln to indulge the Virginia conference, which was generating compromise proposals very similar in spirit and substance to the Crittenden Compromise.

Lincoln brought Seward into line. On the question of slavery extension, he repeated, "I am inflexible. I am for no compromise which *assists* or *permits* the extension of the institution on soil owned by the nation. And any trick by which the nation is to acquire territory, and then allow some local authority to spread slavery over it, is as obnoxious as any other. I take it that to effect some such result as this, and to put us again on the high-road to a slave empire is the object of all these proposed compromises. I am against it. . . ."

Nonetheless, he continued, "as to fugitive slaves, District of Columbia, slave trade among the slave states, and whatever springs of necessity from the fact that the institution is amongst us, I care but little, so that what is done is comely, and not altogether outrageous. Nor do I care much about New-Mexico, if further extension were hedged against."[70]

He told another Republican leader to look upon secessionist politics as blackmail: "We have just carried an election on principles fairly stated to the people. Now we are told in advance, the government shall be broken up, unless we surrender to those we have beaten, before we take the offices. In this they are either attempting to play upon us, or they are in dead earnest. Either way, if we surrender, it is the end of us, and of the government. They will repeat the experiment upon us *ad libitum*. A year will not pass, till we shall have to take Cuba as a condition upon which they will stay in the Union."[71] Thus Lincoln made it clear that the principles of free soil must never be surrendered.

Yet the days in which the Free-Soil struggle was his *primary* challenge were ending. If he meant to block *secession* as well as the extension of slavery, a whole new arena lay before him.

All through the 1850s, Lincoln's powers had been focused on preventing the expansion of slavery. The loathsome scenario of slavery's extension to the North was his worst-case projection. Secession he regarded as in all probability a bluff, since the North could so easily resist it. Surely Southern strategists would know this, Lincoln had presumed, for which reason they would stop before the brink.

But it was suddenly clear in the early months of 1861 that the secessionists had not been bluffing. So it was time for an urgent game of catch-up. It was time to get better information on the state of Southern politics and public opinion. It was time to make practical plans that would use the approach to the prospect of war that Lincoln had developed—the overwhelming use of Northern power—and convert that vision into action. Most importantly, it was time for the president-elect to turn his thoughts to the defense of the Union. It was time for him to craft some manifestos to use against secession.

Like millions of Americans, Lincoln regarded the Union as sacred. But with him there was always a caveat: the worth of the Union was dependent for Lincoln on the strength of its founding principles.

Like many of his fellow Americans, Lincoln had always regarded the Union as a way of refuting the age-old notion that the weakness and depravity of human nature made governance by despots imperative. Yet again, Lincoln added a caveat: human weakness and depravity were *real*. They would manifest themselves in a will for domination that could ruin and degrade the lives of others. Individuals, minorities, and even majorities could act in this despicable manner.

The test for free institutions was "self-government"—not only in the obvious sense of majority rule but also in the *governance of selfish instincts*. "Those who deny freedom to others," he had written in 1859, "deserve it not for themselves." This negative version of the golden rule—a positive form being Jefferson's assertion that "All men are created equal"—was a watchword for guarding the republic through mutual control.

Just as men were essentially equal in their right to basic liberty, Lincoln seemed to believe, they were equal in tyrannical potential. For this reason, the people must restrain one another through legitimate powers of governance. "Slavery is founded in the selfishness of man's nature—opposition to it in his love of justice," he declared in Peoria. "These principles are an eternal antagonism."

Strong governance was needed to suppress the human instinct for tyranny. Strong magistrates were needed to restrain the wolfish tendencies of people. In free institutions, these magistrates must come from the people and answer to the people. Lincoln was determined to be forceful, conscientious, and clever in his role as a magistrate. He would have to be clever enough to prevail without abusing his power, but prevail he must.

If he failed, the nation would unravel or else lose its soul. "If destruction be our lot, we must ourselves be its author and finisher," Lincoln had warned in his Lyceum Speech years before. "As a nation of freemen, we must live through all time, or die by suicide."[72] The Founding Fathers had striven to carry out "a practical demonstration of the truth of a proposition, which had hitherto been considered, at best no better than problematical; namely, *the capability of a people to govern themselves.*"[73]

So the nation had to live—Lincoln had to keep his nation intact, with its definitive evil on the way to a slow termination. Such were his nonnegotiable purposes and goals on the eve of war.

But the constitutional basis for his policy was tricky. Like Daniel Webster and others before him, Lincoln argued that the Union was older than the Constitution, which was really the *second* constitution under which the United States had lived. The full title of the *first* constitution—the Articles of Confederation and Perpetual Union—made the argument for permanent Union appear to be obvious. It was easy for Lincoln to argue that the Union's permanence endured in the Federal Constitution, which, after all, was ordained and established to "form a more perfect Union." How could any perpetual Union become "more perfect" by losing its permanence?

But there remained a significant problem. The Constitution itself said nothing on the issue of permanence. Indeed, the method set forth for its very own ratification was a break in the nation's continuity.

The Constitution provided that as soon as *any nine* of the thirteen states had completed the process of ratification, the federal process would start *among the nine*. This meant that if any four of the original states had decided not to ratify the Constitution, they would *not have been included* in the Union.

The fact that all the states had been given a chance to opt out made the permanent Union effectively a nullity, at least in the view of the political metaphysicians of Confederate secession. What the states had agreed to, the Confederates said, could be voided any time at their discretion.

Historian Kenneth M. Stampp has contended that "the Philadelphia Convention made the historical argument for perpetuity invalid, because the Convention and the ratifying states destroyed the existing Union. Every state had the option of *not* ratifying, and as many as four might have remained independent (as two did for a time) while the other nine entered a new union. . . . The preamble to the Constitution, be it noted, does not propose to make the old Union more perfect but to '*form* a more perfect Union'—that is, to create a new and better one."[74]

Lincoln would insist until the very last days of the war that the Union remained unbroken. He would never refer to "Confederates" as such— they were Confederates "so-called." In his own view, all of them were "rebels"—part of a huge and illegal insurrection that usurped state power in the Southern region of the Union.

A crusade to preserve the Union was a powerful weapon in a number of ways. It could serve as a basis for uniting Republicans and Democrats. But the Democrats could always insist and complain that the Republicans had *caused* the problem—that Republicans were really *to blame* for the crisis of the Union—because they pushed the South into rebellion.

If the war became costly, Democratic support would be essential, especially in Congress. And yet Republican policies and needs would put a very real limit on the politics of coalition.

There were also concerns about the border states. If Maryland proclaimed secession, then the national capital of Washington, D.C., would be surrounded and would have to be abandoned. If Virginia should proclaim secession, a tremendous array of assets would fall into the laps of the Confederates. For all of the undecided slave states, the issue of "coercion" by the federal government was fraught with emotional significance.

As historian Richard N. Current has described the situation, Lincoln faced an apparent dilemma: "If he took a stand, he would run the risk of antagonizing and losing Virginia and other still-loyal slave states. But if he declined to take a stand, he would still risk losing those states, though conferring new prestige and attractiveness upon the Confederacy. And, besides, he would surely alienate many of his adherents in the North."[75]

But he knew what he was going to do. And he knew what he would not allow. He would not allow secession to unravel the American nation. He would not allow secessionists to form a powerful slave-holding nation that would spread its institutions any further in the Western Hemisphere. And, in immediate terms, he would not allow Confederates to take over federal functions in the Southern states. Indeed, he would draw the line *there*. But he would try to play for time as he considered all the military options.

Moreover, he would pick the best ground on which to fight. He would try to force the enemy to fire the first shot, thus arousing and uniting the North.

Lincoln left his home in Springfield, Illinois, on February 11, 1861. The journey by train that would take him from Springfield to Washington, D.C., would take a "winding way," as Lincoln put it, in response to some speaking invitations from a number of Northern cities. When his train reached Indianapolis, Lincoln strove to make fun of the secessionists. He asked "by what principle of original right is it that one-fiftieth or one-ninetieth of a great nation, by calling themselves a State, have the right to break up and ruin that nation as a matter of original principle? Now, I ask the question—I am not deciding anything—[laughter,] . . . where is the mysterious, original right, from principle, for a certain district of the country with inhabitants, by merely being called a State, to play tyrant over all its own citizens, and deny the authority of everything greater than itself. [Laughter.]"[76]

On February 12, in Cincinnati, he recalled the very statements he had aimed across the river to Kentucky less than two years before, "in a playful manner," he admitted, "but with sincere words." He assured the Kentuckians in 1859 that Republicans would always treat them fairly—we will treat you as "Washington, Jefferson, and Madison treated you," Lincoln had said—and he now reaffirmed those sentiments.[77]

In New York City—which harbored a significant amount of Southern sympathy along with considerable Democratic strength—Lincoln made a very interesting statement. The Union was designed for a *purpose*, he reminded the city's Democratic Mayor, Fernando Wood: "There is nothing that can ever bring me willingly to consent to the destruction of this Union . . . unless it were to be that thing for which the Union itself was made. I understand a ship to be made for the carrying and preservation of the cargo, and so long as the ship can be saved, with the cargo, it should never be abandoned. This Union should likewise never be abandoned unless it fails and the probability of its preservation shall cease to exist without throwing the passengers and cargo overboard."[78] In other words, the Union would be saved *Lincoln's way*, and with its fundamental principles preserved. But Lincoln would never sacrifice these principles to preserve the union.

At Trenton, New Jersey, after speaking of the valor of Washington's troops in the American Revolution, he became more emphatic and decisive. "I shall do all that may be in my power to promote a peaceful settlement of all our difficulties," he said. "The man does not live who is more devoted to peace than I am. [Cheers.] None who would do more to preserve it. But it may be necessary to put the foot down firmly. [Here the audience broke out into cheers so loud and long that for some moments it was impossible to hear Mr. L's voice.] He continued:

And if I do my duty, and do right, you will sustain me, will you not? [Loud cheers, and cries of 'Yes,' 'Yes,' 'We will.']"[79]

In Philadelphia, he spoke about war and made it clear that he would wait for Southern violence before he used force. "There will be no blood shed unless it be forced upon the Government," he promised his audience. "The Government will not use force unless force is used against it."[80]

He also spoke of his personal feelings when he first beheld Independence Hall. "I have never asked anything," he said, "that does not breathe from those walls. All my political warfare has been in favor of the teachings coming forth from that sacred hall. May my right hand forget its cunning and my tongue cleave to the roof of my mouth, if ever I prove false to those teachings."[81]

He made a longer speech the next day in Independence Hall: he said that he had "never had a feeling politically that did not spring from the sentiments embodied in the Declaration of Independence," a document, he added, whose purpose "was not the mere matter of the separation of the colonies from the mother land." No, it was "something in that Declaration giving liberty, not alone to the people of this country, but hope to the world for all future time," a promise that "the weights should be lifted from the shoulders of all men, and that *all* should have an equal chance."

Then he made a most stunning declaration: "If this country cannot be saved without giving up that principle," Lincoln proclaimed, "I would rather be assassinated on the spot than to surrender it."[82] The threat was very much upon his mind. Southern hate mail had flooded his home since the election, and it frequently threatened his life.[83] Indeed, sudden news of a plot to murder him had been uncovered just the day before.[84] The killing ground would be Baltimore—the goal was to kill him before he could take his presidential oath—and the killers were a bevy of secessionists who knew he would have to change trains on the trip to Washington, D.C.

So he agreed to employ a disguise, accept the protection of bodyguards, and take a special nighttime train that would arrive in Washington secretly, well ahead of schedule. At dawn on February 23, he arrived in the nation's capital and checked in at Willard's Hotel. His family arrived the next day.

Awaiting his arrival was Secretary of State-designate William H. Seward, the senior member of his cabinet. Other cabinet appointments had been worked out slowly and carefully. Lincoln strove for a nominal "unity" cabinet including former Democrats and Whigs. Salmon P. Chase would be the secretary of the treasury. Montgomery Blair—son of Francis Preston Blair, the old anti-secessionist Democrat who served as a member of Andrew Jackson's "kitchen cabinet" back in the 1830s—would be postmaster general. Gideon Welles, a Connecticut Republican, would head the Department of the Navy. Simon Cameron, a wily machine politician from Pennsylvania would, by dint of a political bargain, be the secretary of war. Seward had continued his dalliance with Virginia's "peace convention," which was meeting in a dance hall adjacent to Willard's Hotel. And while the peace convention was meeting in Washington, another Virginia convention—a secession convention—was meeting in Richmond.

Seward tried to convince his new chief to back down, to negotiate a deal. But the peace convention kept insisting on a package of warmed-over Crittenden measures that would never be acceptable to Lincoln.

Rumor had it that some peace convention delegates had broached a very different deal. They allegedly hinted to Lincoln that if South Carolina secessionists were permitted to occupy the federal fort in the middle of Charleston Harbor—Fort Sumter—it would strengthen the Unionists' hand in the Virginia secession convention.

Most of the federal forts and coastal defenses in the lower-Southern states had been seized already by secessionists. A few held out: Fort Sumter in Charleston, South Carolina, and Fort Pickens in Pensacola, Florida. In January, President Buchanan tried to send a ship with reinforcements to Fort Sumter. But Confederate batteries had fired upon the ship and turned it back.

At Seward's behest, Lincoln had a few talks with some peace convention delegates at Willard's. And yet a "Sumter-for-Virginia" bargain proved to be impossible. None of the Virginia delegates was authorized to bind Virginia to a deal or to adjourn its secession convention.[85]

The most substantive attempt to avert the threat of war was the passage by Congress of a constitutional amendment that would tie the hands of Congress forever on the question of abolishing slavery. This amendment was never ratified, but it demonstrated exactly how far the congressional Republicans and Democrats were willing to go to put an end to the crisis of secession in the early months of 1861.

Lincoln was obliged to respond to this important new development. Importantly—and unbelievably, to some—he accepted the amendment in principle on the day of his inauguration. It behooves us to ask why.

Answers to the question must to some extent remain conjectural: Lincoln never made his reasons for the move clear to anyone, at least so far as we can tell. And yet the reasons can be easily inferred.

In light of everything that Lincoln ever said or did, his acceptance of a measure such as this would be a grudging acceptance at best. But he confronted a genuine conundrum. For years he had predicted that the institution of slavery would wither and die if Americans could manage to contain it.

Especially after the election, he tried to reassure the white South that this containment of slavery would never be a threat to their safety, their property, their interests. Abolition would be left up to them. And so he urged Southern whites to keep calm and reject the secessionist movement—while the nation put a quarantine around them.

Now, if Lincoln had *opposed* this amendment that would guarantee his promise of non-interference with the slave-holding South, then what, may we ask, would have happened? Southern militants would claim that Lincoln's promise was a trick—a guileful and *temporary* promise, not binding on Republican successors, since he fought against a measure that would guarantee a permanent policy. Thus the politics of secession forced a painful decision on Lincoln with regard to this amendment.

Yet Lincoln really seemed to believe that the evil of slavery would die if the nation contained it. He appeared to believe that it was only a matter of time before Southerners would listen to the logic of a voluntary phaseout.

Why should this have been the case? One reason, perhaps, was the fear that had been haunting the South—the fear that became so unbearable after Harpers Ferry. Once the South lost control of the executive branch, an Alabama writer ventured to predict in 1860, "what social monstrosities, what desolated fields, what civil broils, what robberies, rapes, and murders of the poorer whites by the emancipated blacks would then disfigure the whole fair face of this prosperous, smiling, and happy Southern land [?]"[86]

The great fear of the blacks in the South might become so horrific— the great fear of the ever-growing black population that could not be channeled any longer into lands beyond the great quarantine—that it could break down the Southern police state. White Southerners might come to their senses over time and demand a new politics of change.

This particular freedom scenario could never be averted by a constitutional amendment to tie the hands of *Congress*. Lincoln's hope for the "ultimate extinction" of slavery was premised on a *voluntary* phase-out. The *compulsion* that would break the Southern system would arise within the South itself.

And Southern militants feared this scenario. In October 1860, the *Charleston Mercury* warned that if Republicans should capture the executive branch, a dark chain of events would divide the Southern people into factions. With the Republican Party "enthroned at Washington," declared the *Mercury*,

> the *under*-ground railroad will become an over-ground railroad. The tenure of slave property will be felt to be weakened; and the slaves will be sent down to the Cotton States for sale, and the Frontier States *enter on the policy of making themselves Free States*.
>
> With the control of the Government of the United States, and an organized and triumphant North to sustain them, the Abolitionists will renew their operations upon the South with increased courage. . . . They will have an Abolition Party in the South, of Southern men. The contest for slavery will no longer be one between the North and the South. It will be in the South, between the people of the South. . . .
>
> If, in our present position of power and unitedness, we have the raid of John Brown . . . what will be the measures of insurrection and incendiarism, which must follow our notorious and abject prostration to Abolition rule at Washington, with all the patronage of the Federal Government, and a Union organization in the South to support it? . . . Already there is uneasiness in the South, as to the stability of its institution of slavery. But with a submission to the rule of abolitionists at Washington, thousands of slaveholders will despair of the institution. While the condition of things in the Frontier States will force their slaves on the markets of the Cotton States, the timid in the Cotton States, will also sell their slaves. The general distrust, must affect purchasers. The consequence must be, slave property must be greatly depreciated.[87]

Which of course could make a voluntary buyout—perhaps by a new and more powerful American colonization society—financially feasible.

Under cloudy skies, Lincoln rode to his inauguration at the U.S. Capitol on March 4, 1861. He would receive his presidential oath from the lips of Chief Justice Taney.

His Inaugural Address had been revised after numerous reviews by advisors such as Seward and the Blairs. It would stand for all time as a conventional-wisdom exhibit of "Lincoln the moderate," regardless of the numerous strategic issues that affected its contents—and dated its message.

He began by promising the slave states that he would commit no actions that would harm them. "Apprehension seems to exist among the people of the Southern States," he said, "that by the accession of a Republican Administration, their property, and their peace, and personal security, are to be endangered. There has never been any reasonable cause for such apprehension. Indeed, the most ample evidence to the contrary has all the while existed, and been open to their inspection. It is found in nearly all the published speeches of him who now addresses you. I do but quote from one of these speeches when I declare that 'I have no purpose, directly or indirectly, to interfere with the institution of slavery in the States where it exists. I believe I have no lawful right to do so, and I have no inclination to do so.'"[88]

He contended that "the Union of these States is perpetual," asserting that "no government proper, ever had a provision in its organic law for its own termination." Even if the United States were regarded as "not a government proper, but an association of states in the nature of a contract merely, can it, as a contract, be peacefully unmade, by less than all the parties who made it?"[89]

He asserted that the Union was older than the Constitution, explaining that the permanence proclaimed in the Articles of Confederation carried over to the Federal sequel. So it follows, he continued, "that no State, upon its own mere motion, can lawfully get out of the Union,—that *resolves* and *ordinances* to that effect are legally void."[90]

He called secession "the essence of anarchy," contending that majority rule, with appropriate restraints, was the only possible method for governing republics: "a majority, held in restraint by constitutional checks, and limitations, and always changing easily, with deliberate changes of popular opinions and sentiments, is the only true sovereign of a free people. . . . Unanimity is impossible; the rule of a minority, as a permanent arrangement, is wholly inadmissible; so that, rejecting the majority principle, anarchy, or despotism in some form, is all that is left."[91]

With regard to Supreme Court decisions, Lincoln challenged the doctrine of unlimited judicial review. "I do not forget the position assumed by some, that constitutional questions are to be decided by the Supreme Court," Lincoln explained, "nor do I deny that such decisions must be binding in any case, upon the parties to a suit, as to the object of that suit, while they are also entitled to very high respect and consideration, in all paralel [*sic*] cases, by all other departments of the government." Nonetheless, Lincoln reasoned, "at the same time the candid citizen must confess that if the policy of the government, upon vital questions, affecting the whole people, is to be irrevocably fixed by decisions of the Supreme Court, the instant they are made . . . the people will have ceased, to be their own rulers, having, to that extent, practically resigned their government, into the hands of that worthy tribunal."[92]

Lincoln acknowledged that the Free-Soil leaders and the slave-state leaders held different constitutional views about slavery's expansion. But he challenged the South to consider whether separation in merely *political* terms would achieve their objectives. "Physically speaking, we cannot separate," Lincoln said. "We cannot remove our respective sections from each other, nor build an impassible wall between them. A husband and wife may be divorced, and go out of the presence, and beyond the reach of the other; but the different parts of our country cannot do this. They cannot but remain face to face; and intercourse, either amicable or hostile, must continue between them."

In light of this, Lincoln asked, "can treaties be more faithfully enforced between aliens, than laws can among friends? Suppose you go to war, you cannot fight always; and when, after much loss on both sides, and no gain on either, you cease fighting, the identical old questions, as to terms of intercourse, are again upon you."[93]

Lincoln turned to the recent work of Congress; he acknowledged that the sovereign will of the people could approve constitutional amendments. "I can not be ignorant of the fact that many worthy, and patriotic citizens are desirous of having the national constitution amended," he acknowledged. "While I make no recommendation of amendments, I fully recognize the rightful authority of the people over the whole subject . . . and I should, under existing circumstances, favor, rather than oppose, a fair oppertunity [*sic*] being afforded the people to act upon it."

Moreover, he continued, "I understand a proposed amendment to the Constitution—which amendment, however, I have not seen, has passed Congress, to the effect that the federal government, shall never interfere with the domestic institutions of the States, including that of persons held to service. . . . Holding such a provision to now be implied constitutional law, I have no objection to its being made express, and irrevocable."[94]

Nonetheless, he had taken an oath to uphold the *existing* laws, and the people had never conferred an authority "to fix terms for the separation of the States." He urged Southerners to take their time, but made it clear that he awaited their decision on the use of force, and would respond accordingly: "In *your* hands, my dissatisfied fellow countrymen, and not in *mine*, is the momentous issue of civil war. The government will not assail *you*. You can have no conflict, without being yourselves the aggressors. You have no oath registered in Heaven to destroy the government, while *I* shall have the most solemn one to 'preserve, protect, and defend' it."[95]

At Seward's suggestion, Lincoln closed with some conciliatory words: "I am loth to close. We are not enemies, but friends. We must not be enemies. Though passion may have strained, it must not break our bonds of affection. The mystic chords of memory, streching [*sic*] from every battle-field, and patriot grave, to every living heart and hearthstone, all over this broad land, will yet swell the chorus of the Union, when again touched, as surely they will be, by the better angels of our nature."[96]

On his very first day in the White House, Lincoln received bad news. The supplies at Fort Sumter in Charleston were running out.

Fort Pickens down in Florida was better provisioned, and Lincoln ordered it held and defended. But Fort Sumter was in peril. Lincoln, in the course of his inaugural address, had made a promise to "hold, occupy, and possess the property, and places belonging to the government. . . ."[97] So what was to be done about Sumter?

Lincoln asked for the advice of his top-ranking military officer, General Winfield Scott. He also sought advice from his cabinet.

Scott was extremely pessimistic. Seward was convinced that the fort should be evacuated. He started to spread some unauthorized rumors to Confederate agents that the fort would be abandoned very soon.

But Montgomery Blair was committed to holding the fort and he introduced Lincoln to a relative—a retired naval officer named Gustavus Vasa Fox—who had a plan to reinforce and provision Fort Sumter by means of a small flotilla.

A slim majority of Lincoln's cabinet opposed this move. Nevertheless, Lincoln quietly granted Fox approval to travel to the fort at night and assess the situation.

Lincoln also sent an agent of his own into South Carolina to report on public opinion. This agent was a friend named Stephen S. Hurlbut, an Illinois colleague who was born in South Carolina. After visiting Charleston, Hurlbut bluntly told Lincoln there was "no attachment to the Union" in South Carolina. He said that even "a ship known to contain *only provisions* for Sumpter [*sic*]"—in other words a ship containing food but no troops—"would be stopped & refused admittance." He said that an evacuation of the fort would be "followed by a demand for Pickens and the Keys of the Gulf," and that "the attempt to fulfill the duties of the Executive Office in enforcing the laws & authority of the U.S." within the limits of the so-called Confederate States "will be War."[98]

Lincoln called another meeting of his cabinet on March 29. He suggested a modified proposal: He would send an expedition to Sumter and *announce his intention* to secessionists. He would tell them that the fort would be *peacefully* provisioned as long as the Confederates held their fire. The ships would be delivering *food* to feed some hungry men. It almost sounded like a mercy mission. The cabinet supported this proposal, with Seward in dissent.

The sheer cunning of the move has elicited praise and condemnation down the years. For Lincoln's message to the South could be read in very different ways. In the North it sounded mild and innocuous. In the South it was an act of defiance. Lincoln knew from his agent what the South Carolinians would think when he told them of his plans. And he knew what they would do in return. But it was *Northern* opinion that he wanted to bring into line with his Sumter policy.

Historian James M. McPherson has observed that "if Confederates opened fire on the unarmed boats carrying 'food for hungry men,' the South would stand convicted of an aggressive act. . . . This would unite the North and, perhaps, keep the South divided. If southerners allowed the supplies to go through, peace and the status quo at Sumter could be preserved and the Union government would have won an important symbolic victory. Lincoln's new conception of the resupply undertaking was a stroke of genius. In effect he was telling Jefferson Davis, 'Heads I win, Tails you lose.' It was the first sign of the mastery that would mark Lincoln's presidency."[99]

Oblivious to this mastery was Seward, whose judgment had been yielding to a very strange flight from reality. On April 1, he sent Lincoln a presumptuous and pushy memorandum entitled "Some thoughts for the President's consideration." Seward complained that, after drifting for a month, the administration was "without a policy either domestic or foreign."

He counseled the abandonment of Fort Sumter and urged that Fort Pickens alone be defended. He urged Lincoln to rally Union sentiment in Southern states through a naked jingoistic ploy: he should try to pick a quarrel with France or Spain, since both of those nations were asserting their interests in the Western Hemisphere.

Surely, Seward argued, this quarrel could be fanned into a war. And such a war might cancel out secessionist fervor and revive the old patriotic bond between the North and South. The *pièce de résistance* was the suggestion by Seward that Lincoln choose "some member of his Cabinet" to supervise the policy.

Once again, Lincoln had to put Seward quite firmly in his place. He carefully responded to Seward's allegation that the president and cabinet had drifted for a month, and that they lacked a coherent policy. "At the *beginning* of that month," he reminded Seward, he announced in his Inaugural Address:

> "The power confided in me will be used to hold, occupy and possess the property and places belonging to the government, and to collect the duties and imposts." This had your distinct approval at the time; and, taken in connection with the order I immediately gave General Scott, directing him to employ every means in his power to strengthen and hold the forts, comprises the exact domestic policy you now urge, with the single exception, that it does not propose to abandon Fort Sumpter [*sic*]. . . .
>
> Upon your closing propositions, that "whatever policy we adopt, there must be an energetic prossecution [*sic*] of it"
>
> "For this purpose it must be somebody's business to pursue and direct it incessantly"
>
> "Either the President must do it himself, and be all the while active in it, or"
>
> "Devolve it on some member of his cabinet"
>
> I remark that if this must be done, *I* must do it.[100]

Lincoln could have rid himself of Seward. Indeed, Seward had offered in a moody and petulant manner to resign on an earlier occasion. But Lincoln kept him on—and his reason for doing so was probably to keep him *on a very tight leash*, thus containing his potential for mischief.

On April 4, Lincoln met with Fox to put the finishing touches on their plan. Lincoln would notify the governor of South Carolina that a peaceful supply expedition was heading to Sumter. The first boats into the harbor would indeed be unarmed. But if Confederates should fire upon the boats, then some warships held in reserve beyond the harbor would return the fire. Having done so, they would escort the expedition to the fort.

On April 6, Lincoln sent off his message to the governor of South Carolina by courier. He also permitted some leaks to the press with regard to the mission and the peaceful intentions behind it.[101]

South Carolina Governor Francis W. Pickens received Lincoln's message on April 8. At once, the Confederates' military commander in Charleston, General P.G.T. Beauregard, cabled Jefferson Davis in Montgomery, Alabama, and reported the news. Davis's response was immediate: he had a telegram sent to Beauregard commanding him to fire on the Lincoln expedition as soon as the ships arrived.[102]

On April 10, an old friend and colleague of Davis's suggested that he act preemptively. "No one doubts that Lincoln intends war," cabled Louis Wigfall of Texas, who was staying in Charleston. "The delay on his part is only to complete his preparations. All here is ready on our side. Our delay is therefore to his advantage, and our disadvantage. Let us take Fort Sumter before we have to fight the fleet and the fort."[103]

Davis amended his orders to Beauregard, instructing his general to issue an ultimatum to Fort Sumter: evacuate or else. The bombardment of Fort Sumter began on April 12, before Lincoln's ships reached the harbor.

The Union troops at Fort Sumter were finally obliged to evacuate, but the response in the North was almost everything that Lincoln could have wished. Even some of the most flagrantly partisan Democrats were clamoring for war against secessionist traitors. On April 15, Lincoln issued a proclamation calling for seventy-five thousand troops from the state militias to suppress the insurrection in the South. They would serve for a ninety-day term.[104] In the same proclamation, he called a special session of Congress that would start on the Fourth of July.

The militia call tipped the uneasy balance in Virginia's secession convention, which proceeded to vote for secession on April 17. Arkansas proclaimed secession on May 6, with North Carolina following on May 20. Tennessee proclaimed secession in the following month.

Pro-slavery leaders exulted in this turn of events; moreover, they dedicated themselves and their Confederate nation-in-the-making to the triumph of white supremacy. Confederate Vice President Alexander Stephens, for example, had declared in March that the Confederacy has put at rest forever all the agitating questions relating to our peculiar institution—African slavery as it exists among us—the proper status of the negro in our form of civilization. This was the immediate cause of the late rupture and present revolution. Jefferson, in his forecast, had anticipated this, as the "rock upon which the old Union would split." He was right. . . . But . . . the prevailing ideas entertained by him and most of the leading statesmen at the time of the formation of the old Constitution were, that the enslavement of the African was in violation of the laws of nature. . . . It was an evil they knew not well how to deal with; but the general opinion of the men of that day was, that, somehow or other, in the order of Providence, the institution would be evanescent and pass away. . . . Those ideas, however, were fundamentally wrong. They rested upon an assumption of the equality of the races. This was an error. It was a sandy foundation, and the idea of a Government built upon it—when the "storm came and the wind blew, it fell."

Our new Government is founded upon exactly the opposite ideas; its foundations are laid, its cornerstone rests, upon the great truth that the negro is not equal to the white man; that slavery, subordination to the superior race, is his natural and moral condition. This, our new Government, is the first, in the history of the world, based upon this great physical, philosophical, and moral truth.[105]

Many Southerners who fought for the Confederacy would fight to defend their communities, their families, their homes. Nonetheless, it is absolutely clear—and the point demands very strong emphasis— that the impetus for secession had arisen in the slave-holding class of the South.

Many slave-holding Southerners were ever more intent upon expansion. As early as February 1860, the *Charleston Mercury* had spoken of "Mexico and the Tropics" as ripe for the plucking and asked whether any prescient observer could possibly deny that "as in the past, so in the future, the Anglo-Saxon race will, in the course of years, occupy and absorb the whole of that splendid but ill-peopled country, and . . . remove by a gradual process, before them, the worthless mongrel races that now inhabit and curse the land[.]"[106]

The place to begin was New Mexico, the *Mercury* suggested: even though this region was regarded by some as "too barren and arid for Southern occupation or settlement," it nonetheless "teems with mineral resources." For this reason the South should remember that "there is no vocation in the world in which slavery can be more useful or profitable than in mining."[107]

In the summer of 1861, the Confederate States sent military forces to New Mexico. Indeed, as historian Eugene D. Genovese has pointed out, "Confederate troops marched into New Mexico with the intention of proceeding to Tucson and then swinging south to take Sonora, Chihua-hua, Durango, and Tamaulipas. . . . Juárez was so alarmed that he was ready to go to great lengths to help the Union put down the rebellion."[108]

The long-term scope of an empire for Southern slavery appeared unlimited. Alexander Stephens had declared that the Confederate States comprised "the nucleus of a growing power, which, if we are true to ourselves, our destiny, and high mission, will become the controlling power on this continent."[109]

But the short-term Confederate challenge—indeed, the short-term Confederate imperative—was to unify the slave-state bloc. With Virginia in Confederate hands, the state of Maryland should come soon enough. And then Lincoln could sit in his surrounded city to await his capture and its sequel.

"We are prepared to fight," exulted the *Mobile Advertiser*, "and the enemy is not. . . . Now is the time for action, while he is yet unprepared. Let . . . a hundred thousand men . . . get over the border as quickly as they can. Let a division enter every Northern border state, destroy railroad connections to prevent concentration of the enemy, and the desperate strait of these States, the body of Lincoln's country, will compel him to a peace—or compel his successor, should Virginia not suffer him to escape from his doomed capital."[110]

Lincoln was alert to the threat of invasion and he took urgent action to preempt it. In the first week of April he secretly advised Pennsylvania's governor, Andrew G. Curtin, that militia troops would be needed to defend the nation's capital. On April 8, he told Curtin, "I think the necessity of being *ready* increases. Look to it."[111]

A few army and volunteer companies defended the capital when Lincoln issued his militia call on April 15. And more were on the way—a few hundred troops arrived from Pennsylvania on April 18.

The next day, a large mob of secessionists in Baltimore attacked the Sixth Regiment of Massachusetts Volunteers on their way to Washington. Richard N. Current has observed that "many Baltimoreans, including city officials, though not the Mayor, were determined secessionists, and so were most members of the Maryland legislature. In the city, and in the counties adjacent to Washington, there was a secret organization with the ultimate aim of seizing the national capital and setting up a provisional government to serve the interests of the Confederacy." In the aftermath of the Baltimore riot, the "conspirators sent to Richmond for a supply of arms. Responding with alacrity, the

Virginia governor forwarded two thousand muskets and promised twenty heavy guns. President Davis encouraged [Virginia] Governor Letcher. 'Sustain Baltimore, if practicable,' Davis telegraphed to him."[112]

On the night of April 19, some railroad bridges in Baltimore were burned at the order of the city's own officials. This would make the reinforcement of Washington much more difficult.

These events must be clearly understood to make sense of Lincoln's policy in Maryland. On April 19, Lincoln asked his attorney general, Edward Bates, to give him an opinion on declaring martial law in the state. On the same day, he declared a naval blockade of the Confederate states.

On April 25, as more Northern regiments arrived to defend the capital city, he wrote to General Scott with regard to the Maryland legislature. The governor of Maryland, under public pressure, had convened the state's General Assembly. Lincoln worried that they might attempt secession:

> The Maryland legislature assembles to-morrow at Anapolis [*sic*]; and, not improbably, will take action to arm the people of that State against the United States. The question has been submitted to, and considered by me, whether it would not be justifiable, upon the ground of necessary defense, for you, as commander in Chief of the United States Army, to arrest, or disperse the members of that body. I think it would *not* be justifiable; nor, efficient for the desired object.
>
> First, they have a clearly legal right to assemble; and, we can not know in advance, that their action will not be lawful, and peaceful. And if we wait until they shall *have* acted, their arrest, or dispersion, will not lessen the effect of their action.
>
> Secondly, we *can* not permanently prevent their action. If we arrest them, we can not long hold them as prisoners; and when liberated, they will immediately re-assemble, and take their action. And, precisely the same if we simply disperse them. They will immediately re-assemble in some other place.
>
> I therefore conclude that it is only left to the Commanding General to watch, and await their action, which, if it shall be to arm their people against the United States, he is to adopt the most prompt, and efficient means to counteract, even, if necessary, to the bombardment of their cities—and in the extremest necessity, the suspension of the writ of habeas corpus.[113]

The bombardment of their cities: already, the supposedly "moderate" Lincoln was beginning to move toward the policies we call "total war."

Though the legislature of Maryland did not attempt secession, Lincoln nonetheless authorized Scott to suspend the writ of habeas corpus in Maryland on April 27. Two days later he instructed the secretary of the navy to "have as strong a War Steamer as you can conveniently put on that duty, to cruise upon the Potomac, and to look in upon, and, if practicable, examine the Bluff and vicinity, at what is called the White House, once or twice per day; and, in any case of an attempt to erect a battery there, to drive away the party attempting it. . . ."[114]

The city appeared to be safe by the first week of May. But Lincoln's thoughts had been moving very quickly from defensive to offensive options. On May 3, he issued another militia call for forty-two thousand more troops. These troops, however, were required to sign up for *three years*. He expanded the size of the regular army and navy. Congress would be called upon to ratify all of these actions in the special session that Lincoln had summoned for the Fourth of July.

Above all, Lincoln sought to devise an appropriate war plan. As McPherson has noted, Lincoln was "painfully aware that his Confederate counterpart . . . was better qualified than he as a military leader. Jefferson Davis had graduated from West Point, commanded a regiment in the Mexican War, and served four years (1853–1857) as an outstanding U.S. secretary of war. To remedy his deficiencies, Lincoln borrowed books on military strategy from the Library of Congress and burned the midnight oil reading them. His experience as a self-taught lawyer and his analytical mind (for mental exercise he had mastered Euclidian geometry on his own) stood him in good stead."[115]

Indeed, his mental powers were architectonic: he could grasp in a moment the relationship of parts to whole. He could visualize surges of power as they flowed along lines of force. In this way he would quickly surpass the outmoded thinking that was frequently instilled in young military men—thinking that regarded the troops of the enemy as *barriers* standing in the way of proper *targets* like the enemy's capital city. With all due respect to the importance of fixed geographical assets in war—the Confederate capital, for instance, which was moved to Richmond, Virginia, in the latter part of May—Lincoln quickly came to view the Confederate armies as *targets in their own right*. They were *sources of power* that his armies had to conquer or destroy.

Historian T. Harry Williams has said that Lincoln was "a better natural strategist than were most of the trained soldiers. He saw the big picture of war from the start. The policy of the government was to restore the Union by force; the strategy perforce had to be offensive. Lincoln knew that numbers, material resources, and sea power were on his side. . . . He grasped immediately the advantage that numbers gave the North and urged his generals to keep up a constant pressure on the whole strategic line of the Confederacy until a weak spot was found—and a break-through could be made."[116]

In late April, he requested a strategic plan from General Scott. Scott proposed to seal off the rebel states through a naval blockade augmented by control of the Mississippi River. When this had been accomplished, in Scott's opinion, the government should then let the steady pressure of containment impel the Confederate leaders to desist. This "Anaconda Plan," he suggested, would squeeze the life out of the rebellion.

The containment approach came naturally to Lincoln, for it built upon his policy for slavery. Indeed, he had issued his orders for a naval blockade already. But for military purposes, containment was not enough. Williams has argued that "even if the Anaconda worked, it would take years to make its effect felt, and [Lincoln] wanted quicker results. The defect in the thinking of Scott, the military man, was the idea that the war could be won by a single effort of some kind. Lincoln, the civilian strategist, knew better; he knew that many efforts of different kinds would be required."[117]

As military forces came pouring into Washington and elsewhere, he weighed his many options for attacking the Confederate forces. He prepared for the congressional session in July that would commit the nation to the war. The times had become revolutionary. Lincoln tested and exercised his powers of command as the flow of events rushed along.

In June he received some poignant news. Stephen Douglas, "the most dangerous enemy of liberty because the most insidious one," as Lincoln had once called him, had succumbed to a "rheumatic fever." He was dead.

He had visited Lincoln at the White House and offered to help build support for the war, for he had always been a patriotic unionist. But now, like a candle that had "flickered in the socket," he was gone.

Yet his legacy would linger in the form of a white supremacy consensus. This would curb Lincoln's actions for a time, as we shall see— but it could not constrain them forever. A great decision would be coming in a year: the decision to liberate.

FOUR

Lincoln and Emancipation, 1861–1862

LINCOLN'S INSTINCTS appeared to be "moderate" as war began. But in the very first year of the war against secession, he extended his plans to kill slavery. He found a way to move beyond the first step of his moral strategy—containment—to the process of long-term phaseout.

In immediate terms, Lincoln needed three things to beat the rebels: full access to Northern resources, the continued support of a Northern majority, and brilliant commanders in the field. Winfield Scott made it very clear to Lincoln that a younger man should be offered command of the army on the fields of battle. In April, he suggested that Lincoln consider Colonel Robert E. Lee of Virginia. On April 18, Lincoln offered the position to Lee through an emissary, Francis Preston Blair, Sr.

Lee turned down the offer. At the same time, an impressive number of other West Pointers from the South chose to serve the Confederate cause. Lincoln, however, had very little time in which to brood upon the loss of such a large group of capable commanders. In May, two more of the slave states, Arkansas and North Carolina, succumbed to secession. And a lethal fight was beginning in Missouri, as Governor Claiborne Jackson and former Governor Sterling Price tried to take the state out of the Union.

Another border slave state was hanging in the balance: Kentucky's pro-Confederate governor faced off against a determined Unionist majority in the legislature. The legislature managed to hold off secession by proclaiming "neutrality": both Confederate and Union forces were warned to stay out of the state.

Lincoln did his best to support the loyal Kentuckians. He authorized Major Robert Anderson, the commander-to-the-end at Fort Sumter, to establish a recruiting office in Ohio for Kentucky Unionists. But he avoided any short-term actions that could play into the hands of the governor.

When politics permitted fast action, however, Lincoln seized the opportunity and acted. In the western counties of Virginia, the secessionist cause was unpopular. Some leaders in the area began to talk openly of plans for seceding from Virginia. When Confederate troops were dispatched to the region in the latter part of May, Lincoln sent Union troops from Ohio. Just a few weeks later, on June 19, a Unionist convention met at Wheeling, Virginia to begin the slow process that would gradually result in the new state of West Virginia.

So it went, as the Confederates and Unionists scrambled for position not only in the border states but also in the global arena. Robert Toombs, who served as the Confederates' first secretary of state, commenced a major campaign to win big-power allies abroad. One of the Confederates' tactics took over a year to become effective: they proclaimed an embargo on the exportation of cotton in the hope that by withholding a commodity that Europeans needed they could force diplomatic recognition or even make alliances. But the British had a backlog of cotton in their warehouses.

Some other tactical ploys of the Confederates, however, were effective right away. They invoked the great principle of self-determination to project their cause to the world in a favorable light. They tried to cultivate certain aristocrats who viewed the Southern planter class with sympathetic eyes. Viscount Palmerston, the British prime minister, appeared to be receptive.

On May 13, the Confederates won a major skirmish on the diplomatic front. Due to Lincoln's blockade of the rebellious states, the British government declared that the Confederate States should have "belligerent" status under international law. Emperor Napoleon III of France took the cue and declared the same thing.

The conventions of international law regarded naval blockades as acts of war between sovereign nations. In other words, Lincoln's attempt to contain the rebellion was ironically assisting the Confederate claim to nationhood. Working closely with Seward and with Charles Francis Adams, whom Lincoln had appointed as ambassador to Britain, the president struggled with the difficult problem.

As all of these events unfolded, Lincoln found himself compelled to make some very careful choices as he pondered how best to deploy his many forces in the months of May and June. He strove to fine-tune his decisions, paying careful heed to all the micro-politics in each of the distinctive arenas. But he was also careful to relate the variations to the overall strategic picture.

Above all, he used the most powerful theme of bipartisan consensus—Unionism—for all it was worth in terms of money and troops and votes to make war upon secession. His Free-Soil principles were kept under cover as he wrote the long message he intended to deliver to Congress on the Fourth of July. The last thing he needed was to lose Democratic support that was essential for the war.

Lincoln would never retreat from his pledge to keep slavery contained; indeed, his insistence on the gradual extinction of slavery was a non-negotiable element in his Unionism, even in the summer of 1861. For obvious reasons, however, the next phase of his struggle with the slave states demanded an insistently Unionist politics. After all, if the Confederates won their independence, then his plans for the long-term phaseout of slavery were obviously dead.

So any overlap in patriotic feelings that existed in the minds of Republicans and Democrats demanded cultivation. This meant, in effect, that most partisan differences regarding the slavery issue would have to be minimized in Lincoln's politics, at least for the season.

To be sure, the developing circumstances of war began to force the issue of slavery back into prominence. On May 23, a politician who applied for a Union military command, General Benjamin Butler—a Massachusetts Democrat who would gradually become a Republican—issued very significant orders. Butler and his troops were in Fortress Monroe, a United States installation on the southern Virginia coastline. Some slaves had escaped from their masters and crossed into Butler's lines. The General refused to return them, proclaiming they were "contraband of war." Lincoln let Butler's orders stand. But he did not propose going further: there was too much at risk.

On the Fourth of July, Lincoln sent his special message to Congress, a message that requested retroactive approval of the measures he had taken to suppress the insurrection since the fall of Fort Sumter. In addition, he requested authority to raise at least 400,000 more soldiers; he also asked for a congressional authorization of $400 million to finance the war.

Lincoln ridiculed the logic of secession; he argued that statehood, *per se*, was impossible outside of the Union. "The States," he argued, "have their *status* IN the Union, and they have no other *legal status*. . . . The Union is older than any of the States; and, in fact, it created them as States."[1]

The Confederate cause was not secession at all; it was treason pure and simple—even though the rebels tried to cloak their crimes against the nation in the rhetoric of states' rights. Confederates, said Lincoln, "knew that they could never raise their treason to any respectable magnitude, by any name which implies *violation* of law. . . . Accordingly, they commenced . . . an insidious debauching of the public mind" by means of the doctrine of state sovereignty. "With rebellion thus sugar-coated," Lincoln said, "they have been drugging the public mind in their section for more than thirty years . . . until at length, they have brought many good men to a willingness to take up arms against the government the day *after* some assemblage of men have enacted the farcical pretense of taking their State out of the Union."[2] The Confederate cause should be viewed as a "giant insurrection," Lincoln said.[3]

Gigantic though it was, it was led by a despotic minority, according to Lincoln. "It may well be questioned," he argued, "whether there is, to-day, a majority of the legally qualified voters of any State, except perhaps South Carolina, in favor of disunion." To the contrary, he continued, "there is much reason to believe the Union men are the majority in many . . . of the so-called seceded States." Even in Virginia and Tennessee, which submitted their acts of secession to the voters for ratification, the results were suspicious, Lincoln claimed. "The result of an election, held in military camps, where the bayonets are all on one side of the question voted upon, can scarcely be considered as demonstrating popular sentiment," Lincoln said. In both of these states, there was reason to believe that the voters were "coerced to vote against the Union."[4]

The seceders cared nothing for the will of the people, or the rights of the people, or the *cause* of the people, Lincoln charged. He pointed out that in their draft Confederate Constitution "they omit 'We, the People,' and substitute 'We, the deputies of the sovereign and independent States.' Why? Why this deliberate pressing out of view [of] the rights of men, and the authority of the people?"

Essentially, Lincoln argued, this war was "a People's contest. On the side of the Union, it is a struggle for maintaining in the world, that form, and substance of government, whose leading object is, to elevate the condition of men—to lift artificial weights from all shoulders—to clear the paths of laudable pursuit for all—to afford all, an *unfettered* start, and a fair chance, in the race of life [my emphasis]."[5]

Regarding those who rebelled against a people's government, the duty of patriots was clear. Their duty was to "demonstrate to the world, that those who fairly carry an election, can also suppress a rebellion— that ballots are the rightful, and peaceful, successors to bullets; and that when ballots have fairly, and constitutionally, decided, there can be no successful appeal, back to bullets; that there can be no successful appeal, except to ballots themselves, at succeeding elections."[6]

At this point he made a brief and elliptical reference to his Free-Soil program. He treated it as almost incidental to the issue of putting down secessionist treason. "No popular government," he said, "can long survive a marked precedent, that those who carry an election, can only save the government from immediate destruction, by giving up the main point, upon which the people gave the election. The people themselves, and not their servants, can safely reverse their own deliberate decisions."[7] This was not a *Republican* war, he told the Democratic members of Congress in so many words. It was a fight to protect the very principle of popular rule through elections.

Surely Congress had to judge the propriety of what he had done, but he urged bipartisan unity to save the nation. Referring to himself in the third-person, he said "the Executive . . . has, so far, done what he has deemed his duty," adding that the members of Congress must clearly perform their own duty in whatever way they chose. He concluded by urging all American patriots to swiftly "go forward without fear, and with manly hearts."[8]

Congress gave him everything he asked for; indeed, they exceeded his financial request by approving the immense sum of $500 million for the war. Most of the money would be raised through the sale of bonds—deficit spending—though Congress went on to approve the first direct tax on incomes in American history (deferring its collection until 1863).

Thus armed with congressional authorization, Lincoln turned his mind to fast victory: he would aim a decisive blow at the political heart of the rebellion. In his message to Congress he had singled out Virginia for its offer to allow the Confederate government to move its capital to Richmond.[9]

On June 29, Lincoln made initial plans for a Virginia campaign in a meeting with General Winfield Scott and Irvin McDowell, the general in tactical command of the Union forces in the National Capital region. Lincoln wanted to attack the Confederate troops who were gathered at Manassas railway junction near the banks of a stream known as Bull Run, only twenty-five miles southwest of Washington, D.C.

As McDowell got ready to attack, there was good news from western Virginia: Generals George B. McClellan and William S. Rosecrans defeated the Confederates on July 11 in the battle of Rich Mountain. In Washington, a mood of triumphalism reigned and the battle cry of "On to Richmond" was heard through the city. McDowell and his men marched off to Manassas, and they crossed Bull Run on Sunday, July 21. Much of official Washington decided to tag along in carriages.

Their hopes would be shattered when McDowell's forces were driven from the battlefield in panic. The first battle of Manassas was a tactical disaster for the North, and its shock effects in Washington and elsewhere were profound.

But it only made Lincoln more determined. Two days after the battle, he wrote a list of private "Memoranda of Military Policy Suggested by the Bull Run Defeat." Among their other provisions, the memoranda proposed to "let the forces late before Manassas . . . be reorganized as rapidly as possible." He also proposed further action in other theatres.[10]

Lincoln promptly demoted McDowell and summoned George B. McClellan, the victorious commander from western Virginia, to take command of the army in Washington, the army that was soon to be christened the "Army of the Potomac."

In the aftermath of the defeat at Manassas, congressional politics were churning. The Democrats pushed through some stark resolutions on July 22 and July 25 that were aimed at preventing the Republican Party from expanding the war's rationale and political objectives. The Crittenden-Johnson Resolutions, named for John J. Crittenden of Kentucky (the author of the failed Crittenden Compromise of December, 1860) and Andrew Johnson of Tennessee (the only Senator from a Confederate state who refused to resign from his seat in the United States Senate), declared that the war was definitely not to be fought for the purpose of "overthrowing or interfering with the rights or established institutions" of any state, but "to defend and maintain the supremacy of the Constitution and to preserve the Union with all the dignity, equality, and rights of the several States unimpaired."[11] In other words, slavery was not to be molested in any of the states that permitted it, even in the so-called Confederate states.

The politics of war were so delicate that most of the Republicans supported this action, however faint-heartedly. But a few weeks later, Republicans infuriated Crittenden and other pro-slavery Democrats by pushing through a daring new counter-measure. On August 6, Congress passed a new law that would permit the confiscation of any property—including slaves—that Confederates used in their rebellion. Lincoln signed this law, which in many ways built upon the precedent that Benjamin Butler had set through the orders that he issued at Fortress Monroe back in May. Confiscation was not emancipation: the "contraband" slaves who were seized by the army were in no way given their freedom on a permanent basis. But they would not be returned to their owners.

Many anti-slavery leaders were eager to move much farther and to do it quickly. One of them was John C. Frémont, the Republicans' nominee for president in 1856. Frémont had served as an explorer for the Army, and he asked for a commission as a Union general. Lincoln gave him the command of the "Western Department," with his head-quarters at St. Louis. To him would be given the challenge of defeating the Confederate forces in Missouri.

The fighting in Missouri was bitter, and Frémont used the occasion to assert his anti-slavery leadership. On August 30, he issued a military proclamation declaring that the slaves of all the rebels in Missouri were henceforth free.

Three days later, Lincoln sent off a message to Frémont advising him to pay closer heed to all the short-term ramifications of his action. "I think there is great danger," Lincoln said, "that the closing paragraph" of Frémont's proclamation "in relation to the confiscation of property, and the liberating slaves of traiterous owners, will alarm our Southern Union friends, and turn them against us—perhaps ruin our rather fair prospect in Kentucky. Allow me therefore to ask, that you will as of your own motion, modify that paragraph so as to conform to the . . . act of Congress, entitled 'An Act to confiscate property used for insurrectionary purposes,' approved August 6th, 1861, and a copy of which I herewith send you. This letter is written in a spirit of caution and not of censure."[12]

Frémont told the president to *order* him to change the proclamation. Lincoln did so, observing to the general (and also for the record) that since Frémont expressed "the preference . . . that I should make an open order for the modification . . . I cheerfully do."[13] Lincoln began to have serious doubts about the soundness of Frémont's judgment. And since the military efforts of Frémont had been failures, the president relieved him of command.

The Frémont affair prompted further agitation by Republicans who sought to expand the anti-slavery dimensions of the war. Even Senator Orville Browning, an Illinois friend of the president's, was critical of Lincoln's response to Frémont.

In his answer to a letter from Browning, Lincoln said that he would stay within the strictest limits of the law unless Congress *changed* the law. "Genl. Fremont's proclamation," Lincoln wrote, "is purely *political*, and not within the range of *military* law, or necessity." With regard to the military seizure of slaves, Lincoln wrote, "if the General needs them, he can seize them, and use them; but when the need is past, it is not for him to fix their permanent future condition. That must be settled according to laws made by law-makers, and not by military proclamations."

Lincoln then applied the same stipulation to himself: "I do not say Congress might not with propriety pass a law, on the point, just such as General Fremont proclaimed. I do not say I might not, as a member of Congress, vote for it. What I object to, is, that I as President, shall expressly or impliedly seize and exercise the permanent legislative functions of the government."

Lincoln then took time to review the political issues that pertained to Frémont's action. He told Browning that when news of the proclamation by Frémont had reached Kentucky, "a whole company of our Volunteers threw down their arms and disbanded." And to lose Kentucky, Lincoln warned, "is nearly the same as to lose the whole game. Kentucky gone, we can not hold Missouri, nor, as I think, Maryland. These all against us, and the job on our hands is too large for us. We would as well consent to separation at once, including the surrender of this capitol." But if Browning and other Republicans would only be patient, "give up your restlessness for new positions, and back me manfully on the grounds upon which you and other kind friends gave me the election . . . we shall go through triumphantly."[14]

Lincoln had some very pressing reasons to be careful in regard to Kentucky. On September 3, Confederate forces under General Leonidas Polk had occupied Columbus, Kentucky on the Mississippi River. Kentucky Unionists were quick to seize the opportunity afforded by this breach of their "neutrality": through the Unionist legislature, they appealed to Washington for help in repelling the "invaders." Union troops under General Ulysses S. Grant were dispatched to Kentucky only three days later.

On the eastern front, the political pressure in Washington was building for a fast and decisive return to the attack in Virginia. But George B. McClellan, the commander of the Army of the Potomac, was slow to move. He was gradually taking the remnants of the army that was beaten at Manassas and was trying to shape them, along with many thousands of new recruits, into a large and mighty force. This work was McClellan's forte: he was excellent at training and preparation. McClellan was by temperament and experience a military engineer.

He was also a Democratic white supremacist who had voted for Stephen Douglas. Supporting the war in the manner of Douglas, he had no intention of moving in Frémont's direction. In fact, he asked a Democratic confidante to "help me dodge the nigger—we want nothing to do with him."[15] McClellan made no secret of his views on the "negro question." Republicans worried that he might be treacherous, but Lincoln was prepared to give him time. After all, the troops seemed to worship McClellan: they called him "little Mac." Others—especially Democrats—called him the "young Napoleon" and talked to him of presidential prospects.

It went to his head in a manner that elicited arrogance. "I seem to have become *the* power in the land," he wrote to his wife. "I almost think that were I to win some small success now, I could become Dictator or anything else that might please me—but nothing of the kind would please me—*therefore I won't* be Dictator. Admirable self denial!"[16]

This foolish demeanor was linked to some character flaws. McClellan possessed two crippling vices that would doom him to failure as a general. First, his bravado was nothing more than a brittle veneer to conceal a major weakness of will. When the bloodshed started and the casualties rose, this military man would prove weak to the point of timidity. Second, when he lost a battle, he would blame it on his superiors. Ironically, his victories in western Virginia that summer had been won to some extent by the skill of his subordinates.[17]

Lincoln had yet to discover these problems in early October when he wrote a memorandum on military strategy envisioning the next campaigns. His intention was to work for simultaneous, coordinated action in all theatres.[18] But McClellan was still inactive, and congressional

Republicans were starting to suggest that he malingered due to "softness"—perhaps a *Democratic* softness toward the South.

Lincoln suggested that McClellan accelerate his plans, and the general's response was revealing. He said that Winfield Scott, the old general in chief, was to blame for most of the delays. Perhaps retirement for Scott would be the answer, suggested McClellan.[19]

The old general, ill and fatigued, was more than ready to retire and McClellan was appointed on November 1 to command all the Union armies. Early in November, he rearranged some theatre commands. He appointed a military bureaucrat, Henry Halleck, to command a large "Western Department," consisting of Missouri and the western portion of Kentucky. He created a "Department of the Ohio," comprising eastern Kentucky and all of Tennessee, appointing Don Carlos Buell, an officer who shared a great many of his own personal foibles, to command it. McClellan himself would retain direct command of the Army of the Potomac.

All through November, Lincoln visited McClellan at his headquarters, sharing ideas, encouraging action, and attempting to build up rapport with the "young Napoleon." In mid-November, he tried to get McClellan enthused about a new proposal from the Navy Department to attack New Orleans and move up the Mississippi River. McClellan was not impressed.

Lincoln had some other issues to contend with. It was time for him to write his long annual message to Congress, a message transmitted in writing at the end of the calendar year. As December approached, it was beginning to look as if the war might last a long time. For this reason, the politics of war were changing.

For Lincoln, the outlook was guardedly hopeful as winter arrived. Notwithstanding the bitter disappointment at Manassas, the Confederate menace was preliminarily contained. The British held back from any open or decisive recognition of Confederate independence. The Unionist position in the border states had been slowly but dramatically improving. Bipartisan unity in Congress remained when it came to the issue of the *Union*.

But the slavery issue had caused a clear schism when Republicans had pushed through their confiscation bill on an obvious party-line basis—a bill that Lincoln promptly signed. Lincoln's strategy concerning slavery had been weighing on his mind since summer.

After pondering the matter, Lincoln came to a decision in the closing days of 1861: he would use the Civil War as a fitting and perhaps
providential occasion to launch the second phase of his anti-slavery
strategy. With slavery's *containment* on the way to accomplishment—
and the Republicans in Congress were fully intent upon pushing through
a free-soil measure just as soon as the timing seemed right—perhaps
the *phaseout* of slavery could also be pushed if the president could catalyze the process.

The politics, of course, would be tricky, but perhaps it could be
done through coordinated legislative action at the federal and state
levels. The thirteenth amendment to the Constitution that Congress
had passed that spring—the amendment that would tie the hands of
Congress forever on the subject of slavery within the states—had not
been ratified. And so the coast was clear, at least in legal terms, to
launch a gradual phaseout of slavery, propelled with federal funding.

As historian Allen C. Guelzo has suggested, Lincoln truly believed
"from the first" that he should "not leave office without some form of
legislative emancipation policy in place. By his design, the burden would
have to rest mainly on the state legislatures, largely because Lincoln
mistrusted the federal judiciary and expected that any emancipation
initiatives that came directly from his hand would be struck down in
the courts."[20]

Lincoln secretly drafted some plans in late November for a bill to be
passed by the legislature of Delaware—tiny Delaware, whose Unionist
politics and small population of slaves made it seemingly the perfect
place from which to launch emancipation in the border states. Lincoln's
bill, if adopted by the state of Delaware, would *ask* for congressional
financial assistance to rid the state of slavery. "Be it enacted by the
State of Delaware," Lincoln's draft proclaimed, "that on condition the
United States of America will, at the present session of Congress, engage by law to pay . . . in the six per cent bonds of the said United
States, the sum of seven hundred and nineteen thousand and two hundred dollars, in five equal annual instalments [*sic*], there shall be neither
slavery nor involuntary servitude, at any time after the first day of January in the year of our Lord one thousand, eight hundred and sixty-seven,
within the said State of Delaware. . . ."[21] A second version of the plan
would extend the process over thirty years. Lincoln intended to work
behind the scenes for the Delaware bill as he helped the Republicans

in Congress to be ready for the moment when the state would apply for assistance. He would work both ends of the process simultaneously.

As he drafted these proposals, he put the final touches on his message to Congress, which he sent on December 3. While the message restated some points he had made in July, it included some important new proposals.

Lincoln hurled some new barbs against Confederate autocracy, repeating his earlier warnings that Confederate power was a threat to free government itself, observing that the power of the Southern electorate seemed to be shrinking in Confederate states.[22]

Lincoln spoke once again of the free-labor system as "the just, and generous, and prosperous system, which opens the way to all." Regardless of the rights of capital, he said, human "labor is the superior of capital, and deserves much the higher consideration."[23] Property rights, said Lincoln, flowed directly from the efforts of the people, and were grounded in the aspirations of the people. But Confederates meant to invert this principle and make human rights subservient to property.

The great war to suppress the insurrection, said Lincoln, was proceeding rather well, but coordination was essential. And in that regard, Lincoln mentioned McClellan's new position as general in chief, observing that "the nation seemed to give a unanimous concurrence" to the appointment. And yet he added a statement that seemed to imply that he was hedging his bets about McClellan. There was a saying, said Lincoln, that "one bad general is better than two good ones; and the saying is true, if taken to mean no more than that an army is better directed by a single mind, though inferior, than by two superior ones, at . . . cross-purposes with each other."[24] A curious thing for a commander in chief to observe in a message to Congress—unless the actual purpose was to seed the record with expressions of doubt that might be useful later on if McClellan turned out to be incompetent.

Turning to the slavery issue, Lincoln noted his own strict adherence to the letter of the confiscation law. His behavior had been prudent and legal to a fault: "In considering the policy to be adopted for suppressing the insurrection," he declared, "I have been anxious and careful that the inevitable conflict for this purpose shall not degenerate into a violent and remorseless revolutionary struggle. I have, therefore, in every case, thought it proper to keep the integrity of the Union prominent as the primary object of the contest on our part, leaving all questions which are not of vital military importance to the more deliberate action of the legislature." But then Lincoln made a statement that could plausibly be read as a come-on to fellow Republicans: "If a new law upon the same subject shall be proposed," Lincoln said, "its propriety will be duly considered."[25]

And in that connection, he added, it would probably be best to start planning right away *for the freedom of the confiscated slaves.* The slaves who had been seized by the army since Butler's proclamation were "already dependent on the United States, and must be provided for in some way," Lincoln said. Besides, he continued, it was "not impossible that some of the States will pass similar enactments for their own benefit respectively." Consequently, he continued, "I recommend that Congress provide for accepting such persons from such States, according to some mode of valuation, in lieu, *pro tanto*, of direct taxes, or upon some other plan to be agreed on with such States respectively; that such persons, on acceptance by the general government, be at once deemed free."[26]

"Deemed free." There it was—the thin end of the wedge that would open up a path for emancipation. No mention by Lincoln of the embryonic Delaware plan was included in this message to Congress. He was playing a doubled-handed game.

To appease white supremacist Democrats, not only in Congress, not only in the border states, but also in places such as "Egypt" in southern Illinois, Lincoln quickly endorsed the old colonization approach that would send former slaves to other countries when their freedom was granted. He recommended that "steps be taken for colonizing" contraband slaves "at some place, or places . . . congenial to them," adding that "it might be well to consider, too—whether the free colored people already in the United States could not, so far as individuals may desire, be included in such colonization."[27]

Here again, Lincoln's latter-day critics see a white supremacist at work. But the overall sense of his anti-slavery program makes the allegation weak. Lincoln's motive for colonization—at least until he changed his mind about the subject in 1864—was his fear that racial prejudice would undermine the cause of liberation unless, somehow, the racial issue could be gradually defused. He would make this explicit to a group of black leaders later on. Moreover, his concept of colonization was that of a *voluntary* haven—"so far as individuals may desire," had been his words.

There were even a few black leaders at the time who found the vision attractive, in light of the pervasiveness of American white supremacy—though it has to be admitted that blacks as a rule found the colonization idea to be insulting.[28]

Regardless of its feasibility (an open question), the concept of colonization was an obvious device to defuse white supremacist resistance to emancipation. Pennsylvania Congressman Charles Biddle, for example, confided that the "alarm [about emancipation] would spread to every man of my constituents who loves his country and his race if the public mind was not lulled and put to sleep with the word 'colonization.'"[29]

Lincoln's phaseout strategy for slavery was launched in December 1861. And he would push the experiment hard. He concluded his annual message by observing that "the struggle of today, is not altogether for today" but "for a vast future also."[30]

Congressional Republicans were suitably emboldened in December: they showed new strength by reversing their previous action on the Crittenden-Johnson Resolutions, which protected slavery. Fifty-three Republican congressmen changed their position when the issue came up in December. And so the Crittenden-Johnson Resolutions were repealed, and it was no longer possible for anyone to say how far or how fast the anti-slavery cause might propel the next actions of Republicans.

LINCOLN TOOK SOME UNPRECEDENTED ACTIONS to extend his anti-slavery program during the first six months of 1862. And he became more demanding of his generals.

The new year of 1862 dawned angrily and bitterly in Washington. The Army of the Potomac was still on the sidelines, and no one could predict when it would move. Indeed, the war seemed almost at a standstill. Early in December, McClellan came down with typhoid fever and was bed-ridden. Lincoln was left uninformed as to what (if anything) McClellan had been doing to stimulate coordinated action in the other military theatres. At this point, as T. Harry Williams has observed, Lincoln "took over the function of general in chief" until McClellan recovered.[31]

Lincoln wrote to Halleck and Buell, the two western commanders, asking questions and urging action.[32] Buell replied that he could not be optimistic in regard to ambitious attacks in the near future. Lincoln wrote that he was deeply disappointed; he instructed Buell and Halleck to "name as early a day as you safely can, on, or before which you can be ready to move Southward. . . ."[33]

Neither man complied. Indeed, Halleck told Lincoln he was not in a position to commence any action that would really be of benefit to Buell. Lincoln sent off a copy of the message from Halleck to the secretary of war, observing that in Halleck's department, "as everywhere else, nothing can be done."[34]

The secretary of war, Simon Cameron, was another of Lincoln's problems. Cameron was coming under fire by critics who accused him of financial and political impropriety, perhaps to the point of real crookedness. He had also been issuing statements on the slavery issue that were totally at odds with the statements of Lincoln.

Lincoln decided to ease him out of office, and appointed him Minister to Russia. To succeed Cameron, Lincoln promoted the chief legal advisor for the War Department, an attorney named Edwin M. Stanton. Stanton was a Unionist Democrat who had served for a time as attorney general under President James Buchanan—hardly a service to commend him in the eyes of Lincoln. Even earlier than that, he had clashed with Lincoln in a bitter courtroom battle. But Lincoln looked beyond these negative factors, perceiving all the benefits that Stanton could bring to the executive branch: a militant Unionist, Stanton was extremely intelligent and also familiar with the War Department's routine.

Stanton would become a very useful advisor to Lincoln, much as William H. Seward, notwithstanding his earlier lapses, began to be useful to Lincoln in a great many ways when he learned that the president was fully intent upon running his own administration.

As Lincoln made arrangements to remove Simon Cameron, he met with selected generals to get their advice and work around the absent McClellan. By January 13, McClellan was well enough—indeed, he was angry enough when he heard about these meetings behind his back—to attend a council of war with other generals, members of the cabinet, and Lincoln.

McClellan's behavior at this meeting was sulky and disdainful. He said his plans for Virginia were not quite ready, and he had no intention of revealing them unless Lincoln ordered him to do it. But he did acquiesce in the proposition that the forces of Buell should be goaded into action.

On the same day, Lincoln seized the opportunity of writing to Buell for the purpose of offering "encouragement," along with some pointed strategic advice. He sent a copy of this letter to Halleck. He said his "general idea of this war," his grand vision of the gatherings of force that were currently in play on the battlefield, was his insight that "we have the *greater* numbers, and the enemy has the *greater* facility of concentrating forces upon points of collision." Consequently, the Union "must fail . . . unless we can find some way of making *our* advantage an over-match for *his*." The way to do this, Lincoln suggested, was "by menacing him with superior forces at *different* points, at the *same* time; so that we can safely attack, one, or both, if he makes no change; and if he *weakens* one to *strengthen* the other, forbear to attack the strengthened one, but seize, and hold the weakened one."[35] In other words, Lincoln was telling his generals to stretch out the enemy's forces as thin as they could and then smash their way through the weakest point in the enemy's lines.

Though Lincoln was preoccupied with military matters in January 1862, his attention to the slavery issue was keen. Abolitionists and Radical Republicans were much more demanding. Around January 20, two anti-slavery leaders paid a call on Lincoln at the White House. One of them—an abolitionist Virginian named Moncure Daniel Conway—wrote a long account of the meeting years later when he published his memoirs. The account is both convincing and instructive.

Conway was joined at the meeting by William Ellery Channing, a nephew of the great Unitarian clergyman of the same name. Their purpose in meeting with Lincoln was to push him toward emancipation. What Lincoln allegedly revealed to them was extraordinary.

In Conway's account, Channing opened the discussion by declaring "his belief that the opportunity of the nation to rid itself of slavery had arrived." Lincoln responded by asking, "how he thought they might avail themselves of it. . . . Channing suggested emancipation with compensation for the slaves." Lincoln "said he had for years been in favour of that plan."

Then, wrote Conway, "when the President turned to me, I asked whether we might not look to him as the coming Deliverer of the Nation from its one great evil. . . . He said, 'Perhaps we may be better able to do something in that direction after a while than we are now.'"

Conway pressed the point harder. He asked Lincoln whether "the masses of the American people would hail you as their deliverer if, at the end of this war, the Union should be surviving and slavery still in it?'" Yes, said Lincoln, "if they were to see that slavery was on the downhill."

Conway would not let up: he told Lincoln that "our fathers compromised with slavery because they thought it on the downhill; hence war to-day." At this point Lincoln confided some strategic ploys in a manner that deserves a full quotation:

> "I think the country grows in this direction daily, and I am not without hope that something of the desire of you and your friends may be accomplished. Perhaps it may be in the way suggested by a thirsty soul in Maine who found he could only get liquor from a druggist; as his robust appearance forebade the plea of sickness, he called for a soda, and whispered, 'Couldn't you put a drop o' the creeter into it unbeknownst to yourself?'" Turning to me the President said, "In working in the antislavery movement you may naturally come in contact with a great many people who agree with you, and possibly may overestimate the number in the country who hold such views. But the position in which I am placed brings me into some knowledge of opinions in all parts of the country and of many different kinds of people; and it appears to me that the great masses of this country care comparatively little about the negro, and are anxious only for military successes." We had, I think, risen to leave and had thanked him for his friendly reception when he said, "We shall need all the anti-slavery feeling in the country, and more; you can go home and try to bring the people to your views; and you may say anything you like about me, if that will help. Don't spare me!" This was said with a laugh. Then he said very gravely, "When the hour comes for dealing with slavery I trust I will be willing to do my duty though it cost my life. And, gentlemen, lives will be lost."[36]

"You may say anything you like about me, if that will help. Don't spare me!" How often in American politics have we seen a president encouraging others to besmirch his own reputation—to call him names, when it came right down to it—to increase public pressure for actions that he secretly favored but could not yet espouse? Where else in American history does such a remarkable spectacle present itself?

Until public sentiment was ready, Lincoln hinted, he would work toward emancipation by phasing it in, through deception if he felt that it was needed. He would play the role of a *Unionist only* and expand his agenda by cunning, like the druggist who connived to spike a soda for his friend in Maine—"unbeknownst to himself."

This account suggests that Lincoln envisioned his work with abolitionist militants as something of a *synergistic* process. His strategy amounted to an insider/outsider orchestration, with the "outsider" militants building up pressure in a manner that the wily "insider" used. Consider this scenario in light of the account set forth by Senator

Charles Sumner—a Radical Republican who came to believe in Lincoln's judgment—in regard to a meeting with Lincoln in December 1861. Sumner's purpose was very much the same as Conway and Channing's: to push for emancipation measures. According to Sumner, Lincoln told him that their only major difference when it came to the subject was the difference of "a month or six weeks."[37] He was probably alluding to his secret Delaware plan.

On the military front, Lincoln's patience with McClellan was slipping. On January 27 he issued an order designed to be as simple and clear as he could make it, beginning with its title, "President's General War Order No. 1." He commanded a "general movement of the Land and Naval forces of the United States" no later than "the 22nd day of February, 1862."[38]

It worked: at last McClellan unveiled his big scheme for Virginia when the Lincoln orders forced his hand. And in the Western Department, the bureaucratic Halleck permitted a subordinate, Ulysses S. Grant, to attack the Confederates.

The Confederates had been establishing a line in Kentucky with a fallback line to protect Tennessee. In February, Grant destroyed this fallback line; he attacked the Confederate defenses, moving up the Tennessee River with gunboats, attacking the Confederate bastion Fort Henry on February 6. Having captured Fort Henry, Grant moved up the Cumberland River and attacked Fort Donelson, which likewise surrendered to his forces on February 16. With the fall of Forts Henry and Donelson, the rebels' position fell apart. They withdrew not only from Kentucky but also from most of Tennessee and then fled to Mississippi.

In the East, it was a different story. McClellan decided it was time to reveal his grand design, and he did, first to Stanton and then to Lincoln. His plan was to execute a flanking maneuver, to bypass the rebels at Manassas by sending his army on boats down the Chesapeake Bay and then landing his men *in between* the rebel forces at Manassas and the city of Richmond. He would flush the Confederates out of Manassas by threatening their capital city. He proposed to land his army at Urbana, Virginia, on the Rappahannock River.

Lincoln didn't like the scheme at all. He was worried that the plan would leave Washington defenseless, that a gap in the Federal lines would be opened that would give the Confederates a chance to strike at Washington before McClellan hit Richmond. He thought that an overland attack against Manassas would be safer, since it would permit McClellan to switch back and forth from offensive to defensive measures if necessary.

McClellan begged for a chance to make a case for his plan, and Lincoln agreed. But on February 3, Lincoln dashed off a letter to McClellan with a series of questions. "If you will give me satisfactory answers," he told McClellan, "I shall gladly yield my plan to yours." The last of Lincoln's questions was a worst-case contingency issue: "In case of disaster," Lincoln wrote, "would not a safe retreat be more difficult by your plan than by mine?"[39]

McClellan defended his plan in a lengthy report that he sent via Stanton to Lincoln.[40] And so, with tremendous misgivings, Lincoln gave him a preliminary go-ahead. There is very little doubt that in the next six months Lincoln came to regret this decision. But he had no intention of allowing McClellan to behave as if he had a blank check. Indeed, Lincoln supervised the planning for the whole operation.

In February, Lincoln was preoccupied with several other issues, not least of all the fast-breaking action in the West. In addition, two depressing developments haunted him, one of them profoundly disappointing and the other one deeply tragic. In the first place, his Delaware plan was going nowhere. In the second place, on February 20, the Lincolns' next-to-youngest child, William Wallace Lincoln ("Willie") took sick and then died of a fever.

Mary Todd Lincoln was hysterical with grief and the president was terribly shaken. Of all the Lincoln children, young Willie was the closest to Lincoln himself in his personal qualities. Though a number of men who were near and dear to the Lincolns had been perishing in battle, the death of little Willie was a foretaste of all the morbid feelings and events that were soon to engulf both Lincoln and the nation in 1862 and beyond.

Early in March, Lincoln felt a greater urgency than ever on the slavery front. He had to prove to himself that his vision—his long-cherished vision of the gradual phaseout of slavery—would come into being. The emotional imperative was nothing less than this: he had to *force* the great vision into being.

His attempt to begin indirectly was a failure: even Delaware was too far-gone in the ways of the slavery system for hints or behind-the-scene promptings to have an effect. But what if a direct legislative approach by Congress—a direct and official offer of federal funding—could be put on the table? As long as it was framed as a measure to suppress the insurrection, such a measure might withstand the resistance of bigots.

On March 6, Lincoln sent Congress an unprecedented presidential message recommending "a Joint Resolution . . . as follows: 'Resolved that the United States ought to co-operate with any state which may adopt gradual abolishment of slavery, giving to such state pecuniary aid, to be used by such state in it's [*sic*] discretion. . . .'" Lincoln said that such a measure could weaken the Confederate rebellion: it could sever the link between the slave-holding border states and the cotton-belt states that comprised the Confederate nucleus. "The point is not that *all* the states tolerating slavery would very soon, if at all, initiate emancipation," Lincoln said. Yet the process of offering the deal to all the slave states could start a great chain reaction that could split the Southern bloc in two.

"While the offer is equally made to all," explained Lincoln, "the more Northern [of the slave states] shall, by such initiation, make it certain to the more Southern, that in no event, will the former join the latter, in their proposed confederacy." Why should states that were phasing out slavery attempt to secede?

The cost of the plan, said Lincoln, was an issue of money well spent: "In the mere financial or pecuniary view," he argued, "any member of Congress, with the census-tables and Treasury-reports before him, can readily see for himself how very soon the current expenditures of this war would purchase, at fair valuation, all the slaves in any named State."

Lincoln stressed that the plan should be "a matter of perfectly free choice." The decision would remain with the voters in each of the slave states, Lincoln insisted. But he warned that if rebel resistance should continue, "the war must also continue; and it is impossible to foresee all the incidents, which may attend and the ruin which may follow it." In other words, Lincoln was telling the supporters of slavery to take up his offer while it lasted, since sterner measures might follow. In view of "my great responsibility to my God, and to my country," Lincoln said in his conclusion, "I earnestly beg the attention of Congress and the people to the subject."[41]

Three days later, Lincoln dashed off a private letter to the editor of the *New York Times* pointing out that "one half-day's cost of this war would pay for all the slaves in Delaware, at four hundred dollars per head." Indeed, "eighty-seven days cost of this war would pay for all in Delaware, Maryland, District of Columbia, Kentucky, and Missouri at the same price."[42]

The Republicans in Congress proceeded to pass this measure in a near-straight party-line vote. But many Democrats denounced the very concept of "taxes to buy negroes." A new slogan in the North began to make the rounds of white supremacist Democrats: "The Constitution as it is and the Union as it was."

On March 13, the Republicans in Congress passed another anti-slavery measure. It forbade Union military men from returning any slaves who had crossed Union lines. Lincoln signed the new bill into law.

As all of these events unfolded in March, Lincoln's doubts about McClellan kept nagging him. He issued new orders on March 8 to the effect that the Army of the Potomac should not make a move "without leaving in, and about Washington, such a force as, in the opinion of the General-in-chief, and the commanders of all the Army corps, shall leave said City entirely secure."[43]

On the following day, the Confederates forces at Manassas abandoned their position and relocated farther south. This movement was fatal to McClellan's existing plans: the Confederates had moved too close to Urbana for his army to take them by surprise or to get between them and Richmond.

Lincoln seized the opportunity to cut back McClellan's authority: considering the work that was in store for him, Lincoln said, it was fitting to relieve him from his duties as general in chief so he could turn his mind wholly to Virginia. Lincoln did this on March 11.

Lincoln also consolidated the western armies in a new and greatly expanded "Department of the Mississippi," to be commanded by Halleck. Moreover, he created a "Mountain Department" in the Appalachians from western Virginia to the uplands of Unionist East Tennessee, which were still in Confederate hands. At the behest of some powerful congressional Republicans, Lincoln guardedly agreed to give Frémont a chance to redeem himself in this theatre and win a victory. The position of "general in chief" was left vacant for the time being.

While McClellan was chagrined by his demotion, he was all the more determined to revive his Virginia scheme and thus prove himself. So he shifted his landing point southward: his army, he decided, could be landed at Fortress Monroe at the tip of the peninsula created by the York and James Rivers. He would then proceed to take Richmond and end the war.

On March 13, he persuaded his subordinate commanders to endorse this scheme, which he promptly dispatched to Stanton. Lincoln approved it, with some new stipulations, and at last McClellan was ready: his troops began departing on March 17 and McClellan embarked for the peninsula on April 1.

As he left, he sent a letter to the War Department explaining the deployment of his troops. But as McClellan and his army sailed down the Potomac, a furor was developing in Washington: it seemed that McClellan had made some mistakes, or had juggled some numbers, in reporting on the troop deployments. Lincoln and others were worried that the troops who were left in the Washington defense perimeter were far too few. Indeed, the commander of the Washington defenses said as much to the secretary of war. So Lincoln held back a large number of troops—a corps of over thirty thousand commanded by General Irvin McDowell—in the first week of April.

As McClellan's campaign was launched, there were very few people who imagined that the war was approaching a horrific new crisis: that murderous battles would soon be unleashed that would surpass any previous slaughters in American history.

In the western theatre, the armies of Grant and Buell were pursuing the Confederate troops who had fled to Mississippi. Then on April 6, at the crack of dawn, an audacious Confederate counterattack was unleashed against Grant's army at a place called Shiloh Church near the southern Tennessee border. On the first day of battle, the Confederates seemed to be winning. But their commander, General Albert Sidney Johnston, was killed in action. On the second day, Grant succeeded in pushing the Confederates back with assistance from reinforcements he received overnight from Buell.

The fighting at Shiloh was savage; moreover, the death toll was staggering compared to the experience of 1861. The political and personal shock effects of this carnage began to change the atmosphere and politics of war both in Washington and Richmond. The Confederates were prompted to initiate a military draft, and the Union did the same thing a few months later—though the federal draft would be deferred in its direct operations until 1863.

The battle of Shiloh threw a cloud over Grant's reputation that would last for the better part of a year. It almost looked for a while as if Grant were another false hope—another "flash in the pan" whose beginner's luck had run out.

But Union victories resumed in the West. Some Union forces commanded by General John Pope put a major Confederate fortification on the Mississippi River near the border of Kentucky and Tennessee—Island # 10—out of action on the day after Shiloh.

Then, at the end of April, a combined sea-and-land operation carried out by Admiral David Farragut and General Benjamin Butler ventured up the Mississippi River and seized New Orleans. Farragut continued up the river: he captured Baton Rouge, the Louisiana capital, and occupied Natchez. The Confederates' position in the West was unraveling quickly.

In the East, however, it was merely the same old story. As McClellan got ready for his march upon Richmond, his forces at the edge of the Virginia peninsula confronted some Confederate troops who were waiting in the fortifications of Yorktown. The Confederates, commanded by General John B. Magruder, numbered only seventeen thousand. McClellan's own troop strength was somewhere in the eighty- to ninety-thousand range. But he believed himself vastly outnumbered and concluded that a frontal attack on the Confederate position would be suicide.

Lincoln wrote to McClellan on April 6; he told him that in light of the fact that he was currently supplied with "over one hundred thousand troops . . . I think you had better break the enemies' line from York-town to Warwick River, at once. They will probably use *time*, as advantageously as you can."[44]

Three days later Lincoln urged McClellan once again to attack the enemy quickly. This is "the precise time for you to strike a blow," Lincoln said. "By delay the enemy will relatively gain upon you—that is, he will gain faster, by *fortifications* and *re-inforcements*, than you can by re-inforcements alone." The enemy had to be attacked, Lincoln said, and it was no good trying to evade that fact by maneuvering to stave off a battle. "Going down the Bay in search of a field, instead of fighting at or near Manassas," said Lincoln, "was only shifting, and not surmounting, a difficulty. . . . The country will not fail to note—is now noting—that the present hesitation to move forward upon an intrenched enemy, is but the story of Manassas repeated."[45]

Lincoln was also disturbed at the time by the fact that the border-state initiative for phasing out slavery was facing resistance. Political reactions from the border-state leaders had been sullen and defiant. In contrast, Republicans in Congress took another step against slavery. They passed a new law to abolish it forever in Washington, D.C., with provision to compensate the owners and to set aside funds for the purpose of colonization, as Lincoln recommended. Lincoln signed this new anti-slavery measure on April 16.

At the end of the month, the great army of McClellan remained inactive. Lincoln was very angry: on May 1, he wrote that a request by McClellan for some more heavy siege guns "argues indefinite procrastination. Is anything to be done?"[46]

Something was done: the Confederates abandoned their Yorktown position on May 3 and withdrew their forces to Richmond, where General Joseph Johnston was preparing a last-ditch defense of the city. To stiffen the resolve of McClellan, Lincoln worked up a plan to send McDowell's corps to the vicinity of Richmond by land, thus achieving two goals: reinforcing McClellan while positioning McDowell and his men to be available to fend off Confederate attacks upon Washington, if any should develop.[47]

But Confederate authorities in Richmond ordered Stonewall Jackson to stir up some trouble in the Shenandoah Valley, and the onset of Jackson's Valley campaign made a mess of these plans for McDowell. This campaign, which commenced on May 8 and concluded on June 9, was a *tour de force*. In lightning-fast moves, Jackson fell upon the Union forces in the area commanded by Frémont and also by Nathaniel Banks (another political general), prompting Lincoln to re-route McDowell and his men to assist in the fighting.

Lincoln's purpose, however, was more than defensive: what he wanted was to use his military forces to converge upon Jackson and *destroy* him. Accordingly, he goaded his generals and urged them on by telegraph. On May 24, he cabled Frémont to "put the utmost speed into it. Do not lose a minute."[48] He also goaded McClellan. When it looked as if Jackson might cross the Potomac, Lincoln telegraphed McClellan that "the time is near when you must either attack Richmond or give up the job and come to the defense of Washington. Let me hear from you instantly."[49]

Jackson, however, kept his forces in Virginia, so Lincoln kept working to trap him. On May 30 he demanded of Frémont, "Where *is* your force? You ought this minute to be near Strasburg. Answer at once."[50]

In the meantime, Confederate authorities decided to throw the full weight of their Richmond troops against McClellan. On May 31, the Confederate forces in Richmond under General Joseph Johnston lashed out against McClellan and his army. The result was the two-day battle of Fair Oaks or Seven Pines: a tactical standoff. But McClellan was sickened by the gore of this battle and his weakness on the field increased. The Confederate result was different: Joseph Johnston, the Confederate commander, was wounded and had to be replaced. His replacement was Robert E. Lee.

Lincoln's faith in his Virginia commanders—such as it was—was nearly gone by the middle of June. He had given up hope of catching Jackson and his army when Frémont, McDowell, and Banks were so maddeningly slow. His disgust with his Virginia commanders was prompting him to look for replacements. Perhaps it was time to transfer a western commander to Virginia—time to summon a real fighting general and give him a chance to get Virginia under control. Grant's reputation was under a cloud, but there remained the Union general who captured a fortified island: John Pope.

McClellan continued to reiterate his call for reinforcements. He warned Lincoln that the grim responsibility of "saving" his army should "rest where it belongs," in Washington.[51]

Why, one is tempted to ask at this point, did Lincoln tolerate this behavior? It was clear to many members of Congress, as well as to the greater part of the Lincoln inner circle, that McClellan was a prima donna. Even Stanton, who at first was on the friendliest of terms with McClellan, was beginning to loathe him. Why did Lincoln keep him in command?

It seems likely that Lincoln had little intention of retaining McClellan much longer. Yet Lincoln, after all, had been "burned" already by promoting some generals who looked like winners at first but revealed fatal weaknesses later. McClellan himself was such a man, and it appeared that Grant could be another. Lincoln was bringing John Pope to Virginia, but time—and time alone—would determine whether Pope should replace McClellan.

On June 26, Lincoln issued an order consolidating all "the forces under Major Generals Frémont, Banks, and McDowell" into "one army, to be called the Army of Virginia." The command of this army was "specially assigned to Major General John Pope." The Army of Virginia would proceed to "attack and overcome the rebel forces under

Jackson and Ewell, threaten the enemy in the direction of Charlottes-
ville, and render the most effective aid to relieve General McClellan
and capture Richmond."[52]

On June 26, Lee was ready for another attack: he unleashed a tremendous assault upon McClellan. Lee's forces were approximately
ninety thousand strong, with McClellan's in the one hundred thousand range. But McClellan believed that he was vastly outnumbered,
and he panicked as the onslaught grew. In a series of attacks—known
forever after as the "Seven Days Battles"—Lee hurled his forces at
McClellan. In every battle but one (Gaines's Mill), Lee's attacks were
repulsed with heavy losses. Yet McClellan proceeded to retreat. He
dashed off a cable to Stanton proclaiming, "I have lost this battle because my force was too small. . . . The government must not and cannot hold me responsible for the result. . . . If I save this army now, I tell
you plainly that I owe no thanks to you or to any other person in Washington. You have done your best to sacrifice this army."[53]

Lee hammered at McClellan's men: he drove them ever farther from
Richmond. Yet at Malvern Hill, Lee's forces were savaged by the broad-
sides of Union artillery. Malvern Hill was a major Union victory, a victory that could have been decisive. But McClellan refused to follow up.

In the midst of this fighting, Lincoln came to a major decision: he
had to issue another call for troops. If McClellan really faced a gigantic
Confederate army, it was time to do some worst-case analysis. Lincoln
drafted a letter to be carried by Secretary Seward to a meeting of Union
governors; he stated in the letter that the enemy had concentrated "too
much force in Richmond for McClellan to successfully attack."

The best course of action, he said, "is to hold what we have in the
West, open the Mississippi, and, take Chatanooga [sic] and East Tennessee, without more." Then, "let the country give us a hundred thousand new troops in the shortest possible time, which added to McClellan
. . . will take Richmond, without endangering any other place which
we now hold—and will substantially end the war."[54] When Seward
reported to Lincoln that the governors were behind him, Lincoln tripled
his call for volunteers: he sent out a volunteer call for another *three
hundred thousand* troops on July 1.

All the while, he was working on the slavery issue. He was pushing,
pleading, and cajoling the border-state leaders to assist him with the
great second phase of his anti-slavery program. When another Union
general muddied the waters for Lincoln by issuing an anti-slavery proc-

lamation, Lincoln stopped him. General David Hunter had proclaimed emancipation in Georgia, Florida, and South Carolina on May 9; his anti-slavery proclamation had been issued from his base in the Sea Islands off the coast.

Ten days later, Lincoln countermanded this order, observing that the question of "whether it be competent for me, as Commander-in-Chief of the Army and Navy, to declare the Slaves of any state or states, free, and whether at any time, in any case, it shall have become a necessity indispensable to the maintenance of the government, to exercise such supposed power, are questions which . . . I reserve to myself." Between the lines of this message was a big revelation: Lincoln at last might be willing to consider some direct form of presidential action that would strike at slavery.

In the same proclamation, Lincoln added an "appeal" to the leaders of the border states. "I beseech you," Lincoln said, to consider the financial offer that Congress extended in March. "You can not if you would," he argued, "be blind to the signs of the times. . . . This proposal makes common cause for a common object, casting no reproaches on any. It acts not the pharisee. The change it contemplates would come gently as the dews of heaven, not rending or wrecking anything. Will you not embrace it? . . . May the vast future not have to lament that you have neglected it."[55] But they *did* neglect it.

Conversely, the Republicans in Congress passed more anti-slavery laws: in June, the congressional Republicans enacted a free-soil measure barring slavery from federal lands. Moreover, on June 7, the Republican Congress passed a law for the collection of taxes in rebel states, with the stipulation of a lien on the physical property of rebel tax dodgers. Then, the congressional Republicans drafted a stronger confiscation act, as Lincoln had invited them to do in his annual message of December 1861. This act was designed to give freedom to the contraband slaves under certain conditions.

Lincoln's thoughts about the slavery issue were expanding—expanding from the ethical plane to the frankly religious realm. Lincoln was a scoffer in his youth: he had ridiculed the Bible as a hodge-podge of myths.[56] Nonetheless, in the 1850s he had used a number of quotations from Scripture as he sought to express his position on the slavery issue in the language of the golden rule.

Then, after Willie's death, he found himself turning to Scripture more often, not only to console his wife, who in the deepest phase of her depression had locked herself in her room for a great many days, but also to console himself.

In addition, the cost of this war, the great toll in human life that was constantly forced upon Lincoln by the death of his friends—Elmer Ephraim Ellsworth, for instance, who had worked with Lincoln in his law office back in Springfield, and Edward Baker, who had served with Lincoln in the Illinois legislature many years earlier (both of whom were killed in Virginia)—played over his mind as he ordered his generals to *fight* the Confederates, to overcome squeamishness, to smash and annihilate the armies of the rebels—to deal out death without mercy.

He thought about the flickering and transient nature of our life: about the "passing speck of time" he had been given. The enormity of thoughts such as these began to move his vision in a starkly Old Testament direction. In June, he responded to a visit by some anti-slavery leaders who hoped that he "might, under divine guidance, be led to free the slaves." Lincoln told them "he had sometime thought that perhaps he might be an instrument in God's hands" and was "not unwilling to be."[57]

His great purpose in life became clear in the 1850s: he would dedicate himself and his political talents to the gradual elimination of slavery. When his policies had triggered secession, then the fight to save the Union was *added*. To this work in its totality he swore to dedicate his life.

In appealing for hundreds of thousands of additional troops, Lincoln pledged to "maintain this contest until successful, or till I die, or am conquered, or my term expires, or Congress or the country forsakes me. . . ."[58]

Until he died—or was "conquered" or forsaken by the country. What would happen if one (or more) of these gloomy latter visions came to pass? What would happen, for example, if Lincoln should die, by assassination or by illness? His vice president, Hannibal Hamlin, would be forced to cope with the terrible crisis of the nation as best he could.

What would happen if the Union should lose? A successful Confederate republic of slave states would then be positioned for a wave of aggressive conquest. The "golden circle" of white supremacist rule in Latin America could be the result.

What would happen if Lincoln's support in the Northern states were to plummet—what would happen, indeed, if he were voted out of office in the next presidential election? Would the backlash against him be sufficiently great as to wreck the Republican Party, at least for a while? Would the Democrats be willing to terminate the war and then patch things up with the South? Would this development set back the anti-slavery movement for decades on end?

He had vowed to "maintain this contest until successful, or till I die." But could he contemplate the prospect of death without knowing for certain that his country was safely on the proper course for the eventual phaseout of slavery? If his strategy were not in the cards—if the border-state leaders refused to listen to his pleading—then perhaps it would be time for something drastic.

He would make a last appeal to the border states. He would make a final effort on behalf of his gradual plan. But if the border-state leaders continued to be willfully obstinate—if it proved to be impossible for Lincoln to *pay* them to do the right thing—then he would start to handle matters very differently. He would make the great decision very quickly in the month of July.

LINCOLN'S ANTI-SLAVERY STRATEGY would reach the point of radical measures as the second year of war continued. In the summer, he decided on a short-term gamble of extraordinary scope: he would start to free the slaves of the rebels.

Charles Sumner, the Radical Republican senator, was urging Lincoln on. The Union should proceed to attack the real source of the rebellion, he advised the president: put the axe to the root and strike directly at the evil of slavery, Sumner urged.

For months, certain Radical Republicans had argued, in Congress and elsewhere, a case for the war that was profoundly different from Lincoln's. In February 1862, Sumner introduced in the Senate a series of resolutions on the status of the rebel states. In contrast to Lincoln's assertion that the so-called Confederate states were still functional units of the nation (albeit under temporary criminal rule until secessionist treason could be crushed), Sumner, Thaddeus Stevens, and a number of others in the Radical camp began claiming that the rebel states were no longer real states at all: by dint of their treason, the Radicals argued, these Southern jurisdictions had committed a kind of "state suicide." Such states had reverted to the status of federal territories. They were soon to be conquered provinces—richly deserving of whatever new rules the Republican majority in Congress might impose for their political and social reconstruction. Emancipation was just the beginning.[59]

This impatient agenda caused a number of the Radicals to speak in rather hostile or even contemptuous terms when it came to Lincoln's incremental methods. But Sumner, in particular, was firmly convinced that Lincoln's strategy was good for their own. In a letter to a Radical Republican colleague (whose name was deleted from the published correspondence), Sumner claimed that the president agreed with the Radicals on many fundamental issues. He revealed, moreover, he had met with the president on numerous occasions for behind-the-scenes talks at the White House.

Consequently, he told his correspondent on June 5, 1862, "your criticism of the President" was altogether "hasty." If you knew the president, Sumner continued, "you would feel the sincerity of his purpose to do what he can to carry forward the principles of the Declaration of Independence," a course that in Lincoln's estimation "promised the sure end of slavery." In Sumner's opinion, Lincoln's strategy was well worth pursuing. In fact, his invitation to the border states to initiate a gradual emancipation program was a wedge in the door for the anti-slavery movement. Importantly, Sumner himself had once suggested a financial phaseout program for slavery and still supported the concept: "To me, who had already proposed a Bridge of Gold for the retreating Fiend," he explained, the proposal of Lincoln was "welcome." Indeed, "proceeding from the President, it must take its place among the great events of history."

Sumner told his colleague to reflect upon everything that Lincoln had "done in a brief period," and then, "from the past," go on to "discern the sure promise of the future." "If you knew the President," Sumner admonished in closing, you would surely "be grateful that he is so true to all you have at heart."[60]

A month later, however, on the Fourth of July, Sumner called upon Lincoln and told him it was time to escalate his strategy: time to issue a strong presidential decree that would strike at the institution of slavery for military reasons. "You need more men," Sumner told the president, "not only at the North, but at the South, in the rear of the Rebels: you need the slaves." Lincoln told his supporter he was deeply concerned about the backlash that such a decree could provoke: "half the officers would fling down their arms and three more States would rise," Lincoln told the senator.[61]

Perhaps Sumner could sense that the president was secretly receptive to what he was suggesting, as indeed Lincoln was. Yet the president continued to be wary of a white supremacist backlash that, in the event of a worst-case political scenario—defeat on the battlefield, foreign intervention, electoral revolt in the North—could destroy almost everything that Lincoln had achieved thus far.

So he resolved to try again to convince the border-state leaders to go along with his gradual liberation plan. At the same time, of course, he would have to keep his mind almost constantly engaged with the ongoing military challenge.

On July 1, Lincoln issued his call for three hundred thousand more troops. Two days later, McClellan demanded fifty thousand reinforcements—as a minimal condition for resuming the battle with Lee. He later raised that number to one hundred thousand more troops.

Such demands were impossible to meet in the short run: reinforcements on the order that McClellan was demanding could not be delivered for months. Though a large new recruiting drive was getting started in the North—an abolitionist named James S. Gibbons had written a patriotic poem (to be set to music later on by composers such as Stephen Foster) entitled, "We are Coming, Father Abraham, Three Hundred Thousand More"—the lead time for training new recruits would remain considerable.

On July 17, Congress strengthened Lincoln's hand by passing the Militia Act. This law permitted the Department of War to set recruiting quotas for the states. If the states were unable to meet these quotas, a "militia draft" would be created by the federal government.

And yet the troops were only part of the problem. As Commander-in-Chief, Lincoln had to decide how to *use* the new troops, in Virginia most of all. He had to decide what to do about McClellan and his army, at least until General Pope had been tested in battle.

On July 7, Lincoln traveled to McClellan's new James River base at Harrison's Landing near Richmond to inspect his army. As Lincoln departed, he was handed a letter by McClellan. This letter contained some outspoken political advice: ignore the Radical Republicans, McClellan recommended, and keep the emancipation issue out of the war. Lincoln thanked McClellan and left without further comment.

As soon as he returned to Washington, Lincoln summoned Henry Halleck, the theatre commander whose armies had won the big victories out West. Lincoln had decided to elevate this theatre commander to the post of general in chief. He did this upon the strong recommendation of the secretary of war. On July 11, Lincoln ordered Halleck to Washington.

On the very next day, Lincoln turned his attention to the slavery issue again. He met with over two-dozen border-state leaders, imploring them to take up the government's offer of assistance with the gradual phaseout of slavery. "Let the states which are in rebellion see," he told them, "that, in no event, will the states you represent ever join their proposed Confederacy." It was time, Lincoln said, to break the lever of power that the rebels can use in your states: "Break that lever before their faces, and they can shake you no more forever."

After all, Lincoln warned them, the war itself might destroy the institution of slavery through "friction and abrasion—by the mere incidents of war." If so, he suggested, then the capital investment in slaves would be "gone, and you will have nothing valuable in lieu of it." Already, he continued, the pressure to emancipate was strong; by rescinding the orders of General Hunter in May, he confided, "I gave dissatisfaction, if not offense, to many whose support the country cannot afford to lose. And this is not the end of it. The pressure, in this direction, is still upon me, and is increasing."

Therefore, seize the moment, Lincoln told them: it could all be easy in light of the fact that there was "room in South America for colonization." Moreover, "the freed people will not be so reluctant to go" when their "numbers shall be large enough to be company and encouragement for one another."[62] Once again, however, the border-state leaders turned him down.

So he made the great decision at last—the decision to liberate. His feelings at the moment are all too easy to imagine. In all likelihood, the president was angry, supremely angry.

The sheer moral banality of slave owners, coupled with the escalating battlefield carnage, prompted him to raise the moral stakes for which so many lives were being lost. If even the offer of money made no impression on slave owners, so much the worse for them.

The next afternoon, in the course of a carriage ride with William H. Seward and Gideon Welles, Lincoln told the two cabinet members he would issue a decree against slavery in all of the rebellious states. He would do it for military reasons.[63]

This was *not*, however, a decision to abandon his voluntary method in the border states: a decree that was aimed at the slaves of the Confederates could never apply in any slave states fighting for the Union.

So Lincoln kept his offer wide open: indeed, on July 14, he sent Congress a bill that contained a more specific new method for its implementation.

But his secret new decision was a radical addition to his plans. His whole *modus operandi* would be changed: in light of his earlier objection to the notion that he (or any president) should "seize and exercise the permanent legislative functions of the government," as he put it in his letter to Browning, his new decision took him straight to the brink of a political and personal Rubicon.

To be sure, he was counting on some new legislative authority as "cover" for his move: he was writing the decree to be viewed as an *enforcement measure* that he meant to be related—at least in the public mind—to the new and more powerful confiscation act that congressional Republicans were drafting.

The decision by Lincoln in July was important for another reason: it amounted to a mid-course correction in his overall emancipation strategy, a *drastic* correction. His preliminary plan had been to use the border states to demonstrate his program, while hoping their achievement in phasing out slavery would serve as a model for the rebel states later.

Lincoln's choice in July was to reverse this sequence: the *rebel* states would now commence the emancipation process, under federal coercion.

The new confiscation act, which reached Lincoln's desk on July 14, made provision for the permanent forfeiture of property, including, most importantly, the slaves of the rebel traitors. Lincoln read this bill over carefully, and then, on July 17, drafted a long message to Congress on the constitutional issues pertaining to it.

In the message that he sent to the Congress, he made a number of important suggestions for strengthening the bill. For example, he identified a serious problem in the portions of the act that provided for the liberation of slaves belonging to the rebels. Slavery, he hastened to observe, was a state-sanctioned institution. For this reason, he suggested, "it is startling to say that congress can free a slave within a state." Nonetheless, the problem could be solved very quickly through insertion of an intermediate step: "if," the president proposed, "it were said that the ownership of the slave had first been transferred to the nation, and that congress had then liberated him, the difficulty would at once vanish."

Furthermore, Lincoln suggested, the bill contained a problem in regard to enforcement: since only those slaves who belonged to the rebels would fall within the act's jurisdiction, he argued, some procedure would have to be created for determining their status.

Finally, Lincoln objected to the permanent forfeiture of *real estate*. In the president's opinion, this provision was a bill for permanent attainder, which the constitution forbids.

But he quickly reaffirmed that congressional action in regard to the freedom of *slaves* could indeed be permanent: the constitutional ban on such bills of attainder, he continued, "applies only in this country . . . to real, or landed estate."[64] Consequently, any slaves who belonged to the rebels could be freed forever.

When congressional Republicans received Lincoln's message, they revised the new law very quickly. In its final version, it warned that the slaves of individual rebels would be freed if the rebellion should continue more than sixty days. Judicial proceedings would be used to enforce this threat. Moreover, any slaves who escaped to Union lines would be classified as "captives of war," and deemed "forever free." Indeed, such liberated slaves were invited to enlist in the United States Army and fight for the Union. Finally, federal funds were provided for the voluntary colonization of blacks who wished to leave the country. This act was a major transitional step in the radicalization of the war.

In secret, however, the president was drafting a document far more radical than anything the act contained. Lincoln's Emancipation Proclamation would extend the power of the federal government in ways that were far more controversial.

Lincoln presented his secret decree to the cabinet on July 22. It began with legalistic probity:

> In pursuance of the sixth section of the act of congress entitled "An act to suppress insurrection and to punish treason and rebellion, to seize and confiscate property of rebels . . . I, Abraham Lincoln, President of the United States, do hereby proclaim to, and warn all persons within the contemplation of said sixth section to cease participating in, aiding, countenancing, or abetting the existing rebellion . . . on pain of the forfeitures and seizures, as within and by said sixth section provided.

So far, the proclamation was grounded in congressional actions. At the end of the document, however, the president extended his executive authority in bold and unprecedented terms. In addition to the previous warnings and threats, he continued

I, as Commander-in-Chief of the Army and Navy of the United States, do order and declare that on the first day of January in the year of Our Lord one thousand, eight hundred, and sixty-three, all persons held as slaves within any state or states, wherein the constitutional authority of the United States shall not then be practically recognized, submitted to, and maintained, shall then, thenceforward, and forever, be free.[65]

This was nothing less than a revolutionary action: a revolution in the name of maintaining the established legal order. Lincoln was explicitly warning the rebels, both leaders and followers, to lay down their arms by the end of the year or face sweeping, irreversible sanctions. Every slave in a rebellious state—regardless of whether a particular slave could be proven to belong to a rebel—would be freed in the following year just as soon as the armies of Lincoln could reach him, the proclamation warned.

Lincoln's announcement at the cabinet meeting drew very mixed reactions indeed. Montgomery Blair, as a former Democrat, could not support the proclamation; he warned of the political backlash that such a decree might provoke in the congressional elections that fall. Stanton, the former attorney general under Buchanan, supported the measure wholeheartedly. Chase, the antebellum Free-Soiler, was somewhat ambivalent. And Seward, most famously of all, recommended to Lincoln that he wait for a battlefield victory: he should issue his decree from a platform of obvious strength. Lincoln chose to take Seward's advice. But he did tell the public on July 25 that he would implement the new confiscation law in sixty days.

The threat of a white supremacist backlash was real that summer. White supremacists throughout the North began howling as soon as Lincoln had signed the second confiscation act. Democratic editorials warned that millions of "semi-savages" would pour into Northern cities when emancipation started. They would flood the job market. They would perpetrate horrendous crimes. They would pant for political and social equality and lust for racial intermarriage.

A New York headline was typical: "Can Niggers Conquer Americans?" Midwestern opinions were also inflamed: Indiana Congressman George Julian, a prominent Radical Republican, wrote, "our people hate the Negro with a perfect if not a supreme hatred."[66] Racial violence—urban riots against free blacks—broke out in Northern cities that summer.

So the political risk for the Republican Party was clear: if the Republicans should lose their majority in Congress because of a white supremacist backlash during the autumn elections, the Democrats would probably (indeed, almost certainly) repeal the anti-slavery laws that the Republicans had recently passed. The confiscation acts, of course, would be the first to go, but the threat was even bigger than that: the Free-Soil measure that Republicans had passed in defiance of the Dred Scott decision could be wiped off the books as well. This was the tremendous gamble that Republicans had taken in the summer of 1862. Lincoln's secret proclamation would of course raise the ante even more.

Moreover, the political threat to the Republicans' program was broadened when the danger of foreign intervention resurfaced in the early weeks of July. To observers in Paris, London, and elsewhere, the failure of McClellan to capture Richmond had improved the Confederates' prospects. Accordingly, Napoleon III sent a query to the British in regard to the wisdom of recognizing the Confederate States of America as a new nation. Parliament considered the issue on July 18, though without taking action. The prime minister was cautious: he wanted more assurance of Confederate military victory.

But the cotton embargo of the South was beginning to succeed in the summer of 1862: the British warehouse supplies were exhausted and a major "cotton famine" was creating unemployment in the British textile industry. Pro-Confederate sentiment was growing in parliament, and one thing alone held it back: the long-standing anti-slavery feelings of the British electorate. Lincoln's Emancipation Proclamation— so politically risky at home—could bring tremendous benefits abroad. But, would the moment arrive soon enough to avert a Confederate diplomatic coup?

In mid– to late July, Lincoln faced the following challenges: to stave off foreign intervention, to stimulate military action in Virginia, and— most challenging of all—to prepare Northern public opinion for his secret liberation decree.

On July 23, the new general in chief, Henry Halleck, arrived in Washington. Lincoln sent him off promptly with a message for George McClellan: if McClellan would agree to renew the campaign against Lee, then the president could offer him twenty thousand more troops. If McClellan should decline to proceed, then the president intended to withdraw McClellan's army from Richmond and merge it into Pope's.

On July 25, Halleck stated these terms to McClellan and suggested that he put the issue to a vote among his corps commanders. Lincoln's offer was accepted very quickly.

But when Halleck returned to Washington, a message from McClellan was waiting. The general had changed his mind: at least *forty thousand* more troops would be needed to renew the campaign against Lee.

For Lincoln this message was decisive: McClellan was hopeless. The campaign in Virginia, the president decided, would use the army of Pope as its spearhead. McClellan's forces would be siphoned away from the vicinity of Richmond—with stealth, by water, in a manner that would shield the gigantic maneuver from the eyes of Confederate scouts—and then fed in a continuous-flow operation into Pope's new Army of Virginia. Already, John Pope was on the move: he had crossed the Rappahannock and was moving toward Richmond by land.

On the fourth of August, Lincoln ordered McClellan to withdraw from the Virginia peninsula. The general, however, was sulking. He decided to take his own time about withdrawing his troops. In the meantime, as Pope was advancing, the Confederates in Richmond guessed the truth about Lincoln's intentions. Lee decided to attack Pope's army and defeat it as McClellan took his time. He ordered twenty-three thousand Confederate troops under Stonewall Jackson to attack Pope's Army of Virginia.

As the battlefield struggle heated up in Virginia, Lincoln turned his mind to the challenge of preparing the North for his secret decree. In light of the anti-black hatred that was glaringly apparent that summer— hatred that was leading to anti-black violence—Lincoln tried to get his colonization program started in the hope of reducing racial tension.

On August 14, he invited a small delegation of blacks to the White House for the purpose of discussing the concept of colonization with them frankly. He was seeking black leaders to be colonizing pioneers— to join with him in founding a haven for expatriate blacks.

He began by acknowledging the racial evils of America. "Your race," Lincoln told his black visitors, "are suffering the greatest wrong inflicted on any people." Beyond the evil of enslavement, blacks were systematically oppressed all over the country, Lincoln acknowledged. "On this broad continent, not a single man of your race is made the equal of a single man of ours."

In guarded language, Lincoln made it clear to his guests that he shared their emotions with regard to this sordid oppression: it was a "fact, about which we all think and feel alike, I and you." Yet, it was "a fact with which we have to deal," for "I cannot alter it."

Consequently, Lincoln urged his black listeners to start life over in another country—to savor the rest of their lives undiminished by oppression and cruelty. The obvious hardship of starting life over, he said, should be weighed very carefully indeed with the dubious merits of staying in a land that was familiar but relentlessly harsh. Compare yourselves, Lincoln urged them, to General Washington as founders of a nation: "Gen. Washington himself endured greater physical hardships" in fighting for the fullness of his own human freedom "than if he had remained" in the comparative comfort of being "a British subject," Lincoln reasoned. Nonetheless, "he was a happy man"—happier by far in embracing the struggle—because he and his fellow revolutionaries were "cheered by the future."

Moreover, a venture in colonization could facilitate emancipation, Lincoln argued. Free blacks like you, Lincoln told them, "ought to do something to help those who are not so fortunate"—that is, they ought to help free the slaves in the South. In light of the "unwillingness on the part of our people, harsh as it may be, for you free colored people to remain with us," Lincoln continued, a vanguard of free black emigrants could, by starting a triumphant exodus, "open a wide door for many to be made free." Leave the house of bondage, he bade them, put it quickly behind you so that others could follow and flourish.

Consider a move to Liberia, Lincoln suggested, or—if something in the Western Hemisphere were more attractive—in Central America, Lincoln continued, there were excellent places for a colony. "The particular place I have in view is to be a great highway from the Atlantic or Caribbean Sea to the Pacific Ocean," he explained, "and this particular place has all the advantages for a colony." Lincoln promised to support the first colonists with federal funding: "I shall, if I get a sufficient number of you engaged, have provisions made that you shall not be wronged."

Above all, Lincoln told them, he hoped they would free themselves from the constant persecution in white supremacist America. "To your colored race," Lincoln said, the inhabitants of Central America "have no objection," and besides, he continued, "I would endeavor to have you made equals, and have the best assurance that you should be the equals of the best."

Take your time, Lincoln said, and consider this matter with care, for "these are subjects of very great importance, worthy of a month's study, [instead] of a speech delivered in an hour."[67]

As he tried to persuade black leaders to think about colonization, Lincoln looked for corresponding opportunities to soften white resistance to emancipation. He dropped hints that much stronger measures would be coming if Confederate resistance continued. In response to some complaints about the Union occupation tactics in Louisiana, Lincoln warned that such measures were just the beginning.

To Cuthbert Bullitt, a New Orleans attorney, he was blunt and defiant. Regarding complaints about the ways in which "the relation of master and slave is disturbed by the presence of our Army," Lincoln posed some questions for the malcontents of New Orleans. "What would you do in my position," he demanded: "Would you drop the war where it is? Or, would you prosecute it in future, with elder-stalk squirts, charged with rose water? Would you deal lighter blows rather than heavier ones? Would you give up the contest, leaving any available means unapplied[?]"[68]

In a letter to financier August Belmont, he warned, "broken eggs cannot be mended. . . . This government cannot much longer play a game in which it stakes all, and its enemies stake nothing. Those enemies must understand that they cannot experiment for ten years trying to destroy the government, and if they fail still come back into the Union unhurt."[69]

Above all, he pounced upon an editorial by Horace Greeley in the *New York Tribune*. Greeley's editorial, "The Prayer of Twenty Millions," accused the president of weakness on the issue of slavery.

Lincoln's famous answer to Greeley, which he wrote as an open letter to the editor, is central to the "moderate" Lincoln legend. Dated August 22, his letter to the editor ignored the specifics of Greeley's complaints; instead, Lincoln offered propositions of his own that would be useful in preparing Northern public opinion for emancipation.

Lincoln posed as a commander-in-chief who was *solely* devoted to the cause of saving the Union, at least in his official capacity as president. "My paramount object in this struggle," he wrote, "*is* to save the Union, and is *not* either to save or to destroy slavery. If I could save the Union without freeing *any* slave I would do it, and if I could save it by freeing *all* the slaves I would do it; and if I could save it by freeing some and leaving others alone I would also do that. . . . I have here stated my purpose according to my view of my *official* duty; and I intend no modification of my oft-expressed *personal* wish that all men every where could be free."[70]

For years these lines have been read with only minimal comprehension by those who argue that "Lincoln only wanted to save the Union."

But—as we have seen—his entire career as a national leader makes the proposition untenable. Right up to his inauguration, he scorned the notion of saving a Union that was not *worth* saving. He killed the Crittenden Compromise for saving the Union by refusing to engage in any further appeasement on the issue of slavery expansion. It was, after all, Lincoln's Free-Soil platform that *caused* the secession crisis in the first place.

No, the famous letter to Greeley is *not* proof that Lincoln "only wanted to save the Union" in the Civil War. It is rather a stunning demonstration of Lincoln the tactician.

Observe his rhetorical manner: *if* he could save the Union without freeing slaves, then he would do it as an act of duty. This was close to the truth in political and constitutional terms—it was an obvious statement of his constitutional constraints—but it was surely not the whole truth for Lincoln. For he chose not to mention the important fact that he intended to do much more than merely save the Union. He would force a great change in the Union, putting slavery "on the downhill."

Moreover, he chose not to mention the fact that there were things he would refuse to do—back down on the issue of slavery expansion, for example—in his struggle to save the Union.

But observe: in the midst of expressing his commitment to saving the Union by doing whatever it took on the issue of slavery—a commitment so strong that it supposedly trumped any other commitments of his own—Lincoln stated that he might free some slaves.

He was softening public opinion. He was getting things ready for his big and risky revelation. To establish his patriotic platform, to pose as a presidential leader who was far above the fray when it came to the slavery issue, he implied that he was still undecided on the merits of emancipation.

Perhaps, he implied, he would *not* free the slaves at all. He was weighing all his options very carefully. But whatever he did—rest assured, white supremacist voters!—he would do it for the sake of the Union.

This deception has been swallowed by millions of readers who encounter Lincoln's letter to Greeley by itself, and without any knowledge of the president's overall purposes.

Meanwhile, the battlefield struggle in Virginia was approaching a disaster. Lee decided to send Jackson's corps on a march to Manassas, which was serving as a Union supply base. Jackson raided Manassas on August 26, and Pope quickly turned north to pursue him.

Pope's initial assaults upon Jackson were inconclusive. Then, when the rest of Lee's army arrived, Lee was able to conceal the presence of his forces. A surprise attack was in the making. On August 30, Lee gave the order to unleash a tremendous assault upon Pope's unprotected left flank. The Union line crumbled and was driven from the field in rout.

Pope was out-generaled at "Second Manassas," without a doubt. Nonetheless, there was plenty of blame to go around for this Union defeat. As the battle was raging, Henry Halleck did a miserable job in his attempts to coordinate the armies of Pope and McClellan. Halleck was beginning to demonstrate his own kind of weakness in the post of general in chief. According to John Hay, Lincoln's secretary, the dispatches that Halleck wrote to Lincoln at the time of the battle were "weak, whiney [and] vague."[71]

McClellan, moreover, bore a huge amount of the blame for the Manassas disaster. He deliberately dragged his heels when Halleck had asked him to send reinforcements to Pope. In the midst of the battle he had telegraphed Lincoln and suggested that the president "leave Pope to get out of his own scrape."[72]

Lincoln at first was inclined to give Pope a second chance. "We must hurt this enemy before it gets away," he declared. On September 1, Hay recorded in his diary that Lincoln was "singularly defiant" in the aftermath of the battle. After Hay had incautiously "made a remark in regard to the bad look of things," Lincoln quickly rebuked him, saying, "'No, Mr. Hay, we must whip these people now. Pope must fight them.'"[73]

But when Lincoln found out that the troops in Pope's army despised him, he decided that McClellan, at least for a while, was the better man to reorganize the army and restore its faltering morale. Strange and perverse as it seems, the troops continued to worship "Little Mac," whom they regarded as a life-saving friend—a commander who would never sacrifice his troops without a very good reason.

Then a new emergency developed: Lee's army crossed into Maryland. A Confederate invasion had begun, and it looked for a time as if Washington itself could be the target. Here again, resignedly, Lincoln turned to McClellan, the defensive commander and fortifier *par excellence*. He confided to Hay that "we must use the tools we have. . . . There is no man in the Army who can man these fortifications and lick these troops of ours into shape half as well as he. . . . He is too useful just now to sacrifice."[74] Since McClellan and Pope were on the angriest of terms, Pope was sent back out to the West (to fight Indians in Minnesota). The new Army of Virginia was disbanded and merged back into the Army of the Potomac.

But the McClellan arrangement would clearly not last. As historian T. Harry Williams has observed, the president "was determined that McClellan's command would be temporary because he believed the General was incapable of offensive warfare."[75]

Since no attack upon Washington occurred, Lee's army would have to be pursued. Lincoln quietly attempted to recruit a successor to McClellan—a *fighting* general to lead the army into battle. Early in September, the president offered the command to General Ambrose E. Burnside, who had made a name for himself by his capture of Roanoke Island and much of the "outer banks" of North Carolina six months earlier.[76]

But Burnside declined, and so, *again* with tremendous misgivings, Lincoln had to give the field command to McClellan. It would take well over another year for the president to find some commanders whose thinking was similar to his and whose battlefield prowess was equivalent to that of the enemy.

Lee's invasion of Maryland was part of a multi-pronged counteroffensive, a coordinated effort by Confederate armies to pull Union forces out of occupied states and bring war to the Northern people. Confederate victories on Northern soil could tip the balance in the international arena. Southern victories could bring recognition, mediation, *intervention* by the British and French.[77] They could even bring an end to the Republican control of Congress. In a message to Jefferson Davis on September 8, Lee expressed high hope that a successful invasion would enable "the people of the United States to determine at their coming elections whether they will support those who favor a prolongation of the war, or those who wish to bring it to a termination."[78] As

Lee headed north into Maryland, Confederate forces in East Tennessee headed northward into Kentucky. And Confederate troops in Mississippi prepared to strike north.

This tremendous crisis moved Lincoln to reflect once again upon religious themes. If indeed he were called to be an agent of Providence, perhaps he should see the Manassas disaster and the crisis of invasion as goads toward a higher moral outcome. Sometime during the month of September, Lincoln penned the following reflections:

> The will of God prevails. In great contests each party claims to act in accordance with the will of God. Both *may* be, and one *must* be wrong. God can not be *for*, and *against* the same thing at the same time. In the present civil war it is quite possible that God's purpose is different from the purpose of either party— and yet the human instrumentalities, working just as they do, are of the best adaptation to effect His purpose. I am almost ready to say this is probably true—that God wills this contest, and wills that it shall not end yet. By his mere quiet power, on the minds of the now contestants, He could have either *saved* or *destroyed* the Union without a human contest. Yet the contest began. And having begun He could give the final victory to either side any day. Yet the contest proceeds.[79]

In early September, Lincoln made a personal vow: he promised to regard a Union victory in Maryland as nothing less than "an indication of Divine Will" concerning the higher meaning of the war. Indeed, Lincoln vowed to interpret such a victory as a providential sign to "move forward in the cause of emancipation." On September 22, he revealed this vow to his cabinet.[80]

Until victory, however, he would have to keep playing for time. He would have to keep pretending he had not yet decided on emancipation policy. He even chose to play the role of devil's advocate in mid-September and floated a series of arguments *against* the proclamation to achieve this political deception. On September 13, a Chicago delegation of Christian abolitionists called upon Lincoln at the White House. He talked with the group for the better part of an hour in the following manner.

"What *good* would a proclamation of emancipation from me do," he inquired, "especially as we are now situated? . . . Would *my* word free the slaves, when I cannot even enforce the Constitution in the rebel states?" Besides, he continued, if the proclamation turned out to be successful, "how can we feed and care for such a multitude?" Lincoln treated his guests to a dazzling display of mock perplexity.

Mind you, the president continued, he was raising "no objections" at all against a proclamation such as this "on legal or constitutional grounds; for, as commander-in-chief of the army and navy, in time of war, I suppose I have a right to take any measure which may best subdue the enemy." This, of course, was a complete reversal of the constitutional views he expressed to his friend Senator Orville Browning just a year before.

At the end of the discourse the president concluded in a reassuring manner: "I have not decided against a proclamation of liberty to the slaves . . . but hold the matter under advisement."[81] Under advisement indeed! The only matter that was really uncertain in his mind was the *timing* of the great proclamation. And what a devious way of half-revealing/half-concealing the truth in this case through the use of a sly double negative—he had not decided *against* the proclamation, he stated—thus concealing the fact that a positive decision had been made, for the liberating document was written already and was waiting in his desk drawer.

As McClellan moved off into Maryland, he wasted several chances to destroy the Confederate army. Lee, on the march, had divided his army into fragments. On September 13, a most extraordinary windfall was given to George McClellan: a Union private had stumbled by chance upon a copy of Lee's secret orders.

An intelligence coup of this sort must be used very quickly, but McClellan, of course, took his time. An audacious commander—a Stonewall Jackson, for instance—would have pounced upon the isolated pieces of his enemy's army and crushed them before they could unite. But McClellan was fretful and obtuse. When he finally caught Lee at Sharpsburg, Maryland, to the west of Antietam Creek, Lee had almost succeeded in pulling his army together. Even so, a determined attack at this point could have dealt Lee a staggering blow. Yet McClellan continued to hesitate. And so, by the time that he finally attacked, he confronted a consolidated enemy.

Lee's forces, however, were meager when compared to McClellan's: at seventy-five thousand, the Army of the Potomac continued to outnumber the Army of Northern Virginia, which was down to forty-five thousand.

The battle of Antietam, on September 17, was the bloodiest day of the war. The Confederates had not been able to entrench. Consequently, the bloodbath was out in the open, with little more than cornfields, fences, and sunken lanes to provide any cover for the troops. By the end of the day, over twenty-three thousand soldiers had fallen, either dead or wounded.

The battle almost ended the war. At one point, a significant gap was created in the center of Lee's position. At that moment, as T. Harry Williams has observed, "McClellan had victory in his grasp." He had a full corps of troops in reserve. If, in the opinion of Williams, he "had sent this force against the weakened Confederate right, he would have swept Lee from the field. He was at the crisis of his career, and he fumbled the moment completely. . . . He halted the attack for the day."[82]

Lee's army retreated to Virginia, and McClellan simply let it go. He did nothing to harass the retreat of the Confederates' principal army—nothing to finish off the army of Lee when it was ready for the *coup de grace*.

But this victory appeared strong enough to give Lincoln the occasion for which he was praying. On September 22, Lincoln issued the Preliminary Emancipation Proclamation. The proclamation was labeled *preliminary* because it was framed as a *warning*. *If*, the president warned, the rebellion continued into 1863, then a *final* proclamation would be issued to carry out the threat of emancipation.

"I, Abraham Lincoln, President of the United States of America, and Commander-in-chief of the Army and Navy thereof, do hereby proclaim and declare that hereafter, as heretofore, the war will be prosecuted for the object of practically restoring the constitutional relation between the United States, and each of the states, and the people thereof, in which states that relation is, or may be suspended, or disturbed." Lincoln launched his revolutionary plan by assuring the public that the war remained a fight to save the Union.

Before proceeding any further, he attempted to prepare Northern racists for the imminent freeing of slaves. As always, Lincoln used the formula of colonization in hopes of staving off a backlash: "the effort to colonize persons of African descent, with their consent, upon this continent, or elsewhere, with the previously obtained consent of the Governments existing there, will be continued," Lincoln affirmed.

Then, without more ado, the great lines were delivered to the nation:

> On the first day of January in the year of our Lord, one thousand eight hundred and sixty-three, all persons held as slaves within any state, or designated part of a state, the people whereof shall then be in rebellion against the United

States shall be then, thenceforward, and forever free; and the executive government of the United States, including the military and naval authority thereof, will recognize and maintain the freedom of such persons, and will do no act or acts to repress such persons, or any of them, in any efforts they may make for their actual freedom.

"*Maintain* the freedom of such persons," here was a promise to use all the might of the nation to *assist* those slaves seeking freedom in Confederate states if the war continued after 1862. Lincoln warned the rebels that "on the first day of January" he would "designate the States, or parts of states" in which rebellion continued to be active. Lincoln closed with a promise to support the idea of compensation for *loyal* masters in rebellious states who had lost their slaves in the war.[83]

On September 24, a group of admirers arrived at the White House and serenaded Lincoln. Afterward, a crowd of administration revelers gathered at the home of Salmon Chase to continue the festivities. As Lincoln's young secretary John Hay reflected in his diary, "they all seemed to feel a sort of new and exhilarated [*sic*] life; they breathed freer." The new proclamation "had freed them as well as the slaves. They gleefully and merrily called each other and themselves abolitionists. . . ."[84]

Lincoln issued yet another proclamation on the same day invoking martial law against "all Rebels and Insurgents, their aiders and abettors within the United States, and all persons discouraging volunteer enlistments, resisting militia drafts, or guilty of any disloyal practice. . . ." Habeas corpus was suspended for anyone arrested pursuant to the policy.[85] "Stronger measures" were arriving indeed.

There was plenty of reason for the Lincoln entourage to celebrate: Lee's invasion of Maryland was stopped and his army had been forced to retreat. The threat of foreign intervention had subsided, at least for a while. And the revolutionary step had been taken that would elevate the war into a national crusade for liberation.

But there were also causes for brooding in the Lincoln inner circle. If the Northern electorate turned upon Lincoln, then Republicans could lose control of Congress. And while Lee's invasion of Maryland was thwarted, there remained the Confederate invasion attempts in Mississippi and Kentucky.

As it happened, the Confederate attack in Mississippi would be easily stopped. Union forces under Ulysses S. Grant—who had succeeded Henry Halleck as commander in the Mississippi theatre—and William

S. Rosecrans vanquished two Confederate armies in the battles of Iuka on September 19, and Corinth on October 3–4, both in Mississippi.

But the Confederate invasion of Kentucky under Generals Braxton Bragg and Edmund Kirby Smith had been gathering momentum since August. From East Tennessee, these Confederates had slashed through Kentucky, seizing one city after another: Richmond, August 30, Lexington, September 2, and Frankfort, the state capital, September 3. The Union army of Buell was unable to stop them and alarm bells were ringing in the North. Cincinnati was directly in the path of the Confederate invasion.

Moreover, thousands of "contraband" slaves had been seized in Kentucky by the Southern invaders and shipped off to slavery again. Lee's army did the very same thing.[86]

On October 8, Buell finally managed to stop the Confederate invasion in the battle of Perryville, Kentucky. But like McClellan in the aftermath of Antietam, he allowed the Confederate forces to fight another day and gain strength. He refused to deliver the knockout blow that the president demanded.

Lincoln's patience with generals like Buell and McClellan was running out. The only reason he had kept them in command, as he confided a month or so later, was his fear that he "would not find successors to them, who would do better."[87]

Lincoln visited McClellan and inspected his army at Antietam in the first week of October. Then he issued an order, through Halleck, on October 6: McClellan was to cross the Potomac and attack the army of Lee as rapidly as possible. McClellan made the usual excuses as he fumbled and dithered. On October 13, Lincoln wrote him: "You remember my speaking to you of your over-cautiousness. Are you not over-cautious when you assume that you can not do what the enemy is constantly doing?"

The best strategy, the president argued, was to strike in the direction of Richmond in order to force Lee into a battle on favorable ground. Lee's forces were largely in or near the Shenandoah; consequently, "you are now nearer to Richmond than the enemy is. . . . Why can you not reach there before him. . . [?] His route is the arc of a circle, while yours is the chord." Consequently, "to beat him to Richmond on the inside track" should be "easy . . . if our troops march as well as the enemy; and it is unmanly to say they can not do it."[88]

Meanwhile, on October 23, Lincoln fired Buell and replaced him with William S. Rosecrans. And though McClellan at last gave the order to cross the Potomac, his fate with the president was sealed. Lincoln finally relieved him of command on November 5, and replaced him with Ambrose Burnside.

When the Northern electorate voted, the Republicans retained control of Congress. But their margin of control was reduced in the House of Representatives: the Democrats gained thirty-two seats. Moreover, the Democrats took control of the Illinois and Indiana legislatures; they also captured the governorships of New Jersey and New York. Though the outcome could have been worse by far (the Republicans actually gained five seats in the Senate), it had a morbid effect upon Lincoln. "We have lost the elections," the president lamented, and "the ill-success of the war had much to do with it."[89]

But he would not back down from his new emancipation commitment. According to a story in the *New York Tribune*, he told a delegation of "unconditional Union Kentuckians" in late November that "he would rather die than take back one word of the Proclamation of Freedom."[90] Moreover, as he wrote his long message to Congress, he conferred with General Burnside regarding a new campaign against Lee.

Burnside was almost McClellan's opposite. Where McClellan was arrogant, Burnside was modest; where McClellan was cautious to the point of occasional cowardice, Burnside—and here was the rub—would pit his troops against hopeless odds.

Burnside proposed to take the Army of the Potomac toward Richmond as the president wanted. But he preferred to move his forces much farther away from Lee's position near Virginia's Blue Ridge. He proposed to take his army all the way to Fredericksburg, east on the Rappahannock River. Having crossed the Rappahannock, he would move his army toward Richmond. Lincoln approved this scheme, with the proviso that the movement should be fast.

But when Burnside arrived in the Fredericksburg vicinity, the bridges he had ordered for the crossing of the river had not yet arrived. And so he waited. By the time the bridges finally arrived, so had Lee's army.

On November 26, Lincoln traveled by boat to Acquia Creek for an urgent conference with Burnside. In a memorandum of the meeting, Lincoln put it on record that Burnside "thinks he can cross the river in the face of the enemy and drive him away, but that, to use his own expression, it is somewhat risky." These odds were not good enough for Lincoln. Consequently, the president urged a new plan to bring forces to the south of Lee's army in order to engage it as Burnside crossed the river. To Lincoln's chagrin, both Burnside and Halleck rejected the plan as unrealistic.[91]

As planning for the Fredericksburg attack continued, Lincoln sent his long annual message to Congress. In a startling move, he urged Congress to write every feature of his presidential anti-slavery program, both the short-term measures and long-term measures, into law as constitutional amendments.

What better strategic hedge could he have had against the worst-case scenarios that haunted him night and day? After all, if the public were to throw him out of office in the next presidential election, the amended Constitution might nonetheless permit the anti-slavery movement to resume in another generation.

Lincoln advocated three amendments: (1) "Every state, wherein slavery now exists, which shall abolish the same therein, at any time, or times, before the first day of January, in the year of our Lord one thousand and nine hundred, shall receive compensation from the United States. . . ." (2) "All slaves who shall have enjoyed actual freedom by the chances of the war, at any time before the end of the rebellion, shall be forever free; but all owners of such, who shall not have been disloyal, shall be compensated for them. . . ." (3) "Congress may appropriate money, and otherwise provide, for colonizing free colored persons, with their own consent, at any place or places without the United States."[92]

In proposing these amendments, Lincoln was trying to give an anti-slavery thrust to the Constitution itself. The cost of paying for the slaves would be paid through the sale of bonds: through deficit spending. Lincoln argued that prosperity resulting from national growth would make the economic burden acceptable. By the turn of the twentieth century, he reasoned, "we shall probably have a hundred millions of people to share the burden, instead of thirty one millions, as now. . . ."[93]

To assuage racist critics, Lincoln emphasized colonization. But he also decided to challenge American racism. Since his program called for colonization as a *voluntary* venture, he considered the case of free blacks who might insist upon staying. Consequently, he criticized racists who objected to the presence of blacks as free neighbors in America. What was it that the racists were afraid of, Lincoln demanded. They seemed to dread "that the freed people will swarm forth, and cover the whole land." But, Lincoln asked, "are they not already in the land?" If the entire population of American blacks were "distributed among the whites of the whole country . . . there would be but one colored to seven whites," Lincoln observed. Moreover, "there are many communities now, having more than one free colored person, to seven whites; and this, without any apparent consciousness of evil from it."[94]

The real question, he said, was a simple formulation for America: "can we do better?" "The dogmas of the quiet past," he continued, "are inadequate to the stormy present. The occasion is piled high with difficulty, and we must rise with the occasion. As our case is new, so we must think anew, and act anew. We must disenthrall ourselves, and then we shall save our country."

"Fellow citizens," Lincoln concluded, "*we* cannot escape history. . . . The fiery trial through which we pass, will light us down, in honor or dishonor, to the latest generation. . . . In *giving* freedom to the *slave*, we *assure* freedom to the *free*." And so, in the end, "we shall nobly save, or meanly lose, the last best hope of earth."[95]

On December 13, the war's "fiery trial" continued in the eastern theatre. Burnside was ready at Fredericksburg, or so he thought. He ordered his men to attack the Confederates, without the support from subsidiary Union forces that Lincoln had suggested. The result was horrible. Lee's men were entrenched along impregnable heights behind the town. And so the Union army was mauled. Wave after wave tried to storm Lee's position. They were all cut down and slaughtered. The Army of the Potomac suffered 12,600 casualties that day, compared to less than 5,000 Confederate losses.

The casualties at Shiloh back in April (both Union and Confederate) came close to the 20,000 mark; at Fair Oaks, 11,000; in the Seven Days Battles, the Union and Confederate losses had been roughly 31,000; at Second Manassas, close to 25,000; Antietam had cost over 23,000; at Perryville, 7,600. Then at Fredericksburg, on December 13, over 17,000 more.

Lincoln would not back down. As New Year's Day was approaching, people speculated about the president's commitment, both to the Union and to liberation. Would his threat against the rebels hold good? Would the final proclamation be delivered on January 1? Fredrick Douglass, the black abolitionist, a critic of Lincoln since the very beginning of the war, was in Boston on New Year's Day. He recalled the occasion in his memoirs: "Eight, nine, ten o'clock came and went, and still no word. . . . At last, when patience was well-nigh exhausted . . . a man (I think it was Judge Russell) with hasty step advanced through the crowd, and with a face fairly illuminated with the news he bore, exclaimed in tones that thrilled all hearts, 'It is coming! It is on the wires!' . . . My old friend Rue, a colored preacher, a man of wonderful vocal power . . . led all voices in the anthem, 'Sound the loud timbrel o'er Egypt's dark sea, Jehovah hath triumphed, his people are free.'"

Though inspection of the document chagrined certain people who expected it to lash out at slavery everywhere at once, Douglass "saw in its spirit, a life and power far beyond its letter. Its meaning to me was the entire abolition of slavery, wherever the evil could be reached by the Federal arm, and I saw that its moral power would extend much further."[96]

Thus, as the new year began, the war for Union had become a war for freedom. The president who guided the soldiers had two years remaining in his term. But he would have to face the voters again—win or lose on the bloody fields of combat. And only *one* year remained before the critical election year of 1864.

FIVE

Lincoln and the War to the Death, 1863

I N 1863, Lincoln mobilized himself for a political race against time. As he carried out his pledge to free the slaves of the rebels, he was keenly aware of the white supremacist backlash this would provoke. Only one year remained before the next presidential election would be getting under way. And so, as he liberated blacks, he tried desperately to win the Civil War before the end of his presidential term.

On January 1, he put the finishing touches on his final and definitive Emancipation Proclamation. To allay Democratic accusations that he meant to start a war between the races by unchaining Southern blacks, he urged slaves "to abstain from all violence, unless in necessary self-defense." But he also declared that black force would be welcomed and encouraged in the *federal uniform*: freedmen "of suitable condition," he declared, would "be received into the armed service of the United States."[1] In other words, Lincoln had decided to turn the former slaves into soldiers.

The Democrats were shrill as they reviled this "wicked abolition crusade" of the "black Republicans." The so-called "Peace Democrats" or "Copperheads"—the anti-war faction of the party—called for measures to restore the "old Union" as it was in the decades before the Civil War. There was even furtive talk of a new midwestern Confederacy.

As emancipation started, the political question for the president recurred with new intensity: how deep were the racial animosities of Northern whites? Lincoln carefully pondered both the best-case options and the worst-case options for his fragile politics of freedom. It

was characteristic of Lincoln that he tried to make concurrent provision for the best-case and worst-case scenarios. But the tension of his
mood was unmistakable in 1863. His sense that time was running out
would reveal the inner anger that had always been a driving force in his
attacks upon slavery.

His best-case plan on the racial issue was to extend as many opportunities to freedmen as politics permitted. But he continued to assuage
the white supremacist voters by promoting the concept of voluntary
colonization, at least until the middle of the year. He insisted on working both ends of the range of possibility: as he tried to use the valor of
blacks as they fought for the Union to silence or shame white supremacists, he carefully retained his old fall-back position on the racial problem as a hedge in case his strategies should fail.

His worst-case strategy—in anticipation of a possible Democratic
victory in 1864—was to lock in as many of his anti-slavery achievements as he possibly could. He was striving for a way to force a national commitment to his long-term plan for liberation. He was striving,
indeed, to force an irreversible commitment to eliminate slavery. His
proposed constitutional amendments, for instance, if enacted and ratified quickly, would serve to protect the great "beach-head" that he and
the congressional Republicans had gained for the anti-slavery movement.

One of these proposed amendments would guarantee permanent
protection to his wartime emancipation policy: no Democratic judges
would be able to challenge the legality of what he had done to emancipate blacks if the Constitution were amended. Another amendment
would establish his voluntary program for the non-Confederate slave
states as permanent policy.

But if the Lincoln amendments were to founder in Congress (which
indeed would be the case during 1863), only military victory could
rescue both Lincoln and the nation from the worst-case future: the
election of a racist, pro-slavery Democrat in 1864. So Lincoln pushed
his commanders to defeat the Confederate armies with ever-greater
vehemence.

On the last day of 1862, an important battle began in Tennessee.
Union forces under General William S. Rosecrans were fighting the
Confederate troops under Braxton Bragg near the town of Murfreesboro. The battle of Murfreesboro (or Stone's River) raged from December 31 until January 2, when Bragg and his army, unable to break
the Union lines, gave up and withdrew.

Ever since the failure of the three-prong Confederate counteroffensive in the autumn of 1862, Lincoln strove to regain the initiative in all major theatres of war. In each major theatre, Lincoln's goal was two-fold: he sought to wipe out Confederate armies (or to force their surrender) and to seize geographical assets. In the Tennessee theatre, he urged Rosecrans to do what his predecessor, Don Carlos Buell, had repeatedly failed to do: destroy the Confederate presence in the state and capture Unionist-tending East Tennessee with its transportation hub, Chattanooga.

In Virginia, the promotion of Ambrose Burnside had led to disaster. Lincoln found some other duties for Burnside—he sent him to Ohio to build a new army that would operate in pincer-fashion with Rosecrans in East Tennessee—as he turned his mind to the task of selecting yet another commander for the ill-starred Army of the Potomac. Lincoln turned to a corps commander, Joseph Hooker.

In the third major theatre—the Mississippi Valley theatre—Lincoln's goal, in addition to defeating rebel armies, was to open up the Mississippi River. To do this, his armies had to seize the rebel-held and fortified cities of Vicksburg, Mississippi, and Port Hudson, Louisiana.

With the Mississippi River in Union hands, the Confederacy would be split: both Arkansas and Texas would be severed from the other rebel states. Moreover, the control of the river would facilitate Union transportation and tighten the Union's blockade. Lastly, with the state of Mississippi under Union bayonets, a great Union-occupied zone would be established all the way from the southern border of the state of Illinois to the Gulf of Mexico.

Union forces would be mustered for this western campaign just as soon as the Confederate offensive had been stopped in the battles of Corinth and Iuka, Mississippi in the autumn of 1862. From the South, Union forces under General Nathaniel Banks (the political general who had served in the Virginia theatre in 1862) would move north along the Mississippi River and attack Port Hudson, Louisiana. Simultaneously, from the north, Union forces commanded by General John A. McClernand, a Unionist Democrat (and therefore a political general with very strong value to Lincoln), would lead the attack upon Vicksburg.

Though Ulysses S. Grant was in nominal command of this department, he was left uninformed about the nature of McClernand's expedition in the earliest weeks of its development. Perhaps Grant, to a

certain extent, was still "under a cloud" in the mind of Lincoln. But as
soon as Grant learned about the turn of events, he took action to ensure his authority. Indeed, Grant had plans of his own for the capture
of Vicksburg.

In December, Grant ordered a two-pronged attack upon the city.
But all of the attacks in the Mississippi theatre came to grief in the final
weeks of 1862. Banks was unable to fight his way farther up the river
than Baton Rouge, Louisiana. Meanwhile, Grant had been forced to
turn back and regroup because of rebel raiders who attacked and destroyed his supply lines. And Grant's trusted lieutenant William
Tecumseh Sherman discovered that the swampy topography north of
the city made direct assault upon Confederate defensive positions almost hopeless. Vicksburg appeared unassailable.

Grant's strategy was to move his men around the city by the opposite bank of the river. But he quickly discovered that the opposite shore
was just another impenetrable swamp. So he tried to dig *canals* farther
inland on the other side of the river—canals he could use to send gunboats, transports, and troops around Vicksburg to approach it from
the southern side. He would then bring his men across the river for a
final attack upon Vicksburg from good dry land.

On the sociopolitical front, as emancipation policy went into effect,
many thousands of slaves began flocking to the armies of Rosecrans
and Grant, thus belying the lame but extremely influential statement
of historian Richard Hofstadter, who complained years ago that the
Proclamation "did not free any slaves. . . . It simply declared free all
slaves in 'the States and parts of States' where the people were in
rebellion—that is to say, precisely where its effect could not reach."[2]
This observation is frequently repeated by determined critics of Lincoln. But Lincoln's Emancipation Proclamation was a deadly serious
announcement, not only that the slaves in rebel states (and certain parts
of rebel states) were deemed free but that the armies of Lincoln would
promptly set them free just as soon as those armies took control of the
areas in question. Within months, moreover, this threat became a demonstrated deed. And with the actual freeing of slaves in the Confederate states, the great question of the freedmen's status was thrust upon
the nation.

For a while, Lincoln kept alive his colonization proposal, shifting its
point of destination from Central America—where his vision of a colony
settled in the Chiriqui coal region met stiff resistance from the gov-

ernments of Honduras and Nicaragua—to an island off the coast of Haiti: Isle-a-Vache.[3] In December 1862, Lincoln signed a contract with entrepreneurs to resettle five thousand black volunteers, and the project began in the early months of 1863.

Nonetheless, Lincoln pushed the recruitment of blacks for Union armies at the very same time. What he wanted was a group of black army veterans whose help in preserving the nation would deserve an appropriate level of patriotic glory in the years to come. On March 26, he wrote to Andrew Johnson—who had left the United States Senate to serve as appointed civilian governor of occupied Tennessee—as follows: "I am told you have at least *thought* of raising a negro military force. In my opinion the country now needs no specific thing so much as some man of your ability, and position, to go to this work. When I speak of your position, I mean that of an eminent citizen of a slave-state, and himself a slave-holder. The colored population is the great *available* and yet *unavailed* of, force for restoring the Union. The bare sight of fifty thousand armed, and drilled Black soldiers on the banks of the Mississippi, would end the rebellion at once."[4]

As Lincoln used this logic to prevail upon Johnson, he turned to other methods of assisting the slaves whom his armies were beginning to liberate. He supported the creation of policies to offer them jobs on seized plantations. This policy was launched in the early spring of 1863. Specifically, in March he issued orders to Adjutant General Lorenzo Thomas to create a new "refugee" policy for occupied parts of the rebellious Mississippi Valley. Thomas organized a work-for-wages program that was promising in Lincoln's eyes.

Moreover, in the Sea Islands off the coast of South Carolina, yet another important experiment was starting in the early months of 1863. The tax act that congressional Republicans had passed in the summer of 1862 provided for the confiscation of real estate belonging to tax evaders in the occupied rebel states. This particular procedure for the confiscation of land in the South—for non-payment of taxes—was immune from the constitutional problems involved in the effort to seize rebel land as a punishment for *treason*.

Tax commissioners were duly dispatched to the South Carolina Sea Islands in October 1862. On February 6, 1863, Congress passed an important amendment to the tax/confiscation law that allowed these federal agents to reserve a certain portion of the seized lands—which were slated to be sold at auction—as a special "reserve" for educational and charitable purposes. This was euphemistic language for a potent idea: the lands would be sold to the very same slaves who had been tilling the soil for their masters. Accordingly, almost two thousand acres in the South Carolina Sea Islands were purchased by freedmen in 1863. Lincoln took direct action to ensure that these "homesteads" for blacks would be delivered. The rest of the lands in question were sold to investors, who instituted programs of wage employment very similar to those underway in the Mississippi Valley.[5]

Moreover, as all of these events unfolded, the executive branch was at work upon a comprehensive policy for aiding the newly freed slaves. As historian LaWanda Cox has observed, "Secretary of War Stanton established the Freedmen's Inquiry Commission shortly after Lincoln issued the Emancipation Proclamation; it is highly unlikely that he did so without the president's sanction." The members of this commission were "staunchly antislavery men." Their reports during 1863 "went beyond emancipation to outline what has been characterized as a 'Blueprint for Radical Reconstruction.' The blueprint included citizenship, suffrage, and landownership for the freedmen."[6] Moreover, certain Radical Republicans demanded the creation by Congress of a stronger "Freedmen's Bureau" to assist the freed slaves more efficiently. But Congress failed to pass such a law during 1863.

The white supremacist backlash against Lincoln's liberation program grew apace in the Northern states in 1863. Copperhead Democrats were urging white resistance to the Negro-loving "tyrant" or "dictator," Lincoln. They called for "peace"—peace with Southern brethren whose pride and "decency" rebelled against the abolitionists who wished to unleash "semi-savages." The resistance of Copperheads was sure to increase as Congress extended its plans to initiate a federal draft, since recruitment was beginning to falter.

Insofar as racist advocates of "peace" could be charged with interference in federal recruitment or enrollment efforts, Lincoln took strong measures against them. In May, new military forces being mustered in the state of Ohio under Burnside arrested the important Democratic Copperhead Clement L. Vallandigham, who was seeking the Democratic gubernatorial nomination. His prison term, handed down by a military tribunal, was commuted by Lincoln to banishment to the Confederacy.

But strong measures such as these against Copperheads led to even stronger appeals to a war-weary Northern public by Democratic critics.[7] Above all, it was the racial issue that the Democrats, working in the mode of Stephen Douglas, kept using for maximum effect. Accordingly, Lincoln continued to promote his plans for voluntary colonization to calm the racists down.

By May, Lincoln's colonization venture near Haiti was beginning in earnest. Over four hundred Blacks took a chance on the venture and departed for the Caribbean. But the project would prove to be a failure as corruption, disease, and squalor took their toll on the relocated community. When news of this reached Lincoln, he gradually began to move away from the colonization idea. After all, he had promised black leaders that the volunteers for colonization would not be "wronged."

Meanwhile, the war raged on. Early in April, Lincoln visited the army of Hooker, which was still in winter camp across the Rappahannock River from Fredericksburg. The army of Lee had not moved.

Lincoln talked at great length with Hooker, who assured his commander that he would dedicate himself to the speedy capture of Richmond. But Lincoln made it very clear to Hooker that Richmond, at least for a time, was but a secondary goal for the army. He observed that "just now, with the enemy directly ahead of us, there is no eligible route for us into Richmond." Consequently, "our prime object is the enemies' [sic] army in front of us." Lincoln also counseled Hooker to avoid the gross mistake of Burnside: "While he [Lee's army] remains in tact," he suggested, "I do not think we should take the disadvantage of attacking him in his entrenchments; but we should continually harrass [sic] and menace him. . . . If he weakens himself, then pitch into him."[8]

Hooker proposed that his army should cross the Rappahannock at a point far above Lee's position and attack Lee's army from the rear. Lincoln approved this proposal. On April 27, Hooker modified his plan to be a pincer movement: he would leave a Union force across the river from Lee and then move a separate force upriver to hit him from the rear. If Lee abandoned his position, Union forces would converge and destroy him.

Lee's response was the greatest single masterpiece of strategy that he and Stonewall Jackson devised in their Civil War partnership. Lee mimicked Hooker's action: He divided his forces, leaving troops under General Jubal Early to man the Confederate lines behind the city of Fredericksburg. He then marched with the bulk of his men to parry Hooker's thrust near the tiny country crossroads of Chancellorsville.

As soon as he encountered Lee's army, Hooker started to panic. He ordered a withdrawal to defensive positions as the fighting began on May 1. Lee sensed Hooker's weakness, and divided his army yet again, sending Jackson on a sweeping flank maneuver that erupted in a storm-like attack upon Hooker's exposed right flank on the evening of May 2. A Union rout began and Hooker was completely stunned.

Hooker's weakness gave Lee a free hand. When the Union forces that were stationed on the opposite side of the Rappahannock River crossed over and stormed up the heights behind Fredericksburg, Lee divided his army *yet again*. He led a separate detachment from the center of battle to suppress this Union drive.

It was all too much for Joseph Hooker, who withdrew his forces from the battle and re-crossed the Rappahannock on May 6. Chancellors-ville was yet another major triumph for Lee. But it came at a terrible cost: Stonewall Jackson was mortally wounded by the "friendly fire" of his troops, who mistook him in the gathering twilight for an enemy scout.

In the Mississippi Valley the news was much better for the Union. Grant finally abandoned his canal-building scheme and took a calculated risk to get his troops below the guns of Vicksburg. He would send his flotilla of transports and gunboats straight below Vicksburg under cover of darkness; he would do it so quickly as to thwart the Confederate gunners who were always on alert. On a moonless night he succeeded; his ships ran the gauntlet on the evening of April 16. With his ships below the city, he could ferry his troops across the river and move to the attack.

His army now in place, Grant decided on another surprise. Instead of moving directly on Vicksburg, he moved his army rapidly inland. The Confederate defenders of Vicksburg—commanded by General John C. Pemberton and numbering thirty-two thousand—had been recently augmented by another rebel force that was assembled under General Joseph Johnston. Johnston had been gathering an army at Jackson, the Mississippi capital. Grant decided to lunge at these forces and defeat them as the first order of business. He would thereby rid himself of threats to his rear as he turned to the capture of Vicksburg.

At this point the military leadership of Grant began to rise to the level of Lee: with speed and audacity, he severed his supply lines and lived completely off the land. Within weeks he defeated the forces of Johnston, sacked the city of Jackson, turned westward to confront the

Confederate forces of Pemberton, beat them in open engagements, chased them back into Vicksburg, and started a siege of the city. His endgame was simple: he would starve them into submission. Well before the surrender of Vicksburg, Lincoln called this whirlwind campaign "the most brilliant in the world."[9]

Conversely, in the aftermath of Hooker's lamentable performance in Virginia, Lincoln tried to size up the situation. He counseled temporary caution as he played for more time to form a clearer impression of Hooker.

This interlude, however, was drawing to a close, for in the weeks after beating Hooker's army, Lee proposed to stage another invasion of the Northern states. Such a move, he suggested in Richmond, would ease the pressure on Vicksburg, strengthen the Democratic Copperheads, reopen the issue of foreign recognition, and aid the Confederate cause across the board. The Confederate cabinet agreed, and the Gettysburg campaign began. Lee gathered his forces and began to move north in early June.

As he did so, the president reversed his recent guidance to Hooker: instead of caution, Lincoln wanted fast *action* to destroy the rebel army. When Hooker suggested that he try to take Richmond, Lincoln overruled him completely. "I think *Lee's* Army, and not *Richmond*, is your true objective point," Lincoln wrote.[10]

Hooker's army attempted to harass Lee's men as they moved through northern Virginia. An encounter on June 9 at Brandy Station turned into the largest single cavalry battle of the war. Notwithstanding, Lee continued his march. So Lincoln prodded Hooker again: "If the head of Lee's army is at Martinsburg and the tail of it on the Plank road between Fredericksburg and Chancellorsville," Lincoln cabled on June 14, then "the animal must be very slim somewhere. Could you not break him?"[11]

Once again, it was too much for Hooker to bear, and he resigned his command. On June 28, Lincoln quickly promoted General George Gordon Meade, another corps commander of the Army of the Potomac, to succeed him.

Lee's troops had reached Pennsylvania. They were seizing supplies (and also blacks, whom they shipped down their lines into slavery, just as they had done in the Antietam campaign). Their preliminary goal was to destroy and disrupt the important Pennsylvania Railroad line between Harrisburg and Lancaster. On the first of July, a Confederate foraging party ran into some cavalry units from the Army of the Potomac near the town of Gettysburg. The clash widened. By dusk it became a great vortex that drew both armies into battle.

Lee tried to seize the best strategic ground—a line of hills and ridges that stretched like a fishhook below the town—on the first day of battle, and he ordered Richard Ewell, who had succeeded in command of Stonewall Jackson's old corps, to assault the Union-held Cemetery Hill. But Ewell proved overly cautious and he missed this crucial opportunity.

By the second day of battle Meade's army had occupied the hill and the long ridge below it. Lee occupied a parallel ridge and prepared to attack: his plan was to hit both ends of the Union line and then to "enfilade" the line from the tallest hills at the ends. A Confederate attack against the southernmost Union position came close to succeeding, but a desperate series of Union counterattacks on a hill known as "Little Round Top" gradually repulsed it. The lines of Meade's army held firm as the second day of battle played out.

On the third and most fateful day, Lee took a great gamble and unleashed an assault—Pickett's charge—against the center of the Union line, which he mistakenly believed to be weakened. The result was catastrophic for Lee: his forces were slaughtered in a hopeless and wasteful assault. Moreover, on the very next day, which was also the Fourth of July, Grant succeeded in capturing Vicksburg. All Confederate troops in the city surrendered, and a few days later the Confederate defenders of the other major fortified city down the river, Port Hudson, surrendered to the army of Nathaniel Banks. The news of these triumphs took several days to reach the White House.

On the Fourth of July, bearing news of the Gettysburg victory, Lincoln sent to the nation a hymn of thanksgiving, announcing that "the highest honor" had been won by the Army of the Potomac. Lincoln called for the "profoundest gratitude" not only to the army of General Meade but to God, "whose will, not ours," should be done.[12]

Though Lincoln continued to express such feelings in public, he was privately disturbed about the *aftermath* of Gettysburg. Meade was allowing Lee's army to escape, just as George McClellan had done in the aftermath of Antietam. On July 6, Lincoln wrote to Halleck, "I left the telegraph office a good deal dissatisfied." He suspected Meade's intention was to "get the enemy across the river again without a further collision," rather than "prevent his crossing and . . . destroy him."[13] Indeed, Lee and his army crossed into Virginia on the night of July 13.

Lincoln was enraged: to John Hay he exclaimed that "we had them within our grasp. We had only to stretch forth our hands & they were ours."[14] According to Hay, "the Tycoon"—a private nickname that Hay had been using for Lincoln—had gone so far as to say that he "'could have whipped them myself.'"[15] On July 14, Lincoln wrote a long letter to Meade—a letter that he never signed or sent. In this letter Lincoln made it emphatically clear that this war was nothing less than a war to be fought to the death unless the enemy surrendered. "I do not believe," Lincoln concluded, that "you appreciate the magnitude of the misfortune involved in Lee's escape. He was within your easy grasp, and to have closed upon him would, in connection with our other late successes, have ended the war. As it is, the war will be prolonged indefinitely. . . . Your golden opportunity is gone, and I am distressed immeasureably [sic] because of it."[16]

Despite the fact that Lincoln kept this letter to himself, Meade began to get wind of the president's mood and he offered to submit his resignation. But Lincoln kept him in command. Many Northerners regarded George Meade as a hero, and dismissing him might have seemed absurd. So Lincoln kept him on, but in a deeply pessimistic frame of mind. The fight to the death was not succeeding in the summer of 1863. In another brief year, the political conventions would launch the next race for the White House.

IN THE SECOND HALF OF 1863, Lincoln turned his attention more and more to the issue of race. The black troops of Lincoln's armies won distinction in two different battles. Blacks participated in the capture of Port Hudson, Louisiana. And near Charleston, South Carolina, blacks fought a gallant but suicidal action in assaulting a Confederate bastion known as Fort Wagner.

Yet military heroism notwithstanding, whites had still not accepted African Americans as equal citizens. As the Union draft went into effect in July, white mobs turned their wrath upon blacks. The biggest and worst of all the riots took place in New York City, where Democratic mobs went berserk on July 13. As James M. McPherson has observed, "the mob's chief target was the black population. Chanting 'kill the naygers' [many of the rioters were Irish immigrants], they lynched at least a dozen blacks and burned down the Colored Orphan Asylum. Because most of the militia had gone to Pennsylvania for the Gettysburg campaign, the city was especially vulnerable. . . . On the fourth day of rioting, the police and several regiments of soldiers that had been rushed to New York finally brought the city under control."[17] Throughout the riots, according to John Hay, Lincoln was a pillar of strength. A few weeks after the riots, Hay set down the following reflections: "The Tycoon is in fine whack. . . . He is managing this war, the draft, foreign relations, and planning a reconstruction of the Union, all at once. I never knew with what tyrannous authority he rules the Cabinet, till now. The most important things he decides, and there is no cavil."[18]

In August, an angry Lincoln wrote a letter intended to shame the white supremacist Northerners. This public letter was dispatched to a very old acquaintance in Springfield, Illinois: James C. Conkling. This letter to Conkling is a striking example of the methods Lincoln used to dragoon white supremacists by means of patriotic imperatives. It is also an excellent example of the methods Lincoln used to make heroes of the Union's black troops.

"There are those who are dissatisfied with me," Lincoln wrote. "To such I would say: You desire peace; and you blame me that we do not have it. But how can we attain it? There are but three conceivable ways. First, to suppress the rebellion by force of arms. This, I am trying to do. Are you for it? If you are, so far we are agreed. If you are not for it, a second way is to give up the Union. I am against this. Are you for it? If you are, you should say so plainly. If you are not for *force*, not yet for *dissolution*, there only remains some imaginable *compromise*. I do not believe any compromise, embracing the maintenance of the Union, is now possible."

Lincoln tried to make the case that a negotiated Unionist settlement appeared to be impossible as long as the Confederates remained unrepentant and their armies kept fighting. "The strength of the rebellion," he continued, "is its military—its army. That army dominates all the country, and all the people, within its range. Any offer of terms made by any man or men within that range, in opposition to that army, is simply nothing for the present; because such man or men, have no power whatever to enforce their side of a compromise. . . . No paper compromise, to which the controllers of Lee's army are not agreed, can, at all, affect that army. In an effort at such compromise we should waste time, which the enemy would use to our disadvantage; and that would be all."

Lincoln then grabbed the bull by the horns: "But, to be plain, you are dissatisfied with me about the negro. Quite likely there is a difference of opinion between you and myself upon that subject. I certainly wish that all men could be free, while I suppose you do not. Yet I have neither adopted, nor proposed any measure, which is not consistent with even your view, provided you are for the Union. I suggested compensated emancipation; to which you replied you wished not to be taxed to buy negroes. But I had not asked you to be taxed to buy negroes, except in such way, as to save you from greater taxation to save the Union exclusively by other means."

Lincoln turned to the Emancipation Proclamation. This too, he insisted, was imperative to save the Union. "You dislike the emancipation proclamation," he continued, "and, perhaps, would have it retracted. You say it is unconstitutional—I think differently. I think the constitution invests its commander-in-chief, with the law of war, in time of war. . . . Is there—has there ever been—any question that by the law of war, property, both of enemies and friends, may be taken when needed? And is it not needed whenever taking it, helps us, or hurts the enemy? . . . Some of our commanders of our armies in the field who have given us our most important successes, believe the emancipation policy, and the use of colored troops, constitute the heaviest blow yet dealt to the rebellion; and that, at least one of those important successes [Port Hudson, presumably], could not have been achieved when it was, but for the aid of black soldiers. Among the commanders holding these views are some who have never had any affinity with what is called abolitionism, or with republican party politics; but who hold them purely as military opinions."

Like a cross before the face of a vampire, the president brandished the emblem of "Union" in the faces of his white supremacist detractors. "You say you will not fight to free negroes. Some of them seem willing to fight for you; but, no matter. Fight you, then, exclusively, to save the Union. I issued the proclamation on purpose to aid you in saving the Union. Whenever you shall have conquered all resistance to the Union, if I shall urge you to continue fighting, it will be an apt time, then, for you to declare you will not fight to free negroes."

By the end of the letter, Lincoln's deep inner anger was emerging. "Peace," he concluded, "does not appear so distant as it did. I hope it will come soon, and come to stay; and so come as to be worth the keeping in all future time. . . . And then, there will be some black men who can remember that, with silent tongue, and clenched teeth, and steady eye, and well-poised bayonet, they have helped mankind on to this great consummation; while, I fear, there will be some white ones, unable to forget that, with malignant heart, and deceitful speech, they have strove to hinder it."[19]

At the risk of repetition, our question must be asked once again: is it possible to read such a letter as the statement of a racist politician who intended nothing more than preservation of the Union?

To the contrary—Lincoln sought to use every practical means at his disposal to reduce the power of slavery. Consistent with that, he would cautiously elevate the status of the newly freed slaves—either by placing them out of harm's reach beyond the borders of the country or by giving them the rudiments of status (the status, for example, of combat veterans and landowners)—while protecting his program from the backlash that might ruin everything.

He continued to be haunted by a number of worst-case scenarios. Around the time that he sent his long letter to Conkling, he penned the following reflections: "Suppose those now in rebellion should say: 'We cease fighting: re-establish the national authority amongst us—customs, courts, mails, land-offices,—all as before the rebellion—we claiming to send members to both branches of Congress, as of yore, and to hold our slaves according to our State laws, notwithstanding anything or all things which has [sic] occurred during the rebellion.'"

Lincoln was fearful and candid as he contemplated this scenario: "I shall dread, and I think we all should dread, to see 'the disturbing element' so brought back into the government. . . . During my continuance here, the government will return no person to slavery who is free according to the proclamation, or to any of the acts of congress, unless such return shall be held to be a legal duty, by the proper court of final resort. . . ."[20]

As LaWanda Cox has observed, Lincoln was "deeply troubled for the future of his emancipation policy" in 1863.[21] He was not alone; Cox has confirmed that "during 1863 and 1864 antislavery men feared the battle against the South's peculiar institution might yet be lost or compromised. However inevitable slavery's end may appear in retrospect, contemporary concern was real, and not without cause."[22]

So much for the worst-case scenarios: what of the best-case? In the summer of 1863, Frederick Douglass came to Washington to meet with the president concerning the status of blacks who were serving in uniform. This was the first time Frederick Douglass had met Lincoln, and his rich account of the event in his memoirs deserves to be quoted in detail.

"I was induced to go to Washington," Douglass remembered, "and lay the complaints of my people before President Lincoln and the secretary of war; and to urge upon them such action as should secure to the colored troops then fighting for the country, a reasonable degree of fair play." He did not know what to expect: "The distance then between the black man and the white American citizen, was immeasurable.... I was an ex-slave, identified with a despised race; and yet I was to meet the most exalted person in this great republic.... I could not know what kind of a reception would be accorded me. I might be told to go home and mind my business ... or I might be refused an interview altogether."

But Douglass was admitted to an interview with Lincoln on August 10. The president "was seated, when I entered, in a low arm chair, with his feet extended on the floor, surrounded by a large number of documents, and several busy secretaries. The room bore the marks of business, and the persons in it, the president included, appeared to be much over-worked and tired. Long lines of care were already deeply written in Mr. Lincoln's brow; ... his strong face ... lighted up as soon as my name was mentioned. As I approached and was introduced to him, he rose and extended his hand, and bade me welcome."

Douglass stated his mission; the president responded by asking him to "state particulars." Douglass did so:

> I replied that there were three particulars which I wished to bring to his attention. First, that colored soldiers ought to receive the same wages as those paid to white soldiers. Second, that colored soldiers ought to receive the same protection when taken prisoners, and be exchanged as readily, and on the same terms, as any other prisoners, and if Jefferson Davis should shoot or hang colored soldiers in cold blood, the United States government should retaliate in kind and degree.... Third, when colored soldiers, seeking the "bauble-reputation at the cannon's mouth," performed great and uncommon service on the battle-field, they would be rewarded by distinction and promotion....

The president "listened with patience and silence to all I had to say. He was serious and even troubled by what I had said, and by what he had evidently thought himself before on the same points." Lincoln then replied:

He began by saying that the employment of colored troops at all was a great gain to the colored people; that the measure could not have been successfully adopted at the beginning of the war; that the wisdom of making colored men into soldiers was still doubted; that their enlistment was a serious offense to popular prejudice; that they had larger motives for being soldiers than white men . . . that the fact that they were not to receive the same pay as white soldiers, seemed a necessary concession to smooth the way to their employment at all as soldiers; but that ultimately they would receive the same.

"They would receive the same" in due time: Lincoln quietly stated his intention to phase-in equality in wages. As to black promotions, Lincoln left the matter open, while deferring to the secretary of war. Lastly, in regard to Confederate crimes and atrocities against black soldiers, Lincoln said that he feared retaliation was a "terrible remedy," one which, "if once begun, there was no telling where it would end."[23]

Once again, however, Lincoln chose to conceal his hand for some reason. For he had signed precisely the sort of directive on war crimes that Douglass recommended. On July 30, Lincoln signed an order that was drafted by the War Department proclaiming it "the duty of every government to give protection to its citizens, of whatever class, color, or condition. . . . To sell or enslave any captured person, on account of his color, and for no offense against the laws of war, is a relapse into barbarism and a crime against the civilization of the age. . . ." Consequently, Lincoln's order continued, "If the enemy shall sell or enslave anyone because of his color, the offense shall be punished by retaliation upon the enemy's prisoners in our possession. It is therefore ordered that for every soldier of the United States killed in violation of the laws of war, a rebel soldier shall be executed; and for every one enslaved by the enemy or sold into slavery, a rebel soldier shall be placed at hard labor. . . ."[24]

Beyond military issues, the fate of black civilians and families was clearly on the minds of all anti-slavery Americans. As the Sea Island process of land confiscation by the federal tax commissioners continued off the South Carolina coast, Lincoln sent explicit orders to ensure that lots of twenty acres would be set aside for "heads of families of the African race, one only to each, preferring such as by their good conduct, meritorious services or exemplary character, will be examples of moral propriety and industry . . . for the charitable purpose of providing homes for such heads of families and their families respectively."[25]

At the same time, another experiment in black economic liberation was beginning to germinate. The scene was Davis Bend, Mississippi, which included the plantations of Jefferson Davis and his brother Joseph Davis. Both plantations had been seized and confiscated. Historian Eric Foner has described the outcome: "In 1863, General Grant decided that Davis Bend should become a 'negro paradise,' and the following year the entire area was set aside for the exclusive settlement of freedmen." Davis Bend became "a remarkable example of self-reliance, whose laborers raised nearly 2,000 bales of cotton and earned a profit of $160,000. The community had its own system of government, complete with elected judges and sheriffs."[26]

Elsewhere, however, the freedmen encountered some neglect, which Lincoln tried to mitigate. In August, Lincoln wrote to his friend Stephen Hurlbut, who had recently been commissioned as a Union general in occupied Mississippi. Lincoln expressed his concern that while "the able bodied male contrabands are already employed by the Army," the other freed slaves were "in confusion and destitution." Hence, "if there be plantations near you," Lincoln instructed, "which are abandoned by their owners, first put as many contrabands on such, as they will hold—that is, as can draw subsistence from them. If some still remain, get loyal men, of character in the vicinity, to take them temporarily on wages, to be paid to the contrabands themselves—such men obliging themselves to not let the contrabands be kidnapped, or forcibly taken away. Of course, if any voluntarily make arrangements to work for their living, you will not hinder them."[27]

In occupied Louisiana, General Nathaniel Banks issued labor regulations in 1863. These regulations, as Foner has stated, "bore a marked resemblance to slavery. The former slaves, [Banks] announced, must avoid vagrancy and idleness and enter into yearly contracts with loyal planters. . . . Once hired, the blacks were forbidden to leave the plantations without permission of their employers."[28] It is not at all clear as to when (or even whether) Lincoln knew the specific provisions of the code that Banks had developed. But Lincoln knew about the code's existence. And it is true that the president had special reasons to be cautious in Louisiana, reasons to be set forth momentarily.

Nonetheless, he made it clear in a letter to Banks that he wanted arrangements such as labor codes to be "probationary"—that is, temporary. He agreed with the short-term proposition that the state should "adopt some practical system by which the two races could gradually live themselves out of their old relation to each other, and both come out better prepared for the new." Some emphasis is needed: the president said that he wanted the races to live themselves *out* of their previous relation. By the end of summer, this vision was decisively replacing his preference for voluntary colonization. He then continued: "Education for young blacks should be included in this plan."[29]

Lincoln's reasons for exercising caution in Louisiana were complex, but the gist of his reasoning was simple: Lincoln had reason to believe in the summer and early fall of 1863 that Louisiana Unionists stood a good chance of redrafting the state's constitution *to make it a free state*. The new state of West Virginia was admitted to the Union as a free state on June 20, 1863. In terms of constitutional politics, the growth of the free-state bloc was of paramount importance to Lincoln. If Louisiana should succeed in redrafting its state constitution to abolish slavery, a new free state would be added to the Union and the slave states accordingly weakened. Indeed, Louisiana might set a new precedent that other occupied Confederate states could be induced, albeit under military pressure, to copy.

Moreover, in terms of Lincoln's worst-case analysis, the abolition of slavery by action of the loyal citizens state by state could be another important strategic hedge against the politics of Democratic victory in 1864. As Cox has observed, "beginning quietly in the spring of 1863, [Lincoln] moved to obtain emancipation in occupied states through state action, a piecemeal but constitutionally unchallengeable solution."[30]

As Cox has elaborated, the supporters of slavery were quick to try to hinder this action. On May 1, 1863, a group of pro-slavery Louisiana Unionists convened in New Orleans. They proceeded to send "a delegation to ask Lincoln for 'full recognition of all the rights of the State, as they existed previous to the passage of the act of secession, upon the principle of the existence of the State Constitution unimpaired.'"[31] They were obviously trying to cut their losses and return to allegiance with their system of slavery intact. But the president was playing for much higher stakes by the summer of 1863. And since a group of Louisiana Unionists led by Thomas J. Durant, Michael Hahn, and Benjamin Flanders were planning a constitutional convention to repudiate secession on a "free state" basis, Lincoln told the pro-slavery Louisiana Unionists on June 19 that since "reliable information has reached me that a respectable portion of the Louisiana people, desire to amend their State constitution, and contemplate holding a convention for that object," the fact of such a project seemed "sufficient reason why the general government should not give the committal you seek, to the existing State constitution."[32]

Since Banks was an active participant in pushing the project, Lincoln was probably averse to making much of an issue of his labor code, at least for a while. Indeed, Lincoln wished to make his role in Louisiana politics appear to be minimal in order that the free-state movement should appear to be a massive insurgency, which it was not. Lincoln summarized the matter in an August 5 letter to Banks: "While I very well know what I would be glad for Louisiana to do, it is quite a different thing for me to assume direction of the matter. I would be glad for her to make a new Constitution recognizing the emancipation proclamation, and adopting emancipation in those parts of the state to which the proclamation does not apply. . . . If these views can be of any advantage in giving shape, impetus, and action there, I shall be glad for you to use them prudently for that object. Of course you will confer with intelligent and trusty citizens of the State, among whom I would suggest Messrs. Flanders, Hahn, and Durant."[33]

In September, Lincoln turned to reconstruction efforts in occupied Tennessee; once again, he encouraged his allies and agents to redraft the state constitution to abolish slavery. Due to different political circumstances, however, he was far more direct than he had been in his Louisiana dealings. To Governor Andrew Johnson he wrote that "not a moment should be lost. . . . I see that you have declared in favor of emancipation in Tennessee, for which, may God bless you. Get emancipation into your new State government—Constitution—and there will be no such word as fail for your case." Do it quickly, Lincoln added, for "it can not be known who is next to occupy the position I now hold, nor what he will do."[34]

A free-state movement was also under way in the loyal slave state of Maryland. This movement, as Foner has explained, was "bolstered by loyalty oaths administered to voters by army provost marshals. . . . Voting was confined to those who took a strict loyalty oath, which included an avowal that one had never expressed a 'desire' for Confederate victory." With the Maryland electorate reduced in this manner, anti-slavery "Unionists committed to immediate and uncompensated emancipation swept the Maryland elections of 1863 and called a constitutional convention to reconstruct the state."[35]

In all, Lincoln's actions on slavery were heavily prioritized in 1863. He sought to do everything within his power to make emancipation permanent, to eliminate the legal underpinnings of slavery. His policies regarding the freedmen were, though extremely important, less urgent. As Cox has affirmed, both in this and other issues, "what becomes apparent in examining Lincoln's leadership role is his way of placing first things first."[36] And in 1863, the first issue was victory and permanent commitment to freedom, well before the next presidential election put everything at risk.

Though the war had fallen short of Lincoln's hopes in the critical theatre of Virginia, his armies in East Tennessee began moving toward victory late in the summer. Burnside and his newly formed army moved south from Ohio and occupied Knoxville in East Tennessee on September 3. More importantly, Rosecrans was able to flush the Confederates out of Chattanooga on September 9. Braxton Bragg's Confederate army retreated into Georgia, with Rosecrans in pursuit.

The Confederates, however, turned the tables and unleashed a ferocious assault upon the Union forces at Chickamauga Creek, about a dozen miles below Chattanooga, just across the Georgia line. The two-day battle of Chickamauga, which was fought from September 19 to September 20, was a tactical Union defeat. As Rosecrans began a retreat to Chattanooga, a subordinate Union commander of far greater bravery and presence of mind—General George Thomas, a loyalist Virginian—held Confederate attackers at bay and thus prevented the retreat from becoming a rout.

Then Bragg turned the tables again: he threw a siege around Chattanooga, turning Rosecrans and all of his troops into prisoners within the very city they had captured just a few weeks before. From Missionary Ridge and from Lookout Mountain, the Confederate gunners prevented any food or supplies from reaching the Union defenders.

In October, Lincoln sent a great infusion of troops from Mississippi and Virginia to break this Confederate siege. He placed Ulysses S. Grant in command of all Union armies in the West so he could supervise the whole operation. Grant went to Chattanooga himself: he promptly removed William Rosecrans from theatre command and appointed George Thomas in his place.

It bears noting that Lincoln's opinion of Meade was sufficiently low that he was quite nonchalant about reducing Union forces in Virginia. In early September, Meade asked for instructions as to how to proceed against Lee. Lincoln answered, via Halleck, that Meade should "move upon Lee in a manner of general attack, leaving to developments, whether he will make it a real attack."[37] Meade's reply (via Halleck) was extremely depressing to Lincoln. Meade claimed that Lee's defensive position (near the Rapidan River in Virginia) was almost unassailable. In other words, according to Meade, there was nothing whatsoever he could do against Lee—though his forces outnumbered Lee's army to a massive extent.

Lincoln dashed off a series of comments to Halleck in a mood of ill-suppressed disgust. "Let me say," Lincoln wrote, that "if our army can not fall upon the enemy and hurt him where he is, it is plain to me it can gain nothing by attempting to follow him over a succession of intrenched [sic] lines into a fortified city [i.e., Richmond]."[38]

On October 16, Lincoln tried once again to get Meade to consider an offensive. He sent a message to Meade via Halleck: "If Gen. Meade can now attack him on a field no worse than equal for us, and will do so with all the skill and courage, which he, his officers and men possess, the honor will be his if he succeeds, and the blame may be mine if he fails."[39] But Meade continued to demur.

So another Union general was proven quite useless for the total-war purposes of Lincoln. Grant, meanwhile—Lincoln's best fighting general—had his hands full out in Tennessee. So Lincoln drained away some troops from Meade's army and sent them off to Grant. He told Gideon Welles, secretary of the navy, that he regarded Meade as utterly hopeless. According to Welles, the president complained that in the autumn of 1863 it was still "the same old story with the Army of the Potomac. Imbecility, inefficiency—don't want to *do*. . . ."[40] It seemed that winning the war would have to wait until 1864, with all the risks of the election in the balance.

The war had been costly enough that year in terms of human losses: though the overall level of casualties had been light in the Vicksburg campaign, combined Union and Confederate casualties at Murfreesboro had been almost 25,000; at Gettysburg, almost 50,000; and at Chickamauga, almost 35,000.

In November, Lincoln made his famous trip to pay homage to the Union soldiers who were killed in the battle of Gettysburg. Their bodies were being slowly reinterred in the federal cemetery there. He who had commanded a war to the death with such anger and vehemence

Lincoln on November 8, 1863, with his secretaries John Nicolay and John Hay. Photograph by Alexander Gardner. (Library of Congress, Meserve Collection #56)

was privately tortured by the news of each battle's cost. Morbid feelings were all too familiar in the life of Abraham Lincoln. Ever since his youth, his depressive side had been haunted by the death of his loved ones. The loss of Ann Rutledge, his young fiancée, drove him close to a suicidal madness in the 1830s. (This affair, long dismissed as a romanticized legend, has been recently validated by the historian Douglas L. Wilson.)[41] In 1850, he lost a young son—Edward, or "Eddie," Lincoln. Then he lost little Willie in the winter of 1862. He kept pondering the heart-breaking cost of what his policies had forced upon the nation.

The worst-case future—the twisted future of America eaten away at the core by the poison of white supremacy—was being averted. But the price of averting such a sickening future for the nation was utterly grievous: the *personal* futures of the troops who were falling in battle were lost forever.

One thing alone could redeem all the death: a transcendent national rebirth. Lincoln used the occasion of the Gettysburg Address to invoke his old vision from the 1850s—the vision for America he used in his Peoria and Springfield addresses when he castigated Stephen Douglas. America's equality creed, as enshrined in its peerless Declaration of Independence, must be rescued from those who would pervert it. It must be lifted on high through a new infusion of spirit.

The Founders, Lincoln said, had conceived a new nation "dedicated to the proposition that all men are created equal." This war was a test to determine not only whether *this* particular nation but *any* nation "so conceived, and so dedicated, can long endure." This hallowed field would be a monument to those who "gave their lives, that the nation might live."

His listeners were challenged by his solemn invocation of the human cycle and its turnings: conception, birth, endurance, the sorrow of death, and his visions of re-birth.

In the midst of the mourning, it is up to the living, he declared, to "be dedicated here to the unfinished work which they who fought here have thus far so nobly advanced." They must not have died in vain for their country. "The last full measure of devotion" played out upon the field must inspire in the hearts of all the living an "increased devotion" to the cause for which the sacrificed heroes gave everything they had. A "new birth of freedom" must result from the death: the Union, devoted to its quintessential creed, must triumph and triumph completely. If not, then all the dreams that America had stood for would "perish from the earth."[42]

As scholar Garry Wills has observed, the "audacity of Lincoln's undertaking" in the Gettysburg Address was to lift the Declaration of Independence and its ideals of freedom and equality far above the moral reputation of the United States Constitution. Lincoln's critics were quick to observe this. "Some people, looking on from a distance," according to Wills, "saw that a giant (if benign) swindle had been performed" by Lincoln in his Gettysburg speech—a "swindle" by the logic of their white supremacist standards. "The Chicago *Times* quoted the letter of the Constitution to Lincoln—noting its lack of reference to equality, its tolerance of slavery—and said that Lincoln was betraying the instrument he was on oath to defend." The editorial quoted by Wills—an openly white supremacist document—proceeded as follows: "It was to uphold this constitution, and the Union created by it, that our officers and soldiers gave their lives at Gettysburg. How dare he [Lincoln], then, standing on their graves, misstate the cause for which they died, and libel the statesmen who founded the government? They were men possessing too much self-respect to declare that negroes were their equals, or were entitled to equal privileges."[43]

As Lincoln gave the speech, the forces of Grant were preparing to defeat the Confederate besiegers of Chattanooga. On November 24, Joseph Hooker, dispatched from Virginia, took Lookout Mountain in the so-called "Battle Above the Clouds." (Hooker, who had fallen apart when he confronted the challenge of senior command in Virginia, seemed to do quite well when he was placed in subordinate positions). And on the very next day, George Thomas's troops performed the seemingly impossible feat of storming Missionary Ridge, driving Bragg

and his Confederate troops to abandon their position on the heights
and retreat across the Georgia state line.

As news of this great Union victory reached Lincoln, it was time once
again for the president to write his long annual message to Congress.
With the message, which he sent on December 8, came another presidential proclamation: a proclamation of amnesty and reconstruction.

Here is yet another major item in the orthodox legend of Lincoln
the "moderate": his "lenient" plan for reconstruction. But Lincoln's
earliest plan for reconstruction was clearly just a temporary ploy if we
consider his position on the issue as it changed in the months before
he died. His lenient offer in the closing days of 1863 was very closely
related to his improvised "free-state" strategy.

As we have seen, Lincoln hoped to catalyze the drafting of anti-
slavery constitutions in some of the occupied rebel states. He had particular hopes for Tennessee and Louisiana; he was heartened as well
by some recent events in Arkansas. He was quietly encouraging the
free-state movement in Maryland as well as a brand-new movement in
the state of Missouri to eliminate slavery through gradual phaseout. It
was vital to his plans to get the work done *quickly*, before the next
national election.

But the politics were delicate and tricky. In Louisiana, for example,
the drive to enroll a new electorate to frame an anti-slavery constitution had begun to break down. "This disappoints me bitterly," the president wrote to General Banks in early November. "There is danger,
even now, that the adverse element seeks insidiously to pre-occupy the
ground." Consider the danger, Lincoln warned, that would loom "if a
few professedly loyal men shall draw the disloyal about them, and col-
orably set up a State government, repudiating the emancipation proclamation, and re-establishing slavery." Make haste, Lincoln pleaded
with Banks: you should "lose no more time."

Then he turned to the issue of the labor code that Banks had developed. "I do not insist upon such temporary arrangement," the president wrote to Banks, "but only say such would not be objectionable to
me." On the largest issue, however, the president was adamant in fighting for the status of Louisiana freedmen: "my word is out to be *for* and
not *against* them on the question of their permanent freedom."[44]

In overall terms, Lincoln's "lenient" plan for reconstruction must be
understood as a facilitating scheme for his plans to protect emancipation—
a facilitating scheme to *speed the work* of redrafting some rebel state

constitutions. It was also, of course, an experiment to see whether offers of federal pardon might weaken the grip of Confederate leaders
and induce more rebel defections, thus shortening the war.

Lincoln's Proclamation of Amnesty and Reconstruction declared:

> whereas it is now desired by some persons heretofore engaged in . . . rebellion
> to resume their allegiance to the United States, and to reinaugurate loyal State
> governments . . . therefore, I, Abraham Lincoln, President of the United States,
> do proclaim, declare, and make known to all persons who have, directly or by
> implication, participated in the existing rebellion . . . that a full pardon is hereby
> granted to them and each of them, with restoration of all rights of property,
> except as to slaves, and in property cases where rights of third parties shall have
> intervened . . .

Presumably this was a reference to the properties sold to third parties
through tax foreclosures.

Lincoln then insisted on an oath that would have to be sworn by the
penitent rebels; not only would the rebels have to swear to support the
Constitution and the federal government, but, the president ordered,
they would also have to swear to "abide by and faithfully support all
acts of Congress passed during the existing rebellion with reference to
slaves, so long and so far as not repealed, modified or held void by
Congress, or by decision of the Supreme Court. . . ." By the same
token, they would have to support "all proclamations of the President
made during the existing rebellion having reference to slaves."

In other words, the only whites who would vote in rebel states would
be the ones who had sworn to uphold Lincoln's anti-slavery policies.
They and they alone would have the power to redraft the state constitutions. A small group of such people would suffice—a mere 10 percent of the 1860 voting population, to be precise.

Lincoln pointedly excluded from the offer any persons who had
served as Confederate leaders. Having done so, he offered the following terms for political reorganization state by state: in any rebel state,
when a tenth of the voting population (as of 1860) took the loyalty
oath and created a new state government "in no wise contravening said
oath," that government would then be recognized by Lincoln as "the
true government of the State." Moreover, Lincoln promised that if
any "provision . . . may be adopted by such State government in relation to the freed people of such State, which shall recognize and declare their permanent freedom, provide for their education, and which

may yet be consistent, as a temporary arrangement, with their present condition as a laboring, landless, and homeless class," it would "not be objected to by the national Executive."

Then he added some important disclaimers. "To avoid misunderstanding," the president continued, "it may be proper to . . . say that whether members sent to Congress from any State shall be admitted to seats, constitutionally rests exclusively with the respective Houses [of Congress], and not to any extent with the Executive." Moreover, while he stressed that his reconstruction plan of December 1863 was "the best the Executive can suggest, *with his present impressions*, it must not be understood that no other possible mode would be acceptable [my emphasis]."[45] Lincoln clearly implied that his offer of a "lenient" reconstruction *might very well change* if the *circumstances* changed. Lincoln emphasized the very same point in his message to Congress.[46]

Lincoln's message was replete with congratulations and praise for his Union commanders. He was also exultant on the new birth of freedom and its progress. His preliminary announcement of emancipation, the president recalled, "gave to the future a new aspect, about which hope, and fear, and doubt contended in uncertain conflict." Indeed, when the final proclamation had been issued, "it was followed by dark and doubtful days." But now, with the passage of a year, Lincoln wrote, the whole prospect for freedom was changed, triumphantly changed. A new spirit was sweeping the land.

Lincoln wrote that "the movements, by State action, for emancipation in several of the States, not included in the emancipation proclamation, are matters of profound congratulation."[47] As examples, he cited the states of Maryland and Missouri. "Three years ago," Lincoln wrote, neither one of these states "would tolerate any restraint upon the extension of slavery into new territories." But now, it seemed that the only dispute about slavery in each of these states was "as to the best mode of removing it within their own limits." Moreover, in occupied states, some examples could be given of a movement to embrace emancipation under law and make it permanent: "Tennessee and Arkansas have been substantially cleared of insurgent control, and influential citizens in each, owners of slaves and advocates of slavery at the beginning of the rebellion, now declare openly for emancipation in their respective States."[48]

Turning to his scheme for reconstruction, he defended his reconstruction oath and its attempt to force allegiance to the policies of the president and Congress on the issue of emancipation. "Those laws and proclamations," the president reasoned, "were enacted and put forth for the purpose of aiding in the suppression of the rebellion. To give them their fullest effect, there had to be a pledge for their maintenance. . . . To now abandon them would be not only to relinquish a lever of power, but would also be a cruel and astounding breach of faith. . . ." He continued: "I may add at this point, that while I remain in my present position I shall not attempt to retract or modify the emancipation proclamation; nor shall I return to slavery any person who is free by the terms of that proclamation, or by any of the acts of Congress. For these and other reasons it is thought best that support of these measures shall be included in the oath; and it is believed that the Executive may lawfully claim it in return for pardon and restoration of forfeited rights, which he has clear constitutional power to withhold altogether, or grant upon the terms which he shall deem wisest for the public interest."[49]

Lincoln tried to maintain a brave front in this message as he pondered the political prospects for what he had achieved. He told Congress that the nation's anti-slavery measures were enjoying broad public support, both at home and abroad. "These measures have been much discussed in foreign countries, and . . . the tone of public sentiment there is much improved," he stated. "At home the same measures have been fully discussed, supported, criticized, and denounced, and the annual elections . . . [presumably Lincoln was referring to the off-year elections held in 1863] are highly encouraging to those whose official duty it is to bear the country through this great trial. Thus we have the new reckoning. The crisis which threatened to divide the friends of the Union is past."[50]

The crisis was past? Surely Lincoln knew better when he made the assertion: he was obviously seeking to rally his supporters in Congress and the nation at large. He was clearly aware of the ordeal that was in all probability awaiting him.

Lincoln's war would be resumed in the spring with the hope of preempting the results of the 1864 election. But if victory eluded him, the worst-case future was looming, and the president knew it. Everything he had struggled to achieve for the nation could be lost if the politics were wrong. And the Confederates knew it as well. If he ever felt the need for providential assistance, he would feel it to the point of despair in the horrid months ahead.

SIX

Lincoln and the Worst-Case Future, 1864

I N 1864, almost everything that Lincoln had been dreading in regard to the next presidential election began to come true: by the end of the summer, he was certain he would lose the presidency. The election of 1864 would be one of the most decisive in American history—and potentially the most catastrophic.[1]

His very renomination was disputed by Republican dissenters: certain Radical Republicans began to court Salmon Chase, Lincoln's secretary of the treasury. Chase, of course, had been a major contender for the 1860 nomination. His supporters were urging him to risk an open breach with the president. In January and February 1864, the growing "Chase boom" flourished in Washington, and Chase encouraged it. On February 22, Senator Samuel Pomeroy of Kansas sent a circular to newspapers: the statement, signed by a number of influential Republicans, declared that Lincoln's reelection was all but impossible and advocated the nomination of Chase.

The "Pomeroy Circular" backfired. Lincoln's supporters swung quickly into action to counteract it: in both local and state Republican conventions, Lincoln's renomination was urged in the strongest of terms. The Republican National Committee followed suit and support for Chase declined in early March. Yet the damage to Lincoln was significant.

Radical Republicans were angry with Lincoln, in large part because of the provisions of his Reconstruction plan. They were especially angry in regard to Louisiana. In late December, Lincoln wrote to General Nathaniel Banks and instructed him to "give us a free-state reorganization of Louisiana, in the shortest possible time."[2] Since the drive to amend the Louisiana state constitution had been stalling, Banks forced abolition on the state through a faster method. As LaWanda Cox has explained, Banks decided to skip the constitutional convention temporarily and "order an election for governor and other state officials under the antebellum constitution with its slavery provisions declared inoperative and void by military authority. . . . A convention for the revision of the state constitution would be held after the government was organized. . . ."[3]

The elections were held on February 22, and Michael Hahn, the Free State leader, was elected as Louisiana's governor. Per Banks's arrangement, the constitutional convention was scheduled for April.

Blacks were not allowed to vote in these Louisiana elections and a number of them chose to protest. As Eric Foner has explained, "In New Orleans lived the largest free black community of the Deep South. Its wealth, social standing, education, and unique history set it apart not only from the slaves but from free persons of color elsewhere. Most were the descendants of unions between French settlers and black women or of wealthy mulatto emigrants from Haiti. Although denied suffrage, they enjoyed far more rights than free blacks in other states, including the ability to travel freely and testify in court against whites."[4]

On March 12, two leaders of this black community, Arnold Bertonneau and Jean-Baptiste Roudanez, came to Washington and met with the president: they protested the fact that they had not been allowed to cast votes in the Louisiana elections. On the very next day, Lincoln wrote to Hahn and encouraged him to think about the phase-in of voting rights for blacks. "I congratulate you on having fixed your name in history as the first free-state Governor of Louisiana," Lincoln wrote. "Now you are about to have a Convention which, among other things, will probably define the elective franchise." Then he made his secret suggestion: "I barely suggest for your private consideration, whether some of the colored people may not be let in—as, for instance, the very intelligent, and especially those who have fought gallantly in our ranks. They would probably help, in some trying time to come, to keep the jewel of liberty within the family of freedom. But this is only a suggestion, not to the public, but to you alone."[5]

It is hard to overstate the importance of this letter: Lincoln clearly supported giving voting rights to blacks incrementally. This experiment could lead toward the gradual achievement of political equality for blacks all over the nation. Many Northern states also denied blacks the right to vote at the time Lincoln made his suggestion, and the issue was explosive with the electorate.

Lincoln had reached another major milestone: in concept at least, he was moving toward the goal of political equality for blacks.[6] As LaWanda Cox has affirmed, "there is ample evidence to conclude that Lincoln's conception of freedom was expansive and that his personal racial feelings constituted no barrier to pushing the boundaries between slavery and freedom to whatever limit could be sustained by public consent and law."[7]

There was no more talk about colonization by Lincoln in 1864. The brief experiment with black volunteers on Isle-a-Vache had ended. In March, Lincoln sent a Navy vessel to bring back the colonists.

His concern about the fate of freed blacks continued to develop. In the previous October, Lincoln had directed General James S. Wadsworth to investigate conditions for blacks in the Mississippi Valley. In February, Lincoln sent another general, Daniel Sickles, to "make a tour for me . . . by way of Cairo and New-Orleans, and returning by the Gulf and Ocean" to determine "what is being done, if anything, for reconstruction. . . ." Then, the president continued, "learn what you can as to the colored people—how they get along as soldiers, as laborers in our service, on leased plantations, and as hired laborers with their old masters, if there be such cases. Also learn what you can about the colored people within the rebel lines."[8]

Lincoln cared about the fate of these blacks: in a speech that he delivered in Baltimore on April 18, 1864, he likened himself to a shepherd protecting his flock from the fangs of the wolves. "The world has never had a good definition of the word liberty," the president observed, "and the American people, just now, are much in want of one. . . . With some the word liberty may mean for each man to do as he pleases with himself, and the product of his labor; while with others the same word may mean for some men to do as they please with other men, and the product of other men's labor. . . . The shepherd drives the wolf from the sheep's throat, for which the sheep thanks the shepherd as a *liberator*, while the wolf denounces him for the same act as a destroyer of liberty, especially as the sheep was a black one."[9]

At the time that Lincoln gave this speech, the new Louisiana constitution was being drafted. It would later be ratified on September 5, 1864, by the 10 percent electorate permitted under Lincoln's plan.

This new constitution ended slavery in Louisiana. Emancipation would be permanent—at least if this new constitution were upheld as binding and legitimate. It provided for a system of public schools that would be open to blacks as well as whites. And it empowered the Louisiana legislature to confer voting rights upon blacks.

In the view of certain Radical Republicans, however, such results were woefully inadequate. The 10 percent plan was too easy on the South in the view of leading Radical Republicans like Thaddeus Stevens and Benjamin Wade. Many prominent abolitionists such as Wendell Phillips gave angry speeches denouncing Lincoln's plan. Even Lincoln's Radical friend in the Senate, Charles Sumner, was angry: a new breach between Lincoln and Sumner was starting to develop.

The Radicals apparently failed to perceive the way in which Lincoln used his 10 percent plan to push *fast abolition* by tiny *minorities* in each rebel state. By allowing only 10 percent of the 1860 electorate to start Reconstruction, Lincoln made it easy for his agents like Banks to foist emancipation on the racist (and rebel) majority. This was a clever trick. Under Lincoln's scheme, a mere 10 percent of each rebel state's electorate could change the state's constitution and make it a free state.

In the spring of 1864, Lincoln privately pushed his emancipationist free-state agenda in Arkansas. He worked with General Frederick Steele, the military governor, to sponsor elections under the antebellum constitution with its slavery provisions held void. On January 27, the president instructed Steele to force unity among the various political factions in the state, and at the same time to "be sure to retain the free State constitutional provision in some unquestionable form."[10] The Arkansas elections were held in March, and the state's constitution was redrafted months later on the president's free-state principles.

Lincoln also intervened in the free-state politics of Maryland, though the Unionist state was exempt from the provisions of his 10 percent plan. Lincoln wrote that he was "anxious for emancipation to be effected in Maryland in some substantial form." As to gradual versus immediate emancipation, he explained to a supporter that his earlier expressions of a "preference for *gradual* over *immediate* emancipation, are misunderstood. I had thought that *gradual* would produce less confusion, and destitution . . . but if those who are better acquainted with the subject . . . prefer the *immediate*, most certainly I have no objection to their judgment prevailing. My wish is that all who are for emancipation *in any form*, shall co-operate. . . ."[11]

Lincoln's work behind the scenes on behalf of the free-state movement cut very little ice with the Radicals. In addition to all of their complaints about the "leniency" of his Reconstruction offer, they had reasons to protest against his offer to return all confiscated property to penitent rebels, except for their slaves. Indeed, the Radical Republican Congressman George Julian of Indiana introduced a bill in the early months of 1864 to extend the provisions of the 1862 Homestead Act to cover confiscated lands in the South. His intention was to offer such confiscated lands to the freedmen and Union soldiers. While Julian's bill passed the House of Representatives on May 12, it was buried in the Senate by the time that Congress adjourned.

As we have seen, Lincoln firmly supported the redistribution of confiscated lands when they were seized for non-payment of taxes. Nonetheless, we have also seen that he opposed the redistribution of lands that were seized as a penalty for treason. He believed this to be unconstitutional. Congress had deferred to his position by attaching a joint declaration in support of his views to the second confiscation act.

But evidence suggests that Lincoln started to rethink his position on the issue of land redistribution by the spring of 1864. Historian James M. McPherson has suggested that the publication of a book entitled *War Powers Under the Constitution of the United States*, written by a widely respected legal scholar named William Whiting (who was serving at the time in the War Department as solicitor), might have influenced Lincoln on the matter of "bills of attainder." Whiting "argued learnedly that the constitutional prohibition of bills of attainder did not debar Congress from confiscating property permanently by separate legislative act as a punishment for treason."[12] Moreover, Congressman Julian claimed that Whiting's arguments had changed Lincoln's mind.

As McPherson recounts the story, "Julian went to see Lincoln on July 2 [1864], hoping to convince the President of the constitutionality of permanent confiscation. Lincoln admitted

Lincoln in 1864. Photograph by Matthew Brady.
(Library of Congress, Meserve Collection #81)

that when he had forced Congress to adopt the joint resolution in 1862 he had not examined the question thoroughly. William Whiting's written and spoken arguments, the President said, had since convinced him of his error, and he was now ready to sign a bill repealing the joint resolution of 1862."[13]

Important subsequent events (in the early months of 1865) lend strong circumstantial support to this theory that the president was coming around to the position of across-the-board land redistribution. In short, Lincoln and his Radical Republican critics were closer on a number of issues in 1864 than appeared on the surface. Indeed, Radicals embraced the rather daring proposal that *Lincoln* introduced in Congress many months earlier: the amendment of the Constitution to protect emancipation.

Instead of the three-amendment package as proposed by Lincoln in his annual message of December 1862, however, the Thirteenth Amendment, as the Radical Republicans drafted it, eliminated slavery nationwide—and all at once. While this powerful amendment was passed by the Senate in April, the Democratic gains in the elections of 1862 kept it stalled in the House of Representatives.

Moreover, Lincoln worked with the Radicals on early civil rights legislation in the spring of 1864. He signed a series of bills that permitted blacks to testify in Federal courts, forbade discrimination in the streetcar system of the District of Columbia, and (in fulfillment of his pledge to Frederick Douglass) raised the level of pay for black troops.[14]

So much for the common positions of Lincoln and the Radicals in 1864: what about the breach? The Radicals' growing discontent with the president's Reconstruction program prompted Senator Benjamin Wade of Ohio and Representative Henry Winter Davis of Maryland to draft an alternative congressional plan for Reconstruction. The Wade-Davis Bill, as it was called, was more demanding than the Lincoln plan. Instead of permitting only 10 percent of the 1860 electorate to start Reconstruction (after taking a loyalty oath), the Wade-Davis Bill demanded that a minimum of 50 percent should take the oath before the process of Reconstruction could start in any rebel state. Moreover, a constitutional convention was *required* in the Wade-Davis Bill. This was clearly an expression of the Radicals' long-standing theory of "state suicide": Congress, in the Radicals' view, possessed unlimited power to reconstruct any state that had forfeited its statehood.

In its earliest version, the Wade-Davis Bill permitted "loyal" men to vote in rebel states, regardless of their race. In its final version, however, the right to vote was limited to whites. Wade and Davis consented to this latter provision so as not to "sacrifice the bill."[15] (Like Lincoln, in other words, these Radical Republicans were willing to modify their tempo of reform in a manner that was mindful of political realities, especially the danger of a backlash.)

On the other side of the political spectrum, the white supremacist Democrats could hardly wait for their chance to oust both Lincoln and the Radicals from power. In preparing himself for a Democratic backlash, the president was careful to maintain his position as a patriotic Unionist above all else—as a president who put the preservation of the Union *first* in every one of his actions. To a Kentuckian he wrote in early April that his "private" convictions on slavery had never affected his judgment in his struggle to protect the Constitution while saving the Union. He admitted he was "naturally anti-slavery," for "if slavery is not wrong, nothing is wrong." But he had "never understood that the Presidency conferred upon me an unrestricted right to act officially upon this judgment and feeling." He continued: "I aver that, to this day, I have done no official act in mere deference"—note the qualifier, "mere" deference—"to my abstract judgment and feeling." He went on to admit that the national emergency had sometimes convinced him "that measures, otherwise unconstitutional, might become lawful, by becoming indispensable to the preservation of the constitution, through the preservation of the nation." Emancipation, Lincoln argued, had become an "indispensable necessity."

Near the close of his letter, he wrote a famous line, often used as evidence of Lincoln's moderate side: "I claim not to have controlled events," Lincoln wrote, "but confess plainly that events have controlled me."

Like so much of his writing, this "confession" must be read on two levels. At the tactical level, the statement was a calculated ploy. For those who knew him best, for those who watched him in action, such a statement would in all probability have seemed like a "put-on." And one is tempted to compare it to the "foxy" maneuverings of Franklin Delano Roosevelt many years later. The "Tycoon," it appeared, was in "fine whack" again: he was crafty in denying any craftiness, ascribing all his actions to "events." We know better: his unremitting efforts to direct, to rechannel, to coordinate events—his brilliance in strategy, his talent for behind-the-scenes orchestration ("give us a free-state re-organization . . . in the shortest possible time"), his peremptory tone with subordinates who flouted his will ("Answer at once")—make a mockery of any such political "confession" that events had somehow "controlled" him. On this level, surely, Lincoln's statement was a palpable deception. He was making such statements to inoculate himself against attacks by the Copperheads who claimed he was acting like a "tyrant." He was posing as a paragon of probity, responding to events as they happened to occur: just a servant of the people who had pledged himself to save the nation.

On a deeper level, however, there is reason to articulate a very different meaning in the statement. We are forced to acknowledge here a different kind of truth: for events *had indeed* been overriding Lincoln's plans since the onset of war. The coming of secession and the coming of the war had been written off by Lincoln as improbable before they occurred, and yet they *did* occur. The carnage of the war had been appalling and surprising to Lincoln. And the worst-case contingencies were threatening to wipe out all of his achievements if his luck should take a turn for the worse in the coming election.

Even geniuses succumb to the vastness of events: the contingencies determine the outcomes they try to control. The wisest will acknowledge it is all "in God's hands" when they have finished. On this level, surely, the statement by Lincoln was an invocation of Providence: it was a prayer that the Lord would sustain him.

Lincoln made this clear at the end of his letter, while expressing guarded hope that his interpretation of Providence would prove to be prophetic. "Now, at the end of three years struggle," Lincoln wrote, the condition of the nation "is not what either party, or any man devised, or expected. God alone can claim it. Whither it is tending seems plain. If God now wills the removal of a great wrong, and wills also that we of the North as well as you of the South, shall pay fairly for our complicity in that wrong, impartial history will find therein new cause to attest and revere the justice and goodness of God."[16] The theme he would use for his second Inaugural Address was taking shape in his mind already—if God granted him a second term in office.

The key to a second term was victory in the war, and Lincoln had reason to hope that a final major military effort could defeat the Confederate armies before the election. Early in the year, he had made his big decision to promote Ulysses S. Grant to the position of general in chief, and to demote Henry Halleck. "[A]t his own request," as Lincoln put it, Halleck opted for the newly created position of Chief of Staff, the senior clerk who would arrange Grant's paperwork.[17]

Legend has it that when Grant took over as general in chief, Lincoln faded as a military strategist. Such was not the case. Grant's initial strategic conceptions were at odds with the views of Lincoln, and the president was called upon to take some remedial action. In January—just after Grant's victory at Chattanooga and before his promotion to the post of general in chief—he took the liberty of sending the president, by way of Halleck, some important strategic suggestions. Lincoln found them to be deeply flawed.

Grant initially proposed to take the Union forces in East Tennessee and divide them into two smaller armies. One of these armies would pursue the retreating Confederates deep into Georgia; the other would be sent on a mission to the Gulf of Mexico to strike against Mobile, Alabama. Historian T. Harry Williams's research has made it clear that Lincoln forced a change in this plan since he believed, as Williams has interpreted the record, that "the government did not have enough troops in the West to constitute two major striking forces." In particular, according to Williams, Lincoln feared that "if the army at Chattanooga was weakened to build up the force destined for Mobile, there was always the possibility that the Confederates might be able to recover East Tennessee. . . . Lincoln saw the weakness in the plan and vetoed it."[18]

Lincoln's *modus operandi*, both in politics and war, was his constant preparation for the best-case and worst-case contingencies—*both of them at once*. He wanted armies that were poised to attack while positioned to defend. He wanted generals who thought in these terms, but too often what he got were "uneven" commanders who were strong on the one side but pitifully weak on the other. None of the president's commanders, as yet, gave *equal* attention to offensive and defensive positioning.

Grant's suggestion for a new campaign in the eastern theatre was worse than his proposal for the West: he proposed to drain troops from the Army of the Potomac and send them by sea into North Carolina to disrupt the Confederate railroads that serviced Richmond. There was no need for Lincoln to veto this plan, since Halleck took care of it for him. Williams elaborates: "When Halleck read Grant's plan, he knew

Lincoln would not like it. Halleck was so familiar with Lincoln's strategic ideas that he could tell how the President would react to almost any proposal. He informed Grant that he would lay the scheme before Lincoln but that the President would disapprove it. Using almost the same words that Lincoln had employed in several letters to Meade, Halleck emphasized that Lee's army, not Richmond, should be the objective of the Potomac Army. . . ." Moreover, Halleck explained, "when Lee learned that the army facing him had been depleted he would move on Washington, forcing the government to recall the whole Carolina expedition for the defense of the capital."[19]

After Grant had been summoned to Washington and given his command, he and Lincoln had a number of conferences. These conferences led to an overall plan, which Williams describes: "After he talked to Lincoln in Washington, Grant dropped completely his scheme to send an army into North Carolina. His new plan was to make Lee's army the objective and to go after it in Virginia and destroy it. In words that Lincoln might have written, Grant instructed Meade: 'Wherever Lee goes, there you will go also.'"[20]

To ensure the compliance of Meade, Grant would ride along and supervise his army in the field. Consequently, in his new post as general in chief, Grant also assumed the *de facto* command of the Army of the Potomac.

The endgame strategy as Lincoln and Grant worked it up was to send the Union forces in Chattanooga to pursue the Confederate army (now commanded by General Joseph Johnston) into central Georgia. These Union forces would be led by William Tecumseh Sherman. In Virginia, Grant and Meade would go after Lee's army—with a number of peripheral forces adding pressure from the Shenandoah Valley and along the James River.

Late in April, everything was ready, and the armies of Lincoln went to work. John Hay was optimistically expectant. At last, Lincoln's macro-strategic ideas would be used for their maximum effect. "The President," Hay wrote in his diary, "has been powerfully reminded, by General Grant's present movements and plans, of his (President's) old suggestion so constantly made and as constantly neglected, to Buell & Halleck, et al., to move at once upon the enemy's whole line so as to bring into action to our advantage our great superiority in numbers."[21] This would now be the case in all theatres. Lincoln too was expectant.

Early in May, he remarked that the conqueror of Vicksburg and Chattanooga could be trusted to destroy Lee's army. "It is the dogged pertinacity of Grant that wins," the president declared.[22] Grant crossed the Rapidan River on May 4.

BUT IT ALL WENT WRONG, and disaster spread out like a rotten abyss in the summer of 1864.

Grant's army collided with the rebels very close to the battlefield of Chancellorsville in a thick forest called "the Wilderness" by locals. The battle of the Wilderness lasted from May 5 to May 7, and it ended in a tactical draw. It was an ugly and terrifying battle that cost almost twenty-eight thousand causalities (Union and Confederate). An unfazed Grant moved quickly around the flank of Lee's army to flush the Confederates out into the open for the showdown.

But then Confederate strategy changed: Lee decided to entrench with the aim of *denying* his attacker (whom he knew to be his equal) any chance for a wide-open battle. Lee's men dug trenches overnight, so quickly that they were ready for Grant's onslaught *the next day*. The battle of Spotsylvania Court House, which lasted from May 8 to May 19, took the lives of approximately twenty-nine thousand men. It ended in a tactical draw.

For the rest of the month, Grant tried again to move around the flank of Lee's army and force the rebels into the open for the blow that would destroy them. Yet, each time Lee entrenched just ahead of Grant and blocked him. Lee and his army were too fast to be caught in the open.

Grant was leery of attacking these Confederate trenches because Civil War weaponry gave the defenders of fortified positions tremendous advantages. He wanted a wide-open battle, and dreaded the prospect of driving Lee back into the formidable defenses of Richmond. A siege of the Richmond defenses could last a long time, and Grant's army was terribly depleted by the recent casualties. Besides, the president wanted fast action to end the war decisively.

Lee entrenched once again at Cold Harbor, very close to the Richmond fortifications. Grant was running out of time. So at last he gave the order for a frontal attack on June 3. The result was a hideous failure—a slaughter that shocked Grant. The troops themselves had a grim premonition before the charge: many of them had pinned notes to their backs or made final entries in their diaries recording the date as their last day on earth. They were dead men, and most of them knew it. They remembered Pickett's charge; they remembered the troops who attacked the impregnable heights behind Fredericksburg. Now it was their turn. Seven thousand Union casualties occurred within the first half hour. By the end of Cold Harbor, Grant had lost about a third of his army in only a month.

As the news of these casualties began to pour back to the home front, the Copperheads were jubilant. Even Grant's admirers began to deplore his latest actions; his detractors began to call him names like "the Butcher." "The immense slaughter of our brave men," wrote Gideon Welles, "chills and sickens us all."[23]

This suited the Confederates perfectly. It was perfectly in line with their new strategy: bog things down and let the clock run out on Lincoln's presidency. McPherson has criticized the various historians who claim that Grant's intention was to wage a war of attrition against Lee. In truth, he contends, "it was Lee who turned it into a war of attrition. . . . The Confederates could no longer hope to 'win' the war with the tactics or strategy of Chancellorsville or Gettysburg. By remaining on the defensive, however, they could hope to hang on long enough and inflict losses enough on the Yankees to make *them* give up trying to win. This strategy was beginning to work in June 1864."[24]

The Confederates used the same strategy down in Georgia: as Sherman's troops tried to force an open battle, the Confederate army under General Joseph Johnston fell back through successive lines of trenches.

The Republican National Convention was held just four days after Cold Harbor. The party was running very scared. Moreover, a schism had occurred: a group of Radical Republicans had joined with some free-lancing Democrats and they held their own convention in Cleveland. They dubbed themselves the "Radical Democratic Party," and proceeded to nominate John C. Frémont as their presidential candidate. Frémont, the political general, had also been the Republicans' first nominee for the presidency in 1856.

Many of the Radical Republicans who flocked to the banner of Frémont had dabbled in the "Chase boom" a few months before. But the "independent" Democrats who helped out the "Radical Democratic Party" were a very different breed. A number of observers at the time, such as William Lloyd Garrison (the venerable abolitionist), concluded that Frémont was nothing but a dupe—or as McPherson has put it, a "catspaw of wily War Democrats hoping to divide and conquer the Republicans."[25]

The convention of the regular Republican Party was held in Baltimore on June 7. Lincoln, of course, was renominated, but the delegates were seriously worried. Consequently, they changed the party's name for the season to the National Union Party. And they decided to replace Vice President Hannibal Hamlin (a staunchly anti-slavery man) with a Democratic running mate for Lincoln. They selected Andrew Johnson, the Tennessee Democrat who served under Lincoln's supervision as the occupation governor. Johnson had also been the cosponsor of the old pro-slavery Crittenden-Johnson resolutions in 1861. Indeed, he had owned five slaves before the war.

He had changed since then, of course: he had come to support emancipation. But Johnson's reasons for "conversion" were selfish, at least psychologically. As a self-made man from the hills—as a "poor boy" who nursed class resentments—he had loathed the plantation aristocrats who ran the South. Freeing their slaves would be a blow to them, humbling their power, in Johnson's estimation. Years earlier, Johnson had declared that he would "show the stuck-up aristocrats who is running the country."[26]

But Johnson was no friend to the slaves: he was virulently racist. He declared later on that blacks possessed less "capacity for government than any other race of people."[27] Here was Lincoln's new running mate for 1864, and it was definitely not his idea.

Lincoln made no attempt to intervene in the work of this convention, with one exception: he strongly suggested its formal endorsement of the anti-slavery amendment to the Constitution. According to LaWanda Cox, "Lincoln made certain that the Republican national convention held in June 1864 would include a plank calling for the 'utter and complete extirpation' of slavery through constitutional amendment. He called in the Republican national chairman to ask that it be made the core of the chairman's keynote address."[28]

After the convention, Lincoln's problems with his fellow Republicans worsened. His relations with Salmon P. Chase had reached the breaking point at last: Chase became terminally quarrelsome. He petulantly offered to resign, and Lincoln accepted. "Of all I have said in commendation of your ability and fidelity," Lincoln wrote, "I have nothing to unsay; and yet you and I have reached a point of mutual embarrassment in our official relation which it seems cannot be over-come, or longer sustained. . . ."[29] Lincoln's Radical Republican critics started screaming: Chase was one of their cabinet icons.

They screamed even louder after Lincoln decided to pocket veto the Wade-Davis Bill, which Congress passed on the second of July. Six days later, Lincoln offered a terse proclamation. He insisted once again that he was *not* "inflexibly committed to any single plan of restora-tion." But he was "unprepared to declare" at the moment that his free-state regimes in Louisiana and Arkansas should be "set aside and held for nought," as the Wade-Davis Bill would surely do.[30] The Radical Republicans were livid.

To add to the president's woes, faint-hearted Republicans were urg-ing him to think about negotiating peace with the Confederates. The ever-mercurial Horace Greeley wrote to Lincoln in early July. He im-plored him to try negotiations. "Our bleeding, bankrupt, almost dying country," wrote Greeley, "longs for peace" and "shudders at the pros-pect of fresh conscriptions, of further wholesale devastations, and of new rivers of human blood. And a widespread conviction that the Gov-ernment [is] not anxious for Peace . . . is doing great harm now, and is morally certain, if not removed, to do far greater in the approaching Elections. . . . I entreat you, in your own time and manner, to submit overtures for pacification to the Southern insurgents. . . ."[31]

These divisions among the Republicans played into the hands of the Democratic Copperheads. The Democratic Party had scheduled its convention for August.

In the middle of June, Grant finally managed to surprise the Con-federates by shifting the bulk of his forces across the James River in a carefully concealed maneuver. Grant's purpose was to strike at Peters-burg, a railroad hub below Richmond. He aimed to cut off the rail-roads supporting both Richmond and Lee, thus forcing Lee to come and attack him.

But the corps commanders of the Union army made a mess of the attack when they arrived in the vicinity of Petersburg. The town had its own defensive perimeter: a thin line of troops under P.G.T. Beauregard was manning these Confederate trenches. The Union troops who arrived on the scene were afraid to attack—they were suf-fering from "Cold Harbor syndrome." By the time Grant arrived with the bulk of his army, Lee's troops had been given all the time that they needed to arrive in force and man the trenches.

Then Lee found a way to twist the knife. He dispatched a Confederate force under General Jubal Early to accomplish what Lincoln had feared in the first two years of war: a raid against Washington, D.C. Lincoln's capital, protected by its own ring of forts, had been stripped of its garrison by Grant.

Jubal Early and his troops crossed over the Potomac on July 5, and just a few days later they were marching toward the Washington defenses. From Petersburg help was on the way: Grant dispatched a whole corps. But would the troops relieve Washington in time?

As the rebels arrived at the Washington defenses, only boys and some local militia were manning the guns of the forts surrounding the city. On July 11, Lincoln anxiously rode to the scene of the battle at a bastion known as Fort Stevens. In the nick of time, Grant's veterans arrived and put an end to the Confederate attack. But in the midst of the battle something very peculiar occurred: Lincoln stood upon the parapet with bullets flying all around him. A young officer—none other than the future Supreme Court Justice Oliver Wendell Holmes, Jr.— looked up at his commander in chief and shouted, "Get down, you damn fool" before he knew what he was doing or saying. Lincoln obliged and got down.[32]

This episode is easy to dismiss as an odd and momentary aberration, or as a fleeting illustration of the Lincoln eccentricities. But in light of what was really at stake (a successful Confederate attack upon Washington might truly have been the last straw for the administration's credibility that summer), and in light of the increasing inclination of Lincoln to regard such events as providential, it might have been something more serious. Consider the emotional pressure that the president was feeling in the aftermath of the casualty reports from Virginia. He lamented in a speech in mid-June that the war had "carried mourning into every home," that it could "almost be said that the 'heavens are hung with black.'"[33] Was there possibly a reason why Lincoln risked his life under fire? According to historian Gabor S. Boritt, who has mused upon the spectacle of Lincoln on the Fort Stevens parapet, here was "this tall man, six-foot four, with a top hat on to exaggerate his height further, recognizable to all on both sides. He stands there, bullets whistle by, an officer falls close to him, but he just stands there— looking at the enemy." Boritt's thesis? "I see a man standing there looking not at the Confederates, but [at] God, saying silently: if I am wrong, God, strike me down."[34]

At Petersburg, Grant began a siege. But his army was so greatly diminished in size—he had lost almost sixty-four thousand men from the Wilderness to Petersburg—that his options were severely limited. He could not throw a ring around the city and starve it out, as he had done in the case of Vicksburg: his forces would be stretched too thin. And the loss of the corps that he had sent back to Washington diminished his army even further.

In July, some clever troops from the Pennsylvania coal-mining country thought up a new stratagem: they would tunnel right under the Confederate trenches and blow a huge hole in their lines with an enormous charge of gunpowder. At first the attack was a stunning success: the explosives went off in the predawn darkness of July 30. The explosion was horrific, and Confederates fled from their positions in hysteria. But the Union attack through "the Crater" bogged down, and by the time that Grant's troops had been reorganized, the rebels were entrenched once again, to the rear of the Crater.

Grant vowed to keep the pressure on Lee. In mid-August Lincoln telegraphed Grant as follows: "I have seen your dispatch expressing your unwillingness to break your hold where you are. Neither am I willing. Hold on with a bull-dog gripe [sic], and chew & choke, as much as possible."[35]

Lincoln and Grant then developed a plan to destroy the Confederate troops who had tried to raid Washington. The soldiers who had saved the city would be sent to pursue its attackers. Their leader would be Grant's great cavalry commander, Philip Sheridan. Lincoln told Grant to make sure that Early's troops were wiped out. "I have seen your despatch [sic] in which you say 'I want Sheridan put in command of all the troops in the field, with instructions to put himself South of the enemy, and follow him to the death. . . .' This, I think, is exactly right." Lincoln also admonished Grant to check on the progress himself; he wanted no mistakes. "I repeat to you," Lincoln wrote to Grant, that the war to the death "will neither be done nor attempted unless you watch it every day, and hour, and force it."[36]

"Force it": here again, we remember the double-sided meaning of the Lincoln remark that he had not "controlled events." Maybe not, but he was constantly *trying* to control them.

Early's army had been causing more mischief. The Confederate raiders had blackmailed the cities of Frederick and Hagerstown, Maryland, extorting two hundred thousand dollars in "protection money" in return for their promise to spare the two cities from the torch. They made a quick lunge into Pennsylvania and burned the town of Chambersburg. Then they faded back into Virginia. Hunting them down would take time. As Sheridan prepared for this task, Grant worked with his limited forces. He kept tightening the pressure on Lee with continued bombardments, tightening his grip upon Petersburg. This, too, would take a very long time if Lee were clever enough to hold out. And in Georgia, Sherman had pursued the Confederates right to the gates of Atlanta; he had started a siege, which of course would take time.

The pressure was becoming excruciating. Horace Greeley had heard about the presence of some Confederate agents in Niagara Falls (on the Canadian side). He urged the president to sound out the agents as the first step to possible peace talks. Lincoln knew the real purpose of the agents; he knew that they were working with the Democratic Party. So he told Horace Greeley to investigate the matter in person. When Greeley demurred, Lincoln sent John Hay to convince him.

When Greeley conferred with the agents, he learned for himself that they had *not* been sent to negotiate. Lincoln made this information public. To another journalist, Abram Wakeman, Lincoln wrote, "the men of the South, recently (and perhaps still) at Niagara Falls, tell us distinctly that they *are* in the confidential employment of the rebellion; and they tell us as distinctly that they are *not* empowered to offer terms of peace. Does any one doubt that what they *are* empowered to do, is to assist in selecting and arranging a candidate and a platform for the Chicago [Democratic] convention?"[37]

Lincoln even obtained a copy of text that these agents had drafted for the Copperheads. In a private memorandum, Lincoln jotted down some notes from the document. In particular, the president copied down the following lines of abuse that were directed at himself: "The stupid tyrant who now disgraces the Chair of Washington and Jackson could, any day, have peace . . . only that he persists in the war merely to free the slaves."[38]

This anti-Lincoln rhetoric was mild when compared to the abuse that was directed at Lincoln by the Democratic presses in August 1864. Democratic editors vilified the "negro-loving, negro-hugging worshippers of old Abe." One Democratic voice proclaimed, "Abe Lincoln— passing the question as to his taint of Negro blood . . . is altogether an imbecile. . . . He is brutal in all his habits. . . . He is filthy. He is obscene. . . . He is an animal!"[39]

Henry J. Raymond, who was serving as the chairman of the Republican National Committee (he was also the editor of the *New York Times*), wrote to Lincoln on August 22 in a state of despair. "I feel compelled to drop you a line concerning the political condition of the country," Raymond wrote. "I am in active correspondence with your staunchest friends in every state and from them all I hear but one report. The tide is setting against us." He continued: "Two special causes are assigned to this great reaction in public sentiment,—the want of military successes, and the impression in some minds, the fear and suspicion in others, that we are not to have peace *in any event* under this administration until Slavery is abandoned. In some way or other the suspicion is widely diffused that we *can* have peace with Union if we would. It is idle to reason with this belief—still more idle to denounce it. It can only be expelled by some authoritative act . . . bold enough to fix attention and distinct enough to defy incredulity & challenge respect."

Then Raymond suggested his stratagem: "Would it not be wise," he wrote, "under these circumstances, to appoint a Commissioner, in due form, *to make distinct proffers of peace to Davis, as the head of the rebel armies, on the sole condition of acknowledging the supremacy of the constitution,*—all other questions to be settled in convention of the people of all the states?"

The chairman of the Republican National Committee was suggesting that Lincoln offer the Confederates peace *with Union only*—that he abandon his emancipation promise.

Raymond, to be sure, was suggesting the measure as a trick. "If the proffer were *accepted*," wrote Raymond, "(which I presume it would not be,) the country would never consent to place the practical execution of its details in any but loyal hands, and in those we should be safe. If it should be *rejected*, (as it would be,) it would . . . dispel all the delusions about peace that prevail in the North. . . ."[40]

It is a stunning measure of the agony that Lincoln was suffering in August that he briefly considered this suggestion. On August 24, the president drafted a letter to Raymond, authorizing him to proceed.[41] But Lincoln never sent this letter.

At the same time he drafted a letter to a Democratic editor, stating, "if Jefferson Davis wishes, for himself, or for the benefit of his friends at the North, to know what I would do if he were to offer peace and reunion, saying nothing about slavery, let him try me."[42]

But Lincoln never sent this letter either. On August 25, he met with Raymond (in the presence of his cabinet) and told him that the course of action he had recommended would be "worse than losing the presidential contest—it would be ignominiously surrendering it in advance."[43] To some Wisconsin Republicans Lincoln remarked that "there have been men who have proposed to me to return to slavery the black warriors of Port Hudson . . . to conciliate the South. I should be damned in time & in eternity for so doing. The world shall know that I will keep my faith to friends & enemies, come what will."[44]

But he was deeply convinced that he would lose the election in the fall: "I am going to be beaten," he said, "and unless some great change takes place *badly* beaten."[45] On August 23, he wrote a strange memorandum, which he then folded over and sealed. He asked his cabinet members to sign their names on the back, without having read it. The memorandum read as follows: "This morning, as for some days past, it seems exceedingly probable that this Administration will not be re-elected. Then it will be my duty to so co-operate with the President elect, as to save the Union between the election and the inauguration; as he will have secured his election on such ground that he can not possibly save it afterwards."[46]

Lincoln secretly invited Frederick Douglass to call at the White House. "I went most gladly," the black abolitionist remembered. Lincoln's purpose was to start a black exodus—to figure out a method "to induce the slaves in the rebel States to come within the Federal lines. The increasing opposition to the war, in the north, and the mad cry against it . . . alarmed Mr. Lincoln, and made him apprehensive that a peace might be forced upon him which would leave still in slavery all who had not come within our lines."

Douglass continued as follows: "I listened with the deepest interest and profoundest satisfaction" to what Lincoln had to say, "and, at his suggestion, agreed to undertake the organizing of a band of scouts, composed of colored men, whose business should be . . . to go into the rebel States, beyond the lines of our armies, and carry the news of emancipation, and urge the slaves to come within our boundaries."[47] The scouts would relay a simple message: escape from your masters as quickly as you can, so that President Lincoln can free you while he still has the power.

Regarding the freedmen, some bad news arrived that month. John Eaton, an army chaplain who was working with the contrabands in Mississippi, paid a visit to Lincoln in August to tell him that some of them were being mistreated. "Mr. Lincoln's keen face sharpened with indignation," Eaton recalled. Exasperated, the president "exclaimed more than once" that he had "signed no regulations authorizing that!"[48]

Could anything else go wrong in this horrible summer? Yes: on August 30, a group of Republicans demanded a second convention to get rid of Lincoln entirely. This convention, they suggested, should meet in Cincinnati on September 28. After dumping Lincoln, they reasoned, the party might still find a way to pull through. Meanwhile, out in Chicago, the Democrats were gathering in full expectation of triumph. And their candidate: George B. McClellan.

Yes, *McClellan*—the man of the hour. McClellan, who had wanted to "dodge the nigger," and who viewed Lincoln's freedom proclamation as a wicked act.

To his followers, McClellan was a prophet in 1864. Had he not, after all, taken steps to avoid needless bloodshed when he was in command? Had he not advised Lincoln to resist the abolitionists and keep this a war for Union only? All right, then: just look at what had happened to the country after Lincoln had relieved George McClellan.

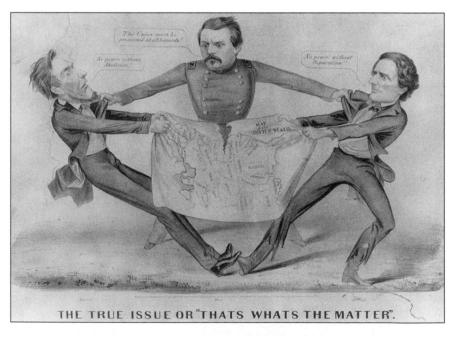

An anti-Lincoln cartoon that was published by Currier & Ives in the election of 1864: the wise and patriotic McClellan tries to mediate between the petulant rivals, Lincoln and Davis. (Library of Congress)

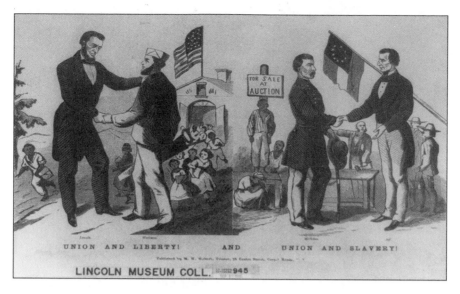

A pro-Lincoln cartoon from the election of 1864: as Lincoln shakes hands with a dignified workman—with the image of a racially integrated school in the background—McClellan shakes hands with Jefferson Davis with a slave auction in the background. This cartoon was published by printer M. W. Siebert. (Library of Congress)

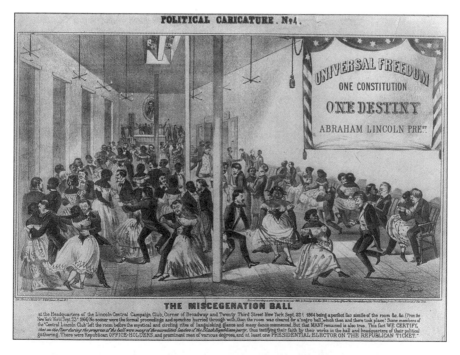

"The Miscegenation Ball": an anti-Lincoln cartoon from the election of 1864 depicting white male Lincoln supporters embracing black women at a dance. This cartoon was published by the printer Bromley & Company. (Library of Congress)

Was Ulysses S. Grant any closer to defeating the rebels after losing almost half of his army?

So it went for Lincoln as he faced the disgusting future in the summer of this year. It appeared that McClellan would win. Like the blowhard he was, he would promise the country to fight for the Union, but his swaggering would probably yield to his deep inner cowardice before very long. He would not have the stomach to fight. A political advisor to McClellan contended that "the General is for peace, not war."[49]

But what kind of peace would he negotiate? Would McClellan abandon the Union and allow the Confederates to build their great empire for slavery? The *Charleston Mercury* predicted that McClellan's election "must lead to peace and our independence . . . [if] for the next two months *we hold our own. . . .*"[50] Alexander Stephens wrote that McClellan's nomination "presents . . . the first ray of real light I have seen since the war began."[51]

If McClellan held out for preservation of the Union, the Confederates would drive a hard bargain. They would play to his obvious weakness— and to his prejudice. They would naturally demand a pro-slavery nation, a nation of the sort that Calhoun or Taney would approve of. Emancipation would be rescinded, and, perhaps, even the free-state regimes in Louisiana and elsewhere would be overturned. The Emancipation Proclamation itself would be discarded.

This wretched scenario was indeed possible, since as Frederick Douglass would later reflect, the institution of slavery was only "wounded and crippled" by 1864, "not disabled and killed."[52]

And what would happen to the thousands of freedmen if McClellan should win? Would he try to send them right back to bondage? Would the blacks troops resist or flee to Canada? Would they riot in the streets, thus inducing McClellan to repress them, or even shoot them down? Would a race war start that would discredit anti-slavery politics for many generations? Would this set back the cause of abolition in America for fifty or a hundred years or longer?

As Harry V. Jaffa has suggested, the wrong resolution of the slavery issue could have happened very easily in nineteenth-century America. The result could have been a long nightmare in which a white minority "would be engulfed in the swirling tides of hatred of an unprivileged majority of a different complexion." Only naked repression could maintain such a system for long: "It is almost inconceivable," Jaffa continues, "that democratic processes could have survived such complications. And we can only shudder to think what the twentieth century would be like if the United States had entered it as first and foremost of totalitarian powers."[53] Does this appear to be "impossible" as well?

Many people recoil at such examples of "what-if" history, dismissing it as "mere" speculation or worse. But as Donald Kagan has argued, "anyone who tries to write history . . . must consider what might have happened; the only question is how explicitly he reveals what he is doing."[54] So let me be very clear: if Lincoln had lost the election of 1864, the United States might very well have lost its last chance to remain a decent country. Everything was hanging in the balance: Lincoln's flickering chances were dependent on the flickering fortunes of his armies. James M. McPherson has emphasized the shifting "contingency that hung over every campaign, every battle, every election during the war."[55] It could all have been disastrously different.

If Lincoln lost the election, then the suffering and sacrifice of hundreds of thousands of Americans would have been in vain. The anti-slavery movement would be weakened and its mission discredited, perhaps for many years to come. Lincoln's brilliance would all have been for nothing. Was there no way out?

SEVEN

Lincoln and the Best-Case Future, 1864–1865

INCOLN'S FORTUNES took a sudden and spectacular turn for the better in the first few days of September 1864: Sherman captured the city of Atlanta. With extraordinary speed, Lincoln's popularity surged as he raced toward an easy reelection. McClellan sounded more and more like the puling defeatist that he was. The power of the Copperheads was broken.

As Lincoln's luck began to change for the better, so did prospects for African Americans. By the time of his death, Lincoln hovered at the brink of endorsing and leading a true civil rights revolution. He never burned his bridges with the Radical Republicans; he frequently agreed with their intentions, even in the miserable summer of 1864. His chief difference with them was a different sense of timing and worst-case risk. As Lincoln's second term began, things had changed: he decided it was time for him to advocate the phase-in of voting rights for blacks, and he did this in public—quite fervently. And he did it in a manner that was carefully chosen to encourage the movement and to soften up public opinion.

The fall of Atlanta made it possible for Lincoln both to win the election and to start his second term auspiciously. Since the capture of Atlanta was the key to all this, it was the military genius of William Tecumseh Sherman that rescued the nation from McClellan and re-empowered Lincoln.

Jefferson Davis had helped in an inadvertent manner. Early in the summer of 1864, the Confederate tactics in Georgia were similar to Lee's. Joseph Johnston (the Confederate commander in Georgia) had been stalling and delaying in the trenches. Delay was inimical to Lincoln in the summer of 1864. With Sherman bogged down in his Georgia campaign and with Grant bogged down in his Petersburg siege, the Confederate logic was obvious: hang on, hurt Northern morale as much as possible, and then cut a deal with McClellan right after the election.

But the pressure on Davis in the summer of 1864 was as brutal as the pressure on Lincoln. Lincoln bent under pressure, in ways that we have seen: he was tempted by others to rescue his party by abandoning his mission on slavery. He had bent under pressure, but he pulled himself together right away: he would rather lose his power, he said, than be "damned in time and eternity."

Davis, on the other hand, broke when the strain was unbearable. The Confederate war of attrition was wearing down Confederate nerves just as surely as it wore down the Yankees. Here was Grant at the outer defenses of Richmond; here was Sherman approaching Atlanta. The pressure on Davis was tremendous. His political enemies attacked him that summer, complaining that Confederates had lost their will to fight when they needed it the most. Of course Robert E. Lee was immune from such attack, for he was almost a saint in the minds of most loyal Confederates. But Johnston cut a very different figure, so Davis relieved him of command on July 17 and replaced him with John Bell Hood, an impetuous fighter.

The result was exactly what Sherman and Grant had been hoping for: battles in the open where the North could use all of its advantages in men and supplies. Hood's attacks upon Sherman were disasters: even Davis sent him orders to call the thing off and get back in place behind the trenches. In the aftermath of these battles, Sherman used his superiority in numbers—he had suffered few casualties, compared with Grant's catastrophe in Virginia—to make his siege of Atlanta effective. Late in August, his raiders struck twenty miles south of the city to cut its railroad links, thus threatening to cut off its food. Hood tried but failed to reopen these lines, and so he had to evacuate the city. Sherman's men marched into the streets of Atlanta on September 3. The result in the North was immediate jubilation.

Lincoln quickly congratulated Sherman and called for a day of thanksgiving and prayer to thank God for "His mercy in preserving our national existence. . . ."[1]

As always, these religious reflections of Lincoln were undoubtedly sincere. On the very next day Lincoln wrote to a Quaker who had visited him at the White House two years earlier, thanking her for helping him to strengthen his "reliance on God." "The purposes of the Almighty are perfect," Lincoln wrote, "and must prevail, though we erring mortals may fail to accurately perceive them in advance. We had hoped for a happy termination to this terrible war long before this; but God knows best, and has ruled otherwise." But Lincoln said he was certain that God "intends some great good to follow this mighty convulsion."[2]

Union victories multiplied: In the Shenandoah Valley, Union forces commanded by General Philip Sheridan attacked Jubal Early's Confederates. In superb displays of battlefield prowess, Sheridan beat the Confederates at Winchester, Virginia on September 19, and again at Fisher's Hill only three days later. As Early's forces retreated, the Union troops began a massive campaign of destruction. Under "total war" directives from Grant, they began to destroy all the farms in the Shenandoah Valley, thus depriving the Confederates of food and other provisions.

In October, as Sheridan prepared to return a great number of his soldiers to Grant—who could use them at Petersburg—he went to Washington to talk about his plans. In his absence, Early struck at his forces in a daring attack at Cedar Creek.

It is interesting to note that Lincoln feared such a move and warned against it. "I hope it will lay no constraint upon you," he had written to Grant in September, "for me to say I am a little afraid lest Lee sends re-enforcements to Early, and thus enables him to turn upon Sheridan."[3]

On October 19, Philip Sheridan was riding back from Washington; approaching Cedar Creek, he heard the sounds of cannon. He spurred his horse, and he encountered his own retreating troops. They cheered him, but he urged them to return to the front. The result was remarkable. Sheridan turned the tide of battle through the force of charisma alone. As McPherson has written, "the effect of this man's presence on the beaten army was extraordinary. By midafternoon, Sheridan had gotten the stragglers into line and organized a counterattack. . . . By nightfall, the blue tide had not only washed back over the four miles lost in the morning but had driven the enemy eight miles farther south. Early's army, thrice routed in a month, virtually ceased to exist as a fighting force."[4]

Lincoln issued another proclamation on the following day, urging citizens to set aside the "last Thursday in November" as a time to thank

God for inspiring their country "with fortitude, courage and resolution sufficient for the great trial of civil war into which we have been
brought by our adherence as a nation to the cause of Freedom and
Humanity." He also urged Americans to "humble themselves in the
dust" as they offered these thanks.[5]

The legend-like details of what Sheridan achieved made the candi-
dacy of McClellan appear almost pitiful in late October. Moreover,
McClellan had managed to unify most of the Republicans: he was viewed
throughout the party as an odious figure, and the party came together
in response. Meanwhile, the "Radical Democratic Party" of Frémont
withered away.

The election of 1864 was a tremendous victory for Lincoln.
McClellan carried only three states: Kentucky, New Jersey, and Delaware. The vote in the electoral college was overwhelming: 212 for Lincoln and 21 for McClellan.

On election night, Lincoln made an impromptu speech to some
cheering serenaders. He seemed to be supremely happy; he said that
"the consequences of this day's work . . . will be to the lasting advantage, if not to the very salvation, of the country. . . . All who have
labored to-day in behalf of the Union organization, have wrought for
the best interests of their country and the world, not only for the present,
but for all future ages. I am thankful to God for this approval of the
people." He added, however, that his gratitude was "free from any taint
of personal triumph . . . if I know my heart."[6]

In response to another group of serenaders, he sought once again to
discourage any gloating by the victors. "It adds nothing to my satisfaction," he explained, "that any other men may be disappointed or pained
by the result. . . . So long as I have been here I have not willingly
planted a thorn in any man's bosom." He urged Americans to use the
Civil War as "philosophy to learn wisdom from," adding that "in any
future great national trial, compared with the men of this, we shall
have as weak, and as strong; as silly and as wise; as bad and as good."[7]

If Lincoln tried to disavow any sense of vainglorious triumph, the
elections were nonetheless a triumph for Republicans, a triumph of
extraordinary magnitude. The Republicans won everything they lost
in the elections of 1862, with some abundant dividends. They would
dominate the House of Representatives by a margin of 145 votes to
only 40. They would dominate the Senate by a margin of 42 to 10.

There was another big reason for Republican satisfaction: Roger Taney, the belligerent racist of "Dred Scott" infamy, had died, thus ridding the United States Supreme Court of a shrill and reactionary enemy. Lincoln nominated Salmon P. Chase as the new chief justice. Moreover, in October the free-state constitution of Maryland was ratified. On this particular occasion, Lincoln *did* permit himself some gloating; when the serenaders called, he was unabashedly righteous: "Most heartily do I congratulate you, and Maryland, and the nation, and the world, upon the event. . . . I sincerely hope it's [*sic*] friends may fully realize all their anticipations of good from it; and that it's opponents may, by it's [*sic*] effects, be agreeably and profitably, disappointed."[8]

After the election, a daring proposal from Sherman came across Lincoln's desk. The general proposed to divide his forces and move them away from Atlanta. Sherman wanted to destroy the Confederate army of John Bell Hood. He also wanted to strike a great blow that would cripple Confederate morale. His proposal was twofold: from his army of ninety thousand, he would send a detachment of thirty thousand to protect Tennessee if Hood should make any moves in that direction. This force would be commanded by General George Thomas. Sherman then proposed to take the other sixty thousand men and march through Georgia while destroying almost everything of value in his path.

T. Harry Williams has shown that both Grant and Lincoln had doubts about the wisdom of the plan. "The general in chief feared that if Sherman set out for the coast the Confederate field army in Georgia would invade Tennessee, and he well knew how Lincoln would react to a movement that might weaken the defenses of the bastion of the West. Grant wanted Sherman to defeat the Confederate army before he left Atlanta. Sherman, however, insisted that he could never destroy the enemy from Atlanta but if he smashed across Georgia the Confederates would have to follow him or attack Thomas in Tennessee. Whichever course the Confederates took, Sherman was sure they would be defeated."[9]

With assurances from Sherman that the Tennessee line would be defended, both Lincoln and Grant approved his "March to the Sea": Sherman left Atlanta on November 15, after ordering the whole population of the city to flee as he torched everything his enemies could possibly use. (The fire destroyed about a third of what remained of the city.) Thomas took his thirty thousand men to Tennessee, where he started to recruit reinforcements.

The next move was up to the Confederates. Hood decided to invade Tennessee, and Thomas readied himself for this blow.

Because of Hood's decision, Sherman was able to march from Atlanta to Savannah almost totally unopposed. His men "lived off the land," and after eating their fill, they put the torch to whatever might be left. Plantation houses, livestock, and crops were all consumed, and many thousands of slaves were set free. They followed Sherman's army by the thousands. The famous Union song that was inspired by the Georgia campaign—"Marching Through Georgia"—contained a message of joyous liberation; "Hoorah," rang the lyrics of the song—"Hoorah! We bring the Jubilee! Hoorah! Hoorah! The flag that makes you free." And it was Lincoln's flag—rededicated by him to its original and founding proposition—that was setting people free.

As Sherman marched to Savannah, Lincoln sent his long annual message to Congress on December 6. He promised war to the bitter end. Judging by the recent election, Lincoln wrote, "The purpose of the people, within the loyal States, to maintain the integrity of the Union, was never more firm, nor more nearly unanimous, than now." Moreover, the *power* to wage war was never stronger. "We have *more* men *now* than we had when the war *began*," Lincoln wrote. "We are not exhausted, nor in process of exhaustion;" indeed, "we are *gaining* strength, and may, if need be, maintain the contest indefinitely."[10] Under these conditions, Union victory was inevitable.

That being the case, he continued, it was time to revisit Reconstruction. Just a year before, he had offered some "lenient" terms to the rebels. "The door has been, for a full year, open to all," the president reflected, "except such as were not in condition to make free choice—that is, such as were in custody or under constraint." But now, he continued, it was time to consider how long that door should stay open. "The time may come—probably will come—when public duty shall demand that it be closed; and that, in lieu, more rigorous measures than heretofore shall be adopted."[11] Lincoln's message was very clear: he was ready to patch up his differences with Radical Republicans.

Lincoln turned to the Thirteenth Amendment—the amendment to abolish slavery everywhere, all at once—which was stalled in the House of Representatives. He exhorted the Congress to pass it and to do so immediately: "At the last session of Congress a proposed amendment of the Constitution abolishing slavery throughout the United States, passed the Senate, but failed for lack of the requisite two-thirds vote in the House of Representatives. Although the present is the same Congress [meeting in lame-duck session], and nearly the same members . . . I venture to recommend the reconsideration and passage of the measure at the present session." Lincoln argued that the very next Congress would pass the amendment, so why not do so at once? "The intervening election," Lincoln wrote, "shows, almost certainly, that the next Congress will pass the measure if this does not. Hence, there is only a question of *time* as to when the proposed amendment will go to the States for their action. And as it is to so go, at all events, may we not agree that the sooner the better?"[12]

Soon after Lincoln sent this message to Congress, the Confederate invasion of Tennessee ended in disaster. Already, a Confederate attack upon a strongly entrenched Union force had been smashed at Franklin, Tennessee, on the last day of November. But Hood persisted. He took his weakened force all the way to the Union defenses of Nashville, where Thomas was waiting. On December 15, Thomas ordered an assault that hit the rebel forces front and rear. McPherson has called the resulting battle "one of the most crushing Union victories of the war."[13] Hood's army was all but destroyed, and its remnants fled toward Mississippi. Lincoln ordered Thomas to pursue them: "Please accept for yourself, officers, and men, the nation's thanks for your good work of yesterday," the president wrote. "You made a magnificent beginning. A grand consummation is within your easy grasp. Do not let it slip."[14]

Thomas made certain he did not "let it slip"; he pursued the fleeing Confederates. Williams summarizes the eventual results: "Only remnants of Hood's army escaped, and it was never an army again."[15]

Then Sherman reached Savannah on December 21; in a message to Lincoln, he offered him the city as a Christmas present. He then proposed to march north, joining forces with Grant to administer the final blow to Lee and Richmond.

In the meantime, Lincoln worked tirelessly to convince the old Congress to approve the new Thirteenth Amendment before it adjourned. As historian Michael Vorenberg has written, "no piece of legislation during Lincoln's presidency received more of his attention than the Thirteenth Amendment."[16] He worked behind the scenes, twisting arms, making deals, and assembling his winning coalition. He even threatened to call the new Congress into special session in March. His tactics worked: on the last day of January 1865, the great anti-slavery amendment was passed, and a huge celebration broke out in the House of Representatives. Republicans began to cheer wildly, and visiting blacks in the galleries—a new rule to admit them had been passed in 1864—cheered and wept.

When a group of serenaders paid a call upon Lincoln, he exulted that the passage of the Thirteenth Amendment was the "King's cure for all the evils." It would settle any lingering disputes about the scope and the validity of what he had achieved with his Emancipation Proclamation. "That proclamation," the president acknowledged, "falls far short of what the amendment will be when fully consummated. A question might be raised whether the proclamation was legally valid. It might be added that it only aided those who came into our lines and that it was inoperative as to those who did not give themselves up, or that it would have no effect upon the children of the slaves." Such arguments would soon be moot forever. The occasion, Lincoln said, was "one of congratulation to the country and to the whole world."[17]

To increase the chances that the Thirteenth Amendment would be ratified, Lincoln actually suggested that the federal government should pay all the slave states to ratify. On February 5, he recommended a joint resolution affirming that

> the President of the United States is hereby empowered, at his discretion, to pay four hundred millions of dollars to the States of Alabama, Arkansas, Delaware, Florida, Georgia, Kentucky, Louisiana, Maryland, Mississippi, Missouri, North Carolina, South Carolina, Tennessee, Texas, Virginia, and West-Virginia . . . on the conditions following, towit: . . . [that] all resistance to the national authority shall be abandoned and cease, on or before the first day of April next; and upon such abandonment and ceasing of resistance, one half of said sum to be paid . . . and the remaining half to be paid only upon the amendment of the national constitution recently proposed by congress, becoming valid law, on or before the first day of July next, by the action thereon of the requisite number of States.[18]

Lincoln's cabinet, however, disapproved of this proposal, so the president quietly retracted it.

In the meantime, as Sherman prepared to move north and turn his wrath upon South Carolina, he decided to do something drastic in order to relieve the pressing needs of the slaves who were following his army. On January 12, he held a conference with a group of black leaders (most of them Methodist and Baptist ministers) from Savannah. It bears noting that Edwin Stanton, Lincoln's secretary of war, attended this meeting. A few days later Sherman issued an extraordinary order—Special Field Order Number 15—granting freedmen "possessory" title to a vast tract of seized rebel lands that would extend from Charleston to Jacksonville. Forty acres would be given to each black family; their titles to the land would be deemed "possessory" until such time as congressional action "shall regulate the title."[19]

Lincoln never countermanded this order, as he clearly had the power to do. It is almost impossible to think that he was ignorant of Sherman's decision, for his secretary of war had been present in Savannah when Sherman had developed the plan. Lincoln probably supported Sherman's order to redistribute this land. It appears that George Julian was telling the truth about his meeting with Lincoln in the previous summer to discuss the constitutional issue of bills of attainder. It seems the president had finally agreed to the redistribution of lands as punishment for treason.

On March 4, Lincoln delivered his second Inaugural Address. As he took the rostrum at the Capitol, a group of the conspirators led by John Wilkes Booth were lurking very close to where he stood. His address was a vision out of Scripture, a vision of a chosen people who had broken their covenant with God. Divine Providence had brought about the war, Lincoln said, and would determine its results in a manner transcending the actions of any participants, including himself. "Neither party expected for the war, the magnitude, or the duration, which it has already attained," Lincoln pointed out. "Each looked for an easier triumph, and a result less fundamental and astounding. Both read the same Bible, and pray to the same God; and each invokes his aid against the other."

Lincoln paused to reflect upon the difference between the two sides: "It may seem strange," he observed, "that any men should dare to ask a just God's assistance in wringing their bread from the sweat of other men's faces." But—he checked himself quickly as he said it—"let us judge not that we be not judged."

"That we be not judged": maybe Lincoln was reflecting on the deeper human sins of which slavery was only a symptom. Perhaps he meant that the sin of forcing others into bondage was a sign of a very deep flaw that lurks secretly in every human heart. It was the quintessential sin of wicked pride.

This sense of Lincoln's message is confirmed in the lines that followed, in which he visualized the war was a punishment designed for the Northern people as well as for the people of the South. God was punishing the nation as a whole.

We must remember that in Lincoln's estimation America was founded as a world-significant experiment in golden-rule ethics. All men were declared to be *equal*, and deserved to be regarded as equal in their rights—treated reciprocally. But Americans continued to *break* that rule by allowing in their midst a vicious social system that reduced other people to the status of beasts of the field. Indirectly or directly, they had done to these suffering people what they obviously wished to avoid having done to themselves. (About a week after giving this Inaugural Address, Lincoln quipped, "Whenever I hear anyone arguing for slavery I feel a strong inclination to see it tried on him personally.")[20]

Now the moment of reckoning had come for the nation of hypocrites. The president continued: "If we shall suppose that American Slavery is one of those offenses which, in the providence of God, must needs come, but which, having continued through His appointed time, He now wills to remove, and that He gives to both North and South this terrible war, as the woe due to those by whom the offense came, shall we discern therein any departure from those divine attributes which the believers in a Living God always ascribe to him?"

Americans should therefore submit to the lash, Lincoln warned, notwithstanding their hopes for God's speedy pardon of their sins. "Fondly do we hope—fervently do we pray—that this mighty scourge of war may speedily pass away." (Note carefully: a scourge is a whip.) "Yet, if God wills that it continue, until all the wealth piled by the bond-man's two hundred and fifty years of unrequited toil shall be sunk, and until every drop of blood drawn with the lash, shall be paid by another drawn with the sword, as was said three thousand years ago, so still it must be said 'the judgments of the Lord are true and righteous altogether.'"[21]

God was *whipping* the American land with a scourge to make it run with the blood of atonement. Every drop of slave's blood that was drawn by a whip would be paid by the blood of fighting soldiers. It was *after* he presented this vision that Lincoln saw fit to deliver those immortal lines about "malice toward none" and "charity for all," about binding up the wounds of the nation and caring for the orphans.

Lincoln supplemented this sermon-like address in an interesting but private letter. New York politician Thurlow Weed had written him a letter in praise of the Inaugural Address. Lincoln replied to him thus: "Every one likes a compliment. Thank you for yours on my . . . recent Inaugeral [sic] Address. I expect the latter to wear as well as—perhaps better than—any thing I have produced; but I believe it is not immediately popular. Men are not flattered by being shown that there has been a difference of purpose between the Almighty and them. To deny it, however, in this case, is to deny that there is a God governing the world. It is a truth which I thought needed to be told; and as whatever of humiliation there is in it, falls most directly on myself, I thought others might afford for me to tell it."[22] The "humiliation" of his sermon, wrote Lincoln, fell "directly" on himself more than others.

But Lincoln's awe in the face of what he took to be the Providence of God placed no inhibitions whatsoever on his penchant for using all the wits that God gave him to improve the lot of others through the arts and skills of politics. In the previous month, he had worked with the Radical Republicans. On March 3, he signed a new bill that established the federal Freedmen's Bureau, an unprecedented social welfare agency. The bureau was designed to give direct assistance to the freedmen: educational, medical, and legal assistance most of all. On the issue of land redistribution, moreover, the bureau was authorized to hold and survey "abandoned" lands and to lease them, in forty-acre tracts, with an option to purchase after three years' time with "such title thereto as the United States can convey." Lincoln signed this bill, which established the bureau on a one-year experimental basis.

Many Radical Republicans were scornful and impatient in regard to the free-state regimes in Louisiana and Arkansas. They refused to admit any members of Congress from these and other Southern states. But Lincoln came to an agreement with some of them: if they would compromise with him and support the regimes he had established already in those two states, he would agree to work closely with them to establish stronger policies elsewhere. According to historian Herman Belz, negotiations between Lincoln and the Radical Republican leader James Ashley began as early as December 1864.[23] McPherson has confirmed that in the months that followed "the President and House Republicans worked out a compromise whereby Congress would recognize the Lincoln-nurtured governments of Louisiana and Arkansas in return for presidential approval of legislation for the rest of the

Confederacy similar to the Wade-Davis Bill vetoed the previous July. This compromise measure initially enacted Black suffrage in the remaining Southern states, but moderates modified it to enfranchise only black army veterans and literate blacks."[24] No bill of this sort could be passed before Congress adjourned. But the newly elected Congress would probably approve such a measure in the autumn of 1865.

The Civil War approached its conclusion as Congress adjourned. Sherman's army of sixty thousand—now augmented to the level of ninety thousand by some troops from the Carolina coast—was storming through North Carolina. The Confederates had managed to assemble a force (of only twenty-two thousand) under General Joseph Johnston to oppose this juggernaut of Sherman. It was no use. And yet a desperate Confederate stratagem was being worked out: if Lee could somehow escape from the Petersburg trenches, swing South, join forces with Johnston, beat Sherman, and then turn to face Grant's army again, perhaps the rebels would still have a chance. A chance of one in a million, no doubt, but a chance all the same.

It was not to be. When Lee attempted his breakout on March 25, Grant counterattacked and forced him back. Then, with Sheridan's cavalry (newly returned from the Shenandoah Valley), Grant threatened to cut the last railroad to Petersburg and Richmond. He sent Sheridan to turn the rebel flank to the south and west of Petersburg. Lee countered this move, and the resulting battle on April 1 at a crossroads known as Five Forks was a massive Union victory. The Confederates abandoned both Petersburg and Richmond: they set their capital ablaze to destroy as many records as they possibly could when they left.

Lincoln was almost on the scene, for he was visiting Grant at his base of operations at City Point, Virginia. From the edge of battle, Lincoln sent back letters that described the sounds of the fighting. To Stanton, the president wrote that on the previous night he had listened to a "furious cannonade" and watched "the flashes of guns upon the clouds."[25] When Richmond was abandoned, Lincoln made up his mind that he would visit the city right away: "I think I will go there tomorrow," he wrote back to Stanton.[26]

As Grant pursued Lee to the west (Union cavalry blocked every one of Lee's attempts to turn south and join forces with Johnston), Lincoln entered the smoldering ruins of the Confederate capital. Black troops escorted him, and Richmond slaves turned out to kneel in his presence. "I know I am free," shouted one of them, "for I have seen Father

Abraham and felt him."[27] Lincoln entered the "Confederate White House," and sat at the desk of Jefferson Davis.

Grant hounded and hammered Lee's troops as he drove them farther to the west, farther toward the mountains. By April 9, it was over: surrounded, outnumbered by a factor of five or six to one, his supplies exhausted and his men nearly dead on their feet, Lee surrendered at Appomattox Court House.

On April 10, an immense cheering crowd asked Lincoln to address them at the White House. Lincoln briefly appeared and requested that they reappear the next evening: "I would much prefer having this demonstration take place to-morrow evening," he explained, when he promised to be better prepared to "say what I have to say."[28] He would give them a speech on Reconstruction.

On the following evening, he began the last speech of his life by acknowledging the joyous tidings from the front. "We meet this evening, not in sorrow, but in gladness of heart. The evacuation of Petersburg and Richmond, and the surrender of the principal insurgent army, give hope of a righteous and speedy peace whose joyous expression can not be restrained."

Then he got down to business very quickly: the business of politics. "By these recent successes the re-inauguration of the national authority—reconstruction—. . . is pressed much more closely upon our attention," the president said. "It is fraught with great difficulty."

He talked about Louisiana: he said that it had come to his attention that he was "much censured for some supposed agency in setting up, and seeking to sustain, the new State Government of Louisiana. In this I have done just so much as, and no more than, the public knows." Of course he did much more behind the scenes than the public would know for many years. But he continued: "In the Annual Message of Dec. 1863 and accompanying Proclamation, I presented *a* plan of reconstruction (as the phrase goes) which, I promised, if adopted by any State, should be acceptable to, and sustained by, the Executive government of the nation. I distinctly stated that this was not the only plan which might possibly be acceptable; and I also distinctly protested that the Executive claimed no right to say when, or whether members should be admitted to seats in Congress from such States."

His own role in the matter was minimal, Lincoln asserted: "When the Message of 1863, with the plan before mentioned, reached New-Orleans, Gen. Banks wrote me that he was confident the people, with his military co-operation, would reconstruct, substantially on that plan. I wrote him, and some of them to try it; they tried it, and the result is known. Such only has been my agency in getting up the Louisiana government. As to sustaining it, my promise is out."

Then he suddenly released upon his audience a sentence that was riveting—almost breathtaking—in its sheer monumental audacity: "But, as bad promises are better broken than kept, I shall treat this as a bad promise, and break it, whenever I shall be convinced that keeping it is adverse to the public interest. But I have not yet been so convinced."

The audacity increased, and the duplicity thickened, as the president digressed to consider some larger issues that pertained to the ex-rebel states. "I have been shown a letter," the president said, "supposed to be an able one, in which the writer expresses regret that my mind has not seemed to be definitely fixed on the question whether the seceded States, so called, are in the Union or out of it. It would perhaps, add astonishment to his regret, were he to learn that . . . I have *purposely* forborne any public expression upon it."

Can we figuratively believe our ears? How on earth could Lincoln deliver such a statement with a straight face? Ever since the beginning of secession the president insisted—in his first Inaugural Address, for example, and his message to Congress on July 4, 1861—that the rebel states were definitely *in* the Union, not "out" of it. Confederate claims of secession, he insisted, were delusions, illegalities, and treason. ("The States," he had written, "have their status IN the Union, and they have no other legal status.") But now Lincoln was saying (or pretending) that he never committed himself on the issue, that he had *purposely* refused to address it. What, may we ask, was Lincoln up to?

In all probability he uttered these words to send a message to the Radical Republicans, a message that he placed between the lines of this address. He was letting them know that if they wished to pursue their old tactic of claiming the Confederates committed "state suicide," he was ready at last to accept their logic and would no longer stand in their way. Listen to his words: "We all agree that the seceded States, so called, are out of their proper practical relation with the Union; and that the sole object of the government, civil and military, in regard to those States is to again get them into that proper practical relation. I believe it is not only possible, but in fact, easier, to do this, without deciding, or even considering, whether these states have even been out of the Union, than with it. . . . Let us all join in doing the acts necessary to restoring the proper practical relations between these states and the Union; and each forever after, innocently indulge his own opinion whether, in doing the acts, he brought the States from without, into the Union, or only gave them proper assistance, they never having been out of it."

Lincoln told the American people to indulge their own "opinions" on a matter of colossal urgency! But this was *not* just a matter of opinion to be privately "indulged" in a state of sweet "innocence." For if Congress should declare that the Confederate states had been *out* of the Union, then the terms of their eventual readmission—or their re-creation as states—could be severe. Lincoln opened up the door to a harsh and demanding Reconstruction in the guise of dismissing an abstract problem that was trivial and almost irrelevant.

Still, Lincoln turned once again to his Louisiana program, and he tried to make the case for retaining it. "Some twelve thousand voters in the heretofore slave-state of Louisiana have sworn allegiance to the Union," Lincoln pointed out; they had "held elections, organized a State government, adopted a free-state constitution, giving the benefit of public schools equally to black and white, and empowered the Legislature to confer the elective franchise upon the colored man. Their Legislature has already voted to ratify the constitutional amendment recently passed by Congress, abolishing slavery throughout the nation. These twelve thousand persons are thus fully committed to the Union, and to perpetual freedom in the state—committed to the very things, and nearly all the things the nation wants—and they ask the nations [*sic*] recognition, and its assistance to make good their committal."

The president admitted there was room for improvement, to be sure; he acknowledged it was "unsatisfactory to some that the elective franchise is not [already] given to the colored man. I would myself prefer that it were now conferred on the very intelligent, and on those who serve our cause as soldiers." Lincoln made the big announcement at last, in a low-key manner—he would favor the extension of voting rights to blacks on an incremental basis. He went on: "Still the question is not whether the Louisiana government, as it stands, is quite all that is desirable. The question is 'Would it be wiser to take it as it is, and help to improve it; or to reject, and disperse it?'"

Lincoln shifted in a moment to a charismatic tone in regard to the issue of voting rights; he said that if the nation should accept the Louisiana achievement, "we encourage the hearts, and nerve the arms of

the twelve thousand to adhere to their work, and argue for it, and pros-
elyte for it, and fight for it, and feed it, and grow it, and ripen it to a
complete success. The colored man, too, in seeing all united for him,
is inspired with vigilance, and energy, and daring to the same end.
Grant that he desires the elective franchise, will he not attain it sooner
by saving the already advanced steps toward it, than by running backward over them?" Could this message be in any way misread? He was
urging all blacks to show vigilance and energy and daring in their fight
to win the vote.

But then, Lincoln took a different tack. He admitted that his 10 percent plan might have to be discarded in the very near future. He observed that "so great peculiarities pertain to each state; and such important
and sudden changes occur in the same state; and, withal, so new and
unprecedented is the whole case, that no exclusive, and inflexible plan
can safely be prescribed as to details and colatterals [*sic*]. Such exclusive,
and inflexible plan, would surely become a new entanglement."

He closed with a hint of some dramatic new policies to come. "In
the present '*situation*' as the phrase goes, it may be my duty to make
some new announcement to the people of the South. I am considering," he pointedly warned, "and shall not fail to act, when satisfied that
action will be proper."[29]

In the audience was John Wilkes Booth. "That means nigger citizenship," Booth hissed to his companions as the president concluded
his speech. "Now, by God, I'll put him through. That is the last speech
he will ever make."[30]

KNOWING AS WE DO the great direction of his life, the cruel murder of
Lincoln by a racist is all the more outrageous—all the more grievous.
Lincoln's plans for Reconstruction would in all probability have led to a
partnership with most, if not all, of the Radicals, a partnership to work
for black civil rights. Success was entirely possible: the times were auspi-
cious for a social revolution in the months that followed Appomattox.

McPherson has conjectured that the "Southern whites might have
submitted to almost any terms of reconstruction the government had
seen fit to impose"; such was the mood of despondency and shock
throughout the South after Lee had surrendered.[31] A South Carolinian lamented that "the conqueror has the right to make the terms, and
we must submit."[32]

The possibilities were outstanding. McPherson has reasoned that "if Lincoln had lived through his second term, the polarization of Executive and Congress after 1865 that turned Reconstruction into a bitter confrontation would not have occurred and the postwar transition from slavery to freedom might have been grounded in firmer and longer-lasting principles of justice and equity."[33] We can only imagine what a like-minded president and Congress could have done to make a civil rights revolution begin after Appomattox.

As it was, crucial months and years went to waste after Lincoln's death, as Andrew Johnson and the Radicals began their political war. Once Johnson took over, he tried to end Reconstruction quickly. He rescinded Sherman's order to set aside the vast "reservation" of confiscated lands for black settlement. He looked the other way in the autumn of 1865 as ex-Confederate states passed a series of "black codes" reducing former slaves to the status of peons. When blacks were shot down as they attempted to vote, Johnson washed his hands of the matter in the name of states' rights and strict construction. When the Radicals voted to extend the existence of the Freedmen's Bureau, Johnson vetoed the bill and condemned it as unconstitutional.

The Radicals forced their way to power and reversed some of Johnson's most flagrant derelictions of duty. By super-majorities, they overturned his presidential vetoes. They renewed the Freedmen's Bureau over Johnson's determined opposition. They passed a civil rights law, pushed through the Fourteenth and Fifteenth Amendments (civil rights and voting rights amendments) to the Constitution, and—for a while—seized control of the army and forced an upheaval in the South that brought blacks into state and local offices, and even into Congress. But the gains were short-lived: a counterrevolution overturned almost all of these advances in the following decades.

By the time the Republicans recaptured the White House in 1869 (with Ulysses S. Grant as president), the public was repelled by the "mess in Washington." The downhill slide was beginning, and the basis for continued Reconstruction would be gone before very long. By the turn of the twentieth century, Americans had come to regard Reconstruction as a "failure," an "age of corruption." The Jim Crow South was the result. It endured until challenged by the "second Reconstruction" of the 1950s and 1960s.

If Lincoln had lived, perhaps the first Reconstruction would have worked. With Lincoln at the helm for another four years—with the savior of the Union working closely with the Radical members of his party—a lasting consensus for black civil rights might have formed in the 1860s.

With such knowledge of the history that *might* have occurred, what form of consolation can we have? For that, we are forced to return to an earlier installment of conjectural or "what-if" history: the history consisting of the danger that Lincoln invoked when he challenged Stephen Douglas in the 1850s, when he warned about the danger of slavery invading the North. By opposing Douglas, by destroying the Crittenden Compromise, by forcing the geographical containment of slavery, Lincoln sought to make certain that the nightmare future of blacks being shipped to the North in stinking cattle cars or in chain gangs—shipped to the North to break strikes in Chicago, in Pittsburgh, and elsewhere—would never come to pass. As political philosopher Jaffa has said, it is "simply unhistorical to say that such a thing *couldn't* have happened because it *didn't* happen. It didn't happen because Lincoln was resolved that it *shouldn't* happen. And nothing but his implacable will made it impossible."[34]

Lincoln stopped such a worst-case future. Then he launched the alternative best-case future: he led the anti-slavery movement to its great consummation, and he did it through his sheer virtuosity in channeling and orchestrating power. He must have felt a secret thrill as he manipulated power in its various forms: political, military, moral, psychological, literary.[35] Perhaps he felt within himself the potential to become a great catalytic force many years before his leadership talent began to blaze forth.

But a discussion of his genius in the uses of power must also force discussion of his fatal lapse in judgment near the end of his life. Lincoln was repeatedly and maddeningly "fatalistic" when it came to the issue of his safety. Assassination threats had increased in the early months of 1865; Lincoln even suffered an eerie premonition through a dream of the White House in mourning. But he tended to dismiss all suggestions for tightening security, asserting that if anyone were truly determined to kill him, they could probably do it regardless of any precautions.

This was nonsense, and Lincoln must have known it. While total security is obviously out of the question, it can be greatly improved through intelligent precautions, and Lincoln was smart enough to know this well: indeed, we *know* that he knew it in the early years of the war.

It is crucial to observe at this point that Lincoln's attitude regarding his personal safety had *changed*. For just consider: he had listened to the warnings back in 1861 when he learned of the assassins in Baltimore. He had traveled, we remember, under cover of darkness, changing trains and wearing a disguise. Months later, when he feared that the Confederates would try to raid Washington, he told his secretary of the navy to "have as strong a War Steamer as you can conveniently put on that duty, to cruise upon the Potomac, and to look in upon, and, if practicable, examine the Bluff and vicinity, at what is called the White House, once or twice per day; and, in any case of an attempt to erect a battery there, to drive away the party attempting it. . . ."[36]

The prudent leader who issued these instructions presents a striking contrast to the spectacle of Lincoln under fire at Fort Stevens, exposing himself to Confederate bullets.

And now a terrible thought begins to dawn—does it not?—the thought that Lincoln under fire at Fort Stevens was a prelude to Booth and Ford's Theater. There is no way to prove such a thing. But one cannot help wondering about it: was the rashness of Lincoln in dismissing the security issue a way for him to somehow "offer himself"—unconsciously, perhaps—to an avenging Lord? Was he offering himself as a gesture in golden-rule ethics—offering to prove to his Maker he was willing to pay the same price as all the hundreds of thousands of soldiers whom his policies had forced to their premature deaths?[37] Remember the tone of Lincoln's lamentations in the previous summer: the war, he reflected, "carried mourning into every home."

We can never pursue any psychological theory in regard to Lincoln's death beyond the limits of a sketchy hypothesis. But we can certainly critique the behavior of Lincoln in regard to his personal safety, behavior that constitutes the greatest single lapse in his career. And we can use this occasion for a more explicit look at Lincoln's spiritual side and what it meant to him.

Theologian Reinhold Niebuhr once wrote that Lincoln's "combination of moral resoluteness about the immediate issues with a religious awareness of another dimension of meaning and judgment must be regarded as almost a perfect model of the difficult but not impossible task of remaining loyal and responsible toward the moral treasures of a free civilization on the one hand while yet having some religious vantage point over the struggle. Surely it was this double attitude that made the spirit of Lincoln's, 'with malice toward none; with

Lincoln as he looked a few days before his assassination. Photograph by Alexander Gardner. (Library of Congress, Meserve Collection #97)

charity for all' possible. There can be no other basis for true charity; for charity cannot be induced by lessons from copybook texts. It can proceed only from a 'broken spirit, and a contrite heart.'"[38]

"A broken spirit and a contrite heart": Niebuhr, of course, is not referring to a state of *despair* in this phrase but to the spiritual *humbling of pride* that is essential to most, if not all, forms of Christian spirituality. Lincoln's keen understanding of the dangers of pride can be traced all the way to the 1830s. Well before he embraced Christian piety,

Lincoln expressed his fear of hubris in his address to the Young Men's Lyceum of Springfield in 1838. He warned that "some man possessed of the loftiest genius, coupled with ambition sufficient to push it to its utmost stretch, will at some time, spring up among us." And he reflected that the people would have to be "united with each other" to "successfully frustrate his designs."[39]

It can certainly be argued that Lincoln's great career as a strategist contained a deep tension: a tension between his awareness of his gifts and his fear that they could lead him into hubris—into sinful pride. But if it led him unconsciously to put himself at risk in a manner that is wholly indefensible except as a gesture of tragic self-sacrifice—if it led him to lay upon the altar of the nation nothing less than his future potential to advance the new birth of freedom—then we are justified in asking whether Lincoln, in the end, reached the point of *excessive* self-effacement that critics of the Christian tradition as diverse in their views and sensibilities as Machiavelli, Hobbes, Gibbon, and Nietzsche have complained about over the centuries. There are, after all, situations where a strong and healthy self-regard is essential to moral accomplishment.

At his best, however, Lincoln reconciled the tension of humility and ego in a manner that Harry V. Jaffa has described in an admirable way: in Lincoln, Jaffa wrote a half-century ago, a man of genius discovered "that the highest ambition can be conceived as consummated only in the highest service, that egotism and altruism ultimately coincide in that consciousness of superiority which is superiority in the ability to benefit others."[40]

In what did this superiority of Lincoln truly consist? It is futile to ascribe it all to Lincoln's sense of "practicality." No less an observer than Theodore Roosevelt attempted to describe it this way and fell sadly short of the mark. Lincoln, said Roosevelt, "did not war with phantoms; he did not struggle among the clouds; he faced facts; he endeavored to get the best results he could out of the warring forces with which he had to deal . . . [And] when he could not get the best he was forced to content himself and did content himself with the best possible."[41]

No, indeed—Lincoln *never* contented himself with the best results he could attain unless they passed a certain threshold of *decency*. And this point is absolutely essential. Lincoln weighed lesser evils with greater, to be sure; he weighed the opportunities of history with countervailing hazards. And he would choose the lesser evil, as Roosevelt has said, but he would do this *only at times when that choice advanced a greater good.* He insisted that the overall "package" of moral results should be good enough to make the subsidiary choices worthwhile. Below a certain level, any "compromise" to Lincoln was worthless or positively evil.

It is only when seen in this light of moral value that the gifts of Lincoln as a strategist can really be considered. But when seen in this light, Lincoln's gifts amounted to the following: (1) His capacity to view the large picture in a flash and to relate the subsidiary parts of a problem to the whole; (2) his capacity to visualize surges of power as they moved along dynamic lines of force; (3) his gift for doing best-case and worst-case contingency planning simultaneously; (4) his ability to develop his plans incrementally, expanding his power by degrees as he diminished the power of his enemies; (5) his ability to practice deception as a ploy within a context of honesty.

All of these abilities were channeled by Lincoln in the following manner when it came to the problem of slavery: (1) He believed it was impossible for him to deal with the institution unless he *condemned* it as an unambiguous evil; (2) however, knowing and saying that slavery was wrong was just a prelude to strong civic *action*; (3) the great challenge for the anti-slavery movement was to deal with the evil *effectively*; (4) the best incremental plan was to revive the early national creed that was inimical to human enslavement: "all men are created equal"; (5) in so doing, one should summon all available power to manipulate the flow of events in this general direction while fighting to prevent any further *erosion* of the national creed.

Harry V. Jaffa has seen in this work an application of "prudential" morality conceived in the Aristotelian tradition. He has suggested that "Lincoln understood the task of statesmanship" as "to know what is good or right, and how much of that good is attainable."[42]

Jaffa's application of Aristotelian principles to Lincoln's moral statecraft is justified. For in his *Nicomachean Ethics*, Aristotle wrote that the challenge of ethical life is essentially the challenge of determining the moral *excellence* or *fitness* of our various responses to the situations we encounter.

In the case of Lincoln, however, one particular issue that figures in the ethics of Aristotle—and especially so if we choose to contrast it to its treatment in the ethics of Kant, who would not condone deception—is deeply provocative: the problem of *honesty*.[43] It is, after all, Lincoln's use of *crafty methods* that appears paradoxical or even inconsistent to some in light of his morality.

Aristotle praises the honest man's nature in no uncertain terms: "falsehood," he writes, is "by its own nature bad and reprehensible." Consequently, "truth [is] a fine and laudable thing."[44] Yet certain key exceptions are presented in the *Nicomachean Ethics*. At one point, for instance, Aristotle speaks in great praise of sincerity, but nonetheless cautions, "by the 'sincere' man I do not mean one who, when he enters into a contract or agreement, puts all his cards on the table."[45] At another point Aristotle states that "the superior man is bound to be open in his likes and dislikes, and to care more for truth than for what people think, and to be straightforward in word or deed." But then he adds this worldly-wise caveat: "His language will be sincere, *unless when he has recourse to irony, which will be his tone in addressing the generality of men* [my emphasis]."[46]

The relationship of truth to untruth in the tactics of Lincoln is a problem that may give the reader pause. But his uses of deception were frequently justified, disturbing though this may seem to be. So let's be *honest*: let us really "put our cards on the table." Most of us demand an inner honesty in those whom we trust. We teach our children to honor the truth, and we teach them to *tell* the truth as well. But do we not, on occasion, teach our children to be wary of the complicated ways of this world? Do we not, as they grow, acknowledge more and more that the problem of honesty relates to situational ethics?

Intellectual historian Jacques Barzun asked the fundamental questions long ago as he reflected on the challenges of twentieth-century "relativism" in relation to the problem of behavior: "Is a man honest who does not always tell the truth? Certainly not! Well then, is he to tell the homicidal maniac where his victim has just gone? Certainly not again. The casuist laboriously works out a rationale: he relates the rule to the circumstance. But if we admit this exception to truth telling, are not people going to hide dishonesty under the name of conditional judgment? No doubt." And the upshot? A *perfect* resolution of the problem is morally impossible. In Barzun's opinion, "there has been no way yet discovered of preventing either absolute or relative rules from . . . cloaking hypocrisies. The only safeguard is in the conscience."[47]

In the conscience. And is there any doubt that Lincoln's conscience controlled his deceptions to achieve moral ends?

Let us leave it at this: Lincoln's genius—in addition to his mastery in shaping historical events—was to force upon those who paid attention to his teachings a "civic religion" that transcended his occasional deceptions.[48] And the message of his creed was as follows: Most of us—even those of gentle nature, it would seem—can be tyrants if our conscience goes to seed. Many of us can be seduced into breaches of morality, some of them minor, to be sure, but some of them as gross as the evil of enslavement. Only principles of self-restraint that are based upon a power of human empathy, a power transcending the self—"all men created equal"—give decency to government of, by, and for the people. Only principles transcending the self can make a free society possible and worth the cost of saving.

Lincoln did much more than merely "save the Union," and he did much more than "free the slaves." At the cost of some occasional deception—and at the cost of some six hundred thousand lives that were lost to the nation, including his own—it can be said that he saved our nation's soul. He was an indispensable genius such as no other figure in our past.

On the day after Lincoln had died, a great banner was stretched across Broadway. The message was powerful and brief. It is a message this book has sought to prove. "The great person," it read, "the great man, is the miracle of history."[49]

Notes

INTRODUCTION

1. Allen C. Guelzo, "A Reluctant Recruit to the Abolitionist Cause," *The Washington Post*, February 11, 2001, "Outlook," B-3. Guelzo's important recent books about Lincoln include *Abraham Lincoln: Redeemer President* (Grand Rapids, Mich.: William B. Eerdmans Publishing Company, 1999) and *Lincoln's Emancipation Proclamation: The End of Slavery in America* (New York: Simon & Schuster, 2004). The former book is an intellectual biography with special emphasis on Lincoln's religious views. The latter is a study of the Emancipation Proclamation, which Guelzo regards as a definitive event in American history, an act both "sincere and profound," and the product of effective "prudential" morality on Lincoln's part. This book conveys a higher estimation of Lincoln by Guelzo than the views he expressed in the above-cited article in the *Washington Post*. Nonetheless, though Guelzo appears to be a great deal more impressed at this writing with the qualities of Lincoln as a moral strategist, he continues to understate or even underestimate the radical side of Lincoln's temperament. Though Guelzo concedes that "Lincoln was not exaggerating in 1858 that he 'hated' slavery," he nonetheless argues that Lincoln was "not enough moved by American slavery's singular injustice to their African captives to call for their immediate emancipation" at the time, as did the full-fledged abolitionists (*Lincoln's Emancipation Proclamation*, 4, 22). While of course it is true that Lincoln called in the 1850s for an incremental emancipation, it hardly follows that his stance in this matter is proof that he was "not enough moved" about slavery's effect upon the slaves. Witness Lincoln's private statements in 1855, in a letter that he wrote to one of his oldest and closest friends, Joshua Speed, to the effect that the status of slaves was "a continual torment to me," that he and many other anti-slavery Northerners "crucify their feelings" on the issue of slavery, and, most directly of all, that "I hate to see the poor creatures [fugitive slaves] hunted down, and caught, and carried back to their stripes, and unrewarded toil" (Lincoln to Joshua F. Speed, August 24, 1855). It is strangely ironic that Guelzo cites the statements quoted above, though without, apparently, being moved by their emotional force.

2. David Herbert Donald, *Lincoln* (New York: Simon & Schuster, 1995), 14–15. For a polite but very strong rebuttal of Donald, see James M. McPherson's book review "A Passive President?" *Atlantic Monthly*, November 1995, 134–40.

3. Statement by Barbara Fields, in Ken Burns et al., *The Civil War* (Florentine Films and WETA-TV, 1989), Episode Four, "Simply Murder (1863)." This particular variation of the argument that Lincoln was shallow or opportunistic may be traced back at least as far as the 1948 essay by Richard Hofstadter, "Abraham Lincoln and the Self-Made Myth." See Richard Hofstadter, *The American Political Tradition and the Men Who Made It* (New York: Alfred A. Knopf, 1948), chapt. 5.

4. James M. McPherson, *Abraham Lincoln and the Second American Revolution* (New York: Oxford University Press, 1991), 42.

5. See, for example: Gore Vidal, *Lincoln* (New York: Random House, 1984) and William K. Klingaman, *Abraham Lincoln and the Road to Emancipation: 1861–1865* (New York: Viking Press, 2001).

6. William Lee Miller, *Lincoln's Virtues: An Ethical Biography* (New York: Alfred A. Knopf, 2002). Miller's book expands upon the writings of political philosopher Harry V. Jaffa, who has analyzed the politics of Lincoln from the philosophic standpoint of ethics, and especially Aristotelian ethics, for half a century. Jaffa's most recent book is *A New Birth of Freedom: Abraham Lincoln and the Coming of the Civil War* (Landover, Md.: Rowman & Littlefield, 2000).

7. LaWanda Cox, *Lincoln and Black Freedom: A Study in Presidential Leadership* (Columbia: University of South Carolina Press, 1981), 1994 ed., 7.

8. Ibid., 43.

9. Søren Kierkegaard, *Fear and Trembling* (1843), in *Fear and Trembling and The Sickness Unto Death*, trans. Walter Lowrie (Princeton: Princeton University Press, 1941; repr., New York: Doubleday, 1945), 37.

CHAPTER ONE

1. Abraham Lincoln, "Speech at Chicago," July 10, 1858, in *Collected Works of Abraham Lincoln*, ed. Roy P. Basler (New Brunswick, N.J.: Rutgers University Press, 1953), II, 500–501.

2. See Harold Holzer's observations, which are based upon a number of authoritative primary-source descriptions, with regard to the charismatic power of Lincoln as a speaker. Holzer writes of "Lincoln's hypnotic manner. . . . his power to amuse and enthrall with a jolt of the head or the flash of an eye." Harold Holzer, *Lincoln at Cooper Union: The Speech That Made Abraham Lincoln President* (New York: Simon & Schuster, 2004), 173. For a persuasive analysis of the role that anger played in the emotional dynamics of Lincoln, see Michael Burlingame, *The Inner World of Abraham Lincoln* (Urbana: University of Illinois Press, 1994).

3. Abraham Lincoln to Joshua F. Speed, August 24, 1855, in *Collected Works*, II, 323.

4. Abraham Lincoln, "'A House Divided,' Speech at Springfield, Illinois," June 16, 1858, in *Collected Works*, II, 461–62.

5. Abraham Lincoln to William Kellogg, December 11, 1860, in *Collected Works*, IV, 150.

6. For those who presume that "Machiavellian" implies an autocratic outlook, a reading of Machiavelli's *Discourses on the First Ten Books of Titus Livy* is a good antidote. Machiavelli preferred republics to monarchies.

7. Abraham Lincoln, "Speech at Chicago," July 10, 1858, in *Collected Works*, II, 500.

8. James Madison, in ed. Max Farrand, *The Records of the Federal Convention* (New Haven: Yale University Press, 1966), I, 486.

9. Thomas Jefferson to Roger C. Weightman, June 24, 1826, in *The Writings of Thomas Jefferson*, ed. Paul Leicester Ford (New York: G. P. Putnam's Sons, 1892–99), X, 390–92. Jefferson's statement was a reiteration of words that were spoken in a 1685 speech on the gallows by Colonel Richard Rumbold, an English Puritan.

10. Thomas Jefferson, "Proposed Constitution for Virginia," (June 1783), in *Writings*, ed. Ford, III, 320–33.

11. John Bernard, *Retrospections of America, 1797–1811* (New York: Harper and Brothers, 1887; repr. New York: Benjamin Blom, 1969) 91.

12. Thomas Jefferson, "Heads of Information given me by E. Randolph," n.d., Library of Congress, M, III, n. 297.

13. The best general interpretations of the role of the Founding Fathers vis-à-vis slavery can be found in William W. Freehling, "The Founding Fathers and Slavery," in *American Negro Slavery*, ed. Allen Weinstein and Frank Otto Gatell (New York: Oxford University Press, 1973), and William W. Freehling, *The Road to Disunion: Secessionists at Bay, 1776–1854* (New York: Oxford University Press, 1990), especially chapt. 7; and Winthrop D. Jordan, *White Over Black: American Attitudes Toward the Negro, 1550–1812* (Chapel Hill: University of North Carolina Press, 1968), parts 3 and 4.

14. Jefferson, *Notes on the State of Virginia* (1785), Harper Torchbook Edition (New York: Harper & Row, 1964), 138, 132–33.

15. John C. Calhoun to Virgil Maxcy, September 11, 1830, Galloway-Maxcy-Markoe Papers, Library of Congress, cited in William W. Freehling, *Prelude to Civil War: The Nullification Controversy in South Carolina, 1816–1836* (New York: Harper & Row, 1965), 257.

16. James Hamilton, Jr., to John Taylor et al., September 14, 1830, *Charleston Mercury*, cited in Freehling, *Prelude to Civil War*, 256.

17. William W. Freehling, *Prelude to Civil War*, 127.

18. *City Gazette and Commercial Daily Advertizer* (Charleston, S.C.), September 14, 1830, and *Proceedings of the States Rights Meeting in Columbia, S.C. on the Twentieth of September, 1830*, 18–42, cited in Freehling, *Prelude to Civil War*, 168.

19. Weld, in addition to his charismatic anti-slavery speeches, assisted several drives to send anti-slavery petitions to Congress. He served in the early 1840s as advisor to the anti-slavery Whigs who were fighting the "Gag Rule."

20. David Walker published an *Appeal to the Colored Citizens of the World* in 1829. Both free black leaders of the North and the black insurrectionaries who hoped to trigger slave revolts were active in the anti-slavery cause before the growth of white militance during the 1830s. In 1817, black leaders met at Philadelphia's Bethel Church to protest the strategy of colonization among white anti-slavery leaders. The first black American newspaper, *Freedom's Journal*, was established in 1827. Its editors were Samuel Cornish and John Russwurm. Over fifty abolition societies were founded by free blacks.

21. See John C. Calhoun, "Remarks on Receiving Abolition Petitions (Revised Report), in the Senate, February 6, 1837," in *The Papers of John C. Calhoun*, ed. Clyde N. Wilson (Columbia: University of South Carolina Press, 1980), XIII, especially 395–96:

> The relation now existing in the slave-holding States between the two [races] is, instead of an evil, a good—a positive good. . . . I hold then, that there never has yet existed a wealthy and civilized society in which one portion of the community did not, in point of fact, live on the labor of the other. . . . It would not be difficult to trace the various devices by which the wealth of all civilized communities has been so unequally divided, and to show by what means so small a share has been allotted to those by whose labor it was produced. . . .

22. See Kenneth Stampp, *The Peculiar Institution: Slavery in the Ante-Bellum South* (New York: Alfred A. Knopf, 1956), Vintage edition, 211:

> Every slave state made it a felony to say or write anything that might lead, directly or indirectly, to discontent or rebellion. In 1837, the Missouri legislature passed an act "to prohibit the publication, circulation, and promulgation of the abolition doctrines." The Virginia code of 1849 provided a fine and imprisonment for any person who maintained "that owners have not right of property in their slaves." Louisiana made it a capital offense to use "language in any public discourse, from the bar, the bench, the stage, the pulpit, or in any place whatsoever" that might produce "insubordination among the slaves."

23. See John Hope Franklin, *The Militant South, 1800–1861* (Cambridge: Harvard University Press, 1956), and David Grimsted, *American Mobbing, 1828–1861: Toward Civil War* (New York: Oxford University Press, 1998).

24. The best work to date on the Free-Soil movement remains Eric Foner's *Free Soil, Free Labor, Free Men: The Ideology of the Republican Party Before the Civil War* (New York: Oxford University Press, 1970).

25. For more information on the use of slaves as rented strikebreakers in Southern industry, see Eugene D. Genovese, *The Political Economy of Slavery* (New York: Random House, 1965), 199, 233, and Robert S. Starobin, *Industrial Slavery in the Old South* (New York: Oxford University Press, 1970).

26. Representative Thomas L. Clingman of North Carolina declared in a speech before the House of Representatives on January 22, 1850, that Southerners would have utilized their slaves in California gold mines if slavery had been given a fair chance to establish itself. (*Selections from Writings and Speeches of Hon. Thomas L. Clingman, of North Carolina* [Raleigh: J. Nichols, printer, 1877], 239). J. D. B. De Bow, in his influential Southern journal *De Bow's Review*, declared in 1850 that it was solely the lack of a protective slave code that deterred Southern owners of slaves from bringing them to California and making it a slave state: "Such is the strength and power of Northern opposition that property, which is ever timid, and will seek no hazards, is excluded from the country in the person of the slave, and Southerners are forced, willingly or not, to remain at home." (J. D. B. De Bow, "California—The New American El Dorado," *De Bow's Review*, VIII, June 1850, 540).

27. Speech by John C. Calhoun in the United States Senate, March 4, 1850, in *Calhoun: Basic Documents*, ed. John M. Anderson (State College, Pa.: Bald Eagle Press, 1952), 298–324.

28. The original Fugitive Slave Law, passed by Congress in 1793, had proven unsatisfactory to slave owners. This law had permitted the owners of escaped slaves to appear in any state or federal court with their captured human property and

then provide legal proof of their ownership. But free-state officials often proved uncooperative. Later, the Supreme Court ruled in *Prigg vs. Pennsylvania* (1842) that enforcement of the Fugitive Slave Law was entirely the federal government's responsibility. Thereafter, a number of free state legislatures passed "personal liberty laws" that interfered with the operations of slave catchers. The stronger Fugitive Slave Law of 1850 attempted to override the personal liberty laws.

29. The most authoritative recent accounts of Lincoln's self-education and early psychological development are Douglas L. Wilson, *Honor's Voice: The Transformation of Abraham Lincoln* (New York: Alfred A. Knopf, 1998), 1999 Vintage edition, especially chapt. 2, and Michael Burlingame, *The Inner World of Abraham Lincoln*.

30. Abraham Lincoln, "Address Before the Young Men's Lyceum of Springfield, Illinois, 'The Perpetuation of Our Political Institutions,'" January 27, 1838, *Collected Works*, I, 114.

31. Edmund Wilson, "Abraham Lincoln: The Union as Religious Mysticism," in *Eight Essays* (New York: Doubleday and Anchor Books, 1954), 190–91, 202.

32. Harry V. Jaffa, *Crisis of the House Divided: An Interpretation of the Lincoln-Douglas Debates* (Chicago: The University of Chicago Press, 1959), 219, passim, chapt. IX.

33. Abraham Lincoln to Mary Speed, September 27, 1841, in *Collected Works*, I, 260.

34. Abraham Lincoln to Joshua Speed, August 24, 1855, in *Collected Works*, II, 320.

35. Abraham Lincoln, "Eulogy on Henry Clay," July 6, 1852, in *Collected Works*, II, 129, 126, 130, 132.

CHAPTER TWO

1. For further information on Quitman and the "filibusterers," see John Hope Franklin, *The Militant South, 1800–1861* (Cambridge: Harvard University Press, 1956), 103–14.

2. See Robert E. May, *The Southern Dream of a Caribbean Empire, 1854–1861* (Baton Rouge: Louisiana State University Press, 1973).

3. M. W. McCluskey, ed., *Speeches, Messages, and Other Writings of the Hon. Albert G. Brown, a Senator in Congress from the State of Mississippi* (Philadelphia: J. B. Smith & Co., 1859), 588–99.

4. *Selections from Writings and Speeches of Hon. Thomas L. Clingman, of North Carolina* (Raleigh: J. Nichols, printer, 1877), 239.

5. On the influence of Fitzhugh's *Sociology for the South*, see Harvey Wish, *Ante-Bellum: Writings of George Fitzhugh and Hinton Rowan Helper on Slavery* (New York: G. P. Putnam's Sons, 1960), 6–8.

6. George Fitzhugh, *Sociology for the South—Or, the Failure of Free Society* (Richmond: A. Morris, Publisher, 1854), Burt Franklin Research and Source Book Series No.102, 179.

7. Abraham Lincoln, "Speech at Peoria, Illinois," October 16, 1854, in *Collected Works of Abraham Lincoln*, ed. Roy P. Basler (New Brunswick, N.J.: Rutgers University Press, 1953), II, 247–48.

8. Ibid., 259.

9. Ibid., 281.

10. Ibid., 266.
11. Ibid., 264.
12. Ibid., 265.
13. Ibid., 266.
14. Ibid., 262.
15. Ibid., 274.
16. Ibid., 255.
17. Ibid., 275.
18. Ibid., 271.
19. Ibid., 271. On the issue of Lincoln and race, see: Benjamin Quarles, *Lincoln and the Negro* (New York: Oxford University Press, 1962); Don E. Fehrenbacher, "Only His Stepchildren: Lincoln and the Negro," *Civil War History* 20 (December 1974): 293–310; and LaWanda Cox, *Lincoln and Black Freedom: A Study in Presidential Leadership* (Columbia: University of South Carolina Press, 1981), 1994 ed., 19–26. Almost fifty years ago, David Herbert Donald came to the conclusion that "the President himself was color-blind . . . and he thought of the black man first of all as a man." (David Herbert Donald, *Lincoln Reconsidered: Essays on the Civil War Era* [New York: Alfred A. Knopf, 1956], 135.)
20. Ibid., 282.
21. Ibid., 255–56.
22. Stephen A. Douglas, "Mr. Douglas's Speech," in "First Debate with Stephen A. Douglas at Ottawa, Illinois," August 21, 1858, *Collected Works*, III, 10.
23. James M. McPherson, *Ordeal By Fire: The Civil War and Reconstruction* (New York: McGraw-Hill, 1982, 1992), 111.
24. William Lee Miller, *Lincoln's Virtues: An Ethical Biography* (New York: Alfred A. Knopf, 2002), 358.
25. Harry V. Jaffa, *Crisis of the House Divided: An Interpretation of the Lincoln-Douglas Debates* (Chicago: The University of Chicago Press, 1959), 383.
26. The "peripheral" status of the abolitionists in no way diminishes their vital catalytic role in the anti-slavery movement. As theologian Reinhold Niebuhr once observed, "Through the whole course of history mankind has . . . reserved its highest admiration for those heroes who resisted evil at the risk or price of fortune and without too much hope of success. Sometimes their very indifference to the issue of success or failure provided the stamina which made success possible." Niebuhr went on to analyze the "paradoxical relation between the possible and the impossible in history." See Reinhold Niebuhr, *The Irony of American History* (New York: Charles Scribner's Sons, 1952), 144–45, passim.
27. For a detailed analysis of the politics behind the 1854 senatorial nomination struggle in Illinois, see Don E. Fehrenbacher, *Prelude to Greatness: Lincoln in the 1850's* (Stanford, Calif.: Stanford University Press, 1962), 37–39.
28. Walker and his government were overthrown in 1857. Three years later, the "grey-eyed man of destiny" met his death—by firing squad—in Honduras.
29. Abraham Lincoln to George Robertson, August 15, 1855, in *Collected Works*, II, 318.
30. Abraham Lincoln to Joshua F. Speed, August 24, 1855, in *Collected Works*, II, 320–22.
31. For a convincing summation of the evidence, see James M. McPherson, *Ordeal by Fire*, 96.

32. Abraham Lincoln, "Fragment on Sectionalism," ca. July 23, 1856, in *Collected Works*, II, 352.

33. Abraham Lincoln, "Speech at Galena, Illinois," July 23, 1856, in *Collected Works*, II, 355.

34. For an excellent and detailed account of the Dred Scott case, see Kenneth M. Stampp, *America in 1857: A Nation on the Brink* (New York: Oxford University Press, 1990), chapt. 4. See also Don E. Fehrenbacher, *The Dred Scott Case: Its Significance in American Law and Politics* (New York: Oxford University Press, 1978).

35. Calhoun expounded this position in a series of resolutions introduced in the Senate in 1847. See James M. McPherson, *Ordeal by Fire*, 64, 104.

36. See Eric Foner, *Free Soil, Free Labor, Free Men: The Ideology of the Republican Party Before the Civil War* (New York: Oxford University Press, 1970), chapt. 3.

37. Ibid., 91–92.

38. Ibid., 96.

39. Abraham Lincoln, "Speech at Springfield, Illinois," June 26, 1857, *Collected Works*, II, 404.

40. Ibid., 404.

41. Ibid., 405.

42. Ibid., 408. See Garry Wills, *Lincoln at Gettysburg: The Words That Remade America* (New York: Simon & Schuster, 1992), 108–10, for an exposition regarding the possible antecedents of this vision in the transcendentalism of Theodore Parker. Parker, in turn, was probably indebted to the international influence of Hegel, whose *Philosophy of History* expounded the doctrine that Absolute Spirit puts forth, as an embryonic "notion," the "idea" of freedom, which develops itself through progressive stages of history. For further development of the Parker-Lincoln connection, see Carl F. Wieck, *Lincoln's Quest for Equality: The Road to Gettysburg* (DeKalb, Ill.: Northern Illinois University Press, 2002).

43. Ibid., 407.

44. Ibid., 405–406.

45. See Alexander Keyssar, *The Right to Vote: The Contested History of Democracy in the United States* (New York: Basic Books, 2000), 142.

46. See Lerone Bennett, Jr., *Forced Into Glory: Abraham Lincoln's White Dream* (Chicago: Johnson Publishing Co., 2000) for a simplistic treatment of the issue based upon erratic skimming of the evidence. For an indirect rebuttal of Bennett, see William Lee Miller, *Lincoln's Virtues*, 353–63.

47. Stephen A. Douglas, "Senator Douglas's Reply," in "Sixth Debate with Stephen A. Douglas at Quincy, Illinois, October 13, 1858," in *Collected Works*, III, 261.

48. Abraham Lincoln, "Fragment on Slavery," ca. July 1, 1854, in *Collected Works*, II, 222–23.

49. Abraham Lincoln, "Fragment on Pro-Slavery Theology," ca. October 1, 1858, in *Collected Works*, III, 204.

50. John Nicolay to John McMahon, August 6, 1864, in *Collected Works*, VII, 483.

51. Frederick Douglass, "Oration by Frederick Douglass, Delivered on the Occasion of the Unveiling of the Freedmen's Monument, in Memory of Abraham Lincoln," in Lincoln Park, Washington, D.C., April 14, 1876," in Frederick Douglass, *Life and Times of Frederick Douglass, written by himself* (Hartford, Conn.: Park Publishing Co., 1881, facsimile edition, Secaucus, N.J.: Citadel Press, 1983), 921.

52. Frederick Douglass, "Draft of Speech," June 1, 1865, Frederick Douglass Papers, Library of Congress.

53. Ibid., 351, 365.

54. Ibid., 373.

55. David Grimsted, letter to the author, January 31, 2002.

56. Lincoln was hardly the first Free-Soiler to perceive the danger, as others have pointed out. As early as March 10, 1857, the Bloomington, Illinois *Pantagraph* reacted to the Dred Scott decision in the following manner: "One little step only remains, to decide all *State* prohibitions of slavery to be void." (See Fehrenbacher, *Prelude to Greatness* 80, 92–93). On November 17, 1857, the *Washington Union* (a pro-slavery Democratic newspaper) ran an editorial condemning as unconstitutional every state law that deprived slave owners of their right to take their slaves with them anywhere in the Union. On March 22, 1858, Stephen Douglas denounced this editorial. At some point Lincoln found out about the matter, for he used it in the Lincoln-Douglas debates to show that Douglas in reality acknowledged the danger that slavery could spread into the North. In so doing, Lincoln modified his charges in the House Divided Speech; he acknowledged that Douglas was perhaps nothing more than a *dupe* of the conspirators Pierce, Buchanan, and Taney.

57. Abraham Lincoln, "Fragment of a Speech," ca. May 18, 1858, *Collected Works*, II, 453.

58. Harry V. Jaffa, *Crisis of the House Divided*, 395. Jaffa continues:

> Even if it were true that the productivity of a system based on free labor is greater than one based on slave labor, it does not follow that it is more *profitable to the men who run it*. A large portion of a smaller sum may still be more than a small portion of a larger one. All we know of the fierce struggles, the long uphill climb, of free labor in the grip of the industrial revolution that followed the Civil War suggests that it never could have succeeded, as it has, if in addition to all the other handicaps the incubus of slavery could have been placed in the scales against it. If the great corporations, the "robber barons" who came to dominate the state legislatures in the postbellum period, had wanted to import slaves as strikebreakers, *then* it would not have required even another Dred Scott decision to spread slavery to the free states.

59. The nomination of a candidate for the United States Senate by a state political convention was audacious and unprecedented. For an illuminating discussion of the politics surrounding the Springfield convention, see Fehrenbacher, *Prelude to Greatness*, chapt. 3.

60. Ibid., 448–49.

61. Abraham Lincoln, "'A House Divided,' Speech at Springfield, Illinois," June 16, 1858, *Collected Works*, II, 461.

62. Ibid., 464–65.

63. Ibid., 467.

64. Ibid., 466.

65. Ibid., 466–67.

66. Ibid., 465–66.

67. Ibid., 468.

68. Abraham Lincoln, "Fragment on the Struggle Against Slavery," ca. July 1858, in *Collected Works*, 482.

69. Abraham Lincoln, "Speech at Chicago, Illinois," July 10, 1858, in *Collected Works*, 489.

70. Ibid., 491.
71. Ibid.
72. Ibid., 492.
73. Ibid., 495.
74. Ibid., 500.
75. Ibid.
76. Ibid., 500–501.
77. Ibid., 501.
78. Abraham Lincoln, "Speech at Springfield, Illinois," July 17, 1858, in *Collected Works*, 519–20.
79. Stephen A. Douglas, "Mr. Douglas's Speech," in "First Debate with Stephen A. Douglas at Ottawa, Illinois," August 21, 1858, in *Collected Works*, III, 9.
80. Ibid., 10.
81. Ibid., 5.
82. Abraham Lincoln, "Mr. Lincoln's Reply," in *Collected Works*, 16.
83. A few years later, Lincoln openly denied that any fight for racial supremacy was truly at stake, while reserving his judgment with regard to the likelihood of such a development in the future. On March 5, 1860, he declared that "the proposition that there is a struggle between the white man and the negro contains a falsehood. There *is* no struggle. *If* there was, I should be for the white man. If two men are adrift at sea on a plank which will bear up but one, the law justifies either in pushing the other off. I never had to struggle to keep a negro from enslaving me, nor did a negro ever have to fight to keep me from enslaving him." "Speech at Hartford, Connecticut," March 5, 1860, *Collected Works*, 10.
84. Ibid., 18–19.
85. Ibid., 23–24.
86. Ibid., 27.
87. Stephen A. Douglas, "Mr. Douglas's Reply," in *Collected Works*, 35.
88. Ibid., 36.
89. Abraham Lincoln, "Mr. Lincoln's Speech," in "Second Debate with Stephen A. Douglas at Freeport, Illinois," August 27, 1858, in *Collected Works*, 39.
90. Ibid., 40.
91. Ibid.
92. Ibid., 40–41.
93. Ibid., 41–42.
94. Ibid., 43.
95. Stephen A. Douglas, "Mr. Douglas's Speech," August 27, 1858, in *Collected Works*, 51–52. For a very long time, historians regarded this response to Lincoln's question as the "Freeport Doctrine" of Douglas. They argued that Lincoln had extracted this answer from Douglas in a clever bid to drive a wedge between Douglas and his Southern supporters. But as Douglas himself pointed out, he had said the same thing many times before, most notably in his reaction to the Dred Scott decision on June 7, 1857. For a good discussion of the issue, see Fehrenbacher, *Prelude to Greatness*, Chapt. 6.
96. Ibid., 53–54.
97. Ibid., 55–56.
98. Stephen A. Douglas, "Mr. Douglas's Speech" in "Third Debate with Stephen A. Douglas at Jonesboro, Illinois," September 15, 1858, in *Collected Works*, 105.
99. Ibid., 112.

100. Ibid., 113.
101. Abraham Lincoln, "Mr. Lincoln's Speech," September 15, 1858, in *Collected Works*, 134–35.
102. Ibid., 130–31.
103. Stephen A. Douglas, "Mr. Douglas's Reply," in *Collected Works*, 140.
104. Stephen A. Douglas, "Senator Douglas's Speech," in "Fourth Debate with Stephen A. Douglas at Charleston, Illinois, September 18, 1858," in *Collected Works*, 176.
105. Abraham Lincoln, "Mr. Lincoln's Rejoinder," September 18, 1858, in *Collected Works*, 179.
106. Abraham Lincoln, "Mr. Lincoln's Speech," September 18, 1858, in *Collected Works*, 146.
107. Stephen A. Douglas, "Senator Douglas's Speech," in *Collected Works*, 171.
108. Stephen A. Douglas, "Mr. Douglas's Speech," in "Fifth Debate with Stephen A. Douglas at Galesburg, Illinois, October 7, 1858," in *Collected Works*, 218–19.
109. Abraham Lincoln, "Mr. Lincoln's Reply," October 7, 1858, in *Collected Works*, 225.
110. Ibid., 230–31.
111. Ibid., 233.
112. Ibid.
113. "Senator Douglas's Reply," in "Sixth Debate with Stephen A. Douglas at Quincy, Illinois, October 13, 1858," in *Collected Works*, 265.
114. Ibid., 267.
115. Ibid., 274.
116. "Mr. Lincoln's Rejoinder," October 13, 1858, in *Collected Works*, 276.
117. Ibid., 278.
118. "Mr. Lincoln's Reply," in "Seventh and Last Debate with Stephen A. Douglas at Alton, Illinois, October 15, 1858," in *Collected Works*, 304.
119. Abraham Lincoln to Norman B. Judd, October 20, 1858, in *Collected Works*, 329–30.
120. James M. McPherson, *Ordeal by Fire*, 111.
121. Ibid., 111–12.
122. Abraham Lincoln to Anson G. Henry, November 19, 1858, in *Collected Works*, 339.
123. Abraham Lincoln to Anson S. Miller, November 19, 1858, in *Collected Works*, 340.
124. Abraham Lincoln to Charles H. Ray, November 20, 1858, in *Collected Works*, 342.

CHAPTER THREE

1. James M. McPherson, *Ordeal by Fire: The Civil War and Reconstruction* (New York: McGraw-Hill, 1982, 1992), 112.
2. Ibid., 113.
3. Don E. Fehrenbacher, *Prelude to Greatness: Lincoln in the 1850's* (Stanford, Calif.: Stanford University Press, 1962), 143.
4. Ibid., 17–18.

5. Abraham Lincoln to Lyman Trumbull, December 11, 1858, in *Collected Works of Abraham Lincoln*, ed. Roy P. Basler (New Brunswick, N.J.: Rutgers University Press, 1953), III, 345.

6. Abraham Lincoln, "Speech at Chicago, Illinois," March 1, 1859, in *Collected Works*, III, 367.

7. Abraham Lincoln, to Henry L. Pierce and Others, April 6, 1859, in *Collected Works*, III, 375–76.

8. Abraham Lincoln, to Samuel Galloway, July 28, 1859, in *Collected Works*, III, 394–95.

9. Abraham Lincoln, to Schuyler Colfax, July 6, 1859, in *Collected Works*, III, 390–91.

10. Abraham Lincoln to Thomas Corwin, October 9, 1859. The discovery and authentication of this long-lost letter from Lincoln was reported by Harold Holzer in the February/March 2005 issue of *American Heritage*. The letter was purchased from the Corwin heirs in 2004 by the Abraham Lincoln Book Shop in Chicago.

11. Fehrenbacher, *Prelude to Greatness*, 144.

12. Abraham Lincoln, "Notes for Speeches at Columbus and Cincinnati, Ohio," September 16, 17, 1859, *Collected Works*, III, 431–32.

13. Ibid., 434.

14. Ibid., 433.

15. Ibid., 434.

16. Ibid., 435.

17. Abraham Lincoln, "Speech at Columbus, Ohio," September 16, 1859, in *Collected Works*, 404.

18. Ibid., 404–405.

19. The complete text of Douglas's article may be found in *In the Name of the People: Speeches and Writings of Lincoln and Douglas in the Ohio Campaign of 1859*, ed. Harry V. Jaffa and Robert W. Johannsen (Columbus: Ohio State University Press, 1959), 58–125.

20. Abraham Lincoln, "Speech at Columbus, Ohio," September 16, 1859, *Collected Works*, 405.

21. Ibid., 414–15.

22. Ibid., 417.

23. Ibid., 417.

24. Ibid., 418.

25. Ibid., 418–19.

26. Ibid., 423.

27. Ibid., 423–24.

28. Ibid., 424.

29. Abraham Lincoln, "Speech at Cincinnati, Ohio," September 17, 1859, *Collected Works*, 440.

30. Ibid., 441.

31. Ibid., 442.

32. Ibid.

33. Ibid., 453.

34. Ibid.

35. Ibid., 453–54.

36. Abraham Lincoln, "Address before the Wisconsin State Agricultural Society, Milwaukee, Wisconsin," September 30, 1859, *Collected Works*, 479.
37. Abraham Lincoln, "Speech at Leavenworth, Kansas," December 3, 1859, *Collected Works*, 502.
38. Ibid, 502.
39. Harold Holzer, *Lincoln at Cooper Union*, 5.
40. Abraham Lincoln, "Address at Cooper Institute, New York City," February 27, 1860, *Collected Works*, 527.
41. Ibid., 527.
42. Ibid., 533–34.
43. Ibid., 536–37.
44. Ibid., 538.
45. Ibid., 543.
46. Ibid., 546–47.
47. Ibid., 547–48.
48. Ibid., 549–50.
49. Abraham Lincoln, "Speech at New Haven, Connecticut," March 6, 1860, *Collected Works*, IV, 18.
50. Quoted in Benjamin P. Thomas, *Abraham Lincoln* (New York: Alfred A. Knopf, 1952), 218.
51. Abraham Lincoln to Samuel Galloway, March 24, 1860, *Collected Works*, op. cit., IV, 34.
52. Abraham Lincoln to Lyman Trumbull, April 29, 1860, *Collected Works*, IV, 45.
53. Don E. Fehrenbacher, *Prelude to Greatness*, 154.
54. Ibid., 157–58.
55. Nathan M. Knapp to Abraham Lincoln, quoted in Thomas, *Abraham Lincoln*, 210.
56. Fehrenbacher, *Prelude to Greatness*, 159.
57. Eric Foner, *Free Soil, Free Labor, Free Men: The Ideology of the Republican Party Before the Civil War* (New York: Oxford University Press, 1970), 215–16.
58. Abraham Lincoln to John B. Fry, August 15, 1860, in *Collected Works*, IV, 95.
59. *Illinois State Journal*, August 9, 1860, quoted in *Collected Works*, IV, 91–92, n. 1.
60. South Carolina's "Declaration of the Causes of Secession," in *The Causes of the Civil War*, ed. Kenneth M. Stampp (New York: Simon & Schuster/Touchstone, 1974), 44–45.
61. Abraham Lincoln to William Kellogg, December 11, 1860, *Collected Works*, IV, 150.
62. Abraham Lincoln to Elihu B. Washburne, December 13, 1860, in *Collected Works*, IV, 151.
63. Abraham Lincoln to Lyman Trumbull, December 17, 1860, in *Collected Works*, IV, 153.
64. Abraham Lincoln to Duff Green, December 28, 1860, in *Collected Works*, IV, 162.
65. Ibid., 162.
66. Ibid., 163.
67. Abraham Lincoln to John A. Gilmer, December 15, 1860, in *Collected Works*, IV, 151–152.
68. Abraham Lincoln to Thurlow Weed, December 17, 1860, in *Collected Works*, IV, 154.

69. Abraham Lincoln to Elihu B. Washburne, December 21, 1860, in *Collected Works*, IV, 159.

70. Abraham Lincoln to William H. Seward, February 1, 1861, in *Collected Works*, IV, 183.

71. Abraham Lincoln to James T. Hale, January 11, 1861, in *Collected Works*, IV, 172.

72. Abraham Lincoln, "Address Before the Young Men's Lyceum of Springfield, Illinois," January 27, 1838, *Collected Works*, I, 109.

73. Ibid., 113.

74. Kenneth M. Stampp, "The Concept of a Perpetual Union," *Journal of American History*, Vol. 65, no. 1, June 1978, 7–8. For a different though problematical interpretation, see Daniel Farber, *Lincoln's Constitution* (Chicago: University of Chicago Press, 2003), 84, 196.

75. Richard N. Current, *Lincoln and the First Shot* (New York: Harper & Row, 1963), Waveland Press edition, 1990, 203.

76. Abraham Lincoln, "Speech from the Balcony of the Bates House at Indianapolis, Indiana," February 11, 1861, *Collected Works*, IV, 195–96.

77. Abraham Lincoln, "Speech at Cincinnati, Ohio," February 12, 1861, in *Collected Works*, IV, 199.

78. Abraham Lincoln, "Reply to Mayor Fernando Wood, at New York City," February 20, 1861, in *Collected Works*, IV, 233.

79. Abraham Lincoln, "Address to the New Jersey General Assembly at Trenton, New Jersey," February 21, 1861, in *Collected Works*, IV, 237.

80. Abraham Lincoln, "Speech in Independence Hall, Philadelphia, Pennsylvania," February 22, 1861, in *Collected Works*, IV, 241.

81. Abraham Lincoln, "Reply to Mayor Alexander Henry at Philadelphia, Pennsylvania," February 21, 1861, in *Collected Works*, IV, 239.

82. Abraham Lincoln, "Speech in Independence Hall, Philadelphia, Pennsylvania," February 22, 1861, in *Collected Works*, IV, 240.

83. See Stephen B. Oates, *With Malice Toward None: The Life of Abraham Lincoln* (New York: Harper & Row, 1977), 195–96.

84. See Benjamin P. Thomas, *Abraham Lincoln*, 242–44.

85. See Richard N. Current, *Lincoln and the First Shot*, 33–35.

86. *Southern Advocate*, December 12, 1860, cited in Stephen B. Oates, *With Malice Toward None*, 188. See also James M. McPherson, *Battle Cry of Freedom: The Civil War Era* (New York: Oxford University Press, 1988), 228–29, and Ollinger Crenshaw, *The Slave States in the Presidential Election of 1860* (Baltimore: Johns Hopkins University Press, 1945).

87. *Charleston Mercury*, October 11, 1860, cited in *The Causes of the Civil War*, ed. Kenneth M. Stampp, 114–15.

88. Abraham Lincoln, "First Inaugural Address—Final Text," March 4, 1861, *Collected Works*, IV, 262–63.

89. Ibid., 264–65.

90. Ibid., 265.

91. Ibid., 267–68.

92. Ibid., 268.

93. Ibid., 269.

94. Ibid., 269–70.

95. Ibid., 271.

96. Ibid.
97. Ibid., 266.
98. See Richard N. Current, *Lincoln and the First Shot*, 72–73.
99. James M. McPherson, *Battle Cry of Freedom*, 271–72.
100. Abraham Lincoln to William H. Seward, April 1, 1861, in *Collected Works*, IV, 316–17.
101. See Richard N. Current, *Lincoln and the First Shot*, 120–21.
102. Ibid., 148.
103. Ibid., 151.
104. Abraham Lincoln, "Proclamation Calling Militia and Convening Congress," April 15, 1861, in *Collected Works*, IV, 331–32.
105. Alexander Stephens, Speech at Savannah, March 21, 1861, in *The Causes of the Civil War*, ed. Kenneth M. Stampp, 116. Jefferson Davis said much the same thing in a speech to the Confederate Congress on April 29, 1861, in *The Causes of the Civil War*, 117–18.
106. *Charleston Mercury*, February 28, 1860, in *The Causes of the Civil War*, 113.
107. Ibid.
108. Eugene D. Genovese, *The Political Economy of Slavery* (New York: Random House, 1965), 258. The penultimate section of Genovese's book, "The Origins of Slavery Expansionism," is a capable refutation of a famous but preposterous 1929 article, "The Natural Limits of Slavery Expansion," by Charles W. Ramsdell.
109. Cited in Richard N. Current, *Lincoln and the First Shot*, 131.
110. Ibid., 160–61.
111. Abraham Lincoln to Andrew G. Curtin, April 8, 1861, in *Collected Works*, IV, 324.
112. Richard N. Current, *Lincoln and the First Shot*, 165.
113. Abraham Lincoln to Winfield Scott, April 25, 1861, in *Collected Works*, IV, 344. Historian Mark E. Neely, Jr., has addressed the apparent incongruity of this letter's closing priorities—specifically, the letter's seeming implication that the bombardment of cities was less momentous than suspension of habeas corpus—as a matter of hasty editing. See Mark E. Neely, Jr., *The Fate of Liberty: Abraham Lincoln and Civil Liberties* (New York and Oxford: Oxford University Press, 1991), 7.
114. Abraham Lincoln to Gideon Welles, April 29, 1861, in *Collected Works*, 348.
115. James M. McPherson, "Tried by War: Lincoln as Self-Taught Strategist," *Civil War Times Illustrated*, November/December 1995, repr. in *Major Problems in the Civil War and Reconstruction*, ed. Michael Perman (New York: Houghton Mifflin Company, 1998), 177.
116. T. Harry Williams, *Lincoln and His Generals* (New York: Alfred A. Knopf, 1952), Vintage edition, 7–8.
117. Ibid., 18.

CHAPTER FOUR

1. Abraham Lincoln, "Message to Congress in Special Session," July 4, 1861, in *Collected Works of Abraham Lincoln*, ed. Roy P. Basler (New Brunswick, N.J.: Rutgers University Press, 1953), IV, 434–35.
2. Ibid., 432–33.
3. Ibid., 427.

4. Ibid., 437.
5. Ibid., 438.
6. Ibid., 439.
7. Ibid., 440.
8. Ibid., 440–41.
9. Ibid., 427.
10. Ibid., 457–58.
11. *Congressional Globe*, 37th Congress, First Session, 222–23, 258–62.
12. Abraham Lincoln to John C. Frémont, September 2, 1861, in *Collected Works*, IV, 506.
13. Abraham Lincoln to John C. Frémont, September 11, 1861, in *Collected Works*, IV, 518.
14. Abraham Lincoln to Orville H. Browning, September 22, 1861, in *Collected Works*, IV, 531–32.
15. George B. McClellan to Samuel L. M. Barlow, November 1, 1861, S. L. M. Barlow Papers, Henry E. Huntington Library.
16. George B. McClellan to Ellen Marcy McClellan, cited in George B. McClellan, *McClellan's Own Story* (New York: Webster & Company, 1887), 82–83.
17. See James M. McPherson, *Ordeal by Fire: The Civil War and Reconstruction* (New York: McGraw-Hill, 1982, 1992), 164. As to McClellan's character flaws, see Stephen W. Sears, *George B. McClellan: The Young Napoleon* (New York: Ticknor & Fields, 1988), xii, 103, 104, 133, 134, 201, passim, in which the biographer, though writing dispassionately, calls McClellan "inarguably the worst" commander of the Army of the Potomac and a man warped by arrogance and self-deception. See also Kenneth P. Williams, *Lincoln Finds a General: A Military Study of the Civil War*, 5 volumes (New York: Macmillan, 1949–1959) and T. Harry Williams, *McClellan, Sherman, and Grant* (New Brunswick, N.J.: Rutgers University Press, 1962).
18. See Abraham Lincoln, "Memorandum for a Plan of Campaign," ca. October 1, 1861, in *Collected Works*, IV, 544–45.
19. See T. Harry Williams, *Lincoln and His Generals* (New York: Alfred A. Knopf, 1952), Vintage edition, 42–43.
20. Allen C. Guelzo, *Lincoln's Emancipation Proclamation: The End of Slavery in America* (New York: Simon & Schuster, 2004) 5.
21. Abraham Lincoln, "Drafts of a Bill for Compensated Emancipation in Delaware," ca. November 26, 1861, in *Collected Works*, V, 29–30.
22. Abraham Lincoln, "Annual Message to Congress," December 3, 1861, in *Collected Works*, V, 51.
23. Ibid., 52.
24. Ibid., 51.
25. Ibid., 48–49.
26. Ibid., 48.
27. Ibid.
28. For a good discussion of divided black opinions on the issue of colonization in the decade preceding the Civil War, see Ira Berlin, *Slaves Without Masters: The Free Negro in the Antebellum South* (New York: Oxford University Press, 1974), 356–62, passim.
29. *Congressional Globe*, June 2, 1862, 37th Congress, Third Session, 2504.

30. Abraham Lincoln, "Annual Message to Congress," December 3, 1861, in *Collected Works*, V, 53.
31. T. Harry Williams, *Lincoln and His Generals*, 53.
32. Abraham Lincoln to Henry W. Halleck and Don C. Buell, December 31, 1861, *Collected Works*, V, 84.
33. Abraham Lincoln to Don C. Buell, January 7, 1862, in *Collected Works*, V, 91.
34. Abraham Lincoln to Simon Cameron, January 10, 1862, in *Collected Works*, V, 95.
35. Abraham Lincoln to Don C. Buell, January 13, 1862, in *Collected Works*, V, 98.
36. Moncure Daniel Conway, *Autobiography, Memories and Experiences* (New York: Houghton Mifflin Company, 1904), I, 345–46. The plausibility of Conway's story is increased by another account of a meeting with Lincoln when the very same "drop o' the creeter" joke—and in the very same connection vis-à-vis emancipation—was used only two months later. In her 1981 book *Lincoln and Black Freedom*, historian LaWanda Cox referred to "a letter of Wendell Phillips which has only recently come to light." It seems that in March, 1862 Lincoln met with Phillips at the White House. The president urged the abolitionist to give him more credit for his anti-slavery initiatives. He told a story to illustrate his point by way of a metaphor. As Cox has paraphrased the letter, "the story was of an Irishman in legally dry Maine who asked for a glass of soda with a 'drop of the crathur [put] into it *unbeknown to myself.*' Lincoln made his point explicit: he 'meant it [slavery] to die.'" See LaWanda Cox, *Lincoln and Black Freedom: A Study in Presidential Leadership* (Columbia: University of South Carolina Press, 1981), 8.
37. Charles Sumner, "Letter to Governor Andrew, of Massachusetts, December 27, 1861," *The Works of Charles Sumner* (Boston: Lee and Shepard, 1870–1873), VI, 152.
38. Abraham Lincoln, "President's General War Order No. 1," January 27, 1862, in *Collected Works*, V, 111–12.
39. Abraham Lincoln to George B. McClellan, February 3, 1862, in *Collected Works*, V, 118–19.
40. For a lengthy documentary account of the written give-and-take between Lincoln and McClellan from January 31 to ca. February 3, 1862, see *Collected Works*, V, 119–25, n. 1.
41. Abraham Lincoln, "Message to Congress," March 6, 1862, in *Collected Works*, V, 144–46.
42. Abraham Lincoln to Henry J. Raymond, March 9, 1862, in *Collected Works*, V, 152–53.
43. Abraham Lincoln, "President's General War Order No. 3," March 8, 1862, in *Collected Works*, V, 151.
44. Abraham Lincoln to George B. McClellan, April 6, 1862, in *Collected Works*, V, 182.
45. Abraham Lincoln to George B. McClellan, April 9, 1862, in *Collected Works*, V, 184–85.
46. Abraham Lincoln to George B. McClellan, May 1, 1862, in *Collected Works*, V, 203.
47. Abraham Lincoln to Irvin McDowell, May 17, 1862, in *Collected Works*, V, 219.
48. Abraham Lincoln to John C. Frémont, May 24, 1862, in *Collected Works*, V, 231.
49. Abraham Lincoln to George B. McClellan, May 25, 1862, in *Collected Works*, V, 235–36.

50. Abraham Lincoln to John C. Frémont, May 30, 1862, in *Collected Works*, V, 250.

51. George B. McClellan to Abraham Lincoln, June 25, 1862, cited in McClellan, *McClellan's Own Story*, 392–93.

52. Abraham Lincoln, "Order Constituting the Army of Virginia," June 26, 1862, in *Collected Works*, V, 287.

53. *War of the Rebellion: A Compilation of the Official Records of the Union and Confederate Armies* (Washington, D.C.: Government Printing Office, 1880–1901), Series 1, Volume 11, Part 1, 61. The last two sentences of this dispatch were deleted by a telegraph officer.

54. Abraham Lincoln to William H. Seward, June 28, 1862, in *Collected Works*, V, 291–92.

55. Abraham Lincoln, "Proclamation Revoking General Hunter's Order of Military Emancipation of May 9, 1862," May 19, 1862, in *Collected Works*, V, 222–23.

56. See Douglas L. Wilson, *Honor's Voice: The Transformation of Abraham Lincoln* (New York: Alfred A. Knopf, 1998), 1999 Vintage edition, 76–85, 186–87, 334–35.

57. Abraham Lincoln, "Remarks to a Delegation of Progressive Friends," June 20, 1862, *Collected Works*, V, 278–79. For studies of Lincoln's evolving sense of spirituality, see: William E. Barton, *The Soul of Abraham Lincoln* (New York: George H. Doran Co., 1920); William J. Wolf, *The Almost Chosen People: A Study of the Religion of Abraham Lincoln* (Garden City: Doubleday & Co., 1959); Elton Trueblood, *Abraham Lincoln: Theologian of American Anguish* (New York: Harper & Row, 1973); Allen C. Guelzo, *Abraham Lincoln: Redeemer President* (Grand Rapids, Mich.: William B. Eerdmans Publishing Company, 1999); Lucas Morel, *Lincoln's Sacred Effort: Defining Religion's Role in American Self-Government* (New York, Oxford: Lexington Books, 2000); and Joseph R. Fornieri, *Abraham Lincoln's Political Faith* (DeKalb: Northern Illinois University Press, 2003).

58. Abraham Lincoln to William H. Seward, June 28, 1862, in *Collected Works*, V, 292.

59. See James M. McPherson, "The Ballot and Land for the Freedmen, 1861–1865," in *Reconstruction: An Anthology of Revisionist Writings*, ed. Kenneth Stampp and Leon F. Litwack (Baton Rouge: Louisiana State University Press, 1969), 133. See also David Herbert Donald, *Charles Sumner and the Rights of Man* (New York: Alfred A. Knopf, 1970), 54–57.

60. Charles Sumner, "'Stand by the Administration,' Letter to _____, June 5, 1862," in *The Works of Charles Sumner*, VII, 116–18.

61. Charles Sumner to John Bright, August 5, 1862, Bright MSS, British Museum, London, cited in David Herbert Donald, *Charles Sumner and the Rights of Man*, 60.

62. Abraham Lincoln, "Appeal to Border State Representatives to Favor Compensated Emancipation," July 12, 1862, in *Collected Works*, V, 317–19.

63. Gideon Welles, *Diary of Gideon Welles, Secretary of the Navy Under Lincoln and Johnson* (New York: Houghton Mifflin Company, 1911), I, 70–71. See also Gideon Welles, "History of Emancipation," *Galaxy* (December, 1872), 842–43.

64. Abraham Lincoln, "To the Senate and House of Representatives," July 17, 1862, in *Collected Works*, V, 329–31.

65. Abraham Lincoln, "Emancipation Proclamation—First Draft," July 22, 1862, in *Collected Works*, V, 336–37.

66. See: V. Jacque Voegeli, *Free But Not Equal: The Midwest and the Negro During the Civil War* (Chicago: University of Chicago Press, 1967), 6; Forrest G. Wood, *Black Scare: The Racist Response to Emancipation and Reconstruction* (Berkeley: University of California Press, 1968), 35; and Frank L. Klement, *The Copperheads in the Middle West* (Chicago: University of Chicago Press, 1960), 14.

67. Abraham Lincoln, "Address on Colonization to a Deputation of Negroes," August 14, 1862, *Collected Works*, V, 370–75.

68. Abraham Lincoln to Cuthbert Bullitt, July 28, 1862, in *Collected Works*, 345–46.

69. Abraham Lincoln to August Belmont, July 31, 1862, in *Collected Works*, 350.

70. Abraham Lincoln to Horace Greeley, August 22, 1862, in *Collected Works*, 388–89.

71. Tyler Dennett, ed., *Lincoln and the Civil War in the Diaries and Letters of John Hay* (New York: Dodd, Mead, 1939), 46.

72. Ibid., 45.

73. Ibid., 46.

74. Ibid., 47.

75. T. Harry Williams, *Lincoln and His Generals*, 161.

76. Ibid., 164.

77. For analysis of the international stakes of the Antietam campaign, see Howard Jones, *Union in Peril: The Crisis over British Intervention in the Civil War* (Chapel Hill: University of North Carolina Press, 1992) and James M. McPherson, *Crossroads of Freedom: Antietam* (New York: Oxford University Press, 2002), 93–94.

78. Robert E. Lee to Jefferson Davis, September 8, 1862, in eds. Clifford Dowdey and Louis H. Manarin, *The Wartime Papers of R.E. Lee* (New York: Bramhall House, 1961), 301.

79. Abraham Lincoln, "Meditation on the Divine Will," ca. September 2, 1862, in *Collected Works*, V, 403–404.

80. Welles, *Diary of Gideon Welles*, I, 143.

81. Abraham Lincoln, "Reply to Emancipation Memorial Presented by Chicago Christians of All Denominations," September 13, 1862, in *Collected Works*, V, 420, 421, 425.

82. T. Harry Williams, *Lincoln and His Generals*, 168.

83. Abraham Lincoln, "Preliminary Emancipation Proclamation," September 22, 1862, in *Collected Works*, V, 433–36.

84. Tyler Dennett, ed., *Lincoln and the Civil War in the Diaries and Letters of John Hay*, 50.

85. Abraham Lincoln, "Proclamation Suspending the Writ of Habeas Corpus," September 24, 1862, in *Collected Works*, V, 436–37.

86. See James M. McPherson, *Crossroads of Freedom*, 77, 114.

87. Abraham Lincoln to Carl Schurz, November 24, 1862, in *Collected Works*, V, 509.

88. Abraham Lincoln to George B. McClellan, October 13, 1862, 460–61.

89. Abraham Lincoln to Carl Schurz, November 10, 1862, in *Collected Works*, V, 493–94.

90. Abraham Lincoln, "Remarks to Kentucky Unionists," November 21, 1862, in *Collected Works*, V, 503.

91. Abraham Lincoln to Henry Halleck, November 27, 1862, in *Collected Works*, V, 514–15.

92. Abraham Lincoln, "Annual Message to Congress," December 1, 1862, in *Collected Works*, V, 530.

93. Ibid., 532.

94. Ibid., 535.

95. Ibid., 537.

96. Frederick Douglass, *Life and Times of Frederick Douglass, written by himself* (Hartford, Conn.: Park Publishing Co., 1881, facsimile edition, Secaucus, N.J.: Citadel Press, 1983), 359–60.

CHAPTER FIVE

1. Abraham Lincoln, "Emancipation Proclamation," January 1, 1863, in *Collected Works of Abraham Lincoln*, ed. Roy P. Basler (New Brunswick, N.J.: Rutgers University Press, 1953), VI, 29–30.

2. Richard Hofstadter, *The American Political Tradition and the Men Who Made It* (New York: Alfred A. Knopf, 1948), 132. Hofstadter's essay on Lincoln is in many ways the worst of all the cameo portraits in this clever but uneven book. His quip about the Emancipation Proclamation was drawn, in part, from a sardonic remark that was attributed to William Seward. See Allen C. Guelzo, *Lincoln's Emancipation Proclamation: The End of Slavery in America* (New York: Simon & Schuster, 2004), 221–22.

3. For an account of the Chiriqui colonization project, from its origins in October 1861 to its termination at the close of 1862, see *Collected Works*, V, 370–371, n. 1.

4. Abraham Lincoln to Andrew Johnson, March 26, 1863, in *Collected Works*, VI, 149–50.

5. See James M. McPherson, "The Ballot and Land for the Freedmen, 1861–1865," in *Reconstruction: An Anthology of Revisionist Writings*, ed. Stampp and Litwack (Baton Rouge: Louisiana State University Press, 1969), 146–47.

6. LaWanda Cox, *Lincoln and Black Freedom: A Study in Presidential Leadership* (Columbia: University of South Carolina Press, 1981), 1994 ed., 30–31.

7. For a full treatment of this issue, see Mark Neely, Jr., *The Fate of Liberty: Abraham Lincoln and Civil Liberties* (New York: Oxford University Press, 1991).

8. Abraham Lincoln, "Memorandum on Joseph Hooker's Plan of Campaign Against Richmond," ca. April 6–10, 1863, in *Collected Works*, VI, 164–65.

9. Abraham Lincoln to Isaac N. Arnold, May 26, 1863, in *Collected Works*, VI, 230.

10. Abraham Lincoln to Joseph Hooker, June 10, 1863, in *Collected Works*, VI, 257.

11. Abraham Lincoln to Joseph Hooker, June 14, 1863, in *Collected Works*, VI, 273.

12. Abraham Lincoln, "Announcement of News From Gettysburg," July 4, 1863, in *Collected Works*, VI, 314.

13. Abraham Lincoln to Henry Halleck, July 6, 1863, in *Collected Works*, VI, 318.

14. Tyler Dennett, ed., *Lincoln and the Civil War in the Diaries and Letters of John Hay* (New York: Dodd, Mead, 1939), 67.

15. Ibid., 67. "Tycoon," a word that was a brand-new addition to American slang, was an anglicized version of a Japanese term that referred to the Shogun.

16. Abraham Lincoln to George G. Meade, July 14, 1863, in *Collected Works*, VI, 318.

17. James M. McPherson, *Ordeal by Fire: The Civil War and Reconstruction* (New York: McGraw-Hill, 1982, 1992), 357–58.

18. Tyler Dennett, ed., *Lincoln and the Civil War in the Diaries and Letters of John Hay*, 76.

19. Abraham Lincoln to James C. Conkling, August 26, 1863, in *Collected Works*, VI, 40610. Conkling orchestrated the release of this letter to the newspapers. See Lincoln-Conkling correspondence, in *Collected Works*, VI, 430.

20. Abraham Lincoln, "Fragment," ca. August 26, 1863, in *Collected Works*, VI, 410–11.

21. LaWanda Cox, *Lincoln and Black Freedom*, 64.

22. Ibid., 4.

23. Frederick Douglass, *Life and Times of Frederick Douglass* (Hartford, Conn.: Park Publishing Co., 1881, facsimile edition, Secaucus, N.J.: Citadel Press, 1983), 350–53.

24. Abraham Lincoln, "Order of Retaliation," July 30, 1863, in *Collected Works*, VI, 357. Lincoln found it hard to carry out the order. On April 12, 1864, Confederate troops under General Nathan Bedford Forrest murdered several dozen black soldiers who surrendered at Fort Pillow, Tennessee, on the Mississippi River. According to James M. McPherson (*Battle Cry of Freedom: The Civil War Era* [New York: Oxford University Press, 1988], 748, n. 48), the facts in this case are "well established and generally accepted." This Confederate action was more than worthy of Hitler's SS, which machine-gunned a contingent of American troops in the Battle of the Bulge after they had surrendered. On May 17, Lincoln sent a letter to the secretary of war in which he seemed unwilling to pursue retaliation in this particular case; "blood cannot restore blood," he stated, and "government should not act for revenge." (*Collected Works*, VII, 345–46.)

25. Abraham Lincoln, "Instructions to Tax Commissioners in South Carolina," September 16, 1863, in *Collected Works*, VI, 457.

26. Eric Foner, *A Short History of Reconstruction, 1863–1877* (New York: Harper & Row, 1990), 27.

27. Abraham Lincoln to Stephen A. Hurlbut, ca. August 15, 1863, in *Collected Works*, VI, 387.

28. Eric Foner, *Short History of Reconstruction*, 26–27.

29. Abraham Lincoln to Nathaniel P. Banks, August 5, 1863, in *Collected Works*, VI, 365.

30. LaWanda Cox, *Lincoln and Black Freedom*, 15.

31. Ibid, 52–53.

32. Abraham Lincoln to E.E. Malhiot, Bradish Johnson, and Thomas Cottman, June 19, 1863, in *Collected Works*, VI, 288.

33. Abraham Lincoln to Nathaniel Banks, August 5, 1863, in *Collected Works*, VI, 364–65.

34. Abraham Lincoln to Andrew Johnson, September 11, 1863, in *Collected Works*, VI, 440.

35. Eric Foner, *Short History of Reconstruction*, 18–19. For Lincoln's justification of this action to the Governor of Maryland, see Abraham Lincoln to Augustus W. Bradford, November 2, 1863, in *Collected Works*, VI, 556–57.

36. LaWanda Cox, *Lincoln and Black Freedom*, 35.

37. Abraham Lincoln to Henry Halleck, September 15, 1863, in *Collected Works*, VI, 450.

38. Abraham Lincoln to Henry Halleck, September 19, 1863, in *Collected Works*, VI, 466–67.

39. Abraham Lincoln to Henry Halleck, October 16, 1863, in *Collected Works*, VI, 518.
40. Gideon Welles, *Diary of Gideon Welles, Secretary of the Navy Under Lincoln and Johnson* (New York: Houghton Mifflin Company, 1911), I, 438–40.
41. See Douglas L. Wilson, *Honor's Voice: The Transformation of Abraham Lincoln* (New York: Alfred A. Knopf, 1998), 114–26.
42. Abraham Lincoln, "Address Delivered at the Dedication of the Cemetery at Gettysburg," November 19, 1863, "Final Text," in *Collected Works*, VII, 23.
43. Garry Wills, *Lincoln at Gettysburg: The Words That Remade America* (New York: Simon & Schuster, 1992), 38–39.
44. Abraham Lincoln to Nathaniel Banks, November 5, 1863, in *Collected Works*, VII, 1–2.
45. Abraham Lincoln, "Proclamation of Amnesty and Reconstruction," December 8, 1863, in *Collected Works*, VII, 53–56.
46. Abraham Lincoln, "Annual Message to Congress," December 8, 1863, in *Collected Works*, VII, 52.
47. Ibid., 52.
48. Ibid., 49.
49. Ibid., 51.
50. Ibid., 50.

CHAPTER SIX

1. For a book-length analysis of this election, see David E. Long, *The Jewel of Liberty: Abraham Lincoln's Re-Election and the End of Slavery* (Mechanicsburg, Pa.: Stackpole Books, 1994).
2. Abraham Lincoln to Nathaniel Banks, December 24, 1863, in *Collected Works of Abraham Lincoln*, ed. Roy P. Basler (New Brunswick, N.J.: Rutgers University Press, 1953), VII, 90.
3. LaWanda Cox, *Lincoln and Black Freedom: A Study in Presidential Leadership* (Columbia: University of South Carolina Press, 1981), 1994 ed., 70.
4. Eric Foner, *Short History of Reconstruction, 1863–1877* (New York: Harper & Row, 1990), 21.
5. Abraham Lincoln to Michael Hahn, March 13, 1864, in *Collected Works*, VII, 243.
6. LaWanda Cox has argued that Lincoln indirectly endorsed black voting rights as early as August 1863 via orders through the secretary of war. His "permission" for enrollment of blacks as voters in occupied Louisiana "was embodied in the order which Secretary of War Stanton gave at the President's express direction to Governor Shepley August 24, 1863. The relevant portion read: 'you will cause a registration to be made in each parish in the State of Louisiana of *all the loyal citizens* of the United States.'" (LaWanda Cox, *Lincoln and Black Freedom*, 77).

    On another matter, historians have long disagreed with regard to the authenticity of a letter that Lincoln supposedly wrote to General James S. Wadsworth ca. January 1864 on the subject of black voting rights that was included in the *Collected Works* edited by Basler et al. For commentary on the issue of this document's authenticity, see Ludwell H. Johnson, "Lincoln and Equal Rights: The Authenticity of the Wadsworth Letter," *Journal of Southern History*

32 (February 1966): 83–87, and Harold M. Hyman, "Lincoln and Equal Rights for Negroes: The Irrelevancy of the 'Wadsworth Letter,'" *Civil War History* 12 (September 1966): 258–66.

7. LaWanda Cox, *Lincoln and Black Freedom*, 36.

8. Abraham Lincoln to Daniel E. Sickles, February 15, 1864, in *Collected Works*, VII, 185.

9. Abraham Lincoln, "Address at Sanitary Fair, Baltimore, Maryland," April 18, 1864, in *Collected Works*, VII, 301–302.

10. Abraham Lincoln to Frederick Steele, January 27, 1864, in *Collected Works*, VII, 155.

11. Abraham Lincoln to John A. J. Creswell, March 7, 1864, in *Collected Works*, VII, 226.

12. James M. McPherson, "The Ballot and Land for the Freedmen, 1861–1865," in *Reconstruction: An Anthology of Revisionist Writings*, ed. Stampp and Litwack (Baton Rouge: Louisiana State University Press, 1969), 143.

13. Ibid., 151–52.

14. See James M. McPherson, *Ordeal by Fire: The Civil War and Reconstruction* (New York: McGraw-Hill, 1982, 1992), 467.

15. Ibid., 141.

16. Abraham Lincoln to Albert G. Hodges, April 4, 1864, in *Collected Works*, VII, 281–82. Another dress rehearsal for the Second Inaugural Address may be found in a letter by Lincoln to a Baptist religious committee. On May 30, 1864, Lincoln wrote the following:

> To read in the Bible, as the word of God himself, that "In the sweat of *thy* face shalt thou eat bread,["] and to preach therefrom that, "In the sweat of *other mans* [*sic*] faces shalt thou eat bread," to my mind can scarcely be reconciled with honest sincerity. When brought to my final reckoning, may I have to answer for robbing no man of his goods; yet more tolerable even this, than for robbing one of himself, and all that was his. When, a year or two ago, those professedly holy men of the South, met in the semblance of prayer and devotion, and, in the name of Him who said "As ye would all men should do unto you, do ye even so unto them" appealed to the christian world to aid them in doing to a whole race of men, as they would have no man do unto themselves, to my thinking, they contemned and insulted God and His church, far more than did Satan when he tempted the Saviour with the Kingdoms of the earth. . . . But let me forebear, remembering it is also written "Judge not, lest ye be judged."

Abraham Lincoln to George B. Ide, James R. Doolittle, and A. Hubbell, May 30, 1864, in *Collected Works*, VII, 368.

17. Abraham Lincoln, "General Orders No. 98," March 12, 1864, in *Collected Works*, VII, 239.

18. T. Harry Williams, *Lincoln and His Generals* (New York: Alfred A. Knopf, 1952), Vintage edition, 295.

19. Ibid., 296–97.

20. Ibid, 304–306.

21. Tyler Dennett, ed., *Lincoln and the Civil War in the Diaries and Letters of John Hay*, 178.

22. Ibid, 180.

23. Gideon Welles, *Diary of Gideon Welles, Secretary of the Navy Under Lincoln and Johnson* (New York: Houghton Mifflin Company, 1911), II, 44–45.

24. James M. McPherson, *Ordeal by Fire*, 423–24.

25. Ibid, 409.
26. Andrew Johnson, quoted in Robert W. Winston, *Andrew Johnson, Plebeian and Patriot* (New York: Henry Holt, 1928), 83.
27. These excerpts from Johnson's annual message to Congress of December 1867, are quoted by Eric Foner, *Short History of Reconstruction*, 84.
28. LaWanda Cox, *Lincoln and Black Freedom*, 18.
29. Abraham Lincoln to Salmon P. Chase, June 30, 1864, in *Collected Works*, VII, 419.
30. Abraham Lincoln, "Proclamation Concerning Reconstruction," July 8, 1864, in *Collected Works*, VII, 433.
31. Horace Greeley to Abraham Lincoln, July 7, 1864, in *Collected Works*, VII, 435, n. 1.
32. See John Henry Cramer, *Lincoln Under Enemy Fire: The Complete Account of His Experiences During Early's Attack on Washington* (Baton Rouge: Louisiana State University Press, 1948).
33. Abraham Lincoln, "Speech at Great Central Sanitary Fair, Philadelphia, Pennsylvania," June 16, 1864, in *Collected Works*, VII, 394. The latter phrase in the quotation was adapted by Lincoln from the first line of Shakespeare's *Henry VI, Part I*.
34. Gabor S. Boritt, "War Opponent and War President," in *Lincoln the War President: The Gettysburg Lectures*, ed. Gabor S. Boritt (New York: Oxford University Press, 1992), 205, 208.
35. Abraham Lincoln to Ulysses S. Grant, August 17, 1864, in *Collected Works*, VII, 499.
36. Abraham Lincoln to Ulysses S. Grant, August 3, 1864, in *Collected Works*, VII, 476.
37. Abraham Lincoln to Abram Wakeman, July 25, 1864, in *Collected Works*, VII, 461.
38. Abraham Lincoln, "Memorandum on Clement C. Clay," ca. July 25, 1864, in *Collected Works*, VII, 459. Clay was one of the Confederate agents in Niagara Falls.
39. *Columbus Crisis*, August 3, 1864, and *Freeman's Journal*, August 20, 1864, quoted in James M. McPherson, *Ordeal by Fire*, 438, 449. See also Forrest G. Wood, *Black Scare: The Racist Response to Emancipation and Reconstruction* (Berkeley: University of California Press, 1968), 53–79.
40. Henry J. Raymond to Abraham Lincoln, August 22, 1864, in *Collected Works*, VII, 517–18, n. 1.
41. Abraham Lincoln to Henry J. Raymond, August 24, 1864, in *Collected Works*, VII, 517.
42. Abraham Lincoln to Charles D. Robinson, August 17, 1864, in *Collected Works*, VII, 501.
43. Quoted by John G. Nicolay, in *Collected Works*, VII, 518, n.1.
44. "Interview with Alexander W. Randall and Joseph T. Mills," in *Collected Works*, VII, 507.
45. Quoted in James M. McPherson, *Battle Cry of Freedom: The Civil War Era* (New York: Oxford University Press, 1988), 771.
46. Abraham Lincoln, "Memorandum Concerning His Probable Failure of Reelection," August 23, 1864, in *Collected Works*, VII, 514.
47. Frederick Douglass, *Life and Times of Frederick Douglass*, 363–64.

48. John Eaton, *Grant, Lincoln, and the Freedmen* (New York: Longmans, Green & Co., 1907), 167–76.
49. Samuel L.M. Barlow to Manton Marble, August 24, 1864, S.L.M. Barlow Papers, Henry E. Huntington Library, quoted in James M. McPherson, *Battle Cry of Freedom*, 771.
50. *Charleston Mercury*, September 5, 1864, quoted in McPherson, *Battle Cry of Freedom*, 772.
51. Alexander Stephens to Herschel V. Johnson, September 5, 1864, in *Battle Cry of Freedom*, 772.
52. Frederick Douglass, *Life and Times of Frederick Douglass*, 360–61.
53. Harry V. Jaffa, *Crisis of the House Divided*, 408.
54. Donald Kagan, *Pericles of Athens and the Birth of Democracy* (New York: Touchstone/Simon & Schuster, 1991), xiii–xiv.
55. James M. McPherson, *Battle Cry of Freedom*, 858.

CHAPTER SEVEN

1. Abraham Lincoln, "Proclamation of Thanksgiving and Prayer," September 3, 1864, in *Collected Works of Abraham Lincoln*, ed. Roy P. Basler (New Brunswick, N.J.: Rutgers University Press, 1953), VII, 533.
2. Abraham Lincoln to Eliza P. Gurney, September 4, 1864, in *Collected Works*, VII, 535.
3. Abraham Lincoln to Ulysses S. Grant, September 29, 1864, in *Collected Works*, VIII, 29.
4. James M. McPherson, *Ordeal By Fire: The Civil War and Reconstruction* (New York: McGraw-Hill, 1982, 1992), 444–46.
5. Abraham Lincoln, "Proclamation of Thanksgiving," October 20, 1864, in *Collected Works*, VIII, 55.
6. Abraham Lincoln, "Response to a Serenade," November 8, 1864, in *Collected Works*, VIII, 96.
7. Abraham Lincoln, "Response to a Serenade," November 10, 1864, in *Collected Works*, VIII, 100–101.
8. Abraham Lincoln, "Response to a Serenade," October 19, 1864, in *Collected Works*, VIII, 52.
9. T. Harry Williams, *Lincoln and His Generals* (New York: Alfred A. Knopf, 1952), Vintage edition, 339.
10. Abraham Lincoln, "Annual Message to Congress," December 6, 1864, in *Collected Works*, VIII, 149, 151.
11. Ibid., 152.
12. Ibid., 149.
13. James M. McPherson, *Ordeal by Fire*, 466.
14. Abraham Lincoln to George H. Thomas, December 16, 1864, in *Collected Works*, VIII, 169.
15. T. Harry Williams, *Lincoln and His Generals*, 344.
16. Michael Vorenberg, *Final Freedom: The Civil War, the Abolition of Slavery, and the Thirteenth Amendment* (Cambridge: Cambridge University Press, 2001), 180.
17. Abraham Lincoln, "Response to a Serenade," February 1, 1865, in *Collected Works*, VIII, 254.

18. Abraham Lincoln, "To the Senate and House of Representatives," February 5, 1865, in *Collected Works*, VIII, 260.

19. James M. McPherson, "The Ballot and Land for the Freedmen, 1861–1865," in *Reconstruction: An Anthology of Revisionist Writings*, ed. Kenneth Stampp and Leon F. Litwack (Baton Rouge: Louisiana State University Press, 1969), 152–53.

20. Abraham Lincoln, "Speech to One Hundred Fortieth Indiana Regiment," March 17, 1865, in *Collected Works*, VIII, 361.

21. Abraham Lincoln, "Second Inaugural Address," March 4, 1865, in *Collected Works*, VIII, 332–33.

22. Abraham Lincoln to Thurlow Weed, March 15, 1865, in *Collected Works*, VIII, 356.

23. Herman Belz, *Reconstructing the Union: Theory and Policy During the Civil War* (Ithaca, N.Y.: Cornell University Press, 1969), 251–76.

24. James M. McPherson, *Ordeal by Fire*, 476.

25. Abraham Lincoln to Edwin M. Stanton, March 30, 1865, in *Collected Works*, VIII, 377.

26. Abraham Lincoln to Edwin M. Stanton, April 3, 1865, in *Collected Works*, VIII, 385.

27. James M. McPherson, *Battle Cry of Freedom: The Civil War Era* (New York: Oxford University Press, 1988), 847.

28. Abraham Lincoln, "Response to Serenade," April 10, 1865, in *Collected Works*, VIII, 394.

29. Abraham Lincoln, "Last Public Address," April 11, 1865, in *Collected Works*, VIII, 399–405.

30. William Hanchett, *The Lincoln Murder Conspiracies* (Urbana: University of Illinois Press, 1983), 37, and Edward Steers, Jr., *Blood on the Moon: The Assassination of Abraham Lincoln* (Lexington: University Press of Kentucky, 2001), 91. Booth made these remarks to coconspirators Lewis Paine and David Herold.

31. James M. McPherson, *Ordeal by Fire*, 493.

32. Ibid., 493.

33. James M. McPherson, "Foreword," in LaWanda Cox, *Lincoln and Black Freedom*, x. In light of Lincoln's audacious actions in the spring of 1865, and in light of the *tone* of his final public address, it is hard to agree with the contention of historian William C. Harris that Lincoln, right down to the end, "sought to restore the South as it existed before the conflict, shorn, however, of the spirit of disunion and the institution of slavery. . . ." See William C. Harris, *With Charity for All: Lincoln and the Restoration of the Union* (Lexington: University Press of Kentucky, 1997), 4. Harris's reading of the evidence betrays the ever-powerful influence exerted by the school of thought that views Lincoln as a consummate moderate. Harris, for example, writes that Lincoln's support for the Freedmen's Bureau was in truth lukewarm in light of his alleged "deep reservations regarding the extension of federal power" (*With Charity for All*, 253–54), a most questionable presupposition in light of the Hamiltonian streak that pervaded the statecraft of Lincoln from his earliest days as a disciple of Henry Clay to the very last weeks of his life.

34. Harry V. Jaffa, *Crisis of the House Divided: An Interpretation of the Lincoln-Douglas Debates* (Chicago: The University of Chicago Press, 1959), 395.

35. Lincoln's interest in the uses and abuses of power—considered as raw and elemental *energy*—was often made explicit. Consider his response to a skeptic in

1864: "Drive back to the support of the rebellion the physical force which the colored people now give . . . and neither the present, nor any coming administration *can* save the Union. . . . It is not a question of sentiment or taste, but one of physical force, which may be measured, and estimated as horse-power, and steam-power, are measured and estimated." (Abraham Lincoln to Charles D. Robinson, August 17, 1864, *Collected Works*, VII, 500). Lincoln said much the same thing in his letter to Isaac M. Schermerhorn, September 12, 1864 (*Collected Works*, VIII, 2).

36. Abraham Lincoln to Gideon Welles, April 29, 1861, in *Collected Works*, IV, 348.
37. Edmund Wilson offers similar speculation with regard to the idea that "this prophet who had overruled opposition and sent thousands of men to their deaths should finally attest his good faith by laying down his own life with theirs" in "Abraham Lincoln: The Union as Religious Mysticism," in *Eight Essays* (New York: Doubleday and Anchor Books, 1954), 202.
38. Reinhold Niebuhr, *The Irony of American History* (New York: Charles Scribner's Sons, 1952), 172.
39. Abraham Lincoln, "Address Before the Young Men's Lyceum of Springfield, Ill.," January 27, 1838, in *Collected Works*, I, 114.
40. Harry V. Jaffa, *Crisis of the House Divided*, 306.
41. Theodore Roosevelt, Speech at Omaha, Nebraska, April 27, 1903, in *Presidential Addresses and State Papers* (New York: The Review of Reviews Company, 1904), I, 331. Theodore Roosevelt's appreciation for Lincoln became more profound in the decade that followed this particular speech.
42. Harry V. Jaffa, *Crisis of the House Divided*, 370.
43. Kant insisted again and again that one's moral *intent* is all-important, regardless of any results that one's moral behavior might deliver, or fail to deliver. "Practical [moral] laws," he proclaimed in his second great critique, the *Critique of Practical Reason*, "refer only to the will, irrespective of what is attained." See Kant's *Critique of Practical Reason* (1788), trans. Lewis White Beck (New York: Macmillan, 1985), 19. For this reason, Kant seemed to allow no exceptions to the moral imperative of truth telling. It bears noting that the ethical system of Kant flowed directly from his underlying metaphysical system, which is highly problematical, especially as he attempted to expand and elaborate it in his second critique.

With regard to Lincoln's moral casuistry, a useful comparison between the statecraft of Lincoln and the later teachings of sociologist Max Weber has been offered by William Lee Miller in his book *Lincoln's Virtues*. Miller emphasized Weber's distinction in his essay "Politics as a Vocation" between the ethic of perfect virtue and the "ethic of responsibility." See William Lee Miller, *Lincoln's Virtues: An Ethical Biography* (New York: Alfred A. Knopf, 2002), 195, 219, 225–26, 483, n. 195. See also Jacques Barzun, "Lincoln's Philosophic Vision," 21st Annual Robert Fortenbaugh Memorial Lecture, Gettysburg College, 1982.
44. Aristotle, *Nichomachean Ethics*, Book 4, chapt. 7, in *The Ethics of Aristotle*, trans. J. A. K. Thomson (Baltimore: Penguin Classics, 1953), 132.
45. Ibid.
46. Ibid., Book 4, chapt. 3, 124.
47. Jacques Barzun, *Darwin, Marx, Wagner: Critique of a Heritage* (New York: Little, Brown & Co., 1941; second revised edition, Garden City, N.Y.: Doubleday Anchor Books, 1958), 348–49.

48. In Lincoln's 1838 Lyceum address, he spoke about the need for a "political religion" to protect America's creed.

49. Carl Sandburg, *Abraham Lincoln, The War Years* (New York: Harcourt, Brace & Company, 1939), Vol. 4, 357.

Select Bibliography

As the corpus of writings on the subject of Abraham Lincoln is vast, this select bibliography is limited to work that was produced in the past half-century.

Anastaplo, George. "Abraham Lincoln's Emancipation Proclamation." In *Constitutional Government in America*, ed. Ronald L.K. Collins. Durham, N.C.: Carolina Academic Press, 1980.

Barzun, Jacques. "Lincoln's Philosophic Vision." 21st Annual Robert Fortenbaugh Memorial Lecture, Gettysburg College, Gettysburg, Pa., 1982.

Belz, Herman. *Reconstructing the Union: Theory and Policy During the Civil War.* Ithaca, N.Y.: Cornell University Press, 1969.

———. "Abraham Lincoln and American Constitutionalism." *The Review of Politics* 50 (Spring 1988): 169–97.

———. *Abraham Lincoln, Constitutionalism, and Equal Rights in the Civil War Era.* New York: Fordham University Press, 1998.

Bennett, Lerone, Jr. *Forced Into Glory: Abraham Lincoln's White Dream.* Chicago: Johnson Publishing Company, 2000.

Boritt, Gabor, ed. *Lincoln the War President: The Gettysburg Lectures.* New York: Oxford University Press, 1992.

———. *The Lincoln Enigma: The Changing Faces of an American Icon.* New York: Oxford University Press, 2001.

Burlingame, Michael. *The Inner World of Abraham Lincoln.* Urbana: University of Illinois Press, 1994.

Carwardine, Richard J. *Lincoln: Profiles in Power.* New York: Longman Publishers, 2003.

Cox, LaWanda. *Lincoln and Black Freedom: A Study in Presidential Leadership.* Columbia: University of South Carolina Press, 1981.

Current, Richard N. *Lincoln and the First Shot.* New York: Harper & Row, 1963.

Davis, Collum, ed. *The Public and Private Lincoln: Contemporary Perspectives.* Carbondale: University of Southern Illinois Press, 1979.

Diggins, John Patrick. *On Hallowed Ground: Abraham Lincoln and the Foundations of American History.* New Haven: Yale University Press, 2000.

Dilorenzo, Thomas. *The Real Lincoln: A New Look at Abraham Lincoln, His Agenda, and an Unnecessary War.* New York: Crown Publishing Group, 2002.

Donald, David Herbert. *Lincoln Reconsidered: Essays on the Civil War Era.* New York: Alfred A. Knopf, 1956.

————. *Lincoln.* New York: Simon & Schuster, 1995.

————. *We Are Lincoln Men: Abraham Lincoln and His Friends.* New York: Simon & Schuster, 2003.

Farber, Daniel. *Lincoln's Constitution.* Chicago: University of Chicago Press, 2003.

Fehrenbacher, Don E. *Prelude to Greatness: Lincoln in the 1850's.* Stanford, Calif.: Stanford University Press, 1962.

————. "Only His Stepchildren: Lincoln and the Negro," *Civil War History* 20 (December 1974): 293–310.

Fletcher, George P. *Our Secret Constitution: How Lincoln Redefined American Democracy.* New York: Oxford University Press, 2001.

Foner, Eric. *Free Soil, Free Labor, Free Men: The Ideology of the Republican Party Before the Civil War.* New York: Oxford University Press, 1970.

Fornieri, Joseph R. *Abraham Lincoln's Political Faith.* DeKalb: Northern Illinois University Press, 2003.

Gienapp, William E. *Abraham Lincoln and Civil War America.* New York: Oxford University Press, 2002.

Greenstone, J. David. *The Lincoln Persuasion: Re-Making American Liberalism.* Princeton: Princeton University Press, 1993.

Guelzo, Allen C. *Abraham Lincoln: Redeemer President.* Grand Rapids, Mich.: Eerdmans, 1999.

————. *Lincoln's Emancipation Proclamation: The End of Slavery in America.* New York: Simon & Schuster, 2004.

Hanchett, William. *The Lincoln Murder Conspiracies.* Urbana: University of Illinois Press, 1983.

Harris, William C. *With Charity for All: Lincoln and the Restoration of the Union.* Lexington, Ky.: University Press of Kentucky, 1997.

Holzer, Harold. *Lincoln at Cooper Union: The Speech that Made Abraham Lincoln President.* New York: Simon & Schuster, 2004.

Jacobsohn, Gary L. "Abraham Lincoln 'On This Question of Judicial Authority': The Theory of Constitutional Aspiration." *Western Political Quarterly* 36 (March 1983): 52–70.

Jaffa, Harry V. *Crisis of the House Divided: An Interpretation of the Lincoln-Douglas Debates.* Chicago: The University of Chicago Press, 1959.

————. *A New Birth of Freedom: Abraham Lincoln and the Coming of the Civil War.* Landover, Md.: Rowman & Littlefield, 2000.

Johannsen, Robert Walter. *Lincoln, the South, and Slavery: The Political Dimension.* Baton Rouge: Louisiana State University Press, 1991.

Klingaman, William K. *Abraham Lincoln and The Road to Emancipation: 1861–1865.* New York: Viking Press, 2001.

Long, David E. *The Jewel of Liberty: Abraham Lincoln's Re-Election and the End of Slavery.* Mechanicsburg, Pa.: Stackpole Books, 1994.

McPherson, James M. *Battle Cry of Freedom: The Civil War Era.* New York: Oxford University Press, 1988.

————. *Abraham Lincoln and the Second American Revolution.* New York: Oxford University Press, 1991.

Miller, William Lee. *Lincoln's Virtues: An Ethical Biography.* New York: Alfred A. Knopf, 2002.

Morel, Lucas. *Lincoln's Sacred Effort: Defining Religion's Role in American Self-Government.* New York: Lexington Books, 2000.

Neely, Mark E., Jr. *The Fate of Liberty: Abraham Lincoln and Civil Liberties.* New York: Oxford University Press, 1991.

———. *The Last Best Hope of Earth: Abraham Lincoln and the Promise of America.* Cambridge, Mass.: Harvard University Press, 1993.

Oates, Stephen B. *With Malice Toward None: The Life of Abraham Lincoln.* New York: Harper & Row, 1977.

Paludan, Phillip Shaw. "Lincoln, the Rule of Law, and the American Revolution." *Journal of the Illinois State Historical Society* 70 (February 1977): 10–17.

———. *The Presidency of Abraham Lincoln.* Lawrence: University Press of Kansas, 1994.

Pressly, Thomas J. "Bullets and Ballots: Lincoln and the 'Right of Revolution.'" *American Historical Review* 67 (April 1962): 661–62.

Quarles, Benjamin. *Lincoln and the Negro.* New York: Oxford University Press, 1962.

Steers, Edward, Jr. *Blood on the Moon: The Assassination of Abraham Lincoln.* Lexington: University Press of Kentucky, 2001.

Strozier, Charles B. *Lincoln's Quest for Union: Public and Private Meanings.* New York: Basic Books, 1982.

Thomas, Benjamin P. *Abraham Lincoln.* New York: Alfred A. Knopf, 1952.

Thomas, John L., ed. *Abraham Lincoln and the American Political Tradition.* Amherst: University of Massachusetts Press, 1986.

Thompson, Kenneth W., ed. *Essays on Lincoln's Faith and Politics.* Lanham, Md.: University Press of America, 1983.

Trueblood, Elton. *Abraham Lincoln: Theologian of American Anguish.* New York: Harper & Row, 1973.

Vorenberg, Michael. *Final Freedom: The Civil War, the Abolition of Slavery, and the Thirteenth Amendment.* Cambridge: Cambridge University Press, 2001.

Wieck, Carl F. *Lincoln's Quest for Equality: The Road to Gettysburg.* DeKalb, Ill.: Northern Illinois University Press, 2002.

Williams, T. Harry. *Lincoln and His Generals.* New York: Alfred A. Knopf, 1952.

Wills, Garry. *Lincoln at Gettysburg: The Words That Remade America.* New York: Simon & Schuster, 1992.

Wilson, Douglas L. *Honor's Voice: The Transformation of Abraham Lincoln.* New York: Alfred A. Knopf, 1998.

Wilson, Major L. "Lincoln and Van Buren in the Steps of the Fathers: Another Look at the Lyceum Address." *Civil War History* 29 (September 1983): 197–211.

Wolf, William J. *The Almost Chosen People: A Study of the Religion of Abraham Lincoln.* Garden City: Doubleday & Co., 1959.

Index